PLAY DIRECTING

Sweeney Todd (Stephen Sondheim) designed by John Rothgeb, USA.

THIRD EDITION

PLAY DIRECTING
Analysis, Communication, and Style

Francis Hodge
UNIVERSITY OF TEXAS

PRENTICE HALL, Englewood Cliffs, New Jersey 07632

Library of Congress Cataloging-in-Publication Data

HODGE, FRANCIS.
  Play directing.

  Bibliography: p.
  Includes index.
  1. Theater—Production and direction. I. Title.
  PN2053.H6 1988   792'.0233   87-17378
  ISBN 0-13-682832-9

Editorial/production supervision: *Edith Riker*
Cover design: *Photo Plus Art*
Manufacturing buyer: *Harry P. Baisley* and *Ed O'Dougherty*

Printed in the United States of America

10 9 8 7 6

ISBN 0-13-682832-9 01

Prentice-Hall International (UK) Limited, *London*
Prentice-Hall of Australia Pty. Limited, *Sydney*
Prentice-Hall Canada Inc., *Toronto*
Prentice-Hall Hispanoamericana, S.A., *Mexico*
Prentice-Hall of India Private Limited, *New Delhi*
Prentice-Hall of Japan, Inc., *Tokyo*
Simon & Schuster Asia Pte. Ltd., *Singapore*
Editora Prentice-Hall do Brasil, Ltda., *Rio de Janeiro*

CONTENTS

List of plays used in photographs

List of authors whose plays appear in photographs

Credits for photographs

I am greatly indebted to the directors and designers who have so generously contributed the many photographs of productions used throughout the book to play "The Game of Visual Perception" (see Chapter 4, pages 77–78, for a full explanation). Without their help I could not have assembled this "game" with such variety in choice of plays, and with directors from so many areas and levels of live theatre production in America.

Each photograph is credited here in the order of its use with the following notation: number of the photograph; title of the play and its author; year of production; level of direction (S = student, F = faculty, RT = regional theatre); specific director, designer, photo credits, and, where appropriate, actor credits, and the place of production. I have used as examples of student work those productions with which I am most familiar—those at the University of Texas at Austin.

Frontispiece: *Sweeney Todd* (Stephen Sondheim); 1985; F; designed by John Rothgeb; University of Texas at Austin.

1 *Pygmalion* (Bernard Shaw); 1985; RT; director, James Moll; scenery, Richard L. Hay; lighting, Wendy Heffner; costumes, Andrew V. Yelusich; photo, 1987 Nicholas DeSciose; actors, Byron Jennings, Michael Winters; Denver Center Theatre Company, Denver.

2 *Beyond the Horizon* (Eugene O'Neill); 1986; RT; director, Royce Gehrels; set, Charles L. Boas; lighting, Joel D. Burns; costumes, Jan Heacock; Different Stages, Austin, Texas.

3 *Extremities* (William Mastrosimone); 1981; RT; director, John Bettenbender; scenery, Paul Owen; lighting, Jeff Hill; costumes, Kurt Wilhelm; photo, David S. Talbott; actors, Eller Barber, Kathy Bates; Actors Theatre of Louisville.

4 *Look Back in Anger* (John Osborne); 1979; S; director, Mark Ramont; scenery, John R. Rothgeb; costumes, Ellen Goodman; lighting, Joel Banks; University of Texas at Austin.

5 *Buried Child* (Sam Shepard); 1980; RT; director, Mike Sullivan; scenery, Mike Sullivan–Catherine Owens; costumes, Peggy Westmoreland; lighting, Greg White; photo, Rex Raymond; The Actors Company, Austin, Texas.

6 *American Buffalo* (David Mamet); 1979; RT; director, John Lutterbie; scenery, Bil Phuderer; costumes, Sarah Byrne; lighting, Mark Loeffler; Center Stage, Austin, Texas.

7 *Taste of Honey* (Shelagh Delaney); 1978; S; director-designer, Julie Davis; University of Texas at Austin.

22   *Curse of the Starving Class* (Sam Shepard); 1980; S; director, Sally Russell; scenery, Sydney Roberts; costumes, Debbie Smith; lighting, Gary Davis; University of Texas at Austin.

23   *Cabaret* (Joe Masterhoff, John Kander, Fred Ebb); 1976; RT; director, Jack Gillum; scenery, Elmer S. Peterson; costumes, Ruth Chase; lighting, John R. Dolphin; photo, Gerald W. Millard; The Milwaukee Players, Milwaukee, Wisconsin.

24   *Death of a Salesman* (Arthur Miller); 1980; RT; director, Donovan Marley; scenery and costumes, Robert Blackman; lighting, Steph Storer; PCPA/theaterfest, Solvang, California.

25   *The Birthday Party* (Harold Pinter); 1987; RT; director, Anthony Taccone; sets, John Bonard Wilson; lighting, Derek Duarte; costumes, Jeffrey Struckman; photo, Ken Friedman; actors, Laurence Ballard, Barbara Oliver; Berkeley Repertory Theatre, Berkeley, California.

26   *The Little Foxes* (Lillian Hellman); 1976; RT; director, James Moll; scenery, Richard L. Hay; costumes, Jeannie Davidson; photo, Hank Kranzler; Oregon Shakespeare Festival.

27   *Children of a Lesser God* (Mark Medoff); 1985; RT; director, Kathryn Long; scenery and lighting, Victor Becker; costumes, Mary Anne Powell; photo, K.C. Kratt; actors, W.T. Martin, Jen Jones, James I. Coleas, Jodene Marie Anicello; Studio Arena Theatre, Buffalo.

28   *Come Back, Little Sheba* (William Inge); 1975; S; director-designer, Alva Haskell; University of Texas at Austin.

29   *Resurrection of Jackie Cramer* (Frank Gagliano); 1980; RT; director, Raymond Benson; scenery, Robert Briggs; costumes, David F. Draper; lighting, James F. Franklin; photo, Anita Feldman; American Theatre of Actors, New York.

30   *The Creation of the World and Other Business* (Arthur Miller); 1978; S; director-designer, Norman Blumensaadt; University of Texas at Austin.

31   *La Ronde* (Arthur Schnitzler); 1979; RT; director, Warren Kliewer; scenery, Sally Locke; lighting, Craig Kennedy; costumes, Gina Taulane; photo, Gary Goodson; actors, Alison MacHale, Richard Sobellico; Equity Library Theatre, New York.

32   *Alice in Wonderland* (Margaret Elizabeth Becker and Gordon Thomas); 1977; RT; director, Margaret Becker; scenery, Michael Sullivan; costumes, Ann Lind; lighting, Bob Selby; Zachary Scott Theatre Center, Austin, Texas.

33   *Child's Play* (Robert Marasco); 1980; F; director, Richard M. Clark; scenery and lighting, Rodney Smith; costumes, Michael Chetterbock; Loretto Heights College, Denver.

33A   *Stuck* (Adele Edling Shank); 1983; RT; director, Theodore Shank; setting, Andy Stacklin and Kurt Landisman; lighting, Patty Anne Farrell; sound, Alaguis-Sincerco; photo, Allen Nomura; actors, Sherry Conner Steffens, Francine Lembi; Magic Theatre, San Francisco.

34   *Undiscovered Country* (Arthur Schnitzler, tr. Tom Stoppard); 1985; RT; director, Nikos Psacharopoulos; sets, David Jenkins; lighting, Arden Fingerhut; costumes, Jennifer vonMayrhauser; photo, Bob Marshak; Williamstown Theatre Festival, Williamstown, Massachusetts.

35   *Peer Gynt* (Henrik Ibsen); 1984; RT; director, Nikos Psacharopoulos; sets, John Conklin; lighting, Peter Hunt; costumes, John Conklin and Dunya Ramicova; actors, Dick Cavett, Dwight Schultz, and ensemble; Williamstown Theatre Festival, Williamstown, Massachusetts.

36   *The Price* (Arthur Miller); 1981; RT; director, Dennis Razze; scenery, Michael Sullivan; lighting, Donald Day; costumes, Gaye Bowen; Zachary Scott Theatre Center, Austin, Texas.

37   *Indians* (Arthur Kopit); 1977; RT; director, Jack Gillum; scenery, Elmer S. Peterson; costumes, Ruth Chase; lighting, John R. Dolphin; The Milwaukee Players, Milwaukee, Wisconsin.

38   *Rosencrantz and Guildenstern Are Dead* (Tom Stoppard); 1979; RT; director, Robert Graham; designer, Bob Dahlstrom; Freddy Wood Theatre, Vancouver, British Columbia.

39   *Servant of Two Masters* (Carlo Goldoni, adapted by Tom Cone); 1987; RT; director, Sharon Ott; photo, Ken Friedman; actors, Sharon Lockwood, Geoff Goyle; Berkeley Repertory Theatre, Berkeley, California.

40   *Orpheus Descending* (Tennessee Williams); 1972; S; director-designer, John Pendleton; University of Texas at Austin.

41   *The Philanthropist* (Christopher Hampton); 1979; S; director-designer, Peter Chapek; University of Texas at Austin.

42   *The Effect of Gamma Rays on Man-in-the-Moon Marigolds* (Paul Zindel); 1979; RT; director, Sally Russell; scenery, Lee Duran; costumes, Eve Bull; lighting, Beki Willis; photo, Marty Bass; Gaslight Theatre, Austin, Texas.

43   *The Lady From The Sea* (Henrik Ibsen); 1980; F; director, James Thomas; scenery, Gregory Gillette; costumes, Dennis Parker; lighting, John Howard; photo, Fred Moore; Mount Holyoke College, South Hadley, Massachusetts.

44   *The Council of Love* (Oskar Panizza); 1982; RT; director, Jim Fritzler; setting, Niki Psomas; lighting and costumes, Jim Fritzler; photo, Bill Leissner; Big State Productions, Capitol City Playhouse, Austin, Texas.

45   *Summer and Smoke* (Tennessee Williams); 1975; S; director-designer, Elota Patton; University of Texas at Austin.

46   *Cabaret* (Joe Masterhoff, John Kander, and Fred Ebb); 1976; RT; director, Jack Gillum; scenery, Elmer S. Peterson; costumes, Ruth Chase; lighting, John R. Dolphin; photo, Gerald Millard; The Milwaukee Players, Milwaukee, Wisconsin.

47   *Misalliance* (George Bernard Shaw); 1970; S; director-designer, Michael McLain; University of Texas at Austin.

48   *The Collection* (Harold Pinter); 1973; RT; director, Michael McLain; scenery, Michael McLain; costumes, Judith Burke; lighting, John Lutterbie; Actors Theatre, Austin, Texas.

48A   *Arsenals* (Jeremy Lawrence); 1986; RT; director, Gwen Arner; scenery, D. Martyn Bookwalter; lighting, Brett Thomas; costumes, Bill Walker; photo, K.C. Kratt; actors, Tanny McDonald, Laurinda Barrett; Studio Arena Theatre, Buffalo.

49   *The Matchmaker* (Thornton Wilder); 1975; RT; director, Laird Williamson; scenery, Richard Seegar; costumes, Robert Fletcher; lighting, Mitch Dana; photo, William Ganslan; A.C.T., San Francisco.

50   *The Wonderful Wizard of Oz* (Polish version, Jan Skotnicki); 1980; RT; director, Lewin Goff, scenery, costumes, lighting, Adam Kilian; Plock, Poland.

51   *You Never Can Tell* (George Bernard Shaw); 1980; RT; director, James Moll; scenery, Lewis Folden; costumes, Andrew V. Yelusich; PCPA/theaterfest, Santa Maria, California.

52   *The Imaginary Invalid* (Molière); 1986; F; director, Gweneth West; scenery, Dana L. Hanson; lighting, Howard Schumsky; costumes, Cristina M. Olivera; technical director, Sterling Shelton; photo, Shary Connella; University of Florida, Gainesville.

53   *The Adding Machine* (Elmer Rice); 1963; S; director-designer, Ray Keith Pond; University of Texas at Austin.

54   *Yerma* (Garcia Lorca); 1963; S; director-designer, Robert Hedley; University of Texas at Austin.

55   *The Effect of Gamma Rays on Man-in-the-Moon Marigolds* (Paul Zindel); 1979; RT; director, Sally Russell; scenery, Lee Duran; costumes, Eve Bull; lighting, Beki Willis; Gaslight Theatre, Austin, Texas.

56   *The Effect of Gamma Rays on Man-in-the-Moon Marigolds* (Paul Zindel); 1979; RT; director, Sally Russell; scenery, Lee Duran; costumes, Eve Bull; lighting, Beki Willis; Gaslight Theatre, Austin, Texas.

57   *Delicate Balance* (Edward Albee); 1971; RT; director, Michael McLain; scenery and costumes, Michael McLain; lighting, Patrick Moore; Actors Theatre, Austin, Texas.

58   *Crimes of the Heart* (Beth Henley); 1978–79; RT; director, Jon Jory; photo, David S. Talbott; actors, Lee Anne Fahey, Susan Kinglsey, Kathy Bates; Actors Theatre of Louisville.

59   *Dear Liar* (Jerome Kilty); 1980; RT; director-designer, Barrie Ingham; Center Stage, Austin, Texas.

60   *South Pacific* (Rodgers, Hammerstein, Logan); 1986; RT; director, Donavan Marley; scenic, Richard L. Hay; lighting, Wendy Heffner; costumes, Jeannie Davidson; Denver Center Theatre Company, Denver.

61   *The Flashing Light Bulb* (Woody Allen); 1987; RT; director, Albert Takazauckas; photo, Larry Merkle; actors, Joy Carlin, Ken Ruta; American Conservatory Theatre, San Francisco.

62   *Suicide in B*$_b$ (Sam Shepard); 1980; RT; director, Kim Kovac; scenery, Kim Kovac; costumes, William Pucilovsky; lighting, Jack Halstead; photo, Dennis Deloria; Paradise Island Express and The Independent Theatre Project, Washington, D.C.

63   *Cowboy Mouth* (Sam Shepard); 1980; RT; director; Kim Kovac; scenery, Kim Kovac; costumes, William Pucilovsky; lighting, Jack Halstead; photo, Dennis Deloria; Paradise Island Express and The Independent Theatre Project, Washington, D.C.

64   *Pantagleize* (Michel deGhelderode); 1980; RT; director, Laird Williamson; scenery, Ralph Funicelle; costumes, Michael Olick; lighting, Dirk Epperson; photo. William Ganslan; A.C.T., San Francisco.

65   *The Visit* (Friedrich Dürrenmatt); 1979; RT; director, Laird Williamson; scenery, Richard Seegar; costumes, Robert Blackman; lighting, Mitch Dana; photo, William Ganslan; A.C.T., San Francisco.

66   *Sunday in the Park with George* (Stephen Sondheim and James Lapine); 1986; RT; director, Laird Williamson; photo, Larry Merkle; actors, Jeff Keller, Lawrence Hecht, Alice Lynn, Anne Buelman, Ruth Kobart, Gina Ferrall; American Conservatory Theatre, San Francisco.

67   *Evita* (Andrew Webber); 1985; F; director, Dennis Razze; scenery, William Winsor; lighting, James McCabe; costumes, Kathleen Janemski; Allentown College, Center Valley, Pennsylvania.

68   *End Game* (Samuel Beckett); 1978; RT; director, Robert Graham; designer, Judith Lee; Vancouver Playhouse, Vancouver, British Columbia.

69   *The Doctor's Dilemma* (Bernard Shaw); 1986; RT; director, Joy Carlin; photo, Larry Merkle; actors, Nancy Carlin, Howard Swain, ensemble; American Conservatory Theatre, San Francisco.

69A *Godspell* (Stephen Schwartz); 1980; F; director, Dennis Razze; scenery, Robert Mond; lighting, James McCabe; costumes, Edward Farley; Allentown College, Center Valley, Pennsylvania.

70   *Love's Labour's Lost* (William Shakespeare); 1972; RT; director, Laird Williamson; scenery, Richard L. Hay; costumes, Jean Davidson; lighting, Steve Maze; photo, Carolyn Mason Jones; Oregon Shakespeare Festival.

71   *School For Scandal* (Richard Brinsley Sheridan); 1986; RT; director, Austin Pendleton; sets, Andrew Jackness; lighting, Roger Meeker; costumes, David Murin; photo, Phyllis Belkin; actors, Tom Tammi, Stephen Hough, George Morfogen, James Naughton, Laurie Metcalf, Richard Kneeland, Diane Venora, Patricia Swanson, Stephen Lawson; Williamstown Theatre Festival, Williamstown, Massachusetts.

72   *Titus Andronicus* (William Shakespeare); 1974; RT; director, Laird Williamson; scenery, Richard L. Hay; costumes, Robert Morgan; lighting, Steve A. Maze; Oregon Shakespeare Festival.

73   *The Imaginary Invalid* (Molière); 1986; F; director, Gweneth West; scenery, Dana L. Hanson; lighting, Howard Schumsky; costumes, Cristina M. Olivera; technical director, Sterling Shelton; photo, Shary Connella; University of Florida, Gainesville.

74   *The Cherry Orchard* (Anton Chekov); 1977; RT; director, Robert Graham; designer, Richard Cook; Westcoast Actors, Vancouver, British Columbia.

75   *The Importance of Being Earnest* (Oscar Wilde); 1979; F; director, Patricia W. Cook; scenery, Bill Sherry; costumes, Jim Swain; lighting, Bob Guthrie; Baylor University.

76   *The Importance of Being Earnest* (Oscar Wilde); 1978; RT; director, Jack Gillum; scenery, Michael McDonald; costumes, Ruth Chase; lighting, John R. Dolphin; The Milwaukee Players, Milwaukee, Wisconsin.

76A *The War of the Roses* (William Shakespeare, arranged by Travis Bogard); 1987; F; director, William Oliver; settings, Henry May; costumes, Warren Travis; photo, Geza Polony; actors, Piper Dellums, Joe Fitzgerald; University of California, Berkeley.

PREFACE

The tradition behind this book dates back more than half a century to the 1930s when courses in play production, with emphasis on directing plays, were first made a formal part of college and university curricula. I am especially grateful to Alexander M. Drummond of Cornell University who taught the enormous value of history of the theatre and dramatic criticism to the directing process. Later on, I worked as a colleague with Shakespearean director B. Iden Payne and costumer Lucy Barton who not only strongly supported this approach in their teaching and practice, but showed how the meaning of theatre lies in strong personal commitment and in a highly developed understanding of all the crafts of the theatre from playwriting and acting to designing and directing. That is the position taken in this book.

This book is therefore dedicated to all those who have helped to keep the theatre alive and well during these years when motion pictures and television have threatened its existence. Some people say that directing is a job for the young in spirit if not in age, and this I believe, for a play is a poem that needs the lyricism and excesses of youthful spirits if it is to fly with the angels.

I want to thank the many students, both undergraduate and graduate, who helped work out the many exercises that appear throughout the text, and the directors at all levels who helped illustrate it with photographs of their productions. I am also indebted to Beulah Hodge, whose many years as a performer/producer in public television helped me clarify the absolute necessity of delineating the live theatre's essential difference from the electronic forms. Thank you to the reviewers for their valuable assistance: Anthony B. Schmitt, Wayne State University; Peter Grego, California State University, Northridge; and Richard M. Clark, Ithaca College.

Finally, this third edition is especially dedicated to three colleagues—John Rothgeb, Mary Margaret Lindsay, and James Moll—now no longer with us, who devoted their life careers to theatre in education and have participated in the pages of this book.

Though the basic theory and approach in this third edition of *Play Directing* is the same as in the previous two, there are many changes throughout. I have had the opportunity to clarify some points, update examples, and especially to rearrange the chapters on communication in Part Two and on style in Part Three to help both instructors and students in navigating this relatively heavy body of material. Previous users of this text will also notice that "The Game of Visual Perception," played throughout the book, has been expanded with additional photographs from several levels of theatre production. In addition, to give greater emphasis to "hearing" a play in production, the director's oral tools have been given a section of their own in Communication 2. And in Part Three a chapter has been added to give some assistance to those who direct new plays, musicals, and operas.

Francis Hodge

CHAPTER ONE
ABOUT THIS BOOK
AND ITS POINT
OF VIEW

This book is about making *live* theatre. Though its content is specifically pointed toward the training of the director, it is intended for all students seriously involved in the study of theatre, whether they be actors, playwrights, designers, or directors, because their goals are the same: the projection of symbolic images to audiences. It is therefore their book as well as the director's.

In line with this intention, the process of directing is arranged in three levels so that you can advance according to your needs as far as course time and curricula allow. To practice what you have learned and to help you make a personal assessment of your development, a major project is placed at the end of each level.

But no matter to what level you advance, you will know a good deal about the directing process because the emphasis is placed on "doing" and not just talking about it. With this approach you will have a firm basis of techniques through which you can make your own discoveries about the nature of theatre and how it works. Whether you intend to be a director or not, you will find much in this study of directing that will apply to your special area of interest.

What can be written about directing is extremely limited simply because it is an activity that is not productive in itself but is entirely reliant on the things other people make—the playscript, the acting, the designs, the theatre architecture. This is precisely why most of the talk about directing concerns how these things are made and how to use them. What follows, then, is a series of detailed discussions, liberally sprinkled with exercises, of how you can make yourself useful in a theatre that for many centuries did without the director, as we know him, and could very likely do so again unless he can prove he is needed. Directing lies in doing, and you must find out what to do, where and when to do it, and how to do it to the best possible advantage. Learning the craft of directing is learning how to *do* and how to *make with imagination and freedom.*

Some of you may think that the process of study outlined in this book is too technical, and too self-conscious, but like all beginning education in any field, you must build from the ground up. From previous courses you already know that plays are artificial objects, that is, man-made rather than natural. But it is pure nonsense to assume that one's natural feelings and responses alone can give life to these artificial bodies. We wouldn't think of letting a carpenter experiment with a surgeon's knife on a real body because he would surely murder it. An uninformed would-be director, no matter how much he loves theatre, would do the same thing to a play, for making art form is a delicate process that requires meticulous care and sensitive skills.

Remember: art is a very personal and individual matter, and there are no shortcuts or halfway measures. Some students drift into theatre training because they have been excited by the stage and want to exhibit themselves on it one way or another; they seem to think that being enthusiastic and feeling strongly are all that is really needed, that theatre art is largely self-expression. But this is unfounded. Any work in the theatre, and this includes directing as a primary study in communication and artistic leadership, requires the utmost in dedication and hard work. Directing means giving to others; it is sharing one's own lifeblood. If you lack the stamina, or the discipline, do not try directing.

Learning directing, as with any craft, is a process of personal discovery—doing basic things over and over until they become second nature. How long the learning process will take is a matter of your capability in perceiving concepts, in getting the message in a very personal way. A book of this sort cannot make you into a director, for no one can actually teach you how to direct any more than he can teach you how to act. What can be done is to put you, as a dedicated learner, on the tracks that can lead to self-discovery. The artist in you will do the rest. The old saying "Life is short and art is long" is true only because artists have been challenged greatly by the demands of their jobs, and then have gone beyond themselves in making their art. If you want to be a director—the artistic leader of others in the theatre—you must learn it all.

The concept of the director in this book, then, is considered to be both a master craftsman in the theatre and the dedicated communicator-leader of all those who work with this art form. To carry out this objective, Part I—Taking a Play Apart—presents a detailed way of examining the structure of a play with the purpose of knowing its insides so well the director will have all sorts of ways to communicate with actors and designers. Part II—Communication—is divided into three sections, with the first two focusing on the physical ways and means a director communicates directly with actors, and the third on how the director communicates to audiences through his design function of choosing options in staging available to him. Part III—Interpretation/Style—again deals with play analysis, but on an advanced and much more sensitive level, designated as *style analysis*. The aproach here is to help the director perceive the inherent *individuality* of each play—its style—and then to help him find his own individual self-expression in producing it—the director's style.

Finally, a note about the use of the masculine pronouns—he, his, him—throughout the text when referring to the director. Just as "director" and "actor" are used nowadays to include both sexes, the pronouns are so used here in lieu of a nonexistent neuter form, or such clumsy words as "one" or "one's." Women have been active in the theatre as directors for over half a century, and as actor-managers for many decades before that. Thus, sexual delineation has no meaning whatever. A director earns the job-title through talent and acquired knowledge of the theatre.

Let's go to work.

EXERCISE

1. Did you notice how "theatre" is spelled here? Back in the nineteenth century, dictionary maker Noah Webster dumped the word into a general category and gave it an "-er" ending, the ending most American publishers have used ever since. But despite this, those who make theatre, especially in New York, have retained the old spelling because of all its special meanings and historical attachments from its European heritage. "Theatre" is a name that connotes heritage, traditions, conventions, public and private communications, mirror images, both visual and aural, great ideas, memorable characters, perceptive sentiments, live audiences, live actors, and much more.

2. How does live theatre, then, differ from the electronic mediums of television and moving pictures beyond the simple fact that it is live?

3. Compare the experience of a theatre performance with that of a religious ceremony. Can you envision the stage director as a "maker of ceremonies" rather than the customary designation, "coordinator" of an entertainment?

4. Why can the director be described as a ritualist who makes rituals?

5. Why is the live theatre more of a "belonging" than watching television or a movie?

6. Is theatre a social institution?

CHAPTER TWO
CAPTURING
THE WILD BIRD
The dramatic poet
and the director's job

THE POET-PLAYWRIGHT AND THE DIRECTOR

A play is like a tropical bird—at once exotic in its song and plumage, half-seen and mystical in its darting flight, and illusive and difficult to capture. Our forebears called the makers of these special stories play*wrights* on the assumption that a play could be made just as other craftsmen could make ships (shipwright) or wheels (wheelwright). His product, to be sure, it is not nearly so concrete, for he is a conscious dream maker who can, with the appropriate use of basic tools, stir up minds and create imaginative flights in others—the audience.

The peculiar characteristic of the playwright's making, the thing that differentiates it from other writing, is that his "dream-flight," his *improvisation,* has to take into account not only vocal and visual instruments—the actors—but also the peculiar place around which or in front of which he can gather his audience to hear and watch the story—the stage. He is a rare artist because what he puts down on paper, at its most demanding level, is not really writing at all in the usual literary sense, that is, writing intended for consumption in solitude by one person at a time, but is the making of a thing that involves live *actors* and *objects* set out in a specific way for seeing and hearing *by a group* meeting together in a group belonging (the audience). What the playmaker leaves out—the gap for the actors to fill in—is usually as important as what he puts in. French actor-director Jean-Louis Barrault described a play as "interrupted silence." This concept moves us entirely away from thinking about a play as a literary product, as merely conversation written down, for we see that it is far more difficult to leave out than to put in. Many celebrated novelists and poets have tried unsuccessfully to make "interrupted silences," but they abandoned their efforts, or audiences forced them to, when they discovered that they didn't have the know-how to devise this sort of skeletal improvisation. Nor did they know what to do with a live audience.

You should not be at all surprised to learn that such famous playwrights as Aeschylus, Shakespeare, and Molière acted in and often directed their own plays. After all, they knew or assumed that they knew, as everybody else did, what their plays were all about. Today, a playwright also hears his words in his mind's ear and sees the actions in his mind's eye when he composes a play. The total thing is the dramatic poem. What the play does to an audience is to arouse its emotions directly. *The process is physical and disturbing,* and it is only *secondarily intellectual,* though the experience requires a perceptive intelligence—not quite the same thing. When it works, it reaches out to grab and thrill; it can cause tears and laughter, chills and anger; it can also exhaust members of an audience as well as exalt them. Its powers are mystical and godlike. As we know, we can retain a well-performed play in our minds for years in the same way that we hold onto an intensively felt personal experience, as characters in plays can seem like exotic friends of many years' acquaintance.

In our day, the playwright seldom directs his own play, nor does he act in it. The pressure of the nineteenth-century world of scientific discoveries, of inventions, and of mechanization so changed playscripts, acting, and the stage machine that a coordinating specialist was needed to hold these forces together. Previously, leading actors with the help of a *"stage-manager,"* (who was—note nineteenth-century spelling—just what his labels implies: a manager of the stage), had given what little direction was considered necessary. But in the last quarter of the nineteenth century, the idea of a separate craftsman began to take shape—a skilled coordinator who understood all the crafts of the theatre and who could devote his full energies to bringing them together into a single, artistic, rhythmic whole in order to express in the best possible way what the playwright had in mind. Thus was born simultaneously twentieth-century theatrical art and the director as the major theatrical artist.

The need for the sort of study developed in this book is obvious. If you are to undertake the job of theatrical artist, you must learn as much as you can about the nature of theatrical art.

THE DIRECTOR'S JOB

It is precisely because he has so much power in the theatre that so much is expected of the director. Yet the curious paradox is that, like the playwright, he is not actually seen *on* the stage but only *through* the actors and the physical staging provided by the designers. In contrast, symphony and opera conductors, and even football coaches, have a physical presence. They visibly run the performance, with the obvious capability of directly affecting coordination, rhythm, and mood. But the director's work can be measured only in what happens when the actors and designers work on the audience. In this sense, he is a silent partner, though his work beforehand is anything but silent. To the contrary, the director is a talker, a verbal imagist, for *his primary work is communication*—not directly to the audience but *to actors and designers* who then transmit his ideas and pressures to the audience.

The director, then, is a communicator of the highest order. This function is his job, his only reason for being. A director may have very strong feelings about a playscript, but sensitivity, though it will help, will not define his directing capabilities. Because the transfer of his ideas must be made through the minds and feelings of others, the challenge for a director lies in the talent for touching the magic springs in others with what he so vividly imagines and feels himself.

This challenge is the director's paradox. All artists operate within some balance of their subjective-objective selves, but it is the subjective that customarily dominates. The director is an exception, for he does most of his work on the conscious side of the scale. Herbert Blau in *The Impossible Theatre,* a stimulating and soul-searching study of the director's function, contends that "The director must be a brain." This statement does not mean that the director works only in a coldly objective, intellectual way. What it does mean is that *the director must trust his feelings to react primitively and vigorously to what he helps make on the stage.* As the practicing critic in the theatre, he must constantly bring *what he feels and thinks to the surface* so that he can communicate readily with others. The director must perceive; he must evaluate; he must make a diagnosis; and he must devise remedies. His effectiveness in all these actions will lie precisely in his outside-inside responses, his objective-subjective balance. To accomplish this balance, the learning director must become intensively aware of the structures of plays, of the prevailing theories and the training processes of acting, of the physical use of the stage, and of the visual capabilities of design, for at the base the director is the total designer of a production—the principal "idea man" who matches concrete form with imagined ideas.

The emphasis in this book may at first seem to make the director too coldly analytical, but the intention is to show the need for the extensive training so necessary to equip a director for his job. Without a wide knowledge of the theatre and a keen understanding of its basic concepts, he is simply ineffective. Although his study may be broad and objective and his development of techniques may follow a self-conscious route, he may not achieve much more than did the nineteenth-century stage-manager unless he has an inherent talent for flight, that is, the ability to let his imagination go wild.

As all artists, the director must first be an adventurous spirit eager to cut new paths, and he must be capable of "soaring" on the level of the dramatic poet. Too often he is regarded as only an interpreter of the creative works of others; yet if he cannot reach some of the same heights as those achieved by the poet he is attempting to reveal on the stage, he is not fulfilling his function. At his best, he will soar with the angels; but at the same time he must be an engineerpilot, a professional who is forever landing and taking off. He knows his plane, his instruments, and his flight plan—the limitations that bind his flight, yet simultaneously make it possible. The stage is a flying machine that must be manipulated with the greatest skill. By knowing the limitations of his art form, he will know which way freedom lies and thus be able to lead others to it. Flight-in-restriction is his goal.

But despite all this high-minded talk, you must never forget that your leading purpose is to entertain—"Make them feel! Make them laugh!" But this can mean dozens of things. Here's the rub: a good director does not make "entertainment" as the end-all, for it is *how* he entertains that matter. A much better phrase than the word "entertain" is "turning on" audiences by getting their *involuntary* attention. This is the sort of attention audiences give despite themselves. It is what you as a director do to members of an audience that makes them sit more on the edge of their seats despite the hold-offs and hang-ups. Never forget that "I've got 'em" is the goal.

In our day, we seem obsessed with violence as entertainment in itself. But what makes good plays is not how people are killed, but why. A shoot-out with the evil ones destroyed and the virtuous surviving, as we can see any night on television, tells us very little, and it merely arouses fears and prejudices and sometimes violence like that portrayed. Remember, good plays—and there are many more that are bad—are made of different stuff. This is the stuff that "moves men's minds and enriches their spirits," says George Bernard Shaw.

You will discover early on how easy it is to entertain, but how difficult it is to make good theatre.

EXERCISE

1. Discuss all the parts of these definitions:
   a. A play is a story brought alive by actors on a stage before an audience.
   b. Plays are musical compositions in dialogue that linger in the memory and are called up with nostalgia like sweet tunes almost forgotten.
   c. Plays move the viewer-listener by plucking the emotional chords that jar loose submerged feelings, and force the turnover of past actions, either happy or unhappy.
2. What is a dramatic poet? Why is a modern writer of drama in prose also a dramatic poet?
3. Without getting involved in the complexities of the differences between serious drama and comedy, why is the writer of comedy also a dramatic poet?
4. The director is an "image-maker." What is an image? Cite images of each of the five senses.
5. From your knowledge of acting and designing, can you see how an audience perceives a play through images? What is the process of transfer?

6. Why do you or anyone else want to direct plays? Although you may be aware of the decreased position given to the theatre in our time because of motion pictures and television, are you fully informed on how the theatre has changed under their strong influences? What effect has the experimentations of the 1960s had on present-day theatre as well as its audiences? The shift of professional theatre away from the commercialism of New York City's Broadway, now more than a quarter of a century ago, to the regional non-profit theatres, supported strongly by state and federal taxes together with private monies, must be taken into any critical evaluation. New York is still of top importance because of its many competing theatres and its large number of newspaper reviewers looking at the same play and its production, but decentralization has made a new/old context across America that is not unlike the city stock company theatres of the nineteenth century. With it has come not only a divergence of theatre centers of quality and many more jobs for actors and playwrights in a rapidly declining media, but it has encouraged and even fostered a widespread network of amateur-professonal groups throughout America.

CHAPTER THREE
STARTING POINT
Basic assumptions; improvisation as a tool

ASSUMPTIONS AT THE BASE OF THIS BOOK

The approach to directing taken in this book, then, is rooted in five basic assumptions:

1. *Play-analysis is of primary importance in the directing process.* Merely feeling about a play is entirely insufficient. Play-analysis (structural analysis) must be mastered as a technique so that it can be used in approaching all aspects of the theatrical art in all plays, historical as well as modern.

2. *The director's core activity is communication.* It is precisely his capability of exact and imaginative communication *with* actors and designers (as distinct from his communication to an audience)—on a sublimated level as well as on a conscious level—that will declare his effectiveness.

3. *The director's training must be very closely allied to the actor's training.* Because the director's primary function is "bringing out" the actor, he must be highly sensitive as to how the actor feels, thinks, and works. Consequently, the approach in this book assumes that most acting instruction falls into two basic categories: the inside-to-outside approach (commonly related to Stanislavskian principles) and the outside-to-inside approach (that assumes a more objective training). But no matter what his initial training in acting may be, in order to work with a wide range of actors a director must become familiar with both approaches.

4. *The director is a master designer.* A produced play is the "physicalization" of a play-script, and it must be cohesive and integrated in all its aspects, from the manipulation of the actor to the manipulation of the stage space and all the materials used on it. An organic approach to theatre history provides an invaluable working tool for this function.

5. *The director is a critic and a stylist.* What the director puts on the stage is a direct statement of what he believes the play contains. Interpretation, as presented in this book, is defined as a sincere attempt at finding an author's ideas in a play and at rendering them honestly and appropriately through theatrical art. The kind of individualization a director uses in this process, without overriding the play, will declare his style for a particular production.

Study these. Know them well. They are the basic premises for all the discussions that follow. This book does not present a method but only an orderly progression of discussions about concepts with which every director must be familiar. The intention is thus far from tying you to any one way of doing things, but instead has the goal of freeing you to your own ways.

PREREQUISITES FOR TRAINING IN DIRECTING

What should the beginning director bring to his training? It is obvious that the study of directing cannot begin until the student has first learned a few basic concepts about the theatre and the skills that make them work.

1. He should be familiar with a body of plays from both modern and historical periods.
2. He should know something about historical stages as well as about conventions in the modern theatre.
3. He should have had some basic training in the crafts of the stage so that he knows how stage materials are made and used and can have ideas about how to put them to work in production.
4. He should have studied acting, including some technical training in voice and speech, *for his work with actors as the principal instruments of his ideas will be his most important contribution to a production.* Directing is not simple manipulation of other people by someone with a dominating ego, but a mature awareness of how to work skillfully with others to bring out the life-force of a breathing and pulsating story on the stage. If he is to capture for an audience the wild tropical bird of the play, a director must be a great deal more than a bird watcher.

PLAY READING

Among the first steps in directing is *reading* many plays. A director who does not avidly read plays, both past and present, cannot go far simply because he will lack a broad knowledge of the most basic tool—the playscript. Therefore, get into a regular habit of reading all kinds of plays and keeping a file card on each play read, with brief notations on ideas, setting requirements, story line, characters, and production possibilities. Once you have acquired such a background, you will be able to understand a particular play much better because of the comparison you can make with other plays.

However, because Parts I and II are principally for the beginning student, this book does not cite a broad range of plays as examples but confines discussions to relatively few on the assumption that the beginning director probably has not read many plays and will not be able to project examples readily in his imagination. All of Parts I and II, including the exercises, can be accomplished if the student is acquainted with the following plays, those usually read in introductory survey courses:

> *Riders to the Sea* (Synge)
> *Hedda Gabler* or *Ghosts* (Ibsen)
> *Candida* (Shaw)
> *Desire Under the Elms* (O'Neill)
> *The Cherry Orchard* (Chekhov)
> *The Little Foxes* (Hellman)
> *Winterset* (Anderson)
> *Murder in the Cathedral* (Eliot)
> *The Bald Soprano* (Ionesco)
> *Oedipus the King* (Sophocles)
> *Hamlet* (Shakespeare)
> Any play by Harold Pinter
> Any play by Tennessee Williams
> Any play by Edward Albee

In contrast, the examples used in Part III range widely on the assumption that by the time the student has been in training for a period of time he will have extended his reading as well as greatly amplified his understanding of the structure of drama. Consequently, he should be able to penetrate groups of plays he could not have handled previously with much perception.

EXERCISE

1. Although director-actor communication will be discussed later, on the basis of your experience as an actor try to list all the methods of communication between directors and actors that you can recall. How do directors "get through" to other people? Simple exposition in words is one of the ways, but it may be one of the poorer methods when it comes to reaching actors. Your answers to this exercise may be largely speculative at this point in your training, but now is the time to call up any experience you may have had along these lines.

2. How do each of the following backgrounds contribute to a student's preparation before beginning directing: acting; designing; the architec-

ture of Shakespeare's stage; what happens in Sophocles' *Oedipus;* what happens in *Hamlet;* a study of phonetics; a study of voice production; an understanding of music and painting.

3. Make a list of *all* the plays you have (a) read or (b) seen. Take care in dividing your experience into these two categories because they are quite different. Date each one, and then examine your actual coverage of drama. How extensive is your background? Where are you weakest? You must make a habit of reading plays regularly to fill in the weak areas.

IMPROVISATION AS A TOOL

In this book the technique of *improvisation* is suggested throughout as a classroom work method. In its early uses, improvisation was thought of primarily as Stanislavskian training for the actor, but as its values and possibilities became more apparent, it was used not only in the relationship between director and actor but also as a basis for play making. Consequently, not only were a number of experimental moving pictures made by using this approach, but the live productions of The Open Theatre and The Living Theatre in the 1960s showed us that unusual theatricals could also be developed through this technique. Though such productions in the 1980s are infrequent, the improvisational approach as a method of freeing both actors and directors in training is still quite valid.

The approach taken in this book, therefore, assumes that stage direction is the process of freeing the master improvisation—the playscript—by freeing actors and designers to make their own improvisations. The imposition of restriction, of limitation, can take place only *after the flight* and not before. One of the great problems in learning directing is in learning this paradox of freedom and restraint. Both are absolutely necessary: without freedom the imagination of an audience is never aroused; without restraint the telling of a story from the confinement of a stage in a theatre with live actors would be impossible.

The director is therefore an improvisor of the first order. In this sense he is very close to the playwright who turns his dreams into forms—all controlled improvisations. The director is forever a game player, always improvising, always making up spontaneously what seems appropriate and believable in a given circumstance.

You will note as you work through this book that many of the exercises require improvisation—spontaneous storytelling in declared or undeclared circumstances. If you have participated in such game playing, you will already know that improvising can make something very much like a play, but it is not a play at all, only an exercise in releasing imagination. The overall intention is to free those persons who play the game—to let them "fly." But in order to do so, several conditions are necessary. Here are a few that must guide you and your classmates when doing improvisations:

1. The participants are not actors; that is, they are neither acting out a portion of a playscript nor are they performing for an audience. Their intention is to *release each other* through full concentration on each other and the situation. Although some given circumstances may be set before an improvisation begins, the participants work "off" one another, with their imagination dictating what to do in a certain context. There is no preplan of action. What happens will happen only as a participant lets his behavior, in reaction to other forces (other people in the same improvisation), be the result of his response to their pressures.

2. The watchers are not an audience. They are privileged to be there when the improvisation takes place. Therefore, they must not participate like an audience, but should watch silently and quietly with no verbal reactions whatsoever, since this would break the "happening" by distracting the participants, thus making them self-conscious. Once the participants have become self-aware, the improvisation is lost because they have become themselves and not participants in an imagined circumstance.

3. The place to develop an improvisation is not a stage nor any location that would resemble it, because the artificial nature of this kind of setting would cause the improvisers to feel self-conscious. For this reason this game should be played in a room, with the space defined only by what the improvisors find necessary.

4. Only the beginning of an improvisation should be suggested, and only in a barely minimal way. What happens afterward is the improvisation.

It is obvious that a good deal that is playlike can happen in improvisations if the participants and watchers observe the conditions. You can see characters in action, with different moods and tempos, and, as a watcher, you can be moved by the truthtelling and believability of such moments. But you must also realize that "achieving" a complex improvisation is not easily accomplished unless you have participants with experience in playing this game, since learning to release fully takes practice. In working through the exercises in this book you must always give yourself seriously and with full concentration to improvisational exercises. If you do, you will find them most rewarding.

EXERCISE

1. Illustrate the difference between restriction and flight by doing the following improvisation: With the use of chairs, tables, or other essentially neutral forms in the classroom, one student composes a four-sided place. The class then tries to guess the *literal* place suggested by the forms and their arrangement by identifying the literal meaning of each form, such as a chair, a bed, a sofa, in the context of other forms. When a consensus has been reached on the literal meaning, the class suggests *alternate meanings* for the forms, with the intention of arriving at more exceptional locations and contexts. Thus, what might at first seem to be a normal suburban living room could be turned into the mountain hideout of a gangster or the primitive hut of a peasant. Repeat this game with several improvised places. The flight takes place as class members move away from

accepted literal meanings of forms in their easily recognizable contexts—their own everyday realities—and begins to let the forms take on imagined places. Thus, *forms become the stimulators of flight,* not hard realities. (Note: This exercise is not that of making a groundplan for a stage, so do not set up the places with a stage in mind but only as places that could exist in real life anywhere.)

2. Continue Exercise 1 with one student arranging a place and then setting in it two people who have a specific relationship to one another, such as mother/son, boss/secretary, boy/girl. The class tries first to declare the literal place and its context; it then tries to identify possible flights by suggesting more exceptional places and relationships of the people.

3. Continue Exercise 2 by having the students in the improvisation *develop a conflict* by using numbers, not words, as dialogue. Example: *A* says: 1, 2, 3, 4; *B* says: 9, 10, 20; *A* says: 2, 3, 6, 7; *B* says: 4, 7, 9, 10. In this substitute for dialogue, the numbers do not mean anything in themselves, but the attitude behind each group of numbers is the basic meaning behind the line. (The use of actual words in improvisations is very difficult for participants because they must think in terms of word choice. Number dialogue is much easier because participants need think only of their attitudes towards other people in the improvisation.) When the improvisers reach an intensity of interresponse, the improvisation can be stopped and the following points discussed:

   a. What is improvisation?
   b. What are the free circumstances of an improvisation?
   c. How was this improvisation like a play and yet not a play?
   d. What is a play? (Try defining it as an expert and highly developed improvisation.)
   e. What did the participants add to the suggested beginning of the improvisation?
   f. What are the limitations in the use of number dialogue?

PART ONE
TAKING A PLAY APART

Play-analysis:
the director's primary study

The poet's eye, in a fine frenzy rolling,
Doth glance from heaven to earth, from earth to heaven;
And, as imagination bodies forth
The forms of things unknown, the poet's pen
Turns them to shapes, and gives to airy nothing
A local habitation and a name.

Theseus in *A Midsummer Night's Dream*

CHAPTER FOUR
HOW TO READ
A PLAY

Do you know how to read a play? Most people don't, but go at it as if they were reading a short story or novel. A play is very different because it is all starts and stops, and full of gaps, silences, and only a bare minimum of descriptions. Furthermore, it is all dramatic action. As a reader you must imagine all of those by supplying in your mind's eye what the actors and the staging are doing. And since a play is all written dialogue, if you don't know what that is and how it works, you will be lost, or confused, or what is worse, take it all for granted as if it is as plain as the nose on your face.

That is what *play-analysis* is for: a way of getting inside plays so you don't miss their real guts.

PERCEPTION: PLAY-ANALYSIS

Perception as it is used here simply implies your own personal discovery of what a playscript is all about—your sense and feel of it.

Many people in the theatre shy away from the phrase *play-analysis* because they think it has a dry, academic ring that implies cold, factual, scientific examination of a playscript, a process that will kill their gut (subjective) feelings about it. They assume that good theatre can be made if one *feels* strongly enough about a playscript; good sense and some general backgrounds in theatre will carry one the rest of the way. This book does not agree at all with that point of view. Certainly, there are aspects of many plays that cannot be described easily in words, but this difficulty does not suggest that a play exists in a mystical world defying logical, mind-oriented examination. Having the right attitude about play-analysis at the beginning is very important.

The word "perception" has specific meanings here because it can imply both strong feelings (the subjective flight and freedom in a director) and a basic objective awareness of how a play is made. It implies much more than a felt reaction on a first reading: "I like that play. It moves me strongly." Perception implies that a penetrating search into a play—play-analysis—is absolutely necessary if one is to understand how a play works.

What a director finds in his play-analysis will depend on how thoroughly he can take a play apart in his own mind and then put it back together again, thoroughly comprehended. Perception is the director's total view of a playscript after he has "felt" it and then "examined" it in detail. If his feelings are strong on first reading, and he knows the job of play-analysis thoroughly, he cannot help but have much greater respect for a play after analysis than he had before. At the very least, he will not be ambivalent about it.

This point of view is predicated on the assumption that a play is not life but art form, a made object that may have a likeness to life but definitely is not life. Even those playscripts that seem most realistic, most like everyday life as we know it, stand this test. You may have heard about Stanislavski's discovery of this difference when he asked his actors to perform a scene from a play by Chekhov out-of-doors in a real garden. Before they began, he assumed that the playscript was lifelike and his players so photographically real in their roles that anyone watching could only think what he saw was actually taking place. He was amazed, and at first greatly disappointed, to discover that the scene produced no such effect; against the reality of nature in the garden the action and the actors were like wax flowers with only a resemblance to reality. He then began to revise his whole theory of making reality on the stage, basing it on the realization that a play is a play, no matter how photographic it seems, and must therefore not be confused with real life.

The nature of art can be defined in many ways, and you should try to clarify in your own mind something about this vast subject as early as possible. Even though such definitions are highly relevant to any discussion of directing, the intention is not to pursue them at this time but only to point out that the more a director knows about the difference between ritual and art form—yet at the same time how they are related—the more he understands about the origins of dramatic and theatrical forms. And the more he understands about the difference between what is real and what is fabricated on the stage, the more he will comprehend not only of theatre as art form but also what he can do as a maker of that art form. Your own definition of art will gradually mature and become part of you as you work in depth with theatrical materials and techniques. However, definitions can be confusing and complicating at first. Therefore, you must accept on faith, if you do not yet comprehend the concept, that a playscript is an artificial object you can disassemble and reassemble as you can any other man-made object.

Play-analysis, then, is the director's objective support *for his feelings* about a playscript. As a technique, it is tied to the primary thesis that directing is not a totally intuitive process but is also an art-creating process in which the director brings the materials (the playscript) of the form to the conscious surface; that is, he becomes *consciously* aware of them in the interest of finding their strengths and weaknesses, their peaks and valleys, and their rhythms, all of which will serve as a basis for theatricalizing the playscript in the best possible way. Adequate play-analysis is no guarantee of success, but it is insurance that the director is at least familiar with his materials.

The playscript is the principal machine of the director, and play-analysis is as basic a reason for his job as is helping the actor. Unless he knows his machine thoroughly, he will be only a stagemanager—a traffic organizer and logistical expert.

EXERCISE

1. Bring some definitions of art to class and discuss their merits. How does the theatre differ from such "fine" arts as painting or sculpture? Can you see theatre as "folk art"?

2. How does a play differ from such literary forms as: (a) a novel; (b) a book of history; (c) a lyrical poem? Why is the stage the natural habitat for a play?

3. Discuss the dangers of "impressionism" if carried out literally—that is, if the student director moves solely out of his feelings. What will it do to his capabilities in communication? What will be his problems with actors who also feel very strongly but perhaps differently about a play?

4. Compare in detail the improvisational reality of an hour of class—the one being experienced at the moment—with what a playwright might do in dramatizing the same hour for the stage. What is dramatic? What is peripherally dramatic? Why is the peripheral more interesting than the obvious that everyone sees?

5. What do we mean when we talk about the "dramatic imagination" in a reader? How does it improve as one reads more plays? Why does such a reader have an advantage over others who do not read and study plays regularly?

6. Discuss with other members of the class your experiences with first readings. Do you make a practice of reading a play in one sitting? Why is this procedure good? What did you *feel* about a particular play after the initial reading? It will be helpful if the class reads the same play for its discussion.

OVERVIEW OF PLAY-ANALYSIS

Study the drawing below very carefully because it is at once a summary of what you will be tangling with not only in Part I on play-analysis but also in Parts II and III as you work at putting a play on stage.

A graphic representation of all playscripts. Note the mid-line: a play begins here, recapturing the past and moving forward to the present.

You should note in the drawing the five major areas to examine in taking a play apart: (1) given circumstances; (2) dialogue; (3) dramatic action; (4) characters; (5) ideas. Two more areas not seen in the drawing will be added to this list: (6) tempos; (7) moods. Although this breakdown is arbitrary for the purpose of explicit discussion, you should recognize at the outset that they overlap, as the drawing illustrates, and that some of these areas are so thoroughly dependent on others that they do not take shape until the force of the others has been determined. Other words might be used to define the same concepts, but this set, when fully delineated, answers the purpose very well. You know that basic communication in textbooks rests on clear definition of the terms used. Therefore, you must recognize at this point that play-analysis in this book is based on the meanings given to the terms here and in the following three chapters. For the purpose of discussion, the seven areas are treated under three major headings: (1) "The Foundation and Facade of the Playscript: Given Circumstances and

Dialogue,'' discussed in Chapter 5, (2) ''The Hard Core of the Playscript: Dramatic Action and Characters,'' discussed in Chapter 6, and (3) ''The Derivatives of Dramatic Action in a Playscript: Idea and Rhythmic Beats,'' treated in Chapter 7.

You must also be alerted at this point to a matter of great importance: each of these words (for example, dialogue) or two-word phrases (for example, given circumstances) stands for a concept. Merely to define them is not to understand them. As in acting, *doing* in directing will lie not in defining terms or in debating concepts but in absorbing them so thoroughly that they are immediately recognizable in all contexts. You must discover for yourself the breadth and depth of these concepts so that they become an intuitive part of your thinking about a play.

In the discussions of the seven areas the terms are first defined and then developed as concepts. Some examples are given to illustrate each step in this technique, but your comprehension will come about only through application of the approach to specific plays. There is no skipping around in this procedure. Try to understand and apply the concept of one term before you go on to the next. The series of seven is developed in an intentional order to show how each draws on what precedes it.

At first, you will be tempted to push aside the examination-in-depth of these concepts. After all, simple impression—''I *feel* it this way''—is much easier. But if you do proceed in this fashion, you will soon discover that you really do not know much about the inside workings of a play and that *you do not really know how to get through to actors.* Once you have mastered the techniques outlined here, you will feel a security you have not known previously, since you will at least know something very specific about your primary tool—the playscript.

Story versus Play-Analysis

Another problem usually confronting the student in his first contacts with play-analysis is the difference between the playscript as mere story and the structure of that story. The story of a play is made up of so many things so well blended together that an unoriented reader merely experiences its final effect: its moods, its feelings. But through play-analysis, the director can get at what makes those moods and feelings. Thus he can have greater assurance of getting the most out of his actors, and in turn, moving audiences. In comparison with live theatre, the moving picture as a form is static because each scene has been perfected through several takes and retakes and is set, impervious to change. In the theatre, however, a playscript is made up of a line of scenes that must be played continuously without interruption, and then repeated at subsequent performances. This living quality is its individuality and its rarity. Your awareness of play structure, then, will give you the seeds for all that can happen later when you put a play into production.

Procedure for Class Discussion

A one-act play of high quality should be selected at this point for an on-going classroom study throughout Part I. J. M. Synge's familiar classic *Riders to the Sea* is so well put together, so well-constructed, that is has withstood nearly a century of picking it apart while still leaving things to wonder about. It has survived all these years because it is a dramatic poem of true stature and intensive meaning. Moreover, it is an example of Early Realism, a style of playwriting begun by Henrik Ibsen, which you should study first as the dominant style in this century if you are to understand much about the changes playwrights have made since. *Unless you can take apart a Realistic play, a play that looks like life around you, and reassemble it fully understood, you will get lost in disassembling those that are not Realistic. Save those until later.* (See note following the exercise at end of this chapter.)

To offset what may seem old-fashioned about *Riders,* your class may want to look regularly at two other Realistic plays, chosen from later periods, to act as "control" plays. One might be a one-act play by Tennessee Williams, written during the 1940s or 1950s (such as *Lord Byron's Love Letter),* and the other a one-act play by William Albee *(The Zoo Story).* However, to make the comparisons work, *the "control" plays must also be Realistic in style.* "Departure" plays will be treated extensively in Part III after you have a sturdy comprehension of Realism. Don't let your enthusiasm to direct recent plays kill off what you must learn now about the structure of all plays. Once you understand the principles of play-analysis, and something about Realism, you will be able to disassemble all kinds of plays, including musicals and operas, and make them work for you on the stage. The theatre will wait for you, but it will not want you if you don't know what is going on there.

EXERCISE

1. Tell the story of the latest play you have read. Did your narration interest your hearers? If it did not, why not? Did you miss the point? Did you try to convey *your* feelings about the play rather than its specific story line?
2. Tell a personal anecdote from yesterday. What made it effective for your listener? Did he get the point quickly or did you need additional explanations?
3. Compare the stories of a recent motion picture you have seen and a play you have either read or seen. What is different about each form? Try to avoid letting your discussion focus on the differences in production, but place the emphasis on the differences in the story lines and how they are developed.
4. What is meant by technique? Why are techniques necessary for people working with art forms?

A note about *style:* It should be sufficient at this point to define *style* as the quality, in a play other than its story, that turns the general form into something individual and specific. These unique markings are therefore always present in a play, but they are difficult to perceive and assess until you have learned a good deal about play-analysis, the technique of taking apart the general form of plays. If you want to know more about the nature of *style* and its relationship to form, you can find a full discussion in Chapter 24 but you will be looking ahead at the risk of confusing matters of *style* with the simplified approach to play structure outlined in this part of the book. Once again: Learn all you can about the Realistic *style,* the one most familiar to you and the one used for exercises in Part I, before you work with other *styles.*

CHAPTER FIVE
THE FOUNDATION
AND FACADE
OF THE PLAYSCRIPT
Given circumstances
and dialogue

After you have read the following pages you will have a better understanding of why "Foundation and Facade" has been chosen to head this chapter. All you need to understand at this point, however, is that both given circumstances and dialogue *frame* the play just as deeply rooted pilings and a covering of glass and steel frame a modern skyscraper. The given circumstances resemble the deeply rooted base of a building—the substructure upon which it is built, its foundation; and dialogue is the outer shell, the facade, the transparent encasement covering the activities that will go on inside. If you keep these images in mind, you will be able to see why the real guts of the play (its hard core) resides in dramatic action and characters, but that they cannot be built into the structure without the foundation of given circumstances and the facade of dialogue.

GIVEN CIRCUMSTANCES (PLAYWRIGHT'S SETTING): THE FOUNDATION

Definition. The term *given circumstances* (playwright's setting) concerns all material in a playscript that delineates the environment—the special "world" of the play—in which the action takes place. This material includes: (1) environmental facts (the specific conditions, place, and time); (2) previous action (all that has happened before the action begins); and (3) polar attitudes (points of view toward their environment held by the principal characters).

Given circumstances versus playwright's setting.   Although Stanislavski's phrase "given circumstances" will be used throughout this text after this initial explanation, the parenthetical phrase *playwright's setting* is used because you are probably more familiar with it. However, as a term, it is so frequently confused with what a designer makes—the actual stage construction—that you should avoid using it altogether. Many readers of plays, including students of the theatre early in their training, commonly assume that the explicit directions describing a room or other location that usually appear in the printed editions of modern plays have been set down by their authors. However, more often than not, they depict the settings used in the first production and thus represent the conception of the designers as recorded by a stagemanager or an editor. Even when such a description comes from an author's own manuscript, a further danger exists because the author may try to play the role of stage designer, a role about which he may know little or nothing at all. If you, as a reader-director, are not aware of this pitfall, you may find it very difficult to free yourself from these initial suggestions because the printed word may seduce you. There is much less harm in reading these directions after you have studied the play, for then you will have a strong conception of the inherent setting, and you can separate what the author considers significant about an environment from a designer's interpretation of it.

Dialogue is the only reliable source of given circumstances.   When you study plays, you quickly become aware that all authors write their settings directly into their dialogue, either overtly or subconsciously. Setting is a matter of feeling about objects and places; it is about time and what has happened before the play begins; and it is about the feelings of the characters for the special world of the play. The totality is what a playwright must communicate to the audience as deftly and as accurately as possible, for what happens in a play will be based on these given circumstances.

You will note in the suggested analytical technique that follows that the first two sections—"Environmental Facts" and "Previous Action"—are far more factual than the third—"Polar Attitudes." Yet it is this last that will actually set up the beginning point of a play because it is the most important aspect of the given circumstances. Look for the facts, yes; but the attitudes of characters toward those facts are extremely important.

Environmental facts.   All plays establish some delineation of the exact place and time of the action as well as give specific information about the environment. These elements are called the facts of the play *whether or not the playwright has been historically accurate,* because they remain fixed throughout the play. The director should isolate them by systematically noting them under the following categories:

1. Geographical location—the exact place. This category should also include climate, since weather often defines specific location and can affect dramatic action.
2. Date—year, season, time of day. What is significant about the date?
3. Economic environment—class level, state of wealth or poverty. If two or more economic levels are used in a play, be certain to record the facts of each level.
4. Political environment—the specific relationships of the characters to the form of government under which they live. Many plays have definite political settings that will strongly affect the behavior of the characters. Many other plays tacitly accept a form of government that has established basic restrictions on the characters. Do not take what you may think is direct omission to mean that it is unimportant. Look carefully for clues throughout the script, for the author may be taking this given circumstance for granted on the assumption that those who read the play will understand the context. But *you* cannot make such an assumption. He will leave a trail of implications behind him, and these you must dig out.
5. Social environment—the mores and social institutions under which the characters live. These facts are extremely important because they may be manifested through their restrictions on the outward behavioral patterns of the characters and consequently may set up basic conflicts in the action of the play.
6. Religious environment—formal and informal psychological controls. Much that applies to item (4) also applies here.

When you study the given circumstances of a play, you must strictly avoid reading anything into the play; all facts must be explicitly stated or implied as is suggested in item (4) of the list. Do not assume anything. Some plays will involve all of these categories; others only some of them. Above all, *do not try to reconstruct your own idea of historical fact* surrounding a play; *if it is not in the play, it does not exist.* A playwright is not writing a history but telling a story; and he may not know his history well at all, or he may be deliberately shifting the facts to suit his own purposes. Do not try to correct him but record his facts exactly as he prescribes them.

Previous action. It is necessary to make a sharp distinction between *present action*—what an audience actually sees *happening* immediately in front of it—and *previous action*—what an audience is *told happened before the present action begins.* All plays begin somewhere in the middle or toward the end of things; thus, given circumstances usually includes some narration of past action so that the present action has a base from which to move forward. More recent plays, those written since the early 1960s, depend very little on past action, whereas others, those of Ibsen, for instance, require much retelling of past events. Both kinds of action—previous and present—are included in what is loosely defined as a story. But the director *always works specifically with present action,* although one of his major problems is to decide how to make the necessary narrations about the past as active as possible. In modern plays based on psychological revelation, the past plays an enormous part in the explanation as it does in a Freudian psychoanalysis; yet, the vital play for audiences lies only in what is actively happening immediately before its eyes.

You must, therefore, learn to separate these two kinds of action. The previous action, though it may take all of the first act and sometimes longer to narrate fully, establishes the point where the present action actually begins. Once you learn how to make this distinction you will know how to make a narration of the past interesting on the stage, for narration in itself is very dull compared to present action. Yet, a good playwright will always make this narration exciting because he will give the character a present action in the process of recalling it; that is, he will arrange for the recounting to do something to a character we are watching. Thus, to the director, *there is never a dull exposition but only a recalling of the past under the excitement and tension of active engagement with other characters in the present.* A director who does not know this point of structure will lose control of his audience very quickly. He will lose the key to handling the plays of Ibsen and Chekhov as well as a great deal of twentieth-century drama.

A technique for separating these two areas of action is the simple one of underlining in the text all lines that *recall* the past. A text by Ibsen contains many such lines, particularly in the first act; and often there are important revelations later in the play, especially when new characters are introduced. If you list these previous actions on one-half of a sheet of paper as they are introduced and put down the present actions, you will see their direct relationship.

A director can obscure a production by careless inattention to previous action, for some playwrights handle the necessary recalling in such subtle ways that an audience will miss important points unless the director carefully sets them out. Plays do not "talk" themselves; they are communicated by actors and directors who know what they are "talking" about. Congreve's *The Way of the World* is a great play, one of the greatest in the English language; but if an audience misses the point, made very briefly in one line, that Mirabell was once a lover of Mrs. Fainall, that he left her pregnant and that he arranged for her marriage to Fainall, the import of most of the action that follows involving Mirabell as well as Fainall will be misunderstood and its significance lost. This example is extreme, but in kind it is forever recurring.

Learn what previous action is and then you will know what to do with it in production.

Polar attitudes.   Every character in a play, as in real life, is conditioned by the "special world" he is caught in, the world of his own prejudices, his own tolerances and intolerances, and his assumptions when he is forced to have relationships with others and must take actions affecting both himself and others. The special world of a character is conditioned, of course, by environmental facts and by previous action. Although it depends on these concrete details, it differs explicitly in that it is the "emotional environment" of a character, the stresses and strains under which he lives. Modern slang would call them his "hang-ups." The special world of the principal character is always declared *at the beginning of a play* because it declares his position vis-a-vis the other characters. This is the *inner environment* of a play, the environment that sets up the conflicts and the problems: the environment of love relationships in and out of marriage; the environment of family pressures that cause love and hate between mothers and sons, fathers and sons, mothers and daughters; the environment of political, religious, and social pressures that forces people to behave in ways that may destroy their families and their relationships to these families; the environments of fear of power, disregard of others, indifference to wealth or love of wealth, indifference to religion or its opposite. A character is caught in this special world, and the play is about how he is destroyed by it or escapes from it.

Here is an important fact about plays: In the course of a play a *principal* character *does not change* in character, but his *attitudes change* under pressures from forces outside his control. The other characters serve as specific instruments to these changes. As the principal character meets these forces, he must adjust to them, and, as he does so, certain capabilities dormant within him (his true character) come to the surface and force him to act. These capabilities have been present all the time, but they have never been called upon and thus recognized as points of character. The development in a play's action, therefore, is composed of the changing attitudes in the principal character towards his *inner* environment, towards *his special world* as it was declared at the beginning of the play.

It is also important to point out that all of the characters in a play do not change their attitudes, but only the principal character, a fact that makes them principal. Secondary characters thus act as instruments in these changes. In a play-analysis it is always the primary characters that concerns us most, for then we can determine the exact force and functions of the secondary characters.

Most plays show radical shifts in the attitudes of their principal characters from the positions they held at the beginning to those they hold at the end. A philosophical way of expressing this shift is to say that a character moves from ignorance to knowledge. He sees the world in which he lives more and more clearly *after* the actions he has been forced to take during the course of the play, than he did before. Therefore, it is necessary to pin down the attitudes towards the inner environment (special world) held at the beginning of a play by a principal character so that a director can clearly see the final pole of this character, and can later help the actor find both poles, as well as help the other characters see their function in the change. What happens in between these poles is the dramatic action.

By setting out the polar attitudes of each principal character, the director can see the scope of what happens in between the poles—the stretch of the characters—and the explicit effects given circumstances have on the characters. Thus, the shape of the play is explicitly declared in the polarities of the principal character.

What we mean by the beginning of a play, then, is the defined positions of the attitudes held by the principal character of the play toward the special world he is caught in and within which he takes action. These positions declare explicitly where the *present action* begins. The characters in most plays (Ionesco's antihero is an exception) will have strong feelings of either like or dislike for the present inner environment in which they find themselves. The plot that follows (present action) will either shake them loose from their liking or bring their dislike to liking (or at least to acceptance). If a character does not finally accept what he dislikes at the beginning of a play, he will probably die or exile himself in the process of resisting the forced change that others bring upon him and become what we call a *tragic hero*. In comedy, if a character strongly resists being pried loose from what he already likes intensely at the beginning, he will survive, but he will be ridiculed and become what we call a *comic fool*. But whatever happens to him, the attitudes he has at the beginning will certainly be radically changed by the end, or if he is a certain kind of comic fool, he may go on blissfully, never realizing that anyone has tried to change him. (See Exercise 5 below.)

An attitude towards the special world at the beginning of a play is usually more general than specific. It is usually something the character has taken for granted as the natural state of affairs, and he is therefore not consciously aware of it, although it most certainly will be pointed out to the audience in one way or another. The action of the play will make him aware of his special world because it will subject him to a test of his attitudes through direct conflict with others. The initial action in a play will usually point out to him where he stands in contrast to others, although he may be very blind about why he stands where he does. The attitudes of characters, then, should be general statements and not tied specifically to the present action which will follow. Here are some examples of initial attitudes.

Men are foolish and romantic and can be manipulated rather easily. (Hedda in *Hedda Gabler*. What is her final attitude?)

The only thing that really matters is money. (Regina in *The Little Foxes*. What is her final attitude?)

"Good" women are dull, embarrassing, and impossible to talk to. (Marlowe in *She Stoops to Conquer*. What is his final attitude?)

A king is sacred and no one can challenge his God-given right to dictate. (Oedipus in *Oedipus Rex*. What is his final attitude?)

Love of women is all romantic adoration and worship. (Marchbanks in *Candida*. What is his final attitude?)

When you have learned to pinpoint the special world of a play, you will understand the secret of its inner workings because you will know what the environmental forces are that hold the principal characters in check at the beginning. This knowledge will show you what they must fight against to overcome those forces in order to arrive at the final pole.

In the actual practice of trying to determine polar attitudes, it is usually easier to find the initial pole for each character by noting what has happened to each character at the end. Remember that the interest of an audience will be focused on what happens between the poles for this is the dramatic action, the specifics that bring about the change in the principal characters. This is what holds the audience riveted to the play and what makes the change so climactic, so theatrical, and so emotionally disturbing.

EXERCISE

1. Using any modern Realisic play (*Riders to the Sea, Ghosts, Hedda Gabler, Desire Under the Elms*), list the environmental facts in the specific categories suggested in the text. What do these facts suggest about a possible stage setting? Can you "see" the setting? Can you visualize some possible costumes? What do they tell you about body movement? About decorum? Do they suggest what the characters think about and what they feel? What does physical circumstance (environmental fact) have to do with human behavior? (Begin the accumulative analysis of your class study-play at this point. See p. 21.)

2. Delineate the previous action in the same play you have studied in Exercise 1 by underlining all the parts of the speeches in the first act that literally refer to actions that have happened *before* the here-and-now of the act begins. If you are looking at *Hedda Gabler* or another play by Ibsen, how many lines by actual count contain references to previous actions? (Be very careful not to include those recountings of actions that the audience has already witnessed as present actions; those narrations are present actions because the playwright intends the audience to weigh and evaluate a character in terms of that character's judgments of what has happened.) In your own judgment, what is the effect of this accumulation of knowledge about the past? Does it have any effect on what is happening in the present? Does it tell us anything about the characters? Can you see why it is unimportant in itself, but only as it affects a character's present action?

3. *Very important:* As an alternate exercise, study several opening pages of a play by listing the previous action on one side of a sheet and the present action on the other. In this way you have a ready comparison of what the playwright is actually doing.

4. In working with the same play used in Exercises 1 through 3, delineate the attitude of each major character toward the special world or the inner emotional environment of the play—what he thinks and feels about life around him. Whether he likes it or not is unimportant; what he likes about it or does not like about it is very important. Look for such hidden attitudes as: love for others, fear of power, disregard of others, indifference to wealth, indifference to religious feeling. Does he admire monarchy? Does he love freedom? Let the emotional environment tell you exactly how each major character reacts to the given world at the beginning of the play.

5. Discuss Archie's polar attitudes in the television situation comedy *All in the Family*. Do you see how he changes during the course of an episode (comparable to a one-act play)? What is the function of "Meathead"? Of Archie's wife and daughter?

DIALOGUE: THE FACADE OF THE PLAYSCRIPT

Now that you understand the roots of a play—where, when, and how it derives from the immediate past (the given circumstances)—you are ready to examine its facade: the clothes on the package. What is inside will be given special attention in Chapter 6, when you study dramatic action and characters. But now you need to become aware that dialogue is not just the things people say, but far more importantly, *what they do*.

Definition.   Although dialogue is obviously the conversation between *two or more* characters in a play, it is not so obvious that *its primary function is to "contain" the dramtaic action,* to be its primary vehicle. In addition, although dialogue may appear as a written line on a printed page, its primary intention is to be *heard* rather than read. It is talk and not writing.

Dialogue is action.   Dialogue is not merely a verbal interchange between characters but an artificial, highly economical, and symbolic intercommunication of *actions* between characters in which each forces his wants and needs on the other. *Dialogue always exists in the present tense* because it comes out of the mouths of speakers who think, as in life, only in the present and who say things to one another to get what they want.

Dialogue is a building process.   *A* says something to *B*, and *B* replies; this talk causes *A* to reply to *B* and *B* to *A* in a continuing cycle. But no matter how refined a line of dialogue may be, no matter how elaborate the choice of words, the purpose is always the same: to seek response out of another person as we do in real life.

Thus, the nature of dialogue is its built-in characteristic of *"forcing."* The words used on the outside may try to conceal this forcing in a very elaborate way, or they may be very direct and not conceal it at all. From a casual reader's view, dialogue looks like it is only the printed text of the play, but its basic function is to contain the heart and soul, the blood and guts of the play—*the subtext* or dramatic action.

Dialogue is in verse or prose.   Plays vary greatly in the choice of language used by characters, a choice that the given circumstances dictates since they specifically delineate the decorum or outward show, that is, how the characters behave—their manners or lack of manners. Most modern plays have prose dialogue because of its likeness to the reality of everyday life; but a few are written in verse forms as were many plays of the past. Verse forms are obviously more artificial in their use of language than is prose, but the basic intent is always the same: the containment of the dramatic action. More will be said about verse later in Part III in the discussion of period acting, but it is sufficient to point out here that verse form is not merely a decorative exterior but a heightened, more compact, exalting language for conveying intense feelings and high actions. The effect of verse is often as potent as physical body movements, simply because verse conveys intensive inner feelings of the highest pitch. It thus has the capability of direct contact with an audience. This is why many playwrights who write dialogue in prose often try to find a language somewhat more elevated than what is used in everyday life, as Arthur Miller did in *The Crucible*.

Dialogue is inner language.   Dialogue should be analyzed in detail to discover its peculiar characteristics in addition to its function as a cover for dramatic action and its direct reflection of given circumstances. Even within the narrow range of the given circumstances for a particular play, an author has a large scope in his choice of words and their arrangement and in the images he may devise. Dialogue is thus said to be *connotative* rather than denotative—much more weighted with feeling and meaning than dictionary usage or definitive meaning. In the human context of plays, characters feel or sense one another (as people who live closely together do in everyday life) and consequently do not talk at one another but *with* one another. Thus, the language of drama is highly subjective, inner language. Realism has used a wide variety of folk-speech patterns—dialects—in the interest of showing how people talk from their "guts" and not from their minds. Moving pictures have fully exploited this aspect of dialogue, particularly in reproducing low-level environments.

Dialogue is heard language.   Any study of a play written in dialect requires penetration beyond the choice of words and the modification of vowels, for an author who has really heard the speech he uses for a certain character will reproduce all sorts of cultural overtones buried in the outer form, a subtle delineation of given circumstances. Thus, the speech sounds of Brooklyn or Dublin or London reflect the hardness of city life, just as Southern American speech reflects the slower rhythm of the rural South. Most recent plays that intend reproduction of local idiom (Harold Pinter's plays, for instance) do not set down the modifications of sound in spelling as playwrights once did, but rely on the specific choice of words or lack of them to convey the inarticulate aspects of the characters. The dialect (sound quality) is thus left to the actor to supply.

Directors must, therefore, learn to hear dialogue in their mind's ear: not only the literal reproductions of sound as they hear it in everyday life, but the reproduction of word-feeling as playwrights set them out in characters. You must learn the craft of matching speech decorum, as perceived in a play's text from the given circumstances, to character decorum. More will be said about this technique later in connection with acting and actors. (See Exercise 2 in this chapter.)

Dialogue is structured of lines and speeches.   As has already been pointed out, dialogue is artificially contrived. A close examination of any good lay text will show that the author has usually arranged his sentence structure to throw the important phrase—the actual point of each line—to the end of the line. This placement makes it climactic. Speeches made up of several sentences are carefully constructed in the same way. When a director is aware of this technique, he can be more certain of getting good line readings from his actors, and he will be more able to accomplish the desirable emphasis that he knows the play requires throughout.

The director's knowledge of line and speech structure can be aided greatly by the study of what is labeled "Interpretation" or "Interpretive Reading" in university curriculums. In that study, the attention is concentrated on word and line values. At its base is the study of grammar, for grammar is the basis of effective speech, although no one actually thinks of grammar in carrying on a conversation. No director can go very far with actors, however, without a full awareness of word forms and their distinctive uses in the interlocking arrangements that comprise sentence structure. Many directors and actors trained in Stanislavskian approaches assume that if the subtext of a line is fully comprehended, the technical delivery of that line is assured. This assumption is simply not true, for the subtext and the text must both be communicated. This double value will be discussed in detail in Chapters 16 and 17 on the oral delivery of the text, but the important thing to understand here is that the *basis* for all dramatic meaning is the subtext—the inner quality of the line. This will be discussed in detail under "Characteristics of Dramatic Action" in the next chapter.

EXERCISE

1. Read aloud some dialogue from *Riders to the Sea,* or another study play, and attempt to reproduce the lines according to the word order and other speech modifications. What does it sound like? Can you get the swing of it? Now play a phonograph recording of an actor speaking in a dialect. (Dublin slum-Irish or London Cockney will do). Why does it sound more genuine than your attempts? Can you pick out any national characteristics in the sound alone? Can you hear social and economic circumstances? Can you hear the specific character traits in the sound?

2. Apply the same test to the television sit-com *Taxi.* Can you visualize a "plain" script without the detailed inflections used by the actors? Why are the dialects so important to the dramatic action?

3. Examine some prose dialogue from a play by O'Neill. Point out the specific characteristics in the choice of words, the length of sentences and speeches, and the climactic build in each speech. Is the important word or phrase at the end? Does he seem to repeat any particular group of "sense" words? What does O'Neill's dialogue sound like when spoken? Try it.

4. Have two actors read aloud from a play by Harold Pinter. Examine in detail Pinter's development of a particular line, and then of a group of lines. Do you hear given circumstances in the lines? What do you sense about the characters, about how inarticulate they are? What sort of dialects does Pinter intend?

5. Read aloud a passage from Maxwell Anderson's *Winterset.* Can you hear his regular beat, his verse form? What does the verse form do that prose

would not do? Repeat the same experiment with T. S. Eliot's *Murder in the Cathedral.* Can you hear his different verse forms? Can you identify their beats (number of stresses in each line)? What does his word choice and verse form add that prose could not accomplish? For contrast, read aloud a passage from Eliot's *The Cocktail Party,* which he wrote in a verse form, although he declared that it ought to sound like prose.

Note: Exercise in the dramatic-action characteristics of dialogue is delayed until after the explanation of dramatic action in the next section.

CHAPTER SIX
THE HARD CORE
OF THE PLAYSCRIPT
Dramatic action
and characters

Dramatic action is the clash of forces in a play—the continuous conflict between characters. Here lies the emotional content that moves audiences. Understanding the action will unlock the play because drama means *doing* or *acting*. The hard core of all plays is thus (1) action and (2) characters—the instruments that effect the action or are affected by it and forced to take action of their own.

Dramatic action and the characters are thus inextricably tied together, a fact of dramatic form that you will understand better as you work through the contents of this chapter. The word *plot* is used here in the way playwrights or literary critics use it to describe the sequential arrangement of the conflict incidents that compose the action. For the purposes of detailed discussion in this chapter, dramatic action and characters are treated separately so that you can see their individual characteristics more clearly in isolation.

Understanding the nature and mechanics of dramatic action is a primary study of the director because action is the lifeforce of a play, and because it is the living blood and viscera out of which all other forces grow. Unless the director comprehends its workings, he cannot possibly command the play in directing the actors or in effecting the physical production. He will always be guessing. Again, what happens in a play is the action; it is what holds an audience, thrills them or makes them laugh.

Unless the student of directing understands the concept of action, unless he pursues it avidly to the core, he will not master the basic tool of his trade. Once he has discovered what action is and how it works in various plays, all the other worlds of play production will open up to him. As has already been pointed out, plays are not realities but artificial devices—contrivances, if you will—that may be likened, through analogy, to a human body. Just as the heart and other vital organs make possible living and breathing in the human being, so dramatic action provides the same lifegiving force to the play.

Since a play is a work of art, it can be examined and taken apart. Thus, a student who fails to study a play's action is proceeding only on the tenuous grounds of his feelings. His job is to find out not what he feels about a play but what the author, the first improvisor, has put into his playscript. The hard-core study in play-analysis is understanding the action.

CHARACTERISTICS OF DRAMATIC ACTION

Present Tense

As has already been noted in the discussion on dialogue, dramatic action exists only in the present tense. Thus, the participants in the action—the characters—are always in a state of "I do," not "I did." This is what gives the living quality to a play and what makes us aware that it is occurring here and now. Whenever two people meet in a play, as in real life, they start "doing" to each other, and this is what we watch through a time sequence. A play turns-on life, and we watch and hear it being lived in front of us. There is never any past tense during a play's life; everthing that happens, even the ways the previous action is conveyed, must occur in the present.

Dramatic Action Is Not Activity

It is important at the outset of this discussion to understand the difference between dramatic action and an actor's activity. The latter is the *illustration* of the action: what one actor or one director may have decided best shows the action. Such illustrations or pieces of business—sitting in a chair, crossing the stage, gesturing with the hand, etc.—can be infinite, but the basic dramatic action is fixed within a narrow range. *Acting is, therefore, the process of illustrating the dramatic action—through activity. Activity is the how; action is the what.*

It is necessary to point out these distinctions, because the nineteenth-century common stage tradition usually accepted by actors and stage managers held that illustrations or pieces of business performed by actors were the actions themselves, a tradition still surviving in opera. This misconception of action has unfortunately been carried over into some theatre training with the result of placing a director's attention on superficialities rather than on basic drives and forces in a play.

Understanding Realistic plays as well as knowing how to exploit the methods of the modern actor both require uncovering the dramatic action, for only then can the search for appropriate illustrations to externalize it take place. *Activities are thus the externalization of dramatic action.*

All Action Is Reciprocal

As defined previously, action is the clash of forces, the forces being the characters. All action, therefore, forces counteraction, or action in two directions with adjustments in between. The cycle goes this way: (1) *A* does to *B;* (2) *B* feels the force of *A*'s action (adjustment) and decides what action to take; (3) *B* does to *A*; (4) *A* feels the force of *B*'s action (adjustment) and decides what action to take. This cycle is then ready to begin again, but this time on a new and different level. This reciprocal process is carried on until either (1) *A* or *B* is destroyed; or (2) some outside force interrupts the progression (another character enters); or (3) the playwright arbitrarily concludes the action (end of scene).

All dramatic action is therefore *reciprocal*; there is no one-way road but always a *returned* action. Forcing goes on in both directions. Note that *a very important part of this cycle lies in the adjustment* that each character must make before taking a new action. As a result, much of the acting an actor does lies in receiving the force of the other character's action and in deciding what action to take himself. This not only excites the audience but moves the scene continuously forward.

The forcing or the doing, however, can take place in so many graduations that it frequently *looks* as if one character were dominating the other so strongly that the scene gives the appearance of one-way action. But this appearance is all a matter of quiet, low-key adjustment, as is the timing of the adjustment; the action will shift in the other direction before long, and the dominated becomes the dominator. Scenes in plays are composed of *A*'s dominance with *B* taking retreating actions; then *B* takes over and dominates *A*, who takes retreating action. The climax of the scene is reached when either *A* or *B* successfully dominates the other completely. But there is always another possible encounter, for a play is made up of delayed adjustments and the new actions they foment. Sooner or later the dominated one will have another chance, with the possibility that he will emerge as the dominant force. A play moves forward, and the audience continues to be interested, just as long as *A* and *B* are in conflict over who will dominate. Once this question has been answered satisfactorily, a state of relative calm prevails, and the play is concluded.

But unless both characters (forces) are destroyed, the end of one play may only set up the given circumstances for the beginning of another one. It is possible, then, if characters are of sufficient interest, for a playwright to write more than one play about their conflicts, as did the Greeks and a few modern playwrights, such as Eugene O'Neill in *Mourning Becomes Electra* or Lillian Hellman with the characters of *The Little Foxes*. All endings of plays are contrived, and some rather unsatisfactorily. Rather than to say the dramatic action ends, it would be better to say that it is in a state of relative quiet, a dormant state awaiting new forces and pressures.

The Divisions of Action: Units

The total action of a play is divided into major sections. Since they intended their plays to be staged without interruption, the Greeks punctuated their major sections of action with choral songs, commenting on the action just seen or forcasting what is to come. Shakespeare ended his scenes with rhymed couplets and may have followed them with brief musical interludes. Today we lower a curtain or the stage lights and give the audience a rest—an intermission—with the audience actually leaving their seats and moving about for ten to fifteen minutes. But whether we play the action continuously or take intermissions, we know that all plays are artificially constructed, that they are broken—plotted—into parts. The plot of a play, then, is the arrangement of the action: what a playwright thinks, out of a total possible story, must be shown to an audience. Thus, the play may be divided not only into acts but also into formal scenes—for example, Act I, Scene 2—each with arbitrary limits.

Printed playscripts in the French theatre, although they follow divisions into acts, further separate the action in a formal way that tells us much about all play construction. Whenever a character enters or exits, a new scene is declared and so marked in the text. This French method of marking scripts shows us that the major sections of action (the acts) in all plays are broken arbitrarily into many sections of action. These are not only declared when a new character enters but whenever characters in concert shift the line of talk (action) in a new direction or shift the dominant focus from one character to another. *A new unit is thus delcared.* The word *unit* is Stanislavski's word for divisions in dramatic action, his word for delineating all the segments of the plotting, even the very smallest ones. This definition provides a far better way for a director to see a play's action than by using the traditional act-scene concept or the division into French scenes, for he can then visualize the total action as one major unit broken into dozens of subunits, all interrelated and all pointing in one concerted direction. But although the large units are easily perceived, the small units are much more difficult to delineate because they vary in size from two or three lines to a dozen or more, or sometimes they may consist of a single line followed by a significant pantomime (silent activity). *Every experienced director knows that audiences can be aroused to excitement only by the clear and explicit acting of these small units,* for a good play is packed with these detailed, revealing moments. The director's mastery of the unit concept is an absolute necessity if he is to understand at all the nature of dramatic action.

The smallest designation of dramatic action is, of course, the line (a speech). Every speech of every character throughout the play, as has already been pointed out in the section on dialogue, contains a dramatic action. If a speech is of more than three or four sentences in length, it may contain additional actions. Do not worry about long speeches until you have mastered the technique of extracting the action from short ones. Then you will be far more sensitive to shifts in action in major speeches.

Thus, each speech contains a forcing—an action—and it is directed toward another character. To repeat the phrasing already used in the above discussion: *A* does to *B* (Speech 1); *B* receives the forcing and adjusts to it; and *B* does to *A* (Speech 2); *A* receives the forcing and adjusts to it; and *A* does to *B* (Speech 3), with the process repeated until that series is stopped suddenly by interruption, pushed aside to be taken up later or climaxed by a joining of the two characters on one side of the separation (love) or by further dividing of the characters (hate). Thus, the actions (speeches) lead to the climax of the unit which then ends, and another unit begins, repeating the process all over again.

Each unit, therefore, has its own *objective*. It is the progressive (always moving ahead) building of these small unit objectives which accumulate into the large unit objectives, which, in turn, finally make the objective for the entire play.

The work of the director is primarily that of helping the actors find not only the speech-by-speech dramatic action in a play but also the objectives of the units throughout the play. At the base of this concept is the hypothesis that all actions are reciprocal (*A* does to *B* and *B* does to *A*), and that the director's function is to see that the appropriate reciprocation actually takes place with the actors. The process of acting is not just doing individual actions, but even more important, reciprocating all actions. Unless *A* does to *B* and *B* does to *A*, nothing will happen for the audience. Emotion can emerge and the audience be moved *only when the reciprocation takes place*, for emotion is a by-product of dramatic action. *Emotion cannot be made directly in itself but is brought about by the forcing of one character by another.* More will be said about this process later in the discussion on acting and the director's relationship to the actor. It is sufficient here to state that the actor who acts alone (without reciprocation) and is permitted to do so by the director cannot possibly produce emotion, for he is not acting but only performing like an individual entertainer in a night club who plays directly to an audience without help from others (except the audience).

A play is always a dialogue—action between two or more characters—and never a monologue. A soliloquy or interior speech, such as that used in *Hamlet*, is not a monologue but an argument carried on between two warring sides within the same character, frequently between his outside self—what others force him to be—and his inside self—what he knows he must be.

Finding and Labeling the Action

Since each speech in a play is intended to do, to force, each speech can be reduced to a verb in the present tense because verbs are the symbol-words for action. The subtext in a sequence of speeches, for example, could be recorded in this way:

A shames
B ignores

A pleads
B berates
A begs
B storms
and so on

Notice how each of these actions is expressed in the present tense and how each successive verb seems to grow out of the preceding verb, thus affecting reciprocation. And notice that *no other qualifying words are used.*

Your problems in using this method will not derive from what you may think is a deficiency in your vocabulary but in discovering what is going on in a line and in a unit. Director-actor language must be simple or it will not work at all. Thus, the problem is one of perception: *if you can sense the action, the verb will come easily to you.* Don't work too self-consciously, too intellectually, but let your feelings and responses tell you what is going on in a series of speeches. Once you catch on to this game, the technique of playing is not difficult at all. But a very real problem will always be there: What is going on in the line? What is the subtext? This question can sometimes be quite baffling. No matter how many years of experience a director or actor may have, or how mature they may be, this problem will always exist. As we have pointed our previously, directors and actors should think of playscripts as the improvisations of others—the playwrights. As such, the inner recesses of their plays may be very difficult to rediscover simply because what goes on may lie outside of the personal experiences of both actors and directors.

But once you, as a director, have learned this technique of looking for the subtext and setting it down in verbal form, you will have at your command the most important key available to the director in communicating with actors, for you can both talk the same language: *the verb-motivations that the actor can act.* Anything less lies in the cloudy, fuzzy realm of "how I *feel* it should go," instead of in "what I (the character) *am doing*"—the only way a director can get through to an actor.

Look again at the examples of verb choice for the sequence of speeches presented on pages 38–39. These are the kind of verbs you should use because *they can be acted.* Some verbs simply cannot be acted. Verbs that are too general, such as those that apply to the nature of dialogue itself, do not "do" to others but merely assert that dialogue is a form of communication. Therefore, do not use such verbs as *ask, tell, say, question, interrogate, explain, show, see, perceive, illustrate, examine, reflect,* and all others that are similar because they are useless in director-actor communication. The question you must always ask is: *Can the verb be acted?* Can it force another character to "do" something? Transitive verbs do this because they always have a direct object. If you do ask the question, you will discover that the search is for *specific* and not for general verbs, for acting is a specific, never a general thing.

Another class of verbs to avoid are those that overtly and directly call up specific illustrations: run, jump, walk, bounce, laugh, smile, etc. Occasionally these verbs can work as dramatic action, but most of the time you will be using them as surface illustrations and not for the deep-lying, motivating actions you must look for. The clearest verbs are those full of direct, though not overtly stated, doing, for they contain the basic passions and emotions.

Again, if the verbs are too general—for example, I love, I hate—they will not stiumlate the actor to specifics, and will not work. Each of these verbs stands for a whole category of gradations, and as such they are too gross when they stand alone. Since the full intention of verbal delineation is to energize the actor, only a specific verb, a verb that delineates the exact gradation, can accomplish that end.

Finally, note that the word used is a verb. Let an initial stand for the character, and *do not use any other qualifying words.* Again, look only for transitive verbs, for in them you will find the action words.

Recording the Action

During the training period, the student director should practice the verb technique by explicitly writing down an analysis of the action. The following procedure is suggested:

1. Divide a short segment of a play (ten minutes with two characters only) into units (usually three to six).
2. Write down in verbal form, as indicated in the example given on pp. 38–39, all the action in each of these units.
3. Now make a summary for each unit by finding a single verb that summarizes the action of each character in the unit. Use this form of expression: *A* does to *B,* and *B* does to *A.* (A more specific example: Mary pleads and George berates.)
    The preceding statement is now a summary for the whole unit; it is reciprocal because both forces are shown; it is reciprocal also because the use of the coordinating conjunction ''and'' ties the two characters inextricably together as if they were on either end of an elastic rope.
4. Record the summaries of all the units that make up the segment of the play selected. These summaries are what you, as the director, can retain in your mind as the unit objectives to be accomplished. The actors may get lost in the details of the action and thus lose sight of the objectives. But if you also lose your way, all is lost. If the summary is well done—if the verbs are well-chosen—the structure of the play can be readily seen. The total play will be only as good as the unit perception, made by you and the actors working together, for you can communicate only what you understand, and if you don't ''see'' very well, neither will the actors or the audience.
5. One further device is of specific use: the titling of units with a nominative phrase. Although not a very accurate way of describing what goes on in a unit, it is still quite useful because it gives you another handle for understanding a scene and holding it in your memory. The phrase must be a simple one: The Arrival; The Close Attachment; The Announcement of the New Plan; The Announcement of the Other Plan; The Head-on Struggle; Left Alone. Such phrases are a good supplement to the reciprocal sentences of the summary as in item 4 above, and can help you find the verbal statements. They are also good phrases to use for conveying the objective of each unit when you are talking to actors. But although they are helpful devices for communication, they are not actable in themselves.

Types of Action

The "types" of action—tragic, comic, melodramatic, farcical—are not treated at this point because they are so complex in theory that they will tend to confuse you as a beginning director during the period when you should be concerned with getting a grasp of techniques for play-analysis. It is sufficient to be aware that there is another level of analysis that you will learn later when you have mastered the basic concepts of play-analysis. From a practical point of view, it is suggested that in choosing plays for projects you select serious ones because of their usual straightforward directness. Dramatic action in comedy is usually not only more difficult to perceive but it presents many more problems for young actors, and thus for yourself.

Action in a Whole Play

In working out the procedures outlined in this chapter for delineating units of action, the beginning director may think he has become lost in detail and won't be able to see the forest for the trees. But remember that once you understand the nature of action and how to find it in a play, you will proceed quickly and spontaneously. The process here is similar to learning to read and play music: reading the notes, observing the bars, and practicing the phrases, eventually attaining the speed that will make a tune. Your desire to want to work with full plays is quite understandable, but you must first learn how to play the notes and join them into units.

Later on, when you do tackle full plays, all you will be doing is expanding the concept of unit structure outlined here to cover the whole play. Exercise 1 following will give you that opportunity. Try it for size just to see the relationships, but then return to work on the *parts* of plays as the best way of comprehending the whole. Learn to crawl before you walk and run.

EXERCISE

The best way to work with dramatic action is to study a one-act play or, better, a 10-minute section of a long play. The instructor could select such an example for class use. Later, each student should work out an action-analysis from a play of his own choice. The following exercises should be done in the order indicated:

1. What are the major divisions of the action of the whole play? Can you find a summary statement for the whole play?
2. Distinguish between an arbitrary division (Act II, Scene 2) and a French scene.
3. Pick out several French scenes.
4. Select a segment of a play (ten consecutive minutes) and do the following:
   a. Isolate the units in the text by drawing a line separating one unit from

another in the text. Note their beginnings and endings; try to find specific speeches on which they occur. Now number the units.
b. Write down noun-phrase titles for each unit.
c. Now write down the dramatic action verbs for each speech, being careful to follow the procedure for such recording.
d. Write out the reciprocal action, summary sentences for each unit.
e. The class should discuss in detail each of these steps.
5. Discuss the playwriting in the television drama *Dallas* by citing aspects of unit structure (action, goal, length, etc.). Does the camera watch the adjustments as much or more than the actions? Why? How does each hour segment build climactically?
6. Illustrate dramatic action "backwards" by setting up a live story-improvision with given circumstances and a brief plot line. (It is described as "backwards" because the class will see an action happening, one that it has not had to analyze from a playscript in advance of the playing.) Be certain that the improvisors know why they are in conflict. Use number dialogue so that the improvisors can concentrate on actions and will not have to think of specific words. They will also be much clearer in their intentions than if they had to improvise both actions and words. The leader can help shape the improvisation through off-stage suggestions (low-volume directions to the participants) while it is in progress. The participants then begin the improvisation. The class instructor lets it run for a few units and then stops it. Immediately he opens up the following discussion:
a. Designate the units.
b. Why did the improvisors make units automatically?
c. Why did some units (name one) not work well? (Did the improvisors know what they were "doing"?)
d. Why is it very easy to delineate the actions behind each speech? (Relate illustration/activity to dramatic action.)
e. Specifically designate some actions behind speeches.
f. How would real dialogue have helped to delineate and intensify the actions behind speeches?
7. Repeat Exercise 6 two or three times until the class can answer all the questions with perception.

CHARACTERS: THE SECOND HARD-CORE ELEMENT IN PLAY-ANALYSIS

Definition

A character is made up of all the dramatic actions taken by an individual in the course of a play. Therefore, *character* can be defined as a summary statement of specific actions. (Note: The word *character* is used here to describe what a playwright makes, which reserves the word *characterization* for use later in this book to define what an actor makes.)

Character Is Action

In the *Poetics*, Aristotle places dramatic action first and character second, with the second flowing out of the first. Although playwrights may not actually write plays in that order since plays can be conceived and evolve from many stimulations, they must achieve this ordered association in the final draft or the character will not have a life of his own. A character does not exist, except in a superficial, external way, through what he says he is or through what others say about him, although these clues help us to see him more clearly. Instead, he exists in what his actions, particularly those under pressing circumstances, tell us he is. Consequently, character is wrapped up in action, and it is for this reason that we can say a *character*, when we analyze his connection with a play, is a *summary statement*.

Mere impressions of a character—what one *feels* he is—are no substitutes for a director's close analysis of the action. An actor, on the other hand, can discover character piece-by-piece in the process of trying to put him together by *doing*—by acting the various incidents in which the character is involved. For this very important reason, during the rehearsal period directors should encourage actors to play the scenes over and over, with new suggestions of action for each playing, rather than discuss the characters in an intellectual way. (Note: Professional directors proceed here with great caution because this is a major part of the professional actor's job. Regardless of how he handles actors, a good director will see this as a crucial point in his directing of a play.)

Simple and Complex Characters

The density of a character—how simple or complex he may be—is determined from how much he participates in the action of a play and from the quality of his participation and what kind it is. It is the density that separates the primary characters from the secondary or supporting characters who act as instruments for revealing the principals. We know much less about these secondary characters than the principals—we know only a few traits—because they have little opportunity in the action to tell us who they are since most of the attention is focused on the principals. A third level—house servants, aides, etc.—we know scarcely at all, although good actors may seem to give them more body (personality) than the playwright actually has. A fourth level, a group or a chorus, a collective body with a collective trait, is obscure to us as individuals because we see only a group mind and a group feeling.

Although a play focuses on all the principal characters, one character usually dominates the action. Since conflicts cannot exist without two forces, a protagonist and an antagonist, the play's action revolves around these two (or possibly three, if there is more than one antagonist). The director must determine during his analysis who the principal character is (*whose* play it is), along with the primary antagonist(s). Thus, another polarity (other than the polarity already discussed in the section on polar attitudes in given circumstances) can be specified if the director understands the nature of character and how characters are used in plays.

A beginning director is sometimes confused by studies of plays (dramatic criticisms) that point out that certain principal characters are very poorly drawn, or that characters—in Greek plays for instance—are very thin. Greek plays have very few incidents to reveal character so they incline to greater simplicity in this respect; but this simplicity does not mean that they will be any less effective. Simple characters in certain contexts can have great power over an audience. One of the characteristics of modern drama, one aspect that delineates the Realistic style beyond the minutiae that make up the given circumstances, is the complexity of character development brought about through a large number of incidents in a play. Many character traits are thus demonstrated to an audience, and what we can say about a character is that we know the complexity of his "psychological self." But we can often become confused because there is so much to assimilate. Good direction is the ordering of this complexity with such clarity and emphasis (which also includes deemphasis) that an audience can readily assimilate the main points, with the secondary points relegated to their proper places.

When a director understands how action reveals a character, he can understand more fully how to direct plays with simple characters ("big" musicals), as well as those with complex characters, and to recognize the different values developed in each. Without this comprehension, he may try to impose the values of the complex on the simple, or vice-versa, and may be confused about why a play does not work.

Character Is Revelation: The Principal Characters

From the preceding discussion, it follows that an actor cannot play his entire character at once. Certainly before a rehearsal period has ended, an actor must be fully aware of the complete body of the character he is acting, just as a playwright must be aware of his whole play; but if he tries to play the full character at the beginning, or even in the middle of a playscript, he will find himself confused and lost. *A character takes shape and is revealed in the course of the action.* Thus, characters do not change; they *unfold.* The stuff a character is made of has always been lying dormant, and only under the impact of conflict—of the forcing of both himself and others—will the buried qualities come to the surface and stand revealed.

As we have already noted in the previous section, dramatic action is a progression of incidents with one incident leading to another. Acting is therefore self-revealing with a sort of inevitability guiding it: "This must be told, this must come out!" As a result, a play is made up of discoveries and surprises. Some are minor; a few are major; and one is exceptional. These are the climaxes. As a character meets each of these moments in a play, something in him comes forward to meet the circumstance—a character trait.

In this way, aspects of character are fully illustrated in a series of climactic moments. An audience can keep these traits in mind because, if the author is a good one, they will have a logical relationship and a close association with the traits still to be revealed in the following climaxes. Thus, the actual progression for the audience, what interests each spectator in the play, is the progressive unfolding of character traits in the protagonist and the antagonists, traits that finally accumulate with clarity and force at the major climax when all the previous character revelations come together. This major clash is of such force that the principal character stands fully revealed, and the audience can see what really makes him work. What follows this climax is usually very brief, for all we need to know is what the principal character is like after his head-on collision with the forces he has tried to overcome.

For the director, analysis of the action is paramount if he is to understand the growth in a character, whether he be secondary or principal, and thus bring about this growing in the actor he will direct. *Progressive unfolding* is the concept he must understand. It will tell him where the climaxes of the play are, what they are about, how important each one is, and what to do with them in getting the play acted. This concept has the most personal significance to a director because he can work intelligently and perceptively with the actors only when he understands these points. Progressive unfolding is at the core of director-actor communication.

Techniques of Character Description

Describing a character by writing it down in your own words is the best way to assure yourself that a character analysis is fully developed and nothing has been missed. But you must be absolutely certain that you determine what a character is by giving the principal attention to an analysis of the action, as has been previously emphasized, for you will be strongly tempted to read the description authors sometimes insert in their plays. If you do the latter, you must keep in mind that the author is providing these suggestions for a casual reading and not for a director, a tip-off to the reader of what to expect. You must remember that a character is determined *only after* his actions, not before. Thus, a playwright's advance suggestions may certainly give you a hint about character, but such suggestions can be quite misleading in the overview and can cause you to miss the dominant traits. See Exercise 8 in this chapter. Consequently, you must treat author descriptions with great caution and perhaps avoid them altogether.

The technique suggested here bases your analysis of a character on your own perception of the dramatic action. Give each of the following areas primary attention and *record your assessment in writing*.

Desire.   Desire is a statement of what a character wants most. He may appear to want a material possession but this is superficial; what he wants is usually far less tangible, such as power or dominance over others. It may also be love for another; self-integrity; dominance over fear; etc.

Will.   Will is a character's relative strength in attaining his desires. How strong or weak is his inner strength? Is it strong enough to push him the full limit, or will he compromise? We take actions in everyday life out of our will power, and in plays we see this clearly and dynamically illustrated.

Moral stance.   A character's moral stance—the stance that will strongly affect the attainment of his desires—consists of his values. How honest is he with others and with himself? Does he have any sense of moral responsibility to others? What is the moral code that governs his inner behavior? What is his sense of integrity? "Evil" characters are usually given low values because, in their view, the end justifies the means. "Good" characters are given higher than average values, a rating we admire in heroes.

Decorum.   Decorum describes a character's physical appearance—what he looks like, his manners, and his poise. Such a projection of the outward appearance of a character is superficial because what a person looks like is no prediction of what he is. Nevertheless, it can be of some value if only to help project the character into the society in which he lives. It is also possible that his physical makeup may be closely related to his mental and emotional temperaments. It can be helpful to make an actual list of a character's physical characteristics seemingly required by the given circumstances, although you may go in the opposite direction when it comes to the point of casting the play. How does he behave in the varying contexts of the play: How does he walk; how does he stand; how does he speak; what is the quality of his voice; and so forth. Is his outward manner affected by his occupation or by the social mores under which he lives? (All of this is a primary consideration in casting a play, but unless a director thinks an actor is capable of getting out the dramatic action, "looking like the part" will accomplish little.)

Summary adjectives.   Summarize all of the categories above by using adjectives only. Do not set down a character's dramatic actions but *only the traits of character they reveal.*

Character-Mood-Intensity.   Character-mood-intensity is *the physical or body-state of the character*—his nervosity—at the *beginning* of the play and at the beginning of each group of associated units. By describing a character's initial physical state, the director has a point of departure for all the ups and downs in the character that follow. In playing a character, if an actor can start at the appropriate level of intensity, assuming good concentration and awareness of the action, he will continue to build from that level. This communication device is very important for the director, for with it he can directly help an actor find the appropriate levels of a character at all times.

Character-mood-intensity thus means the actual physical state of the character: his heartbeat; his breathing; his state of perspiration; his muscular tension or lack of it; and what state his stomach is in—queasy, jumpy, calm, etc. *Nervosity* means all of these—his total nerve vibration, his sensory awareness. Since these states are points of departure, the actual shape of the play can be understood and made evident in the acting.

You should also be aware that each character in a play begins *at a different* character-mood-intensity because each character is independent by definition. Thus, he will feel differently from another character who will be in a different state of nervosity about the same situation. A director's job is often to point out to the actors the difference in these points of departure—*the different beats of the characters.* Defining a character-mood-intensity for an actor is like backing him into a scene: he feels the level of physicality first; then when he plays the dramatic action, he can sense its validity as a beginning point. Since all that follows will be based on this beginning point, he will become aware of the necessity for appropriate departures. The *pitch* of the action can thus be assured.

You must remember that when an actor initially faces a new character, that character will seem strange and odd to him because it is so different from the actor's self. Therefore, for an actor, approaching a new character is like trying on someone else's coat: it hangs too long, or pinches, or smells; it simply does not fit or feel right. In this sense, the character-mood-intensity is the new coat defined, for the actor will know why it does not fit and what he must do to make it fit. The director can directly assist the actor by helping him to delineate the feeling of the character he is trying to play through character-mood-intensity.

EXERCISE

1. Compare Sophocles' *Oedipus Rex* with Ibsen's *Hedda Gabler* in the density of character development. What do you note about each?

2. Compare character density in Shaw's *Candida*, or in another modern Realistic comedy, with Ionesco's *The Bald Soprano.* Try it again with the early scenes in Elmer Rice's *The Adding Machine.* Are the plays by Ionesco and Rice more nearly alike in their development of characters? Why?

3. Read a brief, early scene—one that concerns the principal character—from a class study play (for example, *Hedda Gabler, Ghosts*). How does the action in the scene reveal a character trait? What trait is revealed? Study another scene later in the play and ask the same questions.

4. Continue Exercise 3 with the same character by selecting the climactic scene. What character trait is now revealed?

5. Study the first act of a long play (the same one used in Exercises 3 or 4) and note each incident. What are the character traits revealed in this act? Make a list of what you know by the end of this first act. Be very careful not to include any traits revealed in the previous action. Now study the last act of the same play. How much more do you know?

6. Analyze the principal characters in a study play by applying the technique that has been suggested: desire, will, moral stance, decorum, summary adjectives, character-mood-intensity.

7. Compare the character-mood-intensity of two characters in the analysis made in Exercise 6 at the point where they introduce a formal division

of the play together or very closely together. How different are these character-mood-intensities? A scene can mature only through this difference.

8. Using a study play, list any character traits an author may have inserted in his text as description. Now carefully assess these traits against the action in the play in the interest of discerning their relevance. Note carefully important traits the author does not mention, and whether those he does mention are relevant to the main line of the play. This exercise should convince you that it is necessary to use action instead of an author's description as the primary source of character traits.

CHAPTER SEVEN
THE DERIVATIVES
OF DRAMATIC ACTION
IN A PLAYSCRIPT
Ideas and rhythmic beats

You will recall from Chapter 4 that the structure of a playscript was compared to the construction of a modern building, and that in Chapter 5 given circumstances were pictured as the deeply rooted foundation, and dialogue as the facade. This image was then developed further in Chapter 6 to show that dramatic action and characters formed the inside core of the building, the viscera that provides the life-force and the energy in a playscript. Now you are ready to complete the building by putting on the top—the *idea* in a playscript. You are also ready to put the building into operation by turning on the dynamos of action and characters, with their living vibrations and nerve systems—the rhythmic beats in a playscript.

The word *derivatives* has been used here as the clearest term to describe where ideas and rhythmic beats actually come from; but they are so much the living expressions of dramatic action and characters, so much an inherent part of them and buried in them, that you will have to work hard to see their separateness and their individualities. As in the two previous chapters, idea, tempos, and moods are treated separately here so that you can more readily distinguish their differences and know the force each exerts on the structure of the play.

IDEA

Definition

The *idea* of a play is the core meaning of what it has to say. Idea is derived from an assessment of characters in action and is therefore a summary statement of such action. Consequently, the idea is the sum total of the playscript. (The word "intention" is sometimes used here, but it has a somewhat tentative ring, as if the playwright had not made up his mind.)

Intention or Creative Accident?

Because all good plays appear to be well-ordered, and because some plays seem to "sell" certain ideas very specifically, the unoriented reader could well assume that a playwright begins with formal ideas and then develops them in incidents and characters, as might be done in a formal essay. However, what we mean by creative playwriting is letting things happen. Consequently, a playwright may begin his improvision in any way—for example, with an imaginary character involved with another character, at a particular moment in the action, with a given circumstance, or with a patch of dialogue. But as he works with his characters, letting them be themselves, they will determine the flow of the action and, eventually, the idea. Starting with an idea is more like the writing in this textbook: the definition is set out first and then it is explained with supporting evidence. But such an approach would be far too confining for the creative playwright, although some of the so-called thesis playwrights early in the century appear to have worked in this way.

However, no matter how he goes about putting a play together, sooner or later a playwright must decide what his characters are doing consistently and what they are trying to discover. In other words, he begins to make *unity in the action*, action that is all about one thing, one idea. He may never actually state his idea of the unity directly in words because he believes that creative drama is subliminal, that an audience must experience an idea through *feeling* the action and not be told overtly what it is about. For this reason the idea of a play is usually buried in a subtle way, and pinpointing it may be relatively difficult. But an idea is surely there and the director must find it, for it will declare his comprehension of the unity in the playscript, and subsequently, the unity he will bring to his production.

Meaning in Plays

In the moving-picture version of Jean-Paul Sartre's *The Condemned of Altona*, a principal character says that she clings to the theatre when all else is crumbling because "the theatre is the world compressed, and with meaning." This view may well be Sartre's own personal paradoxical attitude toward drama because in the midst of the absurdist world he describes, the world where men have lost purpose and a reason for being, he still seems to see meaning in writing plays.

He may know that he cannot change the world, but that he can help describe it and perhaps give some of it meaning. And when he can't find that, he tries to make "non-meaning" meaningful.

"The world compressed and with meaning" may be the master paradox of drama: when all else is confusion, it is still possible for man arbitrarily to make an art form that tells him that life is meaningful, that all we need do is compress it in order to see it positively. In this view, plays are artificial devices for reassuring man, for giving him strength, perception, even wisdom. This book is no place to pursue the philosophical aspects of drama, but it is essential to point out that all plays, no matter how poor, have inherent meanings. Pinpointing them is often the problem.

Idea Is Action

To understand the relationship of *idea* to the other elements in play structure, look again at the drawing on page 19. *Given circumstances* provide the underground foundation. *Dramatic action* is at the ground level and moves upward with each incident to unfold characters until the summit—the idea—is reached. The whole structure is covered with a facade of *dialogue*. Thus, *the idea is the result of characters acting out the incidents in the action.* Not until the action, and consequently the characters, is complete, can we assess the meaning, for the major climax and the ending will tell us more explicitly than any other portions of the play what the play is about. (A well-directed play is always delineated from second-rate work by its relentless pursuit in a straight line to the idea.)

Finding the Idea

Although there is no question that the idea of a play will lie in the development of action and characters, two other sources of information are sometimes useful guides: (1) a play's title; (2) a philosophical statement in the dialogue.

A play's title is frequently a symbolic or a metaphorical representation of the inner meaning—a playwright's image of the poetic statement he is trying to make. After reading the plays, few people would have difficulty in discerning the ideas behind such titles as *The Little Foxes, The Hairy Ape, Death of a Salesman. Cat on a Hot Tin Roof*, and *Riders to the Sea* because the essence of each of these plays has been stated quite obviously in the titles given them. But other titles may lead the director into confusion, for instance: *The Bald Soprano, The Birthday Party, Happy Days*. Others tell us very little: *Hedda Gabler, The Lark, Luther, The Homecoming*, although each says something. But when a title is supported by an analysis of the action, the director has a guiding metaphor that will bring him close to the playwright's idea.

Philosophical statements, although occasionally pinpointed in specific speeches, are not very common in plays because most playwrights in their desire to remain on the poetic level shun obvious statements of meaning. They are poets, and they want to reach audiences directly on the most primitive level of understanding: emotional understanding. Intellectual statement is too obvious, too self-conscious.

The principal means of uncovering the idea, then, is to search within the dramatic action of the principal character, or characters: where is the emphasis in the action leading? Why does the principal character take the climatic action that he does? What is the result of that action? There must have been other courses of action he could have taken, so why did he take this one? At the high point of his agony, what seems most important to him? After the climax, what is the effect of the discovery on him and on others? There are many questions a director can ask himself about the action that will lead to the idea. Once he thinks he grasps the idea, he should set it down in words as briefly as possible, and then test his strength backwards against the action.

One of the easier ways to see an idea is to place it in a simple sentence combining characters and action. This sentence will be the idea *stated in action*. Thus: "This play is about a childlike woman who . . . ." By completing the statement of action, the director will still keep the idea submerged up to a point, but bringing it to the surface will be easier because of the emphasis thrown on one character and on the principal action.

You can often find the idea by recording the action in a play, taking great care in setting it down as accurately as you can in the order it occurs. A director should be able to record the action of each act in three or four sentences. This record is a précis or summary, the easiest way to find the focus in an action. You must learn to "tell" an action to others briefly and to the point.

More will be said about "finding ideas" in Part III, which you should pursue only after you have a specific understanding of play-analysis as outlined in this part of the book. It is sufficient at this point for you to know that there are a few other ways of finding meaning, for sometimes it is derived from the values associated with sympathetic characters in contrast to those values associated with unsympathetic characters, and sometimes from symbols and metaphors other than those used in the title. You will also find in Part III a discussion of the work that you may need to do outside play-analysis in order to perceive a play's meaning, for its meaning may escape you if you do not have sufficient background in either the historical or the modern world. Part III will also show you how a play that is not immediately topical in its idea is seldom successful; and that if it cannot be universally applied, it will not endure.

EXERCISE

1. Test the validity of the title of a study play by pinning it down in terms of consistency with the play's action. Do the title and the action say the same thing?
2. Compare the title of a serious play with the title of a comedy. Do you find the latter essentially different? Could it be taken seriously and could a serious action be construed from it?

3. What do you think might be the actions in the plays with the following titles? *Luv; You Can't Take It With You; The Importance of Being Ernest; Ah, Wilderness!; Barefoot in the Park.* Play this exercise as a game with people who have read a play who listen to the comments of the "guessers."

4. Discuss the relationship of the titles to the actions in four or five plays all the members of the group have read.

5. Examine *Riders to the Sea* for a philosophical statement. Do you find one? If certain lines seem to be immediately obvious, are they completely verified in the action? Are they misleading? Remember that *Riders* is also about Nora and Cathleen and not just about Maurya (youth versus age).

6. Arrive at the idea of a play by analyzing the action—that is, by drawing the logical conclusion from the actions. Express the idea in one short sentence. Each student should do this exercise separately, and then the results should be compared. Is there any agreement on the idea? Why may there be differences of opinion?

Note: If there is wide divergence, the action of the play should be reexamined by the group in order to be certain that each member understands exactly what is going on and sees the significance of what is transpiring. Don't overlook the point that understanding the action in some plays may require more maturity than you presently have; but don't let this bother you because even great actors—Olivier, Richardson, Gielgud—have confessed to being puzzled over a playwright's meaning.

RHYTHMIC BEATS

Definition

The *rhythmic beats* comprise the playwright's "music" in a play—its *moods* and *tempos*. They derive from (1) the qualities of the dramatic action in each unit and from (2) the juxtaposition of these actions. Thus, the rhythmic beats give a play its emotional overtones, its poetic qualities, and part of its mystery.

MOODS

Moods are the feelings or emotions generated from the clash of forces in the dramatic action—the result of the action. When taken together in their accumulative effect, moods declare the *tone* of a play. Moods are thus the *tonal feelings* of a play.

Effect on the Audience

The concept of moods can be understood better by going backwards from the play's *effect on the audience* to the playscript itself as the generator of the reception. Of course, there is no question that a director is aware of the moods in a play when he first reads it, and then studies it; but, like tempo, moods are difficult to understand as a concept and particularly illusive to put into words. However, once you understand the nature of mood values and their relationship to the other elements in play-analysis, you can see how to put mood values to work for you.

Moods are not mysterious; it is only explaining them that makes them seem illusive. Moods are basic feelings; they are the disturbances, the excitements we are moved by as we watch a play. When you are a member of an audience, you *experience* the play; that is, if the play is well acted, even you, who may be studying directing and are, therefore, more conscious of what is being done on the stage, will lose your objectivity and become immersed in the play—you will feel it and be moved by it. You are moved by the mood values. This arousal of feelings in the audience can begin early in a performance and accumulate in force throughout, rising to a peak at the major climax of the action and then gradually calming as the play closes.

We all know this arousal to be the ''fun'' of watching a play—the vicarious experience. Experiencing the shifts in the moods not only holds our attention in a performance but, at the end, leaves us tired, or even exhausted, or happy, or ecstatic. We are so busy feeling the emotions generated by the characters in action—empathizing—that we expend almost as much physical energy on the play experience as we might on a real-life happening, even though we know that a play is only an artificial thing, that it is not real life but only a semblance of it. It has been a vicarious experience, to be sure, but it has involved our feelings—all our nervous system. We go to plays because we like the sensation of being aroused, of feeling intensely without the traumas that real-life experiences hold for us.

There is always something in the threatre experience that is akin to the sex life of the average human being. Our minds and our body feelings are so played upon by a performance that we are titillated and aroused to peaks that resemble, in kind, those we experience in real life. These two experiences—the one fake, the other real—are not the same by any means, of course, but they appear to be the same, and plays are removed from us because they happen, not to ourselves, but to other people. We do not feel defrauded by this fake experience because we knew that it was going to be imaginary before we went to the play; but we find something of value, something that makes life richer, by participating in the human behavior of others caught in situations and circumstances that may resemble those possible in our own worlds.

The moods of a play, then, are what move an audience beyond itself into imagined experience.

Dramatic Action and Moods

Again, before discussing the director's work with the printed script, we can get a clearer idea of moods by noting their relationship to dramatic action. Since we think of action in units, so must we also think of moods in the same terms. A play is thus composed of many shifts in moods, with every unit of action having its own specific mood.

As you have already noted in the section on characters, the phrase *character-mood-intensity* means that a character enters a unit of a play at a certain physical (nervous) pitch—the nervosity of the character at that point. And you know that as he participates in the action of the unit, his mood-intensity will shift; if he begins at the right pitch, what he does to another character and what that character does to him will modify his mood-intensity, either making it more relaxed or more tense.

As members of the audience we experience these specific changes in moods, for a play always moves forward in a cause-effect progression. The goal of a unit of action, then, is a mood-goal. Several of these mood-goals put together cause the surge in a play, and, as an audience, we surge with it. The dramatic action, then, is the source of moods, and the characters with their changing mood-intensities are the instruments. Later on in this book we will discuss how the actor makes moods through his technique of acting.

Tone-Goal

The *tone* of a production is, therefore, the *achievement of the appropriate moods* in a playscript. Tone is what the director is striving for, because it is what the playwright felt when he improvised his play. Tone is the maximal state of feeling, the actual purpose of the play. Unless the director achieves this state, he achieves nothing. All of his preparations, all of his production designs are for naught unless he can move his audience in the way the play demands.

The rediscovery of the tone of a play and the achievement of it in production is thus the goal of the director. Note that it is not *a* tone but *the* tone, for the mood-goal will contain the ultimate meaning of a play because the audience receives the meaning subjectively (with only a relative few ever consciously bringing that meaning to the surface). An audience's experience with a play for the most part will depend on the director's perception of the mood-goal and how well he is able to achieve this with his actors.

But although the audience's perception may be subjective, it does not follow that the director can achieve the mood-goal by being subjective himself. He must not only keenly feel the tone of a play on the first or second reading, but he must be able to achieve this tone after weeks of "getting lost" in the details of rehearsals and production.

The Director's Analysis of Mood Values

When most people read a play they sense the shifts in mood; they are impressed or get the impression of mood shift. This response is expected and natural. But the director must be much more aware of and more consciously perceptive to these mood shifts, as well as to the overall tone. Many readings of a playscript together with the disassembling and detailing that goes on during a rehearsal and production period can often obliterate the first feelings a director may have had about a playscript. Since the director's major job is working with actors, if he knows the unit mood goals and the overall tone he wants to achieve, he will not only be able to help the actors find these goals but bring them into a unity within the play.

How to record your initial feelings about a play may at first seem illusive to you because it involves trying to record your personal and very subjective reactions. But once you have worked at this sort of conscious reproduction of your feelings, you will find it of enormous value in communicating with actors.

Moods can be recorded in words in two different ways: (a) through mood adjectives; and (b) through mood metaphors.

Mood adjectives.   Since moods are emotions or feelings, not actions but the result of actions, they can be recorded in the way an actor works because the result of acting is showing others through visual and aural means what a character is feeling. Though the actual process for the actor lies in the execution of the action, out of that execution flows the feeling—the goal. In real life a person can be undergoing a tremendous emotional response to some happening but show very little on the outside. On the stage, however, the actor must demonstrate what is happening. His language of transference is through the physical senses: touching, tasting, smelling, hearing, seeing—all sensations. Therefore, the words that can best describe moods are the adjectives that fall into "sensations" categories. Here are some examples:

touching:	rough, smooth, hard, soft, sandy, cool, hot
tasting:	tart, sweet, puckering, cool, hot, smooth, rubbery
smelling:	pungent, perfumy, stinky, sweet, sour
hearing:	loud, soft, raucous, blaring, piercing
seeing:	red, blue, all words of size and shape, all varying words of lightness and darkness

A number of these adjectives strung together will help you recall unit moods and to talk about them directly. (For example: This unit is rough, tart, pungent, red, big, and loud.)

Mood metaphors.   A metaphor is a figure of speech in which a word or phrase literally denoting one kind of object or idea is used in place of another to suggest a likeness, or analogy, between them. The mood adjectives are highly useful, but they are more limiting than metaphors. The latter allow your imagination to play freely and creatively on a play because you are trying to find images that *resemble* the sensations you have about the units. You therefore say to yourself, "The mood in this unit is like a ———," and you fill in an image. Do not try to think in the "sense" categories suggested for mood adjectives, but let yourself go free. Here are some examples.

The mood in this unit is like:

a moth fluttering around a lamp (the unit mood-goal is nervous, fluttering, indecisive, trembling, etc.);

an air compressor riveting machine (the mood-unit of the unit is noisy, hammering, erratic, jolting, etc.);
lemon juice (the unit mood-goal is sour, flows like liquid, smells fragrant but would pucker the mouth, etc.).

Learn to use metaphors because they are the way of bringing to the surface the subjective sensations of the director. Inherent in metaphors are ways of talking to actors and designers in order to convey something that can really exist only in the doing. They understand symbols too.

Rhythm in Moods

It should now be obvious that the mood structure of a play can declare its basic rhythm. Rhythm has a far wider application than tempos alone, for tempos, like heartbeats, are tied inextricably to the shifts and changes in mood. Further discussion of rhythm at this point may only confuse you, but you must always think of a play as having a rhythmic structure in its moods which rise and fall with increasing intensity as the play progresses.

Atmosphere

The *atmosphere* of a play is the meaning of the mood of the given circumstances. If the circumstances are perceived well, the atmosphere will automatically be evident in the reader's mind and feeling. A director who is thoroughly aware of the atmosphere or aura in a playscript, and can state it in a particular way, will be able to exert a strong command over the design of his production. A director must thus be able both to see and to hear the given circumstances of a playscript, and then be able to translate these feelings into the concrete terms of stage production.

EXERCISE

1. Discuss in class how you receive a play. Try not to let self-conscious attitudes, now developing in your training, interfere with an honest appraisal of your experience as a spectator. This exercise can be done best after your class has watched the performance of a scene or a play.
2. Examine the nature of *empathy*. How does it work in the other arts? It means *feeling out the lines of an object*. Apply empathy specifically to a theatre experience.
3. Examine the difference between a real-life experience you have witnessed and what it would look like as a unit in a play. Be certain it is limited and specific enough for you to make the comparison.
4. Important: Record some mood adjectives for a unit of a study play.
5. Important: Record some mood metaphors for a unit of a study play.
6. Important: Record some units in their mood-goals.

TEMPOS

Tempos are the changing rates or beats of the dramatic action in a play. When a sequential arrangement of tempos is combined—that is, when the varying beats of several consecutive units are strongly felt—you have identified the pulsations of a play—its *rhythm*. Unless a director comprehends the rhythmic markings in a play, he will be powerless in making it work on the stage. The director is a musician in every respect. (The only thing that professional play reviewers seem to recognize as a director's sole responsibility is his *pacing* of a play. His expert "musicianship" is thus a major point of attack.)

Unit Beats

Because all plays are made in units of action, which, though related, are different in content and purpose, each unit has its own particular tempo or, to use a term employed in music, its own *beat*. A play is made up of varying tempos, or *unit beats*. The director must become very much aware of this built-in musical characteristic because it not only strongly determines a play's individuality, but it also declares a primary way the play holds an audience's attention.

A musical sense is one of the marks of talent in the director, one of his best natural tools. If this sense is poorly developed, if he cannot readily discern the difference in beats or have the exact sense of time that an orchestra conductor has, he will not be sensitive enough to the up and down swings of a play. Unlike music scores, where tempos are marked and where the rates of speed of the various passages are indicated by a series of directions such as *largo, molto allegro*, and often by exact metronomic markings, plays have no such textual warnings. The playwright may occasionally insert a word suggesting tempo, but this clue is exceptional. The director and the actors are expected to sense the beats. If a play reader has a strongly developed dramatic imagination, he will also sense them automatically: he will feel the flow. But even the talented director must search each playscript for the unit beats in order to verify and *bring to consciousness* his perceptions of tempo. If your sense of tempo is poorly developed, you must set about improving it through the rhythm exercises provided by dance or music training. Your dramatic imagination will do the rest.

Surges

A play is like the waves on a seashore. As you watch them, you can see the small waves accumulate and finally climax in a major breaker that hurls itself toward the beach to dash its force on the sand; then it disintegrates, loses its force, and draws back toward the sea again. When a storm (the major conflict in a play) is coming, the waves increase in size, and their pattern becomes less regular than before. A play is made up of such surges, retreats, and new surges, all with accumulating force that finally culminates in a climax (the storm). The director, then, must not only see small unit tempos but the cumulative, large ones as well.

His primitive sense of the large surges will tell him, in one way, what the play is about, for a play has these surges built into it; its "music" will be hidden without delineation of these elements of tempo.

One problem with the "ocean" metaphor used above is the danger of assuming that plays have regular surges that only grow in size and intensity. This assumption is quite misleading. Although some plays have this regularity, many are as erratic in their tempos as are some examples of modern music. One of the ways of sensing a play's tempos is to compare beats. This paralleling of form has the distinct advantage of making you aware of the beats without making you too intellectually conscious of them. "Beating a play" or parts of a play on a drum—that is, finding different beats for each unit—also helps bring about a partially conscious awareness of the inherent tempos.

Rhythm

Rhythm refers, in part, to the accumulative effect of the unit beats and is, perhaps, another way of describing surges. Webster's definition is useful as a starter: "The effect created by the elements in a play . . . that relate to the temporal development of the action." From this definition we can see that rhythm is the *effect* of accumulating tempos, and that it is a way of describing *multiple tempos* brought together. But this is only a partial definition of rhythm, for the moods in a play exercise an important effect on rhythm and must be considered in defining it. Because of the illusive nature of the word "rhythm" and because of its double nature when being applied to a play, it is not used much in this discussion. The emphasis has been placed on tempos and moods (note the plural forms of the words) as the keys to discovering rhythm. If you can master these concepts and put them to work for you, you will have a very good understanding of how to find rhythm in a play. Again, a *sense of rhythm* is largely an inherent talent, but it can be developed to an extent through training in music and dance.

Sound and Silence

Do you remember the quotation from Jean-Louis Barrault in the second chapter: "A play is interrupted silence?" Note carefully the idea in that definition. Barrault did not say, "A play is sound interrupted by silence," the way we usually think of it, but he said it the other way around—silence interrupted by sound. This is an extreme view, to be sure, but it is a good way of understanding the concept of drama. In one sense, it can be said that a playwright starts with a silent void and then fills it with sound—the cover of his dramatic action. But if he is a good playwright, he will never completely fill the silence; he will only punctuate it.

What he leaves in the way of silence is the pause—an element of tempo. *Pause* is a silence gap, created first by the playwright, then reproduced by the actor, that has theatrical effect on the stage because its tempo values can be very moving. What is not said is often just as important as what is said. The duration of the pause tells us much. The director should study and mark the pauses in a playscript; again, if he does so, he will have a half-buried device that will tell him much about a play's structure.

The silent moments are also the moments for the actor's pantomimes. Nineteenth-century acting was frequently made up of an alternation of speaking and illustration. Today, because of the demands of Realism, actors are much more motivated to do these two things simultaneously. But in this process we too easily forget the extreme importance of the silent moments—the erratic gaps of tempo. The director's imagination should lead him to a careful examination of a playwright's suggested illustrations for the silent moments. Whether he follows them religiously or not is a matter of personal decision, but at least he knows that the gaps are there, that they form part of the tempo structure of the play, and that they cannot be ignored without causing much damage to the rhythmic structure.

Ostensibly a play is very much like a dance-drama set to music. Without hearing the music—the sound and silence—you almost entirely lose the play's form. If the director has a musical ear, he will *hear* the written play.

RECORDING TEMPOS

Tempos can be readily noted, whether for an entire play or for a succession of units in that play, in two specific ways:

1. Through the use of rate words, such as *fast, medium, slow,* and their variations. If you know musical terms, these can be employed.
2. Through the use of a horizontal graph that shows the relationship of tempos to the horizontal line of the play. In this way the peaks and valleys of the action stand fully revealed. Again, as with the use of the rate words cited in item 1, this can be done with any unit division desired: the three acts of a play, the major scenes of a play, or the units of a specific scene.

EXERCISE

1. With the class aware of the category being illustrated, have one student beat a drum at different, improvised speeds. The rest of the class imagines the following for the rhythms:
    a. Different character types, which each beat prescribes.
    b. Different character-mood-intensities for each beat.
    c. A unit improvisation (one unit only of recriprocal action).

2. One student beats a drum at three different speeds. Try to improvise a story for the three units indicated.

3. One student beats a drum at the speed which he feels expresses a unit from a specific play. The class describes what they feel about the tempo he has played on the drum. They compare their feelings by reading the unit from the playscript.

4. Play some music. What visual images are suggested by the beat of the music? Take care in this exercise not to confuse tempo with moods as you presently understand the latter term.

5. Play some recordings of spoken plays. Note the tempo of the music used between scenes. Does the music contrast with the tempos of the spoken units?

6. Each student finds some music that expresses his feelings for the rhythm of a study play. Compare the findings.

7. Examine a study plan for sound and silence. Pick out the silent moments. What will specifically punctuate them?

8. Suggest improvised business for the opening and closing of a certain section of a study play. How does the visual, as imagined, emphasize the action of this section? What is the tempo of such visual activity?

CHAPTER EIGHT
THE DIRECTOR'S PREPARATION
The basis of communication

A director's preparation is a *written* analysis of given circumstances, dialogue, dramatic action, characters, ideas, and rhythmic beats (moods and tempos). It must be written because this method is the only way a learning director can be certain that he has covered all the points in the improvisation provided by the playwright, and has not substituted his own for the original.

HOMEWORK

No matter how skilled a director may be, no matter if he has been directing for many years, he will always have to do intensive homework—the study of the playscript. After you have done several written analyses, you may not actually record in written detail all of the structural facts about a play, but you will record some of them in your head and some of them on paper—always in the interest of clarifying your ideas and of developing specific communication that will be necessary between you and your actors and designers. But beginning directors must work hard at written analysis, if only to be certain that all its aspects have been covered thoroughly.

Therefore, the basic function of homework is not only to help you ferret out and understand a playscript, but also to put you in a position of extensive and sensitive communication. Homework will make you articulate in the right way. Good directing is not talk, talk, talk—a "gab fest"; it is made up of economical and appropriate suggestions made at the right moments. The job of the actor is to act, to physicalize; it is not the job of a student in a seminar where talking prevails. The director who thoroughly comprehends his primary tool— the playscript—will have a dozen ways of communicating a difficult point to an actor, not just one or two that may emerge after the director has stumbled around in a maze of language. A director's suggestions must be simple, direct, honest, economical, pointed. At the same time, they are imaginative—*imaginal* (full of images) is a better word—not cooly denotative but existing in the half-sublimated language that actors can understand and use.

Directions are also personal because they are directed to a particular actor and not to a puppet, or a robot, or a bit of pasteboard. Actors are not modeling clay. The director who knows his business will be ever ready to make the appropriate suggestion. Plays in rehearsal are built in a ladder-like construction with the director building on what the actor contributes and the actor building on what the director contributes, with this reciprocal process repeated over and over. The prepared director can make it work; but the unprepared director will be forever working out of his own subjectivity, and instead of being able to answer questions he will forever be posing them to his confused actors. The director's job is to lead the actors, not to be led.

The purpose of a director's homework, then, is to place him in the best possible position for communication to actors. He will know not merely a play's skin but its guts, bones, muscles, and blood.

WHY A WRITTEN PREPARATION?

There is something about writing down observations one notes about a playscript that particularizes and pinpoints them. At first, you may think that this procedure is a danger in an artistic process like production, that it could inhibit, or at least restrict, your flight as a director. This fear is nonsense. After you have done an analysis or two and have seen them work, you will know that analysis does just the opposite: *preparation acts as a freeing device.* By writing down your ideas, you see many more possibilities open up. After all, the playwright had to record his improvisations in a written playscript. Why shouldn't the director pin down his own understanding of the playwright's work in the same way? If a scene designer went directly into a shop and began building with only an idea in his head and not recorded in detail on drawing paper, the operation of building a set would be like a recreation hour in a madhouse. Without adequate formal preparation, a young director's work with actors will not only be haphazard but will follow a line of general directing and not of specific directing. A general development is dull and boring; only the specific can hold the attention of an audience. Do not think of a written preparation as an albatross around your neck but as the best possible tool with which you can provide yourself.

A SAMPLE OUTLINE FOR PLAY-ANALYSIS

Although you can plunge into an analysis at any point, a better technique is to approach it systematically. Thus, you should begin with given circumstances and then proceed to dialogue, dramatic action, characters, idea, and wind up with moods and tempos. This procedure works well because the analysis of given circumstances tends to flow into dialogue, and dialogue into dramatic action, and so on. You can also check it, when a fresh idea comes, with what you have already recorded: if it is logical, it will tie in easily, and the freeing process can begin to work.

What follows is a suggested plan for play-analysis. Although this plan is set down here in outline form, an analysis of a scene taken from a long play (ten minutes, with three to five units) or a short one-act play would easily fill several pages; in other words, you must not complete the outline in an abbreviated way as you do in answering a true-or-false question, but develop your answers in detailed exposition.

Work Sheet for Play-Analysis

I.   *Given Circumstances*
    A.   Environmental facts. Discuss under the following numbered headings:
        1.   Geographical location, including climate
        2.   Date: year, season, time of day
        3.   Economic environment
        4.   Political environment
        5.   Social environment
        6.   Religious environment
    B.   Previous action
    C.   Polar attitudes of the principal characters, both in the beginning and at the ending
II.   *Dialogue*
    A.   Choice of words
    B.   Choice of phrases and sentence structures
    C.   Choice of images
    D.   Choice of peculiar characteristics, for example, dialect
    E.   The sound of the dialogue
    F.   Structure of lines and speeches
III.   *Dramatic Action*
    A.   Titles of the units. Number the units in the scene or play and give a nominative phrase as a title for each unit.
    B.   Detailed breakdown of the action. Do this before going on to (C) because the verbs will help you do the summarizing of the units. Separate the action into numbered units. Express the action in each line (speech) by using the initial of each character followed by a present-tense verb. Example: N pleads.
    C.   Summary of the action. Summarizes the action of each unit by following the number of the unit with a compound sentence expressing reciprocal action. Example: A (present-tense verb) to B and B (present-tense verb) to A.

IV. *Characters*
   Treat *each* character under the following headings:
   A. Desire
   B. Will
   C. Moral stance
   D. Decorum
   E. Summary list of adjectives
   F. Initial character-mood-intensity at the scene-opening expressed as:
      1. Heartbeat: rate
      2. Perspiration: Heavy, light, etc.
      3. Stomach condition
      4. Muscle tension
      5. Breathing: rate, depth
V. *Idea*
   A. Meaning of the title
   B. Philosophical statements in the play: Cite actual quotations.
   C. Implications of the action
   D. For the scene in preparation: Cite its purpose and use in the play.
VI. *Moods*
   After the number of each unit express the mood for that unit in two categories:
   A. A list of mood adjectives with one for each of the senses
   B. A mood image
VII. *Tempos*
   After the number of each unit, designate the rate of speed for that unit by using a rate word. Examples: fast, medium slow, *largo*. Also make a horizontal graph of the tempo relationships by inserting connecting perpendicular lines to a horizontal line in order to show the peaks and valleys of tempo change.

EXERCISE

1. Review the outline in detail in class discussion. Be certain you understand all the parts before attempting a complete analysis. The instructor may wish to provide numbered forms for all sections.

2. Select for group study a one-act play or a five-to-ten minute scene from a long play. Each student does his own analysis. The group then examines the play or scene in detail by comparative reporting from the prepared analyses.

   Note: Exercise 2 can be an accumulative one for the entire chapter, if the student writes an analysis of each part as it is studied. In this way, a full play-analysis is prepared during the course of the study of Chapters 5, 6, and 7 and the total analysis will be on hand for discussion at this point.

3. Each student selects a ten-minute scene (four to six units) from a long play and analyzes it.

PART TWO
COMMUNICATION 1
The director-actor relationship: visual tools

. . . .let your own discretion be your tutor;
suit the action to the word, the word to the
action; with this special observance, that
you o'erstep not the modesty of nature. . . .

Hamlet's speech to the Players

CHAPTER NINE
DIRECTING IS
COMMUNICATING

In the previous chapters on play-analysis you learned how the playscript, when intensively studied and taken apart, can give you all sorts of ways to reach actors through special "languages" in the play structure. Now you are cast adrift on your own and are going to learn a new group of "languages" that will help you communicate not only with actors but also with audiences.

You should notice at the outset that this part of the book is specifically devoted to communication, and is divided into three sections with the same major goal of conveying a play to an audience in emotional terms. Yet the processes of communication are quite different. Therefore, each is discussed separately so that you can readily comprehend how each sort of communication works in its own way.

You may have noticed already that Communication 1 consists largely of techniques for communication to actors by placing them on a stage in such a way that they "feel" the elastic tension between them as an aid in finding the appropriate dramatic action. In contrast, Communication 2 gives oral communication a spotlight because most young directors tend to be seduced by the visual and forget that the theatre experience is a carefully balanced composite of the oral as well as the visual. At that point you will be ready to undertake your first major project in doing a scene with live actors. Finally, Communication 3 will focus on the director's function in design, and that is followed by your second major project: designing and directing your own production.

COMMUNICATING: ARTISTIC LEADERSHIP

As has been pointed out, *the director's field of action is communication.* However, you must make a very important distinction. Although the director's ultimate responsibility is to touch and move audiences with a play, he cannot do so by himself but must tell audiences how he thinks and feels through actors and designers—his agents. Consequently, what the director manages to bring about will depend entirely on his talent for, and his capabilities in, communicating with these agents, for he will be successful only if he has a strong faith in their creative abilities and can see his own job as one of encouraging and stimulating them to their highest expression.

But here is the rub! Because he is so devoted to helping others, the director can easily be called a leech, a bloodsucker, a hanger-on; and also a pusher and a bully. Yet at his best, he is also a friend, a confidant, a lover. Once the learning director recognizes that communication is his corework, he will concentrate on using every device he knows to *get through.* But at the same time, because he expects people to pay attention to him, he must go out of his way to pay the closest attention to them. Actors and designers are tender people, and the creative simply does not flourish in an aura of confusion and tension. A director communicates when he is a natural leader who knows how to work *with,* and not *at,* other human beings. Because he loves the artist in himself, he can love the artist in others.

How well you do this will depend on the sort of person you are because touching other people with theatrical ideas is a vastly intricate process largely outside the purely intellectual. A director who thinks that all he need do is talk with actors on a logical, expositional level fails to understand the sort of creative person with whom he is working. Acting problems are not solved *in discussion* but *in doing,* and the director is the freewheeling agent who can find the images or the circumstances that will make doing more likely to succeed.

Communication with actors is, therefore, a matter of a director's interest in and understanding of human beings, and not just an interest in their acting capabilities. Getting through is not a mysterious process; it is based on a director's meticulous homework with the playscript, as well as on his recognition that there are no actors in the abstract but only individual "people" who must be reached on a level of personal feeling. If he understands something about how the creative imagination works, and if he understands the process of acting—the using of the human instrument to effect communication—he will be able to achieve his basic goal of energizing actors in the right way and of inspiring them beyond their usual capabilities. Both actors and directors are working for the same goal—communication of a play to an audience—but only the actors will carry it onstage and bring about the actual contact.

This description of the humanistic director does not at all imply weakness. Though the director must watch his manners at all times—politeness is akin to gentleness—he will find that an appropriate use of directness will not hurt or injure, because it has a professional impersonality about it, and is not open to suspicion or worry on the part of the actor. A good director is a strong director because he does not leave actors, who have equally strong, creative imaginations, in doubt about what he means or intends; consequently, he takes great care to keep his directions clear so that the actors can easily accept and adjust. Appropriately used, strength is not dictatorship but an honest expression of opinion that can be supported and opened to discussion without generating fear and insecurity. The dictator-director is the director who is very unsure of his ground, a condition which actors will quickly detect; and even if they may try to be very cooperative on one level, they will find his leadership hard to accept. There must always be a certain amount of the salesman in the director because he must get across his ideas; yet, it is the soft sell, not the hard one, that will keep him on top of a situation.

THE DIRECTOR IS AN IMAGE-MAKER

All the people who work on a play—the playwright, the actors, the designer, the director—are image-makers. Because a play is an artificial device, an imitation of life and not life itself, its poetic power resides in its capacity to arouse the imaginations of the watcher-hearers. We have already defined this penetration on the sublimated level as *empathy*—an automatic response, if conditions are right, to what is seen and heard. All aspects of the produced play are more symbolic, more typical than they would be in everyday life because they have been carefully selected and simplified, carefully arranged, and carefully unified. And because of this treatment, they possess the inherent capacity of arousing images in members of the audience, each of whom can then connect them with his own personal experiences and view of life.

Thus, we can say that *the produced play actually hovers in the air between the actors on the stage and the audience in the house; it is a froth of images waiting to be rescued and assimilated by the audience.* Consequently, the playgoing experience does not stop with what is literally set out in these images from the stage but continues in a very personal way in the minds and feelings of the viewers. *Everything a viewer sees and hears is converted automatically into his own images.* This conversion is his work on the play, and it is obvious that the process of play production cannot be completed without him. Consequently, the *kind* of images made by the director through the actors is very important in the theatre.

As you can now readily see, if a director is to justify his place in the theatre as a theatrical artist, he will have to be someone who can not only help actors enhance their own capacities for image-making but also someone who can discover *appropriate* images for certain passages of a play, and can see that they are set in motion. As a director in training, you must therefore become highly aware that the theatre experience is primarily a sensuous experience, and that image-making involves the visual and oral deployment of the senses—seeing, hearing, touching, smelling, tasting. That the theatre is sense-arousing we can see readily in a performance of a play when we respond warmly to the color and texture of a costume, to the line of a piece of scenery, or to the sound of something mechanical, such as a clock bell or an offstage airplane engine.

What we are usually not so aware of is how actors continually assault all of our senses by making us constantly taste, smell, and touch, as well as see and hear, in very special ways. We are inclined to take them for granted because much of what a good one does is usually so deftly and subtly done, and is so right and truthful, that we are rarely conscious of the process. Yet, this is the process of acting, for *acting is reaching audience imagination through the direct transfer of sensuous imagery.* What an actor touches, we, as audience, touch in our imaginations; what he smells, we smell, and so on.

The young director, then, cannot be fully responsive to his communication possibilities until he comprehends the sensory-arousing aspects of acting. He will know that he can get through to an audience only when he can bring about in his actors the images with which he wants to assault the audience.

The final goal is, of course, to bring about a high state of *involuntary* attention (unaware or unself-conscious attention) in the audience. How well a director can achieve this goal depends on the sensory inspiration he can bring about in his agents. *A director must first be an image-maker* for his actors if he is to be an image-maker for an audience.

TECHNIQUES OF COMMUNICATION

Intellectual Talk

You should now be aware that there is a good deal more to the communication process between director and actor than exchanging ideas about a playscript on an intellectual level. Of course, a certain amount of useful information can be conveyed in this way, for an actor must understand the intellectual argument in a play, and the part his character plays in it. But when it comes to the hard core of dramatic action and character, such a self-conscious, objective method usually fails. Young directors are often baffled about why they are not getting through to actors because they are unaware that they are trying to reach them largely through objective discussion. Consequently, you must learn to work in many different ways, realizing that *your intention is to free,* rather than to tie up, *the imaginations of actors.* You must remember an actor who thinks too much cannot act. A character is the embodiment of his thought, and he acts accordingly. Consequently, actors must move spontaneously out of natural responses, as we do for the most part in everyday life, relying on their senses, and not on conscious thought.

You must, therefore, learn to restrict intellectual discussion to those matters that do not strongly affect the senses of the actor and you must learn how you can free his imagination, how you can give him flight in as many ways as possible. Objective talk will take your actors only a short way. Image-inducing direction will make him imagize, and that accomplishment will comprise your major communication with the actor. Talk little; do much.

Improvisation: The Inside-to-Outside Process

As you know yourself in your experience as a student of acting, when you started doing improvisations you began to see what acting is all about—that it is not a laid-on process of exterior development but that it starts from inside yourself and is all tied up with relating intensively to other actors. At first, your improvisations were probably arranged to show you how relaxation and concentration could let you show something with honesty and believability, through yourself and without self-consciousness. You probably did brief sense exercises with imaginary objects, and sometimes with real objects. Later you worked with dramatic actions, and eventually you may have tried complex exercises that involved other participants—improvisations that worked only when you learned to play *off* the other improvisor. You learned that improvising requires the utmost attention to what the other improvisor does to you because you have to adjust to him before you know what to do yourself. Do you remember how free you felt without a scenario or an established line of development such as a pantomime would prescribe? You could let the improvisation take form and develop out of that freedom. Did you feel the exaltation and power that freedom gave you?

This is the sort of feeling you must induce in your actors when you use improvisation as a technique of communication. *The goal is discovery in the most personal way possible, for that is what moves from the inside of the actor outward.* Improvisation becomes a device enabling an actor to discover his relationship to another actor on an intimate level (reciprocation); to establish a relationship to another character; to feel the sensation of the dramatic action being expressed; to discover dramatic action; to discover an illustration of dramatic action; to feel the special quality of a given place and its climate; to feel the decorum of a character in a given circumstance; to hear what the voice is like at high volumes and low volumes under forced conditions; to find the extent of movement and body behavior under specifically delineated circumstances.

These are only a few of the enormous number of things that can be accomplished with improvisation, for it is literally imaginative game-playing that can open up a play's mysterious moments. The director is, of course, the leader, and as such he can use improvisation for any purpose he wishes. Some directors use it extensively throughout the rehearsal period and do not actually shape a performance until the later rehearsals.

There are many problems, however, in using only the improvisational approach as the means of releasing actors. Beginning actors will have a particularly difficult time with it simply because improvisation requires experience, and it may not have been part of their training. Advanced actors may do somewhat better, and some will be very good at it. Nevertheless, the primary problem with improvisation is that it has no performance status of its own; that is, although it can lead to very sensitive moments of discovery, they are still only moments, and a performance is made up of many moments joined together. What happens in between making improvisations and making a performance is of primary concern. Some directors try to show the improvisations they have made in rehearsals to audiences without any modifications whatsoever, and then wonder why they do not work. You will keep out of trouble if you remember that improvisations are *highly valuable as devices for discovery,* but they are not intended for performance because they inherently lack the essential power of projection (selection and emphasis), and without that an audience cannot gather the play together.

If you can see improvisation primarily as a rehearsal technique, it may become a valuable tool for you. Used for its proper purposes, it can help you reach many actors on very primitive levels, and make your play that much more sensitive. But recognize at the outset that it is largely a rehearsal and not a performance technique (see the Epilogue for the exception), and that it requires experience and talent in the participants to accomplish successfully.

There will be more comment on the improvisational techniques along with some specific suggestions in Chapter 18. But after you study the intervening chapters on *organic blocking,* you will be in a better position to know what to do with improvisation. A good book to help you learn more about this approach to actor training is Viola Spolin's *Improvisation for the Theater.* If you study her methods of handling actors, you will know a good deal more about what can be done in a specific way.

Organic Blocking: The Outside-to-Inside Process

Organic blocking is the process of stimulating actors to image-making through the use of six visual tools: (1) groundplan, (2) composition, (3) gesture, (4) improvisation with properties, (5) picturization, and (6) movement. Its function is to help actors discover dramatic action by "feeling" its inherent illustration. This "outside-to-inside" process contains rehearsal and discovery techniques, as well as techniques used in performance. (Note: Don't be put off by the use of "blocking," a word professional directors and actors often think is old-fashioned. Once you understand how organic it can be, its seemingly mechanical aspect will be absorbed in the game of using this device.)

In line with the previous discussion of improvisation, you must first understand that these six tools for director-actor communication are used *for the purpose of communicating directly with the actor, who will, in turn, communicate with the audience.* You must, therefore, view these tools as *actor stimulators:* by using them as *external suggestions,* a director can ignite all kinds of chain reactions within an actor. The word "organic" is used to denote that *such blocking is in no way superimposed on a play or forced on an actor,* but it implies that such blocking suggestions derive from the play itself (the organism) and are therefore inherent in it. Organic blocking, then, is not a pictorial process, not a way of making a performance more beautiful through stage arrangements, but *an inherent activation of a playscript through a body of physical suggestions that can arouse imagination in actors.*

At first, this technique may be difficult for you to comprehend, especially if your actor training has been dominantly improvisational with the emphasis always on the inside-to-outside process. However, skillfully used, the outside-to-inside approach to actors can work very well indeed and will not be at all in conflict with the other approach. As a matter of fact, both can be used, and are used, simultaneously. Indeed, many actors like the assurance of the outside-to-inside approach because it is tangible and physical: they know in a physical way where they are going.

The question raised here is what seems to be, in the view of some directors, a strong conflict between using improvisation and blocking at the same time. These directors argue that blocking freezes the actor and that improvisation is the only avenue to his release. The answer to this argument is that *there is no single way to release actors.* Either or both of these approaches can be used effectively and often in combination, paradoxical though that may seem, since blocking is self-conscious and objective, whereas improvisations are largely intuitive and subjective. However, if both are used with care, they do not battle with one another but tend to support and intensify one another. You will need to learn how to do both if you are to take full advantage of available director-actor techniques of communication, for shutting yourself off only with improvisational techniques is to limit greatly what you can do with actors, especially if your actors have been trained in body-release or other physical approaches to acting. In addition, if you should decide to work in the professional theatre, you will find that actors use a wide range of techniques but seldom employ improvisation as a process.

Actors frequently feel quite uncomfortable when they participate in first readings because a play—an ensemble effort—can be very confusing until it has been given some outward form. A director can be of great assistance in helping them get over this initial discomfort by placing them physically in specific relationships to one another in conformity with the dramatic action. This process will not only give an actor time to locate himself, but it will allow him to know who his adversaries in the play are, something he may already know intellectually but not in a physical sense. Anyone who has acted in a play knows the discomfort described here; yet directors who are busy looking elsewhere too easily forget the strangeness and disorientation of first contacts.

When the refinement of illustrations begins later in rehearsal, the concept of aiding the actor with visual suggestions can be stepped up in full force, always with the intention of communicating ideas to the actors—ideas about emphasis, intentions, or shadings in the action. If you keep in mind that transfer to the audience is a transfer of sensory images, you will begin to appreciate the full value of this sort of direction. A good actor will, of course, provide much of this illustration on his own; but illustration is infinite, and the best selection must be made. The director's function is to assist with selection, by constantly working toward what he believes to be refinement and improvement. Where an actor stands on a stage in relation to other characters or other objects, how and why he moves and the nature of that movement, how he handles an object, are all of primary concern to a director for all of these considerations will convey images. The important question is: *do they convey the appropriate images, the ones the director has decided he wants?*

You will have more control over some of these visual tools than you have over others, but they are all tools that you can put to work. Learn to tell the truth with them by finding appropriate images because the tools have great capacity for telling lies; the actor can *speak* one thing and *do* another. Hamlet's advice to the Players quoted on the title page of Part II is the best instruction that can be given to a director: " . . . suit the action [illustration] to the word, the word to the action." This principle is what the actor is learning to apply. If you can exploit his own training to the full, you will find yourself in ready communication with him.

Actors are also great experimenters. Always remember that the process of rehearsing a play is not talking about it but doing it. One thing you must learn is that you should not freeze actor illustrations until late in a rehearsal period when you must consistently use the best ones you have discovered. Some students think that by learning techniques their imaginations will be dried up, that they become more rigid. Just the opposite actually happens. You will certainly be self-conscious when you are learning how to "see" these tools and how to use them, but later they will become second nature to you, and you will know how to exploit them to the fullest possible advantage. Scene discovery or opening up the action will usually depend on experimentation with these visual tools. Gamble on shifting and changing their values as part of the process of actor-discovery in rehearsals.

Organic blocking is developed rather extensively in the following chapters not only because it must be understood in some detail to make it work as a technique of director-actor communication, but also because it provides the process for the projection of a play in performance. As you work through these chapters, you will see how to use these tools to make clear and forceful statements of dramatic action and character statements that may take shape in spontaneous ways during the rehearsal period but can be sharpened and focused during the polishing period.

Organic Blocking Can Be Used on All Stages

You will notice as you work with the six tools that they seem to refer only to the *proscenium stage* where the audience sits directly in front of the stage platform. *This has been done intentionally* at this point so that you can learn how to work on this still dominant form of stage before you progress to others. But it must be emphasized here that organic blocking can be used as a process on *any* stage form, no matter what its shape or where the audience sits, simply because, by definition, *it is a way of getting through to actors and enhancing their illustrations of action.* Later, you will learn how to adapt the techniques to any stage you may be working on. It is very important now that you master the process as a basic technique. Learn some rules that apply to the proscenium stage first, and then you will be able to make the transfer to other stages much more easily. Again: No matter what the stage form may be, blocking is *not* mechanical illustration to be executed by puppet-actors but a *living, breathing process of mutual discovery and communication between actor and director and actor and actor.*

You should also keep in mind when working through the following chapters that the six basic tools have been isolated here as individual working tools. (We never actually see them in such an abstract way when we watch a performance because an actor uses several of these tools simultaneously and so quickly that our eyes cannot readily delineate their separate ways.) Yet, without this detailed separation, you cannot possibly understand the individual force of each tool or know how to exploit each as a way of reaching actors.

The discussion of the tools begins with the groundplan in Chapter 11 and continues in Chapters 12, 13, 14, and 15. So that you will see how they work in concert, Chapter 16 will put them together in a synthesis. Only by understanding the parts as separate tools can you grasp the whole.

EXERCISE

1. Discuss in a group the approaches used in *your* acting training. Try to isolate the different approaches cited. When did you first think you were really acting, as distinct from merely using your exterior personality? What was the experience like?
2. What kinds of communication reach you as an actor? Examine the various approaches directors have used to bring you out as an actor. What worked best? What was least effective?
3. What is an image? Read some short poems and analyze each for its imagery. Look particularly at some five-line Japanese poems and their imagery. Why is poetry so compact? Compare to the compactness of a play.
4. "Talk" to another student in images, using as few words as possible. You will be surprised at how few words are actually needed to convey ideas and human feelings.
5. How does *organic blocking* differ from merely blocking a play? Can you see how the first is deeply rooted in both dramatic action and in actor training, and the second tends toward the pictorial only?
6. Discuss the good and bad points in using improvisation as a director's method of communication.
7. Define the proscenium stage. What is the use of the proscenium wall? How does the "wall" concept differ from the arch concept? Does Realism as a style require the proscenium stage? What is the audience's relationship to the actor on a proscenium stage? What rules do you think should

be observed by actors performing on the proscenium stage? In discussing the proscenium stage, the tendency is to think of it only in terms of set design. How is it also a playwright's stage? An actor's stage? What are its merits? What are its limitations? (The proscenium stage will be discussed in detail in Communication 3; but it is important at this point that you understand it in a minimal way.)

CHAPTER TEN
LEARNING TO SEE
Game of visual perception

"Learning to see"—learning to observe meticulously and perceptively—is a skill the young director must acquire early in order to help him make images that can excite and move audiences. It is not enough to give casual attention to what an actor wears, or the place he tells his story, or how he moves around the stage in relation to other actors. Instead, the director in training must learn to see so incisively that after a single viewing he can recall explicitly every object, every move, the quality of light in the specific place, the color of the upholstery in relation to the color in a costume, and much, much more.

The line drawings used in Chapter 11 will get you started on the "Game of Visual Perception" by asking you to look carefully at stage space, first looking down from above (a groundplan), and then from an elevated angle outfront. As you become more accustomed to looking at groundplans and have learned how to translate them into stage space, photographs of live productions are added throughout the book so that the "Game of Visual Perception" can be practiced with specific examples.

If you will deliberately play this game with the drawings and photographs you will learn how to "see" much better. Learning how to examine *meticulously* the captured moments in the work of others will increase your instant recognition of visual illustration.

In addition to the specific questions suggested with each photograph you should ask: *What did the director do? What would I do?* Don't think of these productions as ideal but as challenges to your own work. *How much can I see?*

The Game of Visual Perception runs throughout the text, with each set of problems assigned to groups as follows:

1. Composition
2. Picturization
3. Choice of Stage
4. Scenery
5. Properties

6. Light
7. Costume
8 Makeup
9. Style in Modern Plays
10. Style in Historical Drama

These photographs have been selected as useful, practical, examples of work being done at different levels of directing. Some are the work of student directors, while others are the work of faculty directors or regional theatre directors, with the latter classification covering the wide range of directing in semiprofessional and professional theatres outside training programs in the schools. A full identification for each photograph can be found in the "Credits for Photographs" at the opening of this book.

CHAPTER ELEVEN
THE GROUNDPLAN
The basic tool in director-actor communication

A *groundplan* is at once a representation of the given circumstances and a tension device for discovering and illustrating the dramatic action of a play *in specific terms of space and of the necessary obstacles that break up that space.* No matter what sort of stage you may be working on—proscenium, arena, thrust—it is still the basic tool in director-actor communication because all the other tools are dependent on it and flow naturally out of it. If you can master the concept of the groundplan as a machine-tool for communication, you will be able to see how the other tools can also work for you.

Although a groundplan is usually represented in a two-dimensional draw-ing, like the architect's floor plan you see in magazines about building homes, it is actually three-dimensional in concept for the drawing represents physical objects occupying vertical space (from the floor upward) as well as space on the plane of the stage floor. A director must, therefore, always think in three-dimensional terms: stage space is a cube and not a rectangle on the floor. Using this point of view, he can see the vertical as well as the horizontal aspects of the design, and he can thus better visualize how he can suggest to actors the feelings and facts about the given circumstances.

For this reason, in devising groundplans for Realistic plays, a director should also include walls, platforms, steps, furniture, and anything else that has height. Only by doing so can he define the cube he and his actors will exploit and his audience will see and feel. Always try to see a groundplan in your mind's eye just as you would if you were looking at a perspective sketch of it with your eyeline slightly above the stage floor.

A groundplan is only incidentally a visual design for an audience. Its primary service is that of *an organic instrument to bring out the dramatic action through director-actor communication.* In composing a play, a dramatist will choose a symbolic place for the dramatic action because he feels that it exerts some particular force on the action itself; that is, he feels the pressure of the place. A director, therefore, must reconstruct this feeling from the dramatic action (not from a physical description the author may have inserted) as nearly as he can, for what he must find is the *appropriate obstacle course for that action.*

Obstacle course is used here because an actor, until he is much advanced, can sense actions much more quickly and keenly with a physical obstacle between him and the opposing force represented in another character than he can when there is no obstacle. A table, sofa, or chair between two actors gives them both something to struggle over, something which prevents them from getting together. This technique is based on the premise that plays are mostly about clashes and not about harmonies. Differences in levels—steps, platforms, etc.—do much the same thing because one character can feel from such juxtapositions his dominance or lack of dominance over another character.

The purpose of a groundplan is, therefore, to give actors strong sensations of tension by placing in their way physical obstacles that must be overcome if they are to reach other characters.

From this discussion, it should be obvious that a director must search for the *appropriate space* for the play he is producing. What he finds will be a specific place, not a general place. The given circumstances will tell him whether that space is large or small; whether it is frequently interrupted by objects or whether it is only occasionally so; whether it has strong vertical possibilities (everything from platforms to balconies) or must be largely horizontal (low-ceilinged, hugging the floor). Good designers also think in these terms, although they are not apt to think about a director's specific communication with actors. (For this reason, it is imperative that directors work intensively at developing their own sense of design for the groundplan. When they work with designers, they can then be certain that the major point of a groundplan—director-actor communication—is accomplished.) The detailing of the space and of the objects can be done by a designer because he can greatly intensify the visual effect. But unless the architecture of a groundplan is well conceived in terms of the dramatic action, not only will the director have lost basic possibilities for communication with his actors, but he will also have reduced the effectiveness of all the other visual tools for director-actor communication that depend on it.

AN IMPROVISATIONAL APPROACH
TO THE CONCEPT OF GROUNDPLAN

You may wish to begin this section on specifics by doing the improvisational approach to "thinking and feeling" about the groundplan outlined in the following exercise. This step-by-step "game" will enable you not only to grasp the difference between a groundplan and a room used in everyday life, but will also give you a much better understanding of the concepts that follow. "Doing" is far better than talking about it.

In order to thoroughly understand why the groundplan is an artistic device for presenting an illusion of reality and that it is not reality itself, do the following set of progressive exercises. Do it carefully step-by-step, and do not proceed to (B) before you have mastered (A), or move to (C) before (B) is fully understood. Remember that the whole exercise is a game that must be played in pieces.

A. Improvise a place with an inside measurement 20 feet wide and 14 feet deep (an average-size living room) by lining up classroom chairs and having them face outward on four sides. In setting up this place, now is the time to practice the technique of rehearsal-room measurement, something you will do over and over again in setting up a rehearsal space, by using the three methods for determining approximate footage: (1) if you know the length of your pace (the distance between your feet—heel to heel—when extended in walking), you can make a fairly accurate measurement by counting the number of your paces walked off; (2) if you know the length of your shoe, you can mark out a desired measurement by placing one foot immediately in front of the other until you have covered the distance; (3) if the rehearsal room floor is made up of square rubber tiles, you can find the exact measurement you want by counting the number of tiles (each tile will probably be 8 to 12 inches wide).

B. When the space is accurately determined, mark off two "entrance doors" to the room by removing chairs in appropriate places. Now arrange living room furniture (classroom materials) in a very similar fashion to that in a room you know in real life—your living room at home, for instance. Note that you will probably be making at least one conversational group with a sofa placed against one wall and chairs placed in relationship to it. It will probably look something like Figure 1.

C. Improvise some dramatic action in this room. Here is a suggestion: A host receives three or four visitors, one at a time. After doing the improvisation, discuss where they sat down (probably in the easiest available spot), and undoubtedly in the conversation group. Also note that most living rooms this size probably have only one conversation group in order that everyone sitting in such a room can be easily included. Note how easy it is for people to carry on conversations in this physical relationship. Try some conversations using "numbers" dialogue. Try two or three other improvisations before going on to (D).

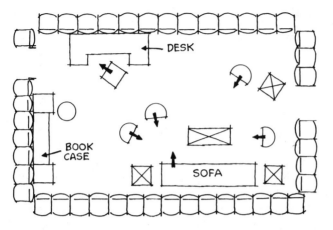

FIGURE 1

D. Now convert the room to a ground plan by:
   1. placing two chairs to represent a proscenium arch 28 feet apart on one long side of the room and centering them on the middle of the room;
   2. removing the chairs on the side and raking the side walls of the room along with any furniture placed against them to meet the proscenium chairs (the chairs mentioned in D, 1). Note that the room will now look like Figure 2. Note also that the walls have been raked to allow good sightlines (so side audiences can see). Thus, it should now be clear to you that a groundplan is an artificial device that is not reality but only an illusion of reality.

E. Increase the departure from reality further by reversing the sofa and coffee table so that they face the audience. It will now look like Figure 3. But this groundplan is still not a good one because it is too simple to provide refreshing illustration for a two-hour play. Rearrange the

FIGURE 2

28 FEET

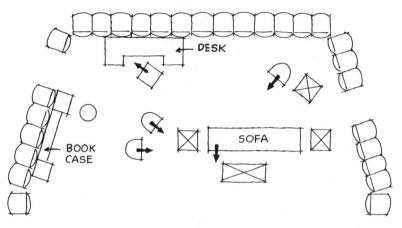

FIGURE 3

furniture even further by placing pieces in the downstage corners of the room (pinning down the corners) and by making a second conversational group on stage right. It should now look like Figure 4.

F. Now increase the architectural "strength" of the room by creating a jog in the upper left corner. Note that this modification makes the room more interesting architecturally because it reduces the obvious symmetry of the wall areas. Add chairs and furniture pieces to make it look something like Figure 5.

G. Now note the following:
   1. An *obstacle course* made of furniture has been established;
   2. Two "conversation" groups allow more flexibility in where people can sit to talk;
   3. The "acting" furniture for the most part occupies the middle planes of the stage—a clear departure from the real room we started with;

FIGURE 4

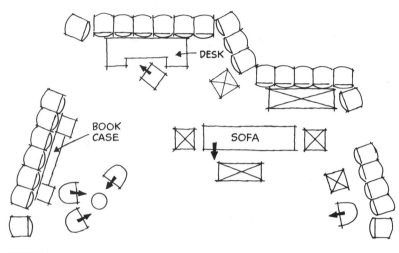

FIGURE 5

4. Multiple acting areas (see the next section) have been established, allowing very flexible use of the groundplan;
5. The corners of the groundplan have been tied tightly to the rest of the plan, thus making the groundplan as a whole seem to hold the stage more solidly and to frame the actors.

ACTING AREAS

Because Realistic plays involve dramatic actions in domestic environments, such as living rooms, bedrooms, kitchens, porches, backyards, and offices, they are ''sit-down plays'' in a literal sense, in contrast to the stand-up nature of historical drama. The groundplan's potential power to illustrate can therefore be measured by strictly defining all the *acting areas*. A very handy technique for doing this sort of advance forecast is the *sit-down rule*. According to this rule, *an acting area consists of two sit-down positions at least six feet or more apart*—that is, two chairs, or a sofa and chair, in different parts of a room. As you can see, this rule arbitrarily excludes *not only all standing positions but also those sitting positions, such as on a sofa, where two people are placed very close together.* Further—and here is the second important part of this rule—*a groundplan must have a minimum of five acting areas* defined in this fashion if it is to be really effective. As you can see, an inherent part of this rule is the concept of keeping characters apart while playing a scene.

Note in Figure 6 how each area is delineated by circling two sitting positions at least six feet apart, and how the merits of the groundplan as a whole can be tested by showing all of the available areas in one drawing (as in Figure 7). Six areas are delineated in Figure 7, but there are at least two or three more not shown because the lines would overlap too much and thus would obscure the drawing as an example.

NOTE: THE AREA CIRCLED
IS #6 IN FIG. 7

FIGURE 6

The use of this *sit-down rule* for estimating the number of acting areas, and thus the flexibility of the groundplan, does not at all imply that standing positions are not constantly used in very effective ways. Quite the contrary. But standing positions will be all the more effective when enough obstacles have been placed in the room to keep the characters at some distance from one another. Each of the obstacles also acts as a physical support to any actor who stands near it because it will emphasize the weight and mass of the actor's body. *If any groundplan has less than five acting areas, it means that the number of obstacles has been so reduced that the possibilities for tension are very limited.*

Learn this sit-down rule because it is an effective safeguard in planning high-tension groundplans. A groundplan conceived on this principle of multiple acting areas will suggest all sorts of illustrative possibilities to actors because of its built-in tension, and you will find that it will become a quick and effective device for communication.

FIGURE 7

TENSION ARRANGEMENTS

A multiple-area groundplan always has high tension values because the possibilities for arranging furniture can be extensive. Your arrangements will need a certain amount of logic, of course, because rooms should more or less look like what they are intended for (likeness to real life). However, appearance is largely a secondary matter. Of much greater importance in a groundplan is its tension-creating possibilities, and if tensions are there, the appearance will probably be more interesting, even more exciting. Here are some specific suggestions for creating tension values:

1. Place your primary objects in space free of the walls so that actors can move easily around them (see Figure 8). *Objects placed against the walls merely create standing spaces with no obstacle course.* They will provide a certain amount of verisimilitude (likeness to real life), but they will not normally provide possibilities for conflict.

VERY WEAK: NO TENSION   STRONG: TENSION CREATING

FIGURE 8

2. Work on the diagonal principle whenever possible because diagonals create more tension than objects parallel to the proscenium line. (Note the direction of the long arrows in Figure 9.)
3. Place objects in contrasting positions that can create tension by their oppositional force. (Note the short arrows in Figures 8 and 9 that show the directions the sitting positions face and, consequently, the oppositional forces they create.)

FIGURE 9

4. Note that walls create tension when they are broken up with jogs and diagonals (Figure 9) because they not only create architectural strength and interest but also cut into and compress the action space.

   The placement of furniture definitely takes these lines into account. Good tension-creating arrangements will arouse strong feelings in actors, thus motivating them to work against tensions as well as with them. You will be amazed at the strength of the compositions automatically created by the actors when there are strong lines of tension in a groundplan.

GROUNDPLAN ON THE PROSCENIUM STAGE

Although creating strong tension values is absolutely essential, you must also arrange the groundplan in accordance with the primary convention of the proscenium stage, the convention that places the audience in front of the stage within an arc of 60° to 70° (see Figure 10). This arrangement implies that some arbitrary rules are automatically put into force in order to help the audience see and hear better. Normally, we are supposed to be looking in at a reproduction of real life, but the placement of the audience makes the use of the proscenium stage quite artificial and not like real life at all. The theory of the proscenium stage will be discussed in Communication 3, but it is essential at this point that you understand that you are trying to overcome the effects of a one-sided view and are compensating for the loss of a true three-dimensional quality.

Here are a few rules you must follow if you are to overcome the flat qualities of the proscenium stage. They will also help your audience see and hear better.

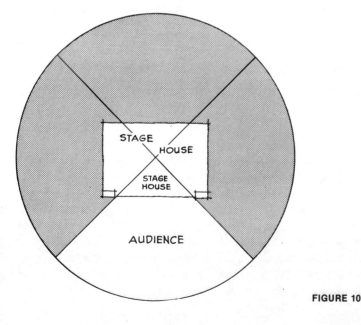

FIGURE 10

1. *Open the side walls to the audience.*   Side walls are usually raked to open up the upstage corners of a setting (Figure 11, a and b), although walls perpendicular to the proscenium line (Figure 11, c) can work if the audience's seating angle to the stage is less than 70° and if entrances are not placed in upstage corner positions. You must never think of the upstage corners as dead areas, for you will need every possible square inch of space to keep your compositions interesting, especially in one-set plays where action is carried on for two to three hours. Always consider the sight lines in composing a groundplan (see Figure 10).

2. *Open the set properties (furniture) to the audience.*   Throughout the seventeenth, eighteenth, and much of the nineteenth centuries, actors faced the audience when they were speaking, just as opera singers still do today. With the introduction of Realism toward the end of the nineteenth century, however, turning away from the audience, even showing the back of the actor—a very shocking behavior to turn-of-the-century theatregoers—replaced the old convention in the interest of creating a semblance of real life. Although a certain amount of psychological truth was revealed in this way, turning away from the audience resulted in obscuring both the actor's voice and face. Since there was much to be said for the old give-it-to-the-audience convention as opposed to the new concealment aesthetic, the new convention as it developed used both ideas, with the emphasis on playing to the house. The groundplan convention has developed in the same way, for the intention has been to help the actor deliver the play in every possible direction, but primarily to the frontal audience. As the furniture placement took on more and more aspects of an obstacle course by occupying the spaces where the actors had always stood, it became general practice to compensate by opening individual furniture pieces to the house. *The general rule thus requires that all much-used furniture pieces be placed prominently as far downstage and as near centerstage as possible.* The *illusion* of reality is thus preserved, although the room is anything but real. Do not think, then, that you will help an actor by placing a chair on the curtain line facing upstage, for you will merely be blocking the audience's view of the stage and forcing the actor, if he sits in the chair, to talk upstage, thus cutting off the audience's hearing as well (see Figure 12). Such placement does not in any way create more reality but instead merely confuses an audience. Avoid such odd theatrics and, instead, comply with the conventions of the proscenium stage.

3. *Pin the downstage corners of the groundplan tightly to the rest of the plan.*   Because the illusion created should be that of a walled room, you will not only help the effect of wall inclosure but also increase the illusion of depth to the room if you place pieces of furniture (chairs or other sitting pieces) at both of the downstage corners of the room and *encourage actors to use them. This arrangement will provide a downstage foreground to contrast with midground and background,* thus tying the groundplan together and intensifying the three-dimensional quality of the staging. This rule is very important because the furniture will help frame the actors in all the positions they take on the stage (see Figure 13). Moreover, without such

SATISFACTORY
100% VISIBILITY
A

VERY POOR
NOTE THE PLAYING
AREA LOST
B

POSSIBLE
ONLY THE UPSTAGE
CORNERS ARE LOST
C

FIGURE 11

FIGURE 12

IMPOSSIBLE AND ILLOGICAL

FIRE PLACE

POOR

FIRE
PLACE

WORKABLE

VERY POOR
(NO FOREGROUND)
A

WORKABLE
(CHAIRS CREATE FOREGROUND)

FIGURE 13

sitting positions, actors will tend to avoid using the downstage corners which will result in only a partial use of the total possible acting area.

INGENUITY IN GROUNDPLAN DESIGN

You must learn to be ingenious in arranging groundplans. Always avoid the dull and trite—what may be called the *no-room*. How dull it is: that bare, three-walled room without architectural jobs for relief; that room with a routine selection and placement of furniture; that room with doors placed in balanced positions in the walls. New ideas about illustrating the action will present themselves to both you and the actors if you think and feel freshly about what makes up a groundplan.

FLEXIBILITY, TESTING, AND IMPROVISATION

You should not make only one groundplan, but several, and then remake them. Since the groundplan is the basis for all the other visual tools, it must be the best possible one you can devise. Therefore, your personal flexibility in this regard is absolutely essential; you must always be ready to discard the groundplan that does not work and start over again, rebuilding on what you have discovered. Making a good groundplan always involves improvisation, for you are trying to project its uses through your own imagination.

One way to approach making a groundplan is to have some specific ideas in mind, and then have the actors help you discover the best possible arrangement. They will enjoy this game of looking for fresh ways of illustrating, and such play will help them to a better understanding of the given circumstances. Remember: *A groundplan is only as good as is its potential to arouse the imagination of the actors who will use it.* They must learn to live in it and to exploit its every possibility. If you are to help them fly, you must help them find the flying machine that will get them off the ground.

Once again: make, test, remake, improvise; make, test, remake, improvise, and so on.

EXERCISE

1. On the basis of the given circumstance of a study play, each member of the class designs a groundplan. (Be absolutely certain to avoid any directions in the playscript that may prescribe a setting. Find all you need in the given circumstances buried in the dialogue, and then let your imagination go free.) Now answer the following questions about the groundplan: Do you have an obstacle course? Is it a no-room? How many acting areas does it contain? What is tension-creating in the plan? How ingenious is it? Now compare your groundplan with those groundplans done by other members of the class. Evaluate the differences carefully. Who has been trite and who original? How many different kinds of furniture has the whole class used?

2. Design groundplans for two or three plays and measure their effectiveness with the same criteria as is used at the end of the improvisational exercise.

3. Set up a groundplan on the classroom floor (be certain to measure the outside dimensions carefully) by using whatever classroom furniture is available, and discuss its effectiveness. After suggestions have been offered, alter the plan to produce a maximum of interest. Repeat this exercise several times, with different students setting up plans and others criticizing their effectiveness and doing the alterations. Work for ingenuity and freshness.

4. Do a group improvisation in one of these plans with number dialogue using three or four improvisors. What did the plan suggest to the improvisors? What can you as a director suggest to them to help their imaginations find different uses of the plan? After discussing the plan and after reviewing the possibilities of dramatic action in the improvisation, redo the improvisation with a different set of participants.

CHAPTER TWELVE
COMPOSITION
Discovering
and projecting
basic relationships

You are now ready to put organic blocking to work (see page 72.)

The techniques discussed in this and the following chapters are devoted to two ways of looking at *activity* on the stage: (1) from the actor's view; (2) from the audience's view. The first is absolutely basic to an actor's understanding of the conflict his character is going through in a play, and the second is about the craft of showing that conflict fully and clearly to an audience. Your attention should be focused primarily on the first objective, but the second, if the first works, will probably be accomplished simultaneously. This is an example of outside-to-inside technique, and it can work in many instances with young actors in training. Later, when you may work with more accomplished actors, you will not need to position them so much because the actors will know how to relate by themselves; they may actually insist on participating in working out their own blocking as they develop their intensive relationships with other characters on the stage. But now, you must learn "to see" in these two slightly different ways. Communication is all a matter of "seeing" first.

DEFINITION

Composition is the physical arrangement of actor-characters in a groundplan for the purposes of discovering dramatic action and of illustrating it in the simplest possible way through emphasis and contrast. *If actors are made aware of basic physical relationships, they will perceive dramatic action in greater depth and be able to transfer this intensity to an audience.*

COMPOSITIONS ON THE PROSCENIUM STAGE

Because the proscenium wall (the wall that separates the house from the stage) has a frame and the audience sits out front and looks through it, all the basic requirements of perspective drawing apply; that is, we must be able to see depth as well as width and height. The director's job, then, is to help arrange the actors in this three-dimensional cube of the stage in a *series of still shots*—a full play would require several hundred such still shots—so that an audience can sense and feel basic forces in a play.

Strictly defined, composition does not involve a movement (transit of the actor from one point on the stage to another). Instead, composition is static. *It is a caught moment. It is a primitive form on which will be superimposed the other elements that make illustration* and which we have yet to discuss—gesture, picturization, and movement. Without the primitive, architectural arrangement of composition, actors cannot convey the meaning of their basic relationship, and thus their feelings about a dramatic action.

Because a play is spoken—an enormously important fact in the theatre—*an actor's body must be relatively, if not entirely, quiet* during much of a play or an audience simply will not be able to hear what the actor says. The animated illustrators (gestures and movement) are so alive and vigorous because of their living and breathing qualities that their meanings are conveyed first (the eye is quicker than the ear); therefore, they must not be allowed to dominate composition. Although you must keep the "still-shot" concept of composition in mind, you should understand that a play in performance is made up of a very great many of these shots that are tied together by movements of the actors that place them on one or another part of the stage. In this sense, *a performed play is a continuous alternation of composition and movement.*

Back in the nineteenth century when the laws of the proscenium stage were taking form, this rule of alternation was observed quite rigidly, and today, as was pointed out previously, we see its holdover in operatic acting where the singer is directed to sing to the audience in set positions, with business interspersed when convenient. With the passing of nineteenth-century poetic drama and with increased emphasis on visual representation in the twentieth-century theatre, the rule of alternation was modifed by allowing actors to move during their own speeches as well as during the speeches of other actors. The easier-to-hear prose dialogue not only made it more feasible to break down the old rule, but it also encouraged the desire for a more completely animated performance. However that modification may be, *a large amount of movement is risky when significant speeches are being delivered.* Consequently, experienced directors and actors learn to stand still and to *hold composition* at important moments. Movies always appear more animated to us than plays because they seem to be continuously moving; but when you watch the work of a good motion picture director you will see an enormous number of still shots (largely close-ups). We hear a film because we are forced to do so by the director's selection of shots, and by actors who learn not to move their heads because they find that moving their eyes and lips—a required motion picture technique—is more effective. *An important principle in acting is learning to hold the body and head still,* so that when they do move, they will "say" something specific.

A composition on the stage is thus a photographic still shot of great value. Once again here is the point: the director must learn the importance of encouraging actors to evolve good compositions because they form the basis of all good illustrations by containing primitive meanings and mood values.

CHARACTERISTICS OF COMPOSITION

Compositions Have Basic Meanings

From the above discussion, you can see that a composition involves *two or more actors* taking specific places on the stage. Try to see composition as made up of bodies *without* moving arms or legs—neutral forms like manikins—who stand on marked points on the stage floor but have the capability of facing the body in different directions or of bending it to kneeling or sitting positions. This neutrality of the body position is very important if you are to see the meanings that come from compositions alone and are not to confuse them with those that come from gestures and movements.

Now observe the relationships of the two bodies in Figure 14. The arrows on the heads represent the directions which the bodies are facing. What does each composition mean? Try to guess their meanings before looking at the suggestions in the following list.

1. *A* and *B* are either like one another or are confronting one another in anger.
2. *A* is playing hard to get, with *B* the weaker.
3. The situation in (2) is reversed with *B* playing hard to get.
4. The relationship between *A* and *B* is disrupted completely with backs turned to one another.
5. Although *A* and *B* face each other, *A* is now much separated from *B*, indicating a coolness, though opposition is still present. If you try these same exercises with *A* or *B* seated, you will see that new meanings emerge. What are they?

Here is the point: All compositions are made of roughly these same juxtapositions. *Characters in a play are either together, apart, or conform to some gradation of these two basic situations.* Composition thus illustrates for us in the simplest possible way the dramatic action—the conflicts—between two or more characters. Without good composition there is no clear storytelling.

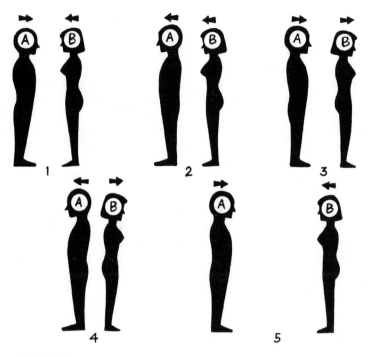

FIGURE 14

Composition as Director-Actor Communication

The communication inherent in composition is now evident. A director can suggest to his actors their basic relationships with other characters by merely placing them in stage arrangements: by keeping the actors apart they can sense some level of their separation; by placing them close together they can sense the intensity of their conflict (love is also conflict). Actors usually accept these hints quickly and are eager to experiment with them.

However, when doing improvisations, young actors, in the interest of developing an action (maintaining improvised dialogue), will forget that composition is a device for illustration. Though the action may be intense in the minds of the improvisors, it will appear to a viewer to be completely internal because it is not illustrated. In other words, the improvisors may understand the action completely, but without employing strong compositional values, they fail to illustrate it (or else they illustrate it very poorly); frequently, they will use the same two or three compositions over and over again. On the other hand, a well-trained actor sees compositions as one of his most valuable tools for illustrating his actions, and he will look for every possible variation to keep that illustration as fresh and as varied as possible.

Composition can be used most effectively as a device for communicating with actors when rehearsals are well-advanced. It is then that a director can communicate his most subtle points about the action by helping the actors find fresh and meaningful compositions, particularly in accord with the set properties in the groundplan. These properties always play a part in composition by becoming animated when they are employed by the actors. *A director who is afraid to introduce new compositions late in a rehearsal period fails to recognize their value as communicative devices, for good illustration of dramatic action can only be found through constant experiment.* The director must learn to gamble with new compositions in the interest of stimulating in the actors new insights into dramatic action.

Composition, therefore, is not something arranged only for its pictorial value to an audience, but it is a *basic device for communicating to actors perceptions about their relationships with other characters.* If this arrangement is dynamically effected, even though a composition holds a set place on the stage floor, it will move an audience. There is certainly something pleasurable in the harmonic balance of a stage picture, but that matter is secondary. If the action is illustrated honestly and intensively, its beauty will emerge in all its truth.

TECHNIQUES OF COMPOSITION

The actor, as well as the director, must learn all of the following basic techniques of composition in order to know as many ways as possible of bringing variety to stage illustration. Holding an audience for two to three hours requires much skill in finding variety, especially if only one setting is used.

The Individual Actor

When we talk about composition, we mean the arrangement of two or more actors on the stage. *But the director and actor must be fully aware of the compositional force of each individual on the stage before any arrangement of groups can take place.* We seldom see actors on the stage alone, and the purpose here is not to discuss that special circumstance but to see the individual isolated in order to assess his potential force in a group arrangement.

Body positions.   Stage right and stage left are the actor's right and left as he faces an audience. Now face the body to the major points of a circle, and you have the body positions (see Figure 15). Note the designations for these positions; full front, one-quarter left, etc.

The force of body positions is very great in any composition, for turning your back on another actor has one meaning, and facing him has another, as we have already suggested in Figure 14. Variations between these extremes give us the necessary nuances. Beginning actors either want to face the audience because they don't understand the concept of reciprocation in acting, or they want to face other actors continuously, thus losing the freshness and new illustrations brought about by varying the body's position.

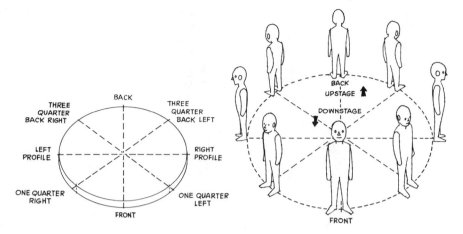

FIGURE 15

EXERCISE

1. Six actors assume different body positions, with the members of the class identifying each. Be absolutely certain that each actor observes the neutral position, that is, arms at the sides, head facing the same direction as the body, no facial expression.
2. At a signal from the instructor, each actor takes a different body position, and the class identifies all the different positions. Repeat this exercise many times until the positions are thoroughly learned and can easily be identified in the stage terminology indicated in Figure 15.
3. What is the basic meaning of the full-back position? The full-front? Either profile?
4. Can one actor force another (dramatic action) through his use of body position?

Levels.   By levels we mean the actual *head level* of the actor. He is at his highest level when standing and any variation that takes his head toward the floor is a change in level (see Figure 16).

When he uses an artificial level introduced in a set design, such as platforms or steps, his level changes even more drastically (see Figure 17).

FIGURE 16

FIGURE 17

EXERCISE

1. Without using any artificial levels, have three actors (observing the rule for the neutral actor as far as possible) assume different body levels. Identify these levels. Now, at the instructor's signal, each actor assumes a new level. Identify and repeat.

2. Repeat Exercise 1 with artificial levels (platforms, chairs, etc.), beginning first with fully erect actors then progressing to variations in body level. Identify and repeat several times. Be sure to observe neutrality as far as possible.

3. What are the meanings of the various levels? Compare the meanings of a standing actor with those of a sitting actor, then with those of a reclining actor. Do you see how each position conveys a general meaning? Keep in mind that until Realism came to the stage in the nineteenth century, actors seldom sat on chairs or other objects but performed plays in standing positions. As noted previously, Realism is sometimes defined as "sit-down drama" in contrast to the "stand-up drama" before the middle of the nineteenth century.

4. Contrast the meanings conveyed by an actor when he first stands on a high platform and then reclines on the floor. You must suggest the most basic meaning, not the story-telling or pictured meaning, such as making a speech or sleeping, because the actor could be doing a dozen different things in each position. How dominant would he be in the elevated position? How weak would he be in the reclining position?

5. Can one actor force another (dramatic action) through the use of levels?

6. Combine body positions and levels by having three actors work with separate chairs. At the instructor's signal, each actor takes a different body position and different level. Note the variety and contrast that is possible.

Planes. The concept of stage *planes* applies only to the proscenium stage where the term is used as a way of pointing out that the proscenium stage has depth as well as width. When we talk about an actor "moving through the stage planes," we mean that he moves upstage or downstage. *Up* and *down* are terms which have been used by theatre people for nearly 300 years to indicate directions mainly because stages were raked; that is, stage floors actually *inclined upward* toward the rear of the stage, some of them very steeply, as can still be seen in the famous Teatro Farnese, built in 1619 in Parma, Italy, where an actor quite literally walks *up*hill or *down*hill, depending on which way he goes on the incline. In modern times stage floors are flat so that scenery can be erected with little difficulty at any place on the stage. But the old stage terms are still used to specify depth, and therefore the concept of stage planes. To compensate for the loss of the incline, theatre architects have inclined the audience, and very steeply in some recently built theatres.

Although planes are purely imaginary, you could see them easily in a physical way if you were to hang several drops on stage battens located two feet apart, and then were to look at them either from overhead or from the side (see Figure 18). Each drop would represent a plane.

Now remove the drops but keep the idea of the positions they occupy by placing actors in each plane (see Figure 19).

A human being is about a foot thick. But since we cannot actually see much difference in planes if they are too close together, we think of each plane on the stage as being about two feet deep. And more important, because the audience sits directly facing the stage in proscenium theatre, objects close to them seem much larger than those farther upstage. Thus, instead of seeing actors or objects as they are represented, we see them as they appear in Figure 20.

Understanding the concept of planes is valuable to an actor because then he can think in terms of moving from or toward an audience as well as crossing

FIGURE 18

PERSPECTIVE VIEW
FROM A CORNER OF
THE STAGE

FIGURE 19

PERSPECTIVE VIEW
FROM THE FRONT, SLIGHTLY
ABOVE THE THEATRE

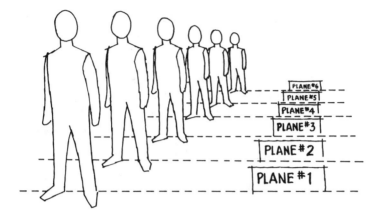

FIGURE 20

in front of it. Most beginning actors and directors think only in terms of the latter and do not see the strong dramatic ideas that can be conveyed by the graduated upstage and downstage positions.

EXERCISE

1. If your class is working on a stage, lower some battens and try to imagine drops hanging from them. Count the number of lines on your stage and note the space between each of them.
2. Place six actors, all facing full-front, in six successive planes (two feet apart) in a slanting row upstage. Observe neutrality. Can you see the different planes? Can you see the difference in size? Squinting will help you see better.
3. Now place six actors, all facing full-front, in different planes but in various parts of the stage. Observe neutrality. Identify the planes.
4. Place one actor in an extreme upstage plane and another in an extreme downstage plane, both in full-front positions. What is the meaning of each position? Why is the one nearer to you stronger?

Horizontal locations.   Just as planes are the designations of depth on the proscenium stage, so horizontal locations declare the position of an actor on the width of the stage. Thus, we say *stage right* (SR), *stage left* (SL), or *center stage* (CS). We often divide the width into even more precise locations, left center (LC) or right center (RC) as in Figure 21. This concept of horizontal location implies that the stage has horizontal meaning as well as depth meaning. We also see differences in the actual location simply because in a proscenium theatre, where the audience sits in front, the center can be seen well by everyone. Thus, we declare the center location to be strongest and the two side extremes less strong in the same way that we can see differences in the extremes of upstage and downstage.

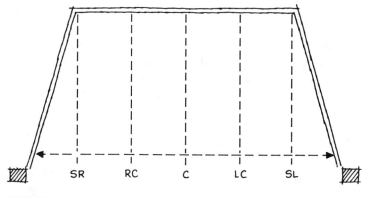

FIGURE 21

EXERCISE

1. Place five actors, facing full-front, in the five horizontal locations designated above. Observe neutrality. Identify each position.
2. What meaning does an actor have in the center location? What is the meaning at either the extreme right or extreme left location?

The Group: Creating Emphasis

Since all compositions are made up of two or more actors, a problem immediately arises over which actor (or character) will have the emphasis. If a director looks at a composition purely as a member of an audience, he realizes that *he must create that emphasis or the audience cannot follow the dramatic action simply and effortlessly;* that is, it will be difficult to tell who is talking or who is strongest in the action. But when the director looks at his possibilities for director-actor communication, he knows that his best hope of finding the appropriate emphasis is to convey to his actors what he thinks is important in the action and how important it is. Only out of this sort of suggestion will a natural emphasis flow. He thus encourages specific groupings to suggest not only literal meanings to the actors but sublimated ones as well; he is again working on the principle that sensitive and varied compositions will arouse appropriate tensions in the actors (organic blocking), who will then communicate directly and much more sensitively to an audience. An actor who is given a dominant position will certainly exploit it fully in his forcing of other actor-characters.

Emphasis, then, is a basic necessity in good composition. You create it by contrasting the four variables of composition—body position, levels, planes, and horizontal locations—in the following group arrangements: focuses, diagonals, triangles, space and mass, repetition or support, climactic compositions, different stage areas, and compositions with furniture.

Focuses.   There are two kinds of focuses: (1) *eye focus,* in which one actor looks directly at another actor (see Figure 22); and (2) *line focus,* in which one actor turns his body directly toward another actor, and may emphasize it further by pointing with arms, legs, or torso, or all three simultaneously (see Figure 23). Both kinds of focuses work on the principle of imaginary lines which run from one actor to another; the lines may be only partially suggested, but such is the nature of the imagination that it is able to complete the lines by seeing them in the mind's eye. (Note the dotted lines in Figures 22, 23, and 24.) We frequently use both eye and line focuses at the same time (Figure 24).

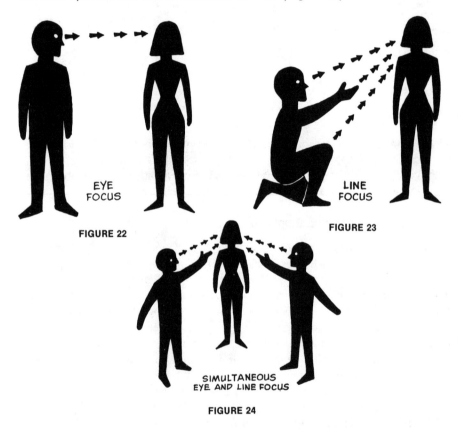

EYE
FOCUS

LINE
FOCUS

FIGURE 22

FIGURE 23

SIMULTANEOUS
EYE AND LINE FOCUS

FIGURE 24

EXERCISE

1. Illustrate eye focus by placing two actors in contrasting one-quarter positions with eyes straight ahead. Without moving his head, have *A* turn his eyes on *B*. What is the effect? Now have *A* turn his head and look full-face at *B*. Is the effect even stronger? Now have him turn his body as well. What is the effect? Repeat this exercise many times in all variations of eye contact and head positions. What do the actors feel?

2. Illustrate line focus by setting up many compositions like the examples given in Figures 22, 23, and 24. *Be sure to be at a distance from the compositions so that you can actually see the lines.* What do the actors feel? What do the compositions mean? You can actually see the lines in a literal way if you use a piece of cord attached to each actor. A large piece of rubberized material, such as an elastic band, works even better because the tension between the two actors can be literally illustrated.

Diagonals. A composition of two actors may be made with the actors in the same plane. This is a *shared* composition because each actor has equal emphasis (if the level and body positions are similar), as in Figure 25. However, they will take on different meanings if the planes are contrasted, thus creating an imaginary diagonal line (see Figure 26). Noe that the emphasis here is on the upstage figure. *The diagonal is more emphatic than a line parallel to the front line of the stage* because it moves both horizontally and vertically (upstage) in the imagination of the spectator. Directors learn to employ diagonal compositions because of the tension which they readily create.

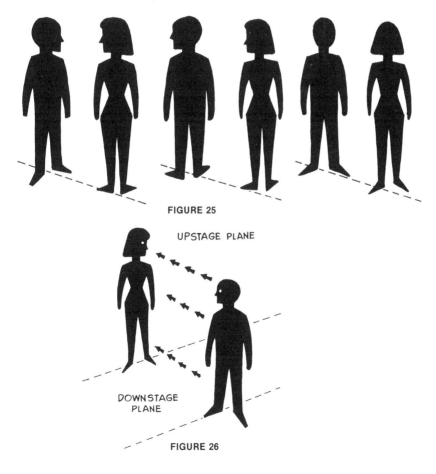

FIGURE 25

FIGURE 26

EXERCISE

Illustrate the strength of diagonals by showing the contrast they make to those lines parallel to the front of the stage. What do the actors feel?

Triangles.   Compositions of three or more actors are arranged in *triangles*. It is obvious that if three actors stood in the same plane, they could not easily see one another, for the actor in the center would block the vision of the other two (see Figure 27). In addition, triangles employ diagonals, the dynamic lines on the stage. By varying the four basics of composition (body positions, levels, planes, horizontal locations) at the points of the triangle, a variety of meanings will emerge.

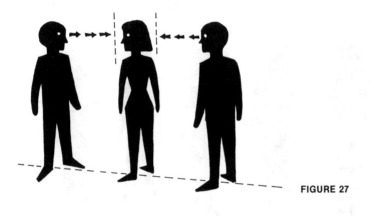

FIGURE 27

An endless variety of interesting compositions can also be made by varying the triangle in the following ways:

1. Shortening or lengthening of the legs of the triangle (see Figure 28)
2. Increasing or decreasing the angles (see Figure 29)
3. Changing the total area of the triangle (see Figure 30)
4. Changing the position of the base leg from a line horizontal to the front stage line (see Figure 31) to a line that runs diagonally to it (see Figure 32)
5. Breaking the legs of triangles when there are more than three actors by inserting actors at points in the legs (see Figure 33)

You must learn to avoid *flat* triangles (those having little depth) because they can neither be seen by an audience nor can they convey to actors much sense of character relationship. Make a rule for yourself not to allow triangles less than two or three planes in depth (see Figure 34).

FIGURE 28

FIGURE 29

FIGURE 30

FIGURE 31

FIGURE 32

FIGURE 33

FIGURE 34

EXERCISE

Illustrate the use of triangles by placing live actors *in all the examples described in this section.* Identify the location of the points of the triangles and the length of the lines. Make some flat triangles and illustrate their ineffectiveness in contrast to deep ones. What do the actors feel? Do you see differences in meaning as the triangles change?

Space and mass. Effective compositions can be made by isolating one actor on one part of the stage and contrasting that isolation with a number of actors on the other side (see Figure 35). The single actor is thus surrounded by *space,*

FIGURE 35

which gives him emphasis and individuality, and the others make a *mass* with only group identification.

EXERCISE

Do several illustrations of making emphasis through space and mass. Evaluate each of them.

Repetition or support. When four or more actors are used, the dramatic action frequently places them on two opposing sides. The supporting actors who stand behind the principal actors are said to *repeat* or *support* the principals, thus giving emphasis to the principals (see Figure 36).

FIGURE 36

EXERCISE

Do several illustrations of making emphasis through repetition or support, and evaluate each.

Climactic compositions. As we have previously noted, old compositions give way to new compositions continuously throughout a performance because they are the still shots that an audience can easily comprehend simply because it knows who has emphasis (and thus who is speaking). *These changes consist of variations on the actual distance of separation between actors,* which depends on the illustration needed to show the forces between the actors. Thus, two actors may play at the extremes of the stage or very close together, with each composition having explicit meanings. *When they are close together (less than six feet) they are in a climactic composition.*

FIGURE 37

Climactic compositions should be used for only two actions, including all their variations: (1) extreme love, in which the actors are about to embrace; or (2) extreme hate, in which they are about to fight. *Climactic compositions must therefore be saved for the climactic moments* of a play. Young directors and actors incline to overuse climactic compositions on the stage as a matter of course because they see them so continuously used in motion pictures and television where it is necessary to bring two people close together to get them on camera. But they forget the alternating use of multiple isolation shots (close-ups) that make the actors appear to be well separated. This technique of breaking long shots, however, cannot be used in the theatre where the continuous long shot is the way of life. *A climactic composition, therefore, has the force of a close-up and must be used sparingly for this purpose or it will have no meaning at all.*

It is necessary to think of compositions as a succession of shots that show actors in successive stages of either making contact or breaking it (see Figure 37).

EXERCISE

Illustrate climactic compositions by first setting one up, and then by dispersing the actors to extreme positions. *What do the actors feel?*

Stage areas. Compositions may occupy (1) the entire stage, (2) the left or right halves of the stage, or (3) a quarter of the stage (see Figure 38). Compositions that occupy less space are usually climactic and can be placed in any location on the stage. But since climactic compositions must be used sparingly, the director must learn to use a wide variety of larger compositions placed contrastingly in all the areas (see Figure 39).

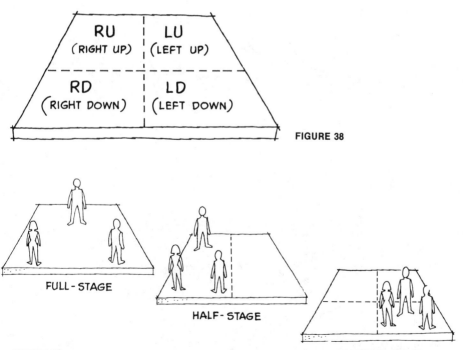

FIGURE 38

FULL-STAGE

HALF-STAGE

FIGURE 39

QUARTER-STAGE

EXERCISE

Illustrate stage areas by setting up compositions on (1) the full stage; (2) a half stage; (3) a quarter stage. At an instructor's signal, shift the composition to different areas. Evaluate.

Compositions with furniture.   Figures 22 through 39 have assumed a bare stage because the intention was to show the techniques of making good compositions; but the bare stage is, of course, a very exceptional circumstance in Realistic drama. The problem is to see compositions in the midst of furniture (properties) placement. If a workable groundplan has been devised, compositions will fall naturally into it, for actors will feel relationships on the basis of where they can sit or stand. *Groundplan designing thus always gives prime consideration to how composition can be exploited by the actors and the director.*

One important aspect is how furniture pieces participate with actors in compositions. Without actors, they are dead objects; but when actors move around them and use them, they take on an animation resembling that of silent actors. Triangles in all their variations can be made in this way, with two actors and a piece of furniture as the third point. Again, if you and the actors think of a

WRONG

RIGHT

FIGURE 40

groundplan as an obstacle course, good compositions will mature of themselves. Remember: using the stage compositionally does not imply clearing the space for the actors to move in front of the furniture pieces, but it means allowing the pieces to interrupt space (obstacle course concept) and, thus, to interrupt an actor's goal to reach and touch another actor (see Figure 40).

An obstacle course will automatically defeat the desire of actors to make climactic compositions, which can then be saved for the appropriate moments. An actor moves *in* a groundplan, not in front of it, for the basic concept declares that the only space available is that space falling between objects. Consequently, the more objects there are in a groundplan, the more difficult it will be for one actor to reach another. If your groundplan is skillfully devised, you can suggest to actors compositions that will impede them—that is, compositions that will keep actors from reaching one another easily, with the result that they will unknowingly intensify the illustrations of their dramatic actions.

COMPOSITIONS AS ACTOR COMMUNICATION
VERSUS PICTORIAL COMMUNICATION

It is not the purpose of this book to take up an extended discussion of composition in terms of pictorial design. Rather, the intent is to view composition from the standpoint of director-actor communication. This presupposes that the only aspect of theatre which really matters is to move an audience through dramatic action and characters, and therefore that the principal function of directing is to arouse actors to assume the positions that will be most effective in communicating appropriate imagery to an audience. Furthermore, although it would be possible to delineate more rules of pictorial design, it is assumed that the young director can neither absorb them nor can use them at this point.

However, as you grow more experienced, you will develop your own sense of the pictorial, or, like some recent directors, you may regard the pictorial as superficial and relatively nonessential in conveying the meaning of some plays. But this approach is exceptional. At this point, you must learn all you can about the effect of the pictorial. The more you know about composition as the liaison between actor and audience, the better you will be able to communicate. Practice composition diligently from every point of view, for good direction is also good picture making.

SUMMARY OF EXERCISE FOR ALL ASPECTS
OF COMPOSITION

1. Coordinate all the exercises inserted throughout this chapter by setting up a groundplan (with furniture pieces) on the classroom floor and by arranging compositions within it. Use three actors to change locations, thus

making new compositions, when the instructor gives a signal (clapping hands). Other students should identify all the elements in each composition and then evaluate the effectiveness of the elements in the groundplan.

2. Each student should compose at least three different groundplans, and then set up multiple compositions on each. Intensive practice in this problem will prepare the director for all that is to follow, for without a basic understanding of the techniques and the uses of composition, he will not be able to bring about truthful illustrations in a play.

GAME OF VISUAL PERCEPTION 1: COMPOSITION
(See pages 77–78)

1. Identify in each photograph: Body position; planes; areas; eye-focus; line-focus.
2. Can you see possible acting areas other than the ones being used?
3. Are obstacle courses provided?
4. Do you see the triangulation: size, length of legs, upstage apex, relation of the base line to the proscenium line if visible?
5. Are the levels in the groundplan being exploited?
6. What character has the focus in each photograph and why?
7. Do you see how actors are tied to set properties?
8. How is dramatic action conveyed through composition in each photograph?
9. Can you see how composition can be effectively developed with only one actor in the context of a setting?

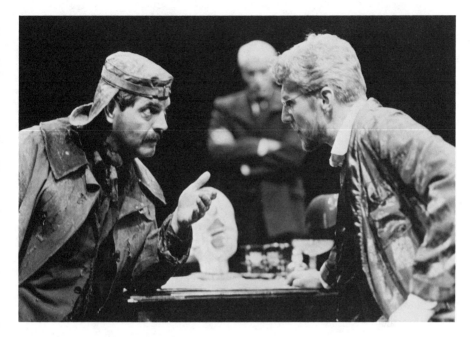

PHOTO 1 *Pygmalion* (Shaw)

PHOTO 2 *Beyond the Horizon* (O'Neill)

PHOTO 3
Extremities (Mastrosimone)

PHOTO 4
Look Back in Anger (Osborne)

PHOTO 5 *Buried Child* (Shepard)

PHOTO 6
American Buffalo (Mamet)

PHOTO 7   *Taste of Honey* (Delaney)

PHOTO 8   *The Creation of the World.* . . (Miller)

PHOTO 9
Fool for Love (Shepard)

PHOTO 10 *They Knew What They Wanted* (Howard)

PHOTO 11
Streetcar Named Desire (Williams)

PHOTO 12   *Food from Trash* (Hill)

PHOTO 13 *Awake and Sing* (Odets)

PHOTO 14 *South Pacific* (Rodgers, Hammerstein, Logan)

CHAPTER THIRTEEN
HELPING THE ACTOR
INTENSIFY
Gesture
and improvisation
with properties

Gesture and improvisation with properties, as tools of director-actor communication, perform similar functions in organic blocking because they help actors not only discover the subtleties of dramatic action but also build character illustration with imagination and sensitivity. The two previous chapters have shown how the groundplan and composition can lead actors into discoveries about given circumstances and relationships in dramatic action, and thus to basic image making. This chapter will show how you can lead actors into making highly detailed and refined visual illustrations.

GESTURE

As noted in the preceding chapter, preserving body neutrality is absolutely necessary to see composition as a powerful force in itself. In this chapter you will see neutrality abandoned and the body fully animated through gesture. Here are two dictionary meanings of gesture:

> The use of motions of the limbs or body as a means of expression
> A movement usually of the body or limbs that expresses or emphasizes an idea, sentiment, or attitude

Note that these definitions suggest three things: (1) that the body is set in one location; in other words, that gesture is not movement, an activity that takes the body from one point to another on the stage; (2) that *gesture is the animation of all the moveable parts of the body*; and (3) that gesture is capable of expressing ideas, sentiments, or attitudes. Now go one step beyond these definitions by thinking of this activity as taking place in the body's sphere—the sphere that stretches from tiptoe to the fullest extension of the arms in all directions. Here are some illustrations of what we mean (see Figure 41).

Think of gesture as extending outward from the center of the body's sphere and occupying whatever space an actor's imagination wishes to give it. Frequently, only part of the space is used, as in the figure on the far right. Gesture can be as large or as small, as free or as restricted, as an actor desires in expressing character.

Again, in contrast to composition, which is architectural and abstract and always expressed in terms of the neutral body, gesture is the living quality of the body—the body's animation. Although it may seem that certain ethnic groups, such as the Italians and the French, speak with more gestures than others, all human beings employ gestures in very great numbers. Shakespeare's line "the hand is instrument to the mouth" is the very essence of gesture, for we always use the hand in the hope of amplifying the meanings of the language we use, or, in the words of one definition quoted above, "to emphasize an idea, sentiment, or attitude." *Words are one kind of symbolic expression and gestures are another, with each having specific uses in conveying ideas.*

Gesture is, therefore, a prime means of actor communication. The suppression or the controlling of gesture is what we usually designate as poise, the body behavior we usually associate with refinement and cultivation. We tend to designate levels of cultivation by the amount of gestures employed, with the inference that the more a person can suppress his gestures, the closer he is to being dominated by his mind. Thus, in plays and movies we are apt to see lower-class characters illustrated with many gestures and upper-class characters with relatively few; that is, there are few until they lose control of themselves and revert to the animalism that hovers in all men.

FIGURE 41

Gesture can convey ideas simply and clearly, as is illustrated in its use by the deaf who not only "talk" in sign language with their hands and fingers, but also indicate attitudes with their whole bodies. Watch them closely and you will see how really animated they are in their own type of conversation, much more so than people with normal hearing. As an animated tool of illustration, gesture can thus rephrase and intensify the crude meanings of composition into highly refined and subtle ones. But the actor must learn some very important lessons early in his training, principally that indiscriminate use of gestures will convey very little meaning, that he must be highly selective, and that he must, above all, start from the neutral position of basic composition.

Gesture in Director-Actor Communication

So subjective is gesture that it is primarily an actor's, and not a director's tool for communication. Yet, the director who is unaware of its force does not know how to reduce or increase its use. It is very important to note: *An actor who does not stand still or hold his head still cannot be heard by an audience, or is heard poorly.* Repeat this over and over to yourself, as well as the saying, "the eye is quicker than the ear." The director must also know how to strip an actor of gestures and to help him build new gestures that will reveal the character he is playing, not just himself as an actor (what we call actor mannerisms) or the gestures belonging to another character. Certain gestures, as well as their size or the state of their control, can also be suggested by the director and thus can become subtle ways of communicating dramatic action from the director to the actor. An actor, when learning to characterize, will discover that the appropriate use of gesture—always within the range of his character and always economically—provides the subtle visual clues to a character's states and feelings.

Decorum

As was just suggested, an actor can declare some aspects of a character by the gestures he uses, gestures that can indicate not only a character's inner feelings but also his outer position in life—his position in society. *Decorum* means specifically *the outward show of a character*—an appropriate reflection of the given circumstances in a play. A king moves like a king because he leads a life of ceremony and is as much symbol as person. Similarly, a ditchdigger moves like a man who uses his body continuously in physical labor. Decorum is simple symbology for what we expect from these occupations, but they are nevertheless prototypes. In real life, we notice this relationship often enough to expect it, but the rules of decorum do not always hold, a fact which encourages actors to look for the exceptions that can be carried over to the stage as fresh observations.

Because decorum is the outward show of a character, a director and an actor must search for the appropriate decorum for a character. Without this, the outward show will lie about his given circumstances, and the audience will be left in confusion about what to expect. Occasionally, directors exploit this confusion with the full intention of misleading an audience into fresh thinking about a character.

So much pressure is placed in actor training on developing the inside core of character—that is, of insuring full comprehension of the dramatic action— that actors frequently give little attention to the force of the exterior look of a character. In contrast, good professional actors always look for the appropriate decorum of a character in order to convey given circumstances quickly to an audience, just as a designer does with his stage scenery. By imaginative suggestion to an actor about a character's decorum, a director can arouse fresh ideas about interior action because the actor can see more clearly the contrast and conflict between the outer and inner selves of a character. The director can also encourage an actor's sense of physical illustration and thus be able to convey many more specific and appropriate images to an audience.

EXERCISE

1. Have one actor demonstrate the "sphere concept" of gesture by assuming different positions that will occupy the full sphere. Repeat with the full class. Get the feeling of the sphere. Compare and contrast formal dance (full use of the sphere) with acting by illustrating the use of gesture in both forms and showing how they differ.

2. Repeat Exercise 1 by using several actors who change positions at the instructor's signal. Try to keep the positions within the boundary of everyday human behavior. These illustrations will show not only the full opportunity an actor has in occupying the limits of the sphere but also how his movements stretch outward from the center point of the body.

3. Do a series of huddled gestures to show how head, arms, and legs can also be drawn inward toward the body.

4. Have one actor sit on a chair in front of the class. At the instructor's signal, he changes his gestures to convey different inner feelings (dramatic action). Identify the meaning of each. How do the gestures help his face? Repeat with three actors, unrelated to each other.

5. Place two actors in a composition in a groundplan and encourage them to add gestures after telling them, out of the class's hearing, of their relationship to each other (dramatic action). Have the class describe the gestures and their meanings.

6. Have two actors illustrate decorum by sitting or standing in their spheres after you have suggested (only to the actors) different occupations (an aspect of given circumstances) to each one. Do not let them move from one place to another on the floor, but encourage them to take within their spheres any positions that they like. Have the class identify the occupations they suggest. Can other aspects of decorum be recognized?

7. Do Exercise 6 in the opposite direction by suggesting a decorum to an actor and letting him improvise dramatic action through that decorum. Repeat extensively with other actors.

IMPROVISATION WITH PROPERTIES

Hand Properties

Definition.   *Hand properties*—any objects that can be held in the hand and easily manipulated—*are extensions of gesture because they increase the variety of possible illustrations with the arms and hands and, frequently, with the legs and head.* Because the director, as part of his design function, can suggest the use of specific hand properties and how to use them, he can make them specific tools of director-actor communication.

Concept.   Although a hand property has inherent meaning—that is, an umbrella is something to ward off rain or sun; a book is something to read; a cigar is something to smoke; or a cup is something to drink from—*most of the hand properties used on the stage should be employed for reasons other than what their literal functions intend.* Only occasionally do we draw an audience's attention to a hand property in its functional use, that is, a knife for cutting, a gun for shooting, a weapon of any sort for murdering. Nor are hand properties used merely to provide the obvious exterior reality of everyday life in the interest of saying "this is the environment" and "these are the things people use in it." By and large, *audiences should notice them only peripherally and should not be made to concentrate on them*, except in unusual circumstances when attention is obviously drawn to them. Hand properties have many more values than their functional qualities.

The principal use of hand properties is to help actors "talk" through gestures, for they can: (1) extend the length of the arm (with a pointer); (2) increase the size of the hand (with a book); (3) make the hands and fingers active (with a cigarette); (4) produce sound (by closing a book); (5) show nervousness (with a handkerchief), etc. *Everything an actor touches, if he uses it properly, can convey a sensory impression simply because an audience can actually feel the way the actor touches it and can empathize with him.*

The primary purpose of a hand property, then, is not its functional use but its potential for underlining dramatic ideas—the subtle aspects of characterization. In one sense, properties provide an additional pair of eyes for the actor. Because the members of an audience vary in their actual distance from the stage, with a large number actually unable to see the detailed eye movements of the actors, the skillful use of hand properties by the actor can actually tell even the farthest reaches of the audience what his eyes are doing, so closely is such amplified gesture allied with inner feeling. The motion picture with its closeups has no such problem, but the stage must rely on significant illustrative tools such as properties to augment the eyes, particularly with Realistic drama.

Characteristics of hand properties.   Along with actors, directors should be highly aware of the qualities and characteristics of hand properties. It is *how* an actor uses a property that will convey idea, and the *how* can be exploited only if the property is completely understood. As a director, you must develop a keen imagination with properties if you are to learn how to exploit them fully. Make a habit of looking carefully at a property: what are its peculiar and individual characteristics? If it is smooth, can it be rubbed against the face? What are its "sound" characteristics (does it snap, pop, etc.?), and how can they be exploited? Will its weight cause it to do certain things in the hands of an actor? Can it be stretched or rubbed against other materials? Can it be torn or pulled apart? All questions of this sort open up the imaginative, fresh use of properties. The trite use of a property by an actor implies that he does not actually *see* and *feel* the property, does not actually know its nature and its possibilities.

As you can see, then, all of the preceding questions are pursuing the same point: how can a hand property be used effectively by an actor to illustrate dramatic action in a fresh, active, and sensitive way. *The purpose is to reveal a character's state of mind, not to show the property itself.* The audience's attention must be on the feelings of the characters, and not on the object, except in those rare instances when an object becomes momentarily the dramatic action itself—a gun doing the forcing because a character is no longer able to rely on his own "weapons" of speech and body.

For these reasons, you can see that such an action as eating is not intended to improve the health of the character in front of the audience or to give a reason for sitting at a dining table. Instead, it gives an actor some hand and mouth tools for illustration. A book in an actor's hand might possibly be read to show the audience that the character is improving his mind, or that he is the intellectual sort; but usually it is used to illustrate nervousness, to emphasize a point by banging the book closed or by banging it on a table, or to show preoccupation and interior disturbance. Hand properties appropriately used possess the inherent capability of revealing detailed psychological states in characters in line with the structural core of modern prose drama; *they have distinctive capacities for revealing subtext.*

Improvisations with hand properties. The word *improvisation* is used here to denote what the actor and director must do in order to find the best illustrations. Only through constant experimentation can a property be fully exploited or another property substituted to make the necessary revelations. Actors should always work with real hand properties just as soon as their hands are free from carrying scripts because properties will suggest buried dramatic action to the actor, as well as tell him how to show what he already understands. Only when the use of a property has been fully exploited in rehearsal does it become a set piece of business in the old sense. Even if a playwright requires specific use of a hand property, the actor must work with it improvisationaly to exploit its highest potential. The old idea of set pieces of business handed down through tradition is irreconcilable with modern training in acting in which each actor must first decide whether a property is needed to illustrate a dramatic action, and then must discover for himself how *he* can best make it meaningful.

EXERCISE

1. What is the difference between hand properties and set properties? Look ahead at the definition at the beginning of the following section if you do not know. The distinction is an important one.
2. Have the class look at one hand property placed on a table for five to ten seconds. Remove the property and then have each student write a complete description of it: its size, shape, weight, color, etc. Compare results. Repeat several times.
3. Repeat Exercise 2 except for the description. In its place, define the characteristics of the property—what its special nature is; what its peculiar characteristics are.
4. Repeat Exercise 3, and add to it all your suggestions of how it could be employed to illustrate dramatic action.
5. Place a dozen chairs evenly distributed in a 15-foot circle facing away from the center. Now have a dozen students stand facing center on the inner side of the chairs. At a signal, each student places a hand property (something personal) on the chair behind him, being careful not to look at objects placed by other students. At the instructor's signal, the students start revolving around their circle, always facing center. At the instructor's signal, they all stop, and one student is designated to pick up the property behind him and to describe its characteristics to the group. Repeat several times.
6. Now repeat Exercise 5 in a spontaneous improvisation. The student who picks up the object examines it for a few seconds, then, employing the object as illustration, selects another student in the circle and does a dramatic action with the other student. The class then evaluates the use of the object. Was it used too literally or with imagination? Did the student really find the peculiar characteristics of the object? Repeat several times.
7. Have each member of the class do improvisations, each with a different hand property. The intention is not to call attention to the property but to use it as a means of revealing dramatic action. (Example: The improvisor enters a store to buy a hat. A hat becomes a mere illustration for an intensive conflict with the saleswoman or manager.) This exercise is invaluable in pinning down the difference between using objects for their own sake and using their qualities for illustration. Therefore, it should be repeated several times to reinforce the concept.

Set Properties

Definition.   *Set properties* are those large items, usually pieces of furniture, permanently placed in a groundplan. *They are specific tools of director-actor communication and not merely set decoration because they amplify and intensify objects given life by actors.* On occasion, such as when an actor moves a chair, they can become hand properties.

Concept. In Chapter 12, we emphasized that pieces of furniture not only come to life when they are used by actors but they also participate directly in compositions because of their space-occupying characteristics. You will also remember that the groundplan was referred to several times as an obstacle course that must be "run" by actors in illustrating a Realistic play. Again, you must be *fully aware* of the dramatic storytelling strength of this use because you must learn to exploit set properties in this way.

"*Tie into the furniture,*" which you may have heard experienced directors say to actors, tells them that their composition will be stronger if they stand near or touch a piece of furniture. It has significant validity as a director's suggestion because furniture pieces not only give mass to the actor by extending his stage values, but they also help him discover subtleties in the dramatic action. Members of an audience will take for granted that an actor sits on a chair or sofa, but a great deal more is being done for them than they imagine. If the specific piece of furniture on which an actor sits is well-selected, it will help tell the actor what to do and how to do it, just as hand properties do. Even more important is what a well-selected piece of furniture can do to encourage sensitive reciprocation between two actors. A suggestion given to one actor to use a chair in a certain way may immediately arouse ideas for adjustment in the other actor—adjustment that can set off a chain of physical illustrations around the set piece which will communicate strong feelings to a watcher.

Furniture selection creates activity areas. Every area of your groundplan should be potent with "activity" possibilities because they will encourage actors to "use" those areas for illustration. This is *organic blocking* in its best sense. Actors must have things to do, and you can help their motivation for crosses or uses of certain areas by providing reasons to use those areas. Downstage corners (foreground plane) that have other uses than merely sitting (telephones, desk work, bookcase, plant stand) will make an actor feel comfortable about moving there. Upstage areas (background plane) can also be set up this way (cabinets, bookcases, drawer for concealing objects used in the play, work tables, sinks, refrigerators, storage areas, coat rack, dish shelf, private collection of objects, etc.) The midstage arrangement is the most important because most of the activity will take place on these planes. Achieve a variety in furniture placement by experimenting with all parts of conversational groupings. Increase your lines of tension in the placement to insure full exploitation.

Variety in using pieces of furniture is a necessity if the illustrations are to be fresh and alive. Sitting on the backs of sofas or on tables is, of course, valid if the given circumstances permit characters such behavior; but chairs and sofas can be used in dozens of ways without employing exceptional uses. As with hand properties, the director must be fully aware of the characteristics of the set properties he introduces for actor use if he is to exploit them. Fresh uses of beds, desks, stools, cabinets, etc., all lie within an actor's imagination, and the director can make them come to life with perceptive suggestions.

EXERCISE

1. Have three members of the class "play" on and around chairs without moving them, each actor doing something different with his chair at the instructor's signal.
2. Try the same exercise with a table and a chair. Each actor should continue to work independently.
3. With one student as the leader, have the class improvise a usable groundplan. Criticize and revise the plan to get as much ingenuity into it as possible. Now have two actors use the groundplan, changing locations on signals from the instructor. Have the class judge the freshness of their uses of the set properties.
4. Repeat Exercise 3 several times, each time trying to find ingenious uses of furniture pieces. Have students, acting as directors, suggest specific uses to the actors.
5. Have two actors improvise a dramatic action around and on a chair. Warn them that they must not point the functional use of the chair but must employ it only in finding contact with one another. *Let the chair tell them what to do.* Repeat the exercise with a table, with a sofa, etc.
6. Combine the use of hand properties and set properties in the same improvisation as outlined in Exercise 5.

CHAPTER FOURTEEN
PICTURIZATION
Group intensification

DEFINITION

Picturization is *detailed storytelling* brought about by the combined use of composition (the arrangement of the group), gesture (the individual moving within his own sphere), and improvisation with properties (objects added to composition and gesture) *for the specific purpose of animating the dramatic action.* Note that although gesture pertains only to the individual, *picturization concerns a group of actors* in which each actor uses the gestures appropriate to his own character. *Picturization,* then, *is a still picture containing detailed storytelling illustrations brought about by individualizing and personalizing composition through the use of gesture and properties.*

CONCEPT

Picturizations are what we actually see in the performance of a play, the same pictures we see in real life when two or more people are involved in a close physical relationship. Again, you must remember that a *staged scene of a play is composed of a succession of still shots, with a new composition born every time the physical relationships of the basic elements are changed.* We use the term *picturization* in order to say that we have added the *storytelling details* of gesture and properties to composition. But remember that composition is an abstraction because we never actually see it in its clear form except in exercises; nor do we see gesture stopped and held as in a tableau. In actual practice, when we set up compositions ''we wipe gestures from our eyes'' in order to see whether we have established a good composition; then ''we put them back in our eyes'' to see if we are making a good picturization. Can you see the logic of this reverse order?

Picturization means that each actor in a group is presenting the dramatic action of his character with the decorum of that character. *The aim is to create the appropriate psychological relationship between characters* because out of this relationship the strong feelings to which an audience reacts emerge. Remember, *only when a group of actors plays the action intensively will feelings emerge.* Picturizations are thus the projections of group feelings. So the actors must find the proper character-mood-intensities for the picture in order for it to project the desired emotional truth. And remember also that picturizations are *visual* illustrations—only part of the full illustration that involves speech as well as movement.

TECHNIQUES

Good picturization involves expert use of a well-conceived groundplan because the obstacles in such a plan will suggest all sorts of picturization ideas to actors. Thus, the groundplan is again a primitive means of communication. As understanding of the action grows, actors will physicalize much more intensively and in greater and greater detail. If the basic composition is right, fresh ideas about gesture—the individual in the sphere—will emerge, and along with it, the improvisational use of properties. Thus, picturization will grow.

Here are some specific suggestions:

1. Encourage picturization over and around obstacles (see Figure 42). Remember: *Obstacles prevent climactic compositions and thus intensify conflict.* They also help to emphasize actors by taking on animate qualities in compositions.

2. Encourage space separations between characters, and the use of different planes, levels, and body positions (see Figure 43 and 44; *A, B, C* are characters).

3. Look for intimate climactic picturizations (see Figure 45), and encourage actors to touch one another.

4. Look for the appropriate character-mood-intensities of the different characters. This procedure will declare the tension levels in the pictures by encouraging the actors to find illustrations at the levels of their nervosity in the scene. All pictures will contain character-mood-intensities of some sort, but the major problem is finding the *appropriate* intensities so that the illustrations will tell the truth. Here gestures play an important part in picturization values.

5. Exploit gesture in every possible way by encouraging actors to vary their illustrations within their spheres by taking them, on occasion, to the full limits and withdrawing them to the opposite extreme.

6. Encourage the continuous use of triangles in setting up compositions, but vary them in as many interesting ways as possible. *There is nothing so dull in picture-making as*

FIGURE 42

FIGURE 43

FIGURE 44

the repetitious use of triangles of the same size and shape. Remember that a good composition must be at the base of every good picture, so make your composition first; then add details.

7. Encourage the use of hand properties because they have high picture-making potential in forcing body positions, levels, etc.

8. When you have exhausted all the director-actor communication possibilities for making good pictures by insuring that the actors understand every detail of the action, you can turn to the secondary functions of picturization, which include:

    a. Balancing the stage. Remember that your picture on the proscenium stage is in a frame, and it is possible for you to make a visually beautiful picture if you follow some of the rules of good perspective painting. Picturizations thus have pictorial values that can give pleasure to an audience whether it is conscious of them or not. Study the groupings in Medieval and Renaissance paintings to see how the masters made exciting picturizations.

    b. Exploiting the stage cube. Remember that you are composing pictures in a cube and not on the floor of the stage. Thus, you can find many unusual storytelling pictures through the use of high levels such as stairways, balconies, etc. Learn to exploit the contrasts in levels to the fullest.

    c. Exploiting the extremes of the stage floor. This means using the full depth of your groundplan by encouraging actors to play the upstage and downstage extremes and by using the full horizontal width through an insistence on far-right and far-left positions. If you play the extremes, you will have the other places to go to; if you cannot, your pictures will seem cramped and underillustrated.

FIGURE 45

EXERCISE

1. Arrive at a picturization by (1) starting with composition, (2) adding gesture, (3) adding hand properties, and (4) then adding picturization. Improvise the following:
   a. A group of three actors decides on a given circumstance and an action.
   b. It sets up a composition, being extremely careful to keep the neutrality of composition.
   c. It now moves the composition to a previously set-up groundplan and uses one of the furniture pieces as an obstacle.
   d. Each actor in turn adds gesture to his part of the composition by experimenting until he finds fresh gesture, and then holding it in tableau.
   e. At least one actor, possibly two, works with a hand property.
   f. When the actors have added gestures and hand properties, they adjust to one another (in terms of the dramatic action) and form the picturization.
   g. The class now identifies the picturization as accurately as possible. What story does it tell? What is its emotional level? The class also comments on the various stages of the exercise.
   h. Repeat this abstract exercise (abstract because it isolates the stages in forming a picturization in a mechanical way) several times because it will clarify all the stages that lead to good picturization.
2. Improvise picturizations that involve furniture pieces and hand properties with two or three actors. Set up three teams of actors to use the same furniture pieces and hand properties, and then change pictures at the instructor's signal. Note how each group will do something different. Have the actors work for as fresh an expression as possible.
3. Improvise picturizations with three or four actors in a present groundplan. *Shift pictures at the instructor's signal, with the class closing its eyes so that it will see only picturizations and not the movement from one location on the stage to another.* Repeat in other groundplans.
4. After you have looked at the photographs attached to this section, play the "Game of Visual Perception" on a "live" level by setting up the same picturizations you see in the photos. Describe the values in each.
5. Repeat Exercise 4 by using the photographs at the end of the chapter on composition.

GAME OF VISUAL PERCEPTION 2: PICTURIZATION
(See pages 77–78)

1. In each photograph answer the following:
   a. Who has the center of attention?
   b. Do you see the added strength of eye-focus?
   c. What function do the characters in the background provide?
   d. What are the functions of the pieces of furniture?
   e. Can you see triangulation?

2. What is the psychological drama (story) being played out in each photograph?
   a. Can you see how picturization creates the dramatic moment?
   b. Has "group intensification" really taken place?
   c. Why is each photograph effective as a photograph?

PHOTO 15 *A View from the Bridge* (Miller)

PHOTO 16 *Independence* (Blessing)

PHOTO 17
Playboy of the Western World
(Synge)

PHOTO 18   *Hedda Gabler* (Ibsen)

PHOTO 19   *Oliver!* (Bart)

PHOTO 20   *When You Comin' Back, Red Ryder* (Medoff)

PHOTO 21
The Couch (Kaufman)

PHOTO 22   *Curse of the Starving Class* (Shepard)

PHOTO 23
Cabaret (Masterhoff/Kander/Ebb)

PHOTO 24 *Death of a Salesman* (Miller)

PHOTO 25   *The Birthday Party* (Pinter)

PHOTO 26
The Little Foxes (Hellman)

CHAPTER FIFTEEN
THE DYNAMIC TOOL
OF MOVEMENT

This is a short chapter, but *movement* is so important as a tool in organic blocking that it must be given a spotlight.

Up to this point in our discussion of the visual tools in director-actor communication, we have been concerned with how you, as the director, can help actors penetrate the subtext of a play through suggestions that have been, with the exception of gesture, primarily of a static nature. The intention in this chapter is to reveal the *dynamics of movement as the most powerful* of all the tools in *organic blocking.*

DEFINITION

Movement is the actual transit of an actor from one point on the stage to another. Although it includes gesture in that the body sphere is always animated during the process of movement, it is a separate tool from gesture in that the actual *distance* traveled, the *route* of travel, and the *speed* of travel all declare specific values, in themselves distinct from gesture.

Concept

Think of movement as continuous lines on the floor of the stage between points (see Figure 46). When a point is reached, an actor stands still and we have a composition. Movement thus takes place *between* compositions. In order to see

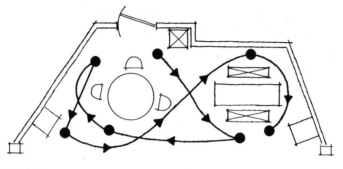

FIGURE 46

movement on the stage, that is, in order to see its meaning, *the distance traveled must be five feet or more,* for anything less will look like gesture (the body in the sphere). Movement is, therefore, climactic since all the other tools—groundplan, composition, gesture, picturization—must be operating before movement can take place; and since it is climactic, it is the most overtly powerful of all the tools of director-actor communication. Because it is large, because it is continuous, because gesture animates it, movement can convey illustrations to an audience quickly and with force. An actor walking conveys a very different idea from an actor running or sauntering; and walking *toward* an actor means something very different from walking *away* from him. Movement, therefore, has tempo values; it takes place in time.

EXERCISE

Illustrate movement by setting up two points and having an actor pretend he is rolling a ball with himself inside it from one point to the other. Repeat with two or three actors, each taking a turn at doing this, and using three or four points as destinations. Repeat a third time with the actors holding compositions long enough for each, in turn, to speak a line of numbers dialogue.

THE DIRECTOR AS CHOREOGRAPHER

In a more restricted sense, a play performed on stage looks like a dance. Just as a dance starts and stops, a play alternates between movement and composition, with gesture working continuously. Thus, a director tries to find the appropriate dancelike movements to punctuate the still shots. If he and the actors find them, their production will have the appropriate animation—the rhythms—inherent in the playscript.

In the movies we see many close-ups that punctuate the long or medium shots, shots that usually contain movement, either that of actors in transit as we have defined movement here, or that of the camera moving. *But on the stage, compositions act as close-ups and movement as the long and medium shots.* Yet, a playgoer always sees both at relatively the same distance from his eye, whereas movies can vary the size of images greatly. In this comparison, the stage is enormously limited. And this limitation can be overcome in part only by intensely articulate and highly selected movement—movement that is potent with meaning and ideas. Because of its dynamics, then, all movement must be inherently motivated directly out of the dramatic action; *it cannot be laid on but must be generated from within.* For this reason, some directors prefer to have the actors improvise their own movement because it can flow freely from their inherent comprehension of the action. But this approach also has limitations because actors often prefer gesture to movement for illustration. The director must, therefore, learn to motivate actors to articulate specific dramatic action through his suggestions for movement.

KINDS OF MOVEMENT

Although all movement must be motivated by the dramatic action, it is convenient to note the different kinds of movement in order to see the full range of this valuable tool.

Playwright's Movement

This kind of movement is formally prescribed by the playwright—what he considers the basic playscript requirements. They include all entrances and exits, as well as those movements to locations on the stage prescribed by the author as necessary for the completion of certain business absolutely requiring that location by the dramatic action. Thus, if an actor must climb a scaffold to man a machine gun mounted thereon because the playwright has located his action there, an actor is performing *playwright's movement.* If actors are required to dance, to play a game that requires movement, to participate in a military parade, to fight a duel, to crawl around on hands and knees looking for dropped jewels because a character has instructed them to do so, they are performing playwright's movement. As you may note, these movements are quite arbitrary in their demands. However, except for exits and entrances, most playwrights prescribe a minimum of this kind of movement. Be wary of directions for movement written into a printed play, for they are very likely to be the movements inserted by the director of the first production of that play on a specific groundplan and not the playwright at all. (Do Exercise 1 at end of chapter.)

Technical Requirements

The choreographing of a play is not entirely free improvisation but is partly mechanical because two hours of staging a play, often in one location (one setting), creates an immense traffic problem. How to get actors on and off the stage quickly and efficiently, particularly if there are many characters, and how to bring about the performance of business in appropriate areas of the stage are of utmost importance to the director. Thus, parts of playscripts must be blocked by directors, either in their minds or on paper, to be certain that they are exploiting their groundplans in the most imaginative ways.

A director will, therefore, occasionally require an actor to move arbitrarily from one location to another, and only then look for the motivation to support it—motivation which can always be found if the actor is imaginative enough. The actual placement of a piece of business may be extremely important to the revelation of character; so the director arbitrarily locates the scene for his actors, and then decides, with the actors, how they get there. Actors may thus be required (1) to cross the stage at a certain time; (2) to uncover from behind other actors who may stand in front of them; or (3) to close in or spread out as the business requires; etc. This manipulation is always essential when several actors are involved. *The intention is to make arbitrary arrangement, when motivations are added, look like spontaneous improvisation.* In arranging group scenes, a director may want to distribute the actors in a particular way to show balance or imbalance. The movements by which they reach their assigned points, though otherwise motivated, are probably technical movements. "Probably" is used here because actors can frequently reach assigned positions through primary dramatic action. The skillful director will use technical movement only as a last resort when the use of primary dramatic action simply will not solve the traffic problems. (Do Exercises 2 and 3.)

Movement Derived from Dramatic Action

Ninety-five percent of all movement in staging a play *is derived from the dramatic action—what the subtext tells the actors and the director to do.* Actors who know their trade will move spontaneously and knowingly out of their strong feelings about the action in a play. The director's job in that case becomes that of suggesting more movement or less movement, in actual quantity; more selective movement; more or less speed on certain movements; and often the specific destination of these movements in order to indicate to the actors the next important composition. But *beginning actors,* on the other hand, are *movement bound;* that is, they will not move unless required by the director to do so because they have not yet learned the illustrative values of movement. In handling such actors, directors often suggest much of the movement that will eventually be absorbed into the performance. If it is used skillfully, it can open up the subtext to the actors in a very real way—the outside-in approach, organic blocking. However, if is not well-conceived, it can impede actors' imaginations.

What is difficult about all of this—whether the actors develop movement on their own or the director suggests it to them—is finding the *appropriate* movement directly inherent in the playscript. As we have said several times in this book, every line of dialogue is a word-statement of a dramatic action, and a dramatic action is the forcing by a speaking character of another character. Thus, it is in the forcing or in the reception of the forcing (adjustment) that the movement inherently lies. For this reason, we use verbs to express dramatic action, for a verb is a statement implying activity. We note this point readily in such obviously active verbs as run, jump, tear apart, rip, cry, grab, pull, caress, kiss, etc., because these verbs are verbs of *visual activity,* a class of verbs we avoid when writing down dramatic action (see p. 40). The verbs we use to express dramatic action are not nearly so obvious. Note that there are no obvious visual hints in such verbs as plead, command, seduce, adore, hate, and all modifications of such verbs; yet, they contain movement (and gesture) in exactly the same way as the others, although we do not associate typical body behavior with them as we do with run and jump. If you always think of verbs as possessing inherent movement, you will see how actors and directors can readily devise this sort of illustration. (Do Exercise 4.)

Therefore, the director must study the dramatic action of a play intensely, for he must be certain that, whether an actor presents a movement or he suggests it to the actor himself, the truth is being told about an action. Movement can tell a bold-faced lie; it can even tell the opposite of what is intended. Therefore, both director and actors must be certain that actions that go ''towards'' and actions that ''retreat'' actually do so in the visual movement unless opposite movements are consciously intended for very specific reasons.

There are only two directions of movement on the stage: *the advance* and *the retreat.* Whichever one is used depends on the meaning of the subtext. Movement is played like a cat-and-mouse cartoon, with characters switching to play Cat or to play Mouse depending on the meanings of the actions. One character will always be the aggressor and one the pursued; and the change in roles will occur very frequently, perhaps as often as every minute or two. (Do Exercise 5.)

MOOD VALUES IN MOVEMENT

Movements have many mood values that need the most careful control if they are to be continuously expressive because (1) they occupy space when actors move from one location to another, (2) they require time periods (duration), (3) they are large and dynamic, and (4) they can vary greatly in their rates. Here are some of the values you must consider:

Length of a Movement

Long movements tend to be weaker than short ones unless they are used with the greatest care; yet, they can have strong mood values when used in the appropriate places. Remember that all movements, if they are to be seen and recognized as movements, *must traverse five feet or more.* Continuous short movements, however, unless specifically intended, have a choppy effect, something like a series of simple sentences. Learn to vary the lengths of movements with the moods you want illustrated. On the whole, inexperienced actors tend toward short movements; therefore, when working with such actors, you will need to show them how relaxation and ease can be illustrated in generous movements. (Demonstrate long and short movements.)

Movement and Space

Although movement technically occupies space only when it is being made, it possesses the psychological value of tying areas of the stage together, thus making it seem as if movement occupies more space than it actually does. Learn to exploit this value by interrupting long patterns of movement with momentary compositions that will occur each time an actor stops. *Travel the diagonals of the stage* because they will give the feeling of occupying the upstage areas and the far corners of the downstage areas. If the movement zigzags with interrupted stops, it will appear to occupy space. The mood values of small-space occupation are quite different from those of large-space occupation. You must learn to use each appropriately. (Demonstrate.)

Size and Dynamics

Movements vary in size according to the number of gestures employed while making them. If an actor plays his character-decorum and his character-mood-intensity appropriately, he will vary the size and dynamics of his movements. Encourage the use of the sphere (gesture) while moving if you would increase or decrease the size of a movement, and thus affect the mood values it reflects. (Demonstrate.)

Rate or Tempo

The rate of speed of movements is most important in expressing mood values because audiences are so easily affected by rate. The major problem with actors lies not just in helping them discover when and where to move but in how to vary the tempos of the movements in line with the character-mood-intensities of the scenes. The tendency with inexperienced actors is to take all movements at the same rate of speed, so that movement as illustration becomes quite ineffective. *You must therefore be certain that actors move at their appropriate character-mood-intensities,* a condition which will come about only if they understand their dramatic action thoroughly. Two characters never have the same rate but each moves according to his nervosity. Only by understanding this concept can actors learn to make moods through the use of movement. (Demonstrate.)

Movements in Series

You must learn how to plan movements so that they are joined in a series, with each move proceeding from the logic of the previous one. Thus, movements are more interconnected than they would seem to be, and moods can evolve out of their accumulation. If you learn to play this "chess game" sensitively, you will find that you can control the moods of a play more through movement than through any of the other visual tools. (Demonstrate.)

Movement in Relation to Speeches

Movement is so dynamic, so eye-catching, that it exerts great power over line-reading illustration. Thus, the exact point at which a movement is made becomes extremely important, something that you and the actor must decide together. To accent a line, the actor moves *before* he says the line. To accent a movement, that is, to have the movement actually say more than the line, the actor moves *after* the line. It is for these reasons that actors tend to move on the lines because by making such movements most of the time they can then save the pointing of a line or movement for special moments. However, you can readily see that unless your actors are fully aware of the values of "pointing", many of them will not use movement as illustration at all, and thus you will lose the most valuable tool in your directing kit. Therefore, you must learn to mix up the speech-movement relationship and to exploit it in every possible way. (Demonstrate with numbers and dialogue.)

Quantity of Movement

At first you will not need to worry about putting too much movement into a scene because you will have difficulties in finding enough of it. But after you understand the value of movement and learn the knack of arousing such illustration in your actors, you will learn to select all movements with extreme care. *Excessive movement, that is, movement on nearly every line, can kill the other tools of expression; but insufficient movement will mean underillustration.* You will also learn that experienced actors do not need as much movement as the less experienced because they know how to exploit *all* the tools of illustration and not just one or two. But to help the inexperienced you must learn how to suggest movement to them, for these suggestions will build their confidence by giving them something specific to do, and will lead to the use of the other tools as well. *The quantity of movement, then, must be determined not only by the character of the play you are producing, but just as much by the quality of the actors you are using.* You must learn to judge both with care and objectivity.

Because young directors tend to ignore movement as a tool of illustration, *you are encouraged at this point to work as much movement into a scene as you possibly can, and then remove, at a later stage of rehearsal,* what you consider excess. Movement can be your most potent tool in helping actors discover the dramatic action because when they move, they feel on the outside the way they should on the inside, and that feeling will give them a strong hint about what they should be doing in the dramatic action. This is an example of *organic blocking* put to work. (Do Exercise 6.)

EXERCISE

1. Examine a class study play by first marking out *all* the directions in the script that prescribe movement, except for "playwright's movement" as described above. Now underline all entrances and exits by noting the beginning of units where characters either leave or enter the scene (French scenes). How many are there? What other movement does the playwright formally prescribe in the action? (look for the use of objects that the playwright has specifically placed and then incorporated in the required visual illustration.)

2. Select a play for study that requires a group (*Riders to the Sea* at the point where Bartley is carried in and the villagers follow is useful), and actually block the entrance of the group with live actors. Who will enter first? How many together? Where will they move to on the groundplan? How will the principal characters adjust to this entrance? Now arrange an exit. What problems does this arrangement involve?

3. Improvise a living room/dining room scene with six to eight characters (*Ah! Wilderness!* is a suggestion). Play an action in the living room, and then move the actors to seated positions around the dining table. Note the extra movements required to bring this change about effectively and efficiently. Improvise the same action, but use the whole groundplan for the first action before moving the group to the table. What problems does this procedure involve?

4. Assign verbs to several actors. Have each one improvise movements to illustrate his verb.

5. Improvise an action involving two actors. Using "number" dialogue, have them play the action. Did they use much movement? If so, was it meaningful? If not, why not? Now play the same action with the aid of the instructor who urges movement, when necessary, from the side lines, and who also, on a signal, demands that the actor playing "Cat" start playing "Mouse," and vice-versa.

6. Each student, working alone, blocks the movements in a class study play. In class, one student directs live actors through two or three units, using his preconceived movements. Class discussion follows. Repeat several times.

CHAPTER SIXTEEN
COORDINATING VISUAL TOOLS IN DIRECTOR-ACTOR COMMUNICATION

COORDINATION

It was emphasized in Chapter 9 that a separate treatment of each tool would be necessary in order to see their values and strengths in director-actor communication. Although isolating them has made them more abstract, the better you learn to see in great detail everything that happens in a physical way on the stage, the easier it will be for you to see the simultaneous use of these tools. So, while you are learning, you must run the film at quarter speed if you are to isolate these tools at all. Yet, we know that the strengths of a scene's moods depend greatly on highly selective uses of these visual tools. A director who fully understands them will know how to exploit them.

Coordination, then, means using all the tools with as much variety and freshness as possible, a technique that can come about only if you constantly remind yourself of the many tools at your command. The most frequently neglected tool is movement; the dullest is usually the groundplan; the tritest in its uses is hand properties; the least exploited is composition. And so it goes. Not until you have all the tools working for you will you be of genuine help to actors in search of dramatic action and how best to illustrate it.

The director's job is to make a scene work by *"bringing out"* the actors through *appropriately illustrated reciprocation* of dramatic action. Once you fully comprehend that dramatic action cannot be conveyed movingly without convincing and believable visual illustrations employing all the tools, you can begin to consider yourself on the way to becoming a director. Play production is the articulation of idea, not the invention of the idea itself—something the playwright has already done.

USE OF THE TOOLS ON OTHER STAGES

You must give the proscenium stage all your attention at this point if you are to learn in a progressive way, for *all the tools are readily adapted to other stage forms—* thrust, arena, forestage, proscenium—adaptations that will be given special attention in Chapter 21. But now you must concentrate on how to help the actor on the proscenium stage through the use of the tools of communication. Don't confuse the form of the stage with this central purpose. The strongest director is one who knows how to bring the actor to his highest achievement.

BLOCKING

Some professional directors take a negative attitude toward blocking plays, saying that they do little of it and that they leave stage positions and movement up to the improvisation of their actors. However, they fail to mention that professional actors, through multiple experiences, know how to show themselves to best advantage on the stage—an awareness amateur actors seldom have. Don't let such statements mislead you; learning about how to direct is quite a different process than leading skilled performers in a professional production. Do your homework first.

Although a director in training should gradually move toward the goal of controlled improvisation with actors, he must practice *paper blocking* as a necessary step in learning the values of all the tools of communication. Paper blocking is the homework preceding rehearsal periods when a learning director can improvise in the quiet of his study without all the confusion and speed of a rehearsal situation where he will likely be more self-conscious and less able to concentrate than the actors he may be working with. *Since his job is to help actors, he must be, in one sense, a big jump ahead of them in his knowledge of the playscript and what he wants done with it.* His blocking homework, then, is a playing of the scene in his own imagination: what he thinks it might look like visually. And because he has quiet and time, he can experiment with several ways until he arrives at what he thinks at that time is the best.

Paper blocking, then, is in no sense an arbitrary director's decision that he will force on the actors, but a preexamination of possibilities for director-actor communication. Instead of leaving himself with only one way to illustrate a scene, a director has investigated the possibilities widely enough to enable him to move in several directions with actors, although he may personally think that one is superior to the others. *Paper blocking opens up a director's imagination instead of closing it,* for a dozen suggestions are far better than one. Moreover, the job of rehearsal is to keep the actors working. If they must wait around while the director makes up his mind about how he thinks a play should go, actors will be tense and will not concentrate well. Imagination in rehearsing is often released in the appropriate speed and rhythm of a scene; too much slow-moving playing may dry up the actors' imaginations.

THE PROMPTBOOK

The *promptbook* is your original design for a live production of a play. After you have studied Part III it will be much more inclusive, but at this point the promptbook must be based on what you have learned in Parts I and II. It is, therefore, a testing of how well you have grasped the concepts of play-analysis and the six visual tools, as well as the techniques for making them work for you.

In order to provide sufficient space for all the necessary notations, prepare a working promptbook by taking the playscript apart, if it is a printed text, and mounting each page on an 8½ × 11-inch sheet of unruled paper. One procedure, if you are working with a printed script, is to cut windows in the paper so that both sides of the text are visible, thus requiring only one playscript. Now insert a blank page between the pages of the text so that each page of text has its own work page. You should make a practice of binding the promptbook in either a hard-bound notebook cover or a strong folder-type cover with metal fasteners. A director, as with any craftsman, is known by the condition of his tools, in this case his promptbook. Therefore, don't be sloppy about making this primary work tool that will undergo a great deal of use.

Groundplan Design and Testing

Since a groundplan for a Realistic staging is the floor plan of a walled setting, the plan should show the lines of the enclosing walls, the doors, windows, levels (platforms), and all furniture pieces. *Always make an accurate drawing to scale.* Free-hand improvisation will only get you into serious trouble because you will not be accurate with the space relationships and will be misled by what you think you have instead of by what you actually have. Figure 47 is a sample drawing, but *you should follow the principles you have learned in your scene design class.* You must take the greatest care with the groundplan, following explicitly the procedures discussed in Chapter 11, for all the other director-actor communication tools will either depend directly on it or be strongly influenced by it. Remember: a dozen groundplans are better than one in trying to find the best choice because your imagination and improvisational force will be released. Select the furniture pieces with unusual care in the interest of projecting how they can act as "activity centers" in stimulating actors to fresh illustration.

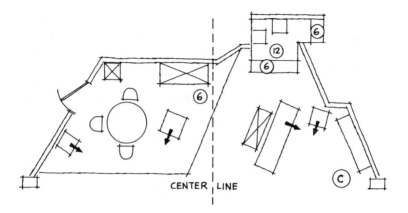

FIGURE 47

Test your groundplan by answering the following questions: (1) Does it have a minimum of five to seven acting areas? (2) Does it have strong upstage-downstage movement possibilities as well as stage right/stage left possibilities? (3) Are strong diagonals possible? (4) Have you created tension in the placement of your furniture pieces? (5) Is it an obstacle course? (6) What is the potential for strong compositions and picturizations? (7) Is it ingenious? (8) Will it provoke actors to fresh and imaginative illustrations? (9) *Have you avoided the no-room?*

Perspective Sketch

A *perspective sketch* of the groundplan is needed at this point to show more nearly what the groundplan looks like in the stage cube. Does your plan exploit levels as well as give ideas of proportion, balance, etc.? It will tell you whether the room looks like a room and whether the areas have all been exploited. The mood of the *setting*—and it is now a setting with the walls added, except for color treatment and modifying details—will be declared largely on the basis of the distribution of furniture pieces, the sense of space created, and the size of the setting.

Composition and Movement Notation

Now that you have the groundplan designed and the promptscript ready for use, you are in a position to record your compositions and movement suggestions in a detailed way. You will already have many ideas in mind from your work on the groundplan, but your intention now is to assess the groundplan in a specific way by seeing how well it will work continuously throughout the scene. If you have done a good job in design, you will find that this detailed procedure will move rapidly and excitingly. *Do not labor over making everything work, for if you move too slowly with this sort of notation you will lose the rhythm of the scene* and what you intend doing with it; blocking is like a chess game that you always project five moves ahead. Remember that the blocking you ''see'' now will meet its crucial test only when you suggest it to the actors who will play the scene, and that the intention of advance planning is to put yourself in as flexible a position as possible.

Now enter on the upper half of each blocking page all the movements for that page of text (see Figure 48). Number each movement on this page consecutively and then place the same numbers in the text. By setting down the movements you will automatically imply the compositions and also, at least in your imagination, some projection of the picturizations. Now prepare a small pasteboard cutout (a template) of your groundplan *drawn to scale* and reproduce it on the lower half of each blocking page. *Draw* all the *movements* for each page on this reproduction of the groundplan, and indicate each character by a triangle with its initial inside (△). Show the direction of each movement by arrows on the lines and by the same number of the movement you have used in the written directions and in the text. A different color for each character will aid in keeping them separate.

Although gestures cannot be shown, as ideas come to the director they can be noted on the blocking page. Similar notes can also be made for improvisation with set and hand properties.

1. AMY X'S TO LS TO FP
2. TED X'S TO CHAIR
3. AMY SITS SOFA
4. TED X'S DRC
5. TED X'S TO BACK OF SOFA

FIGURE 48

Master Movement Plan

When all the detailed blocking has been done for each page of text, the director should *enter all movement on a single groundplan*, this time by using enlarged dots to show compositional positions (see Figure 49) and colors to show movements. When you finish doing this procedure, the drawing will look like a scribbled

FIGURE 49

mess. Yet, it can reveal very quickly your exploitations of the groundplan—whether the movement, and thus the composition, has been concentrated in only one or two areas; whether the central planes have dominated, thus reducing the vertical use of the groundplan; whether the full groundplan has been exploited, etc. This check is quick and reliable to see how well the groundplan has been thought through. Here is an example that shows the exploitation of all the areas.

List of Properties

You have already made decisions on set properties when you designed your groundplan. At this point, you should review them carefully to be certain that you have selected the most activity-exciting furniture pieces you can think of that apply specifically to the given circumstances you are trying to suggest. *Strive for freshness and ingenuity, and regard the trite and dull as sure death as far as director-actor communication with the groundplan is concerned.*

Now proceed to select with the greatest care the hand properties you think might stimulate actors. Verisimilitude to the given circumstances is again necessary, but remember that it is secondary, and that the primary value of a hand property is to aid an actor in his use of gestures. If too few properties are used, a scene will very likely be underillustrated, but too many can distract an audience by throwing emphasis on the properties themselves. So you must give your *appropriate* list your primary attention, with the accepted intention of adding other properties later as they are needed or withdrawing the ones you first selected if they prove inadequate.

EXERCISE

1. With the class using a common study play (a one-act play), each student prepares a promptbook incorporating the following:
   a. Playscript and blocking pages

    b. The full play-analysis you did at the end of Chapter 8

    c. Groundplan to scale

    d. Perspective sketch

    e. Blocking notations for the entire play

    f. Master movement plan

    Note: If these exercises have been done with a study play en route, all that needs doing at this point is the "Master Movement Plan."

2. Discuss "coordination" in all of its aspects.

3. Discuss "organic blocking" as a primary procedure in working with actors in training.

PART TWO
COMMUNICATION 2
The director-actor relationship: oral tools

Speak the speech, I prey you,
As I pronounced it to you, trippingly
On the tongue; but if you mouth it, as many
Of your players do, I had as lief the
Town-crier spoke my lines. . .

Hamlet's speech to the players in *Hamlet*

CHAPTER SEVENTEEN
ORAL VERSUS
VISUAL BALANCE
IN DIRECTING

Now that you have a grasp of the visual tools used in director-actor communication, you are ready to attack the much more difficult problem of getting the actors to speak the play with dynamic intensity. Reaching an audience—moving it, persuading it, keeping its attention—will depend greatly on your awareness of speaking as the core meaning of theatre. After you have tried to work with this aspect of directing, you will look back at the visual as readily controllable. Now you are treading on the real heart of acting, and you may have a very difficult time.

As you may have already noticed, this section, Communication 2, is relatively brief. At first, it may seem inadequate to you in view of the extensive discussion of the visual tools in the preceding chapters, and especially after Chapter 9 stressed that *good directing means a visual-oral balance in production.*

In explaining this apparent shortage of material on the oral side, the learning director should appreciate the fact that *highly developed seeing also means highly developed hearing,* or at least provides ideal circumstances for hearing. Thus, part of the oral communication process has already been examined in the preceding chapters on the visual tools. Furthermore, the development of the voice and technical capability in speaking are largely problems of the individual actor, the essential tools he must provide himself with if he is to become effective on the stage, and is not a major subject of this book. The only aspects of the acting process discussed here are those that immediately concern the director in his communication with actors. If actors can bring to rehearsals an adequate voice and body instrument, the directing process can be what it should be: the development of an ensemble of players who can, through appropriate imagery, transfer to an audience the sort of play a director has in mind. If they do not, as is too often the case in the amateur theatre, the director's problems will be greatly increased, for his job is to shape a play in production, not to train the actors.

HEARING VERSUS SEEING AS DIRECTOR EMPHASIS

Because some directors believe they can reach audiences directly, they begin relying much too heavily on visual design as the aspect of production they can more readily control. They tend to concentrate on all the visual elements from groundplan to movement, to settings, lighting, and costumes, in the interest of obtaining a high degree of specific communication. But there is no question that this sort of approach can greatly reduce the effectiveness of the spoken play. Unless a director is highly aware that a visual-oral balance must exist in production, when he works with imaginative designers his good fortune may well turn into misfortune because overladen visual design may well kill the acting. Many actors and directors could tell you that the best performance of their play took place in the final rehearsal period before the physical staging elements were added. What they mean is that the strong feelings in the spoken play—*the sound of the dramatic action*—emerged in the rehearsal because the play was about human behavior in conflict, and that *without* the trappings of production the actors were strong enough to make the play come through with great force.

Nevertheless, the visual designs can add greatly to a play's total feeling *if the appropriate balance is found.* Although Aristotle placed spectacle at the bottom of his list of the six basic elements required in a playscript, he nevertheless intended it to be a part; and ever since the seventeenth century, when painted scenery was added to the staging of plays, the theatre has had spectacle in great quantity.

The director's problem, then, is largely one of keeping the visual elements under control because he understands the great significance of the oral elements. His problem is one of balance. In Shakespeare's day, people talked about going to *hear* a play, not to ''see'' one as we say today. This distinction is important because it tells us where the emphasis too often lies in our contemporary theatre.

We have become so accustomed in the twentieth century to the power of the visual that we have literally forgotten that *great acting before our time was spoken acting.* There is no question that the twentieth century has discovered through the camera a more highly developed sense of seeing than any other age has ever experienced. We look at everything, even such strange things as microorganisms enlarged thousands of times, or representations of such abstractions as sound waves and heart beats. On television, it is run-of-the-mill to see things at the exact time they happen, so we participate in wars in our living rooms by going directly to the absolute reality of the battlefield. In motion pictures, so greatly have lenses and film quality been improved, that we are seeing close-ups of human beings in intimacies no age has ever witnessed. Actors often appear without makeup; and in a 15- to 20-foot picture, sometimes even larger, we see the hair on their skin, their natural perspiration, body blemishes, warts, and moles, in the greatest detail. In real life, we all come to know a few persons in this way, but never have we been allowed to look so closely at so many different people as we are now permitted to do.

The theatre, consequently, has an enormous task in competing with this sort of visual assault on our senses because we can never see acting on the stage this close. Stage makeup has always been used to enlarge and simplify features of the face, or masks have been made with typical or symbolic meanings. Even if a member of an audience sits close to the stage, say within the first five rows, although he will certainly see the actors in much more personal detail, he may not actually receive any more of the play than those sitting several rows to the rear or in galleries above. There is certainly a limit to the size of a playhouse, but that limitation is not made on the basis of the visual but on the basis of the oral—what can be readily heard.

Good directing, then, provides an aural (hearing) as well as a visual experience for an audience, and *a director's communication to actors must be poised to emphasize this point.* He will constantly work at bringing about in them the power of a well-delivered play. Poetry in the theatre (though the actual language used may be lowly prose) is achieved in the aural experience because it allows us to *hear* humanity caught in tragic dilemma, not just to watch its pitiful suffering. *A play is not a moving picture on a stage; it is an assault on the ear as well as the eye.* Without the sensitivity to and delight in the musical aspects of the human voice in the theatre, a director will have great difficulty in communicating to an audience.

THE CONCEPT OF ORAL AND AURAL

We do not have a comparable word in the English language for the speaking-hearing process that is quite like "visual," which denotes the double process of making something visible and seeing it at the same time. In the case of theatre, visual means both the actor doing the illustration and the audience receiving it. The closest we can come when we talk about spoken dialogue is to use the two words that actually sound very much alike but have different meanings: *oral,* or the speaking of language or the making of sound through the vocal apparatus, and *aural,* or the hearing of sound through the ears. In real life we take this reciprocal process for granted, assuming that all anyone has to do is speak and we will hear. Yet, we are constantly asking people to repeat what they say, and when they do, even then we may puzzle over the meaning of what they have said and may ask them to rephrase or explain further. But a play is an artificial contrivance in which an audience can do neither of these things. *What is spoken usually must be heard and understood the first time it is said,* although occasionally, if a playwright is particularly anxious to be certain a particular point is well heard, he may have characters ask for repetition, or he may have a character repeat the same material in different scenes to different characters. But this technique is more exceptional than typical, for usually 80 to 90 percent of a playscript is new material to a hearer. For these reasons, most dialogue in plays must be heard the first time it is spoken or it will not be heard at all.

Bringing this about is much more difficult to achieve than it first appears because hearing what an actor says, if he is at all competent in his craft, frequently has little to do with the volume he uses or his actual capability in articulation (the precise production of individual sounds in speech). Playgoers frequently complain that they cannot hear young and inexperienced actors because they mumble and do not speak up. But more than likely the fault is not low volume because there are so many things that prevent hearing besides the actor's actual volume-articulation capability. Chief among these are (1) the distraction of the visual; (2) the deemphasis of the actor as speaker; (3) the actor's faulty speaking of the subtext, and (4) an audience member's actual capability of hearing.

The paradox of the visual is that its intention is to support the actor in his dramatic action (subtext) in every possible way; yet, the exact opposite frequently occurs. As we have noted previously, the visual tools can tell lies as well as truths; that is, actors and directors can unknowingly contradict themselves, contradictions that lead audiences into confusion because merely hearing the words is not understanding their contextual meaning. Physical production (the staging) when not performing its appropriate function, can also interfere with hearing by setting up irrelevant distractions between the actor and the audience. A playscript may have great clarity in its writing; yet a production can cover up, smudge, or push aside that clarity, and, consequently, make it difficult for audiences to hear the play very well. *The director's job is to find a balance between the visual and the oral that will permit easy hearing.* Again, hearing is comprehension of what is said, not merely receiving the words.

The oral-aural process, then, is given the best chance to work in the absence of distraction, for hearing a play well is a matter of intense concentration by both the actor and the audience. In one sense, a member of an audience has a right to blame an actor if he cannot hear, although the director and, through him, the designers often may actually be the guilty parties. The director's job is to hold the audience's attention by reducing distractions to an absolute minimum. The motion-picture director is able to control this by means of close-ups, careful editing, and high-volume projection that cuts out all other sound interference. The close-up specifically lets us watch both the mouth and eyes of the actor in great detail, and we hear better because we are better lip readers than we think we are.

AUDIENCE CAPABILITIES

But in another sense, a member of an audience can unfairly blame a production and those who have made it because he is totally unaware that he is incapable of receiving it, despite the fact that it may have been perfectly delivered. Mature plays are stories "told" to an audience, and to assume that they are going to reach everyone at all ages and with all backgrounds is assuming far too much. If you, as a member of an audience, cannot hear a play well, it may not at all be the fault of poor delivery by the actors, or because the dialogue is difficult as language, but because you are not mature enough or experienced enough to comprehend its content; you may understand the superficial elements but not the complexities.

We talk blithely about universals in drama, but by that term we do not mean simplemindedness. And often plays that may look utterly simple, *Oedipus Rex,* or *The Bacchae,* for instance, can be most complex at their cores. Hearing, then, involves audience capabilities as well as director-actor capabilities. But with comprehension pushed aside, it is quite possible that audiences have lost the "knack of hearing" in the live theatre of our time because of the visual onslaughts of television and motion pictures.

EXERCISES

1. What is the aural (hearing) experience of radio? Can you reconstruct all that you do in listening to that medium?
2. Have you ever heard a radio play? If you have, how does it differ from the TV experience? If you haven't heard one, try closing your eyes and listen only to a play on television. Why do you want to watch, rather than only listen?
3. Play an album of a recorded performance of a comedy or drama. What is the aural experience? Can you also "see" the action? Can you tell a trained actor from an untrained one? Do you admire a good actor's oral capabilities?

CHAPTER EIGHTEEN
DIRECTING TOOLS
IN ORAL
COMMUNICATION

The art of the theatre, then, does not lie in the visual but in its balance with the oral-aural experience. Because the visual close-up is not possible in the theatre, the only thing that can take its place is the actor's voice because it comes from deep inside him. That voice is what moves us. And how very rare that experience is.

So much attention is placed today in actor training on the interior approach in order to develop subtextual awareness that young actors lose sight of the fact that without a voice and the capability of using it, they can get nowhere on the stage. Small, realistic voices are possible in motion pictures and television, but certainly not in the cavern of the theatre. The voice is, therefore, an actor's prized possession because it is his principal tool of communication, and a director who does not comprehend this fact is simply bypassing his most potent means of reaching audiences. Reliance on the visual, although it may seemingly enhance a production with inexperienced beginners who have no voices, is certainly not the answer to mature performance. *Acting is speaking in a very real sense.* Instruction in acting cannot take the voice for granted but must make voice development a dominant part of the training.

Oral delivery is, perhaps, the one major difference between the amateur and the professional actor. "Talent" is often designated on this basis, for the voice speaks from inside the nervous system of the human being; it "drags out the guts," so to speak, and forces hearing on the basis of its revealing intimacy. In this sense the voice has a greater capability than the visual close-up, since it can move more deeply simply because it becomes a heart-to-heart contact between actor and members of an audience. *A character literally lives in his human voice and not merely so much in what he looks like or illustrates visually.*

The mature art of acting, then, is speaking.

THE ACTOR'S SPEAKING OF THE SUBTEXT

As we have just noted, an actor may possess a fine voice and excellent articulation and yet be quite incapable of being well heard—well understood—by an audience. *Much of the problem may lie in his failure to understand the subtext.* If an actor speaks the way *he* thinks and feels, he may not speak at all in the way that the character he wants to portray thinks and feels. Finding the character means finding the subtext, and this is where the director plays an enormous role in the oral-aural process. After all, it is his job, as we have pointed out before, to help the actor find the subtext and to insist on its presentation.

Although prose dialogue in modern drama, because of its careful selection and intensification, is not an exact reproduction of everyday speech, it is very close to everyday speech. And because of this closeness, it is often assumed that if an actor comprehends the dramatic action behind the actual words of a dialogue, he can make the words provided by the author his very own; that is, he can speak like the character. Although there are definite pitfalls the actor can fall into if he relies only on this one approach, there can be no question of its basic validity because dramatic action is *character.*

This is precisely the core use of the director's intensive work on play-analysis, particularly his detailing of the dramatic action in verbal form as described in Chapter 6. In his communication with actors, he probably will not use the exact verbs he has set down in his play-analysis, for they may be too pure, too formal, for ready communication; but he will be able to imagize and stimulate in many different ways because he knows what must come out. The flexibility of his communication with specific actors is very great, and in working closely with them, in sensing and building on every contribution an actor may make, he can shape the action as he thinks necessary.

And again, to repeat the point of the discussion in Chapter 6, *the director's most important job is to bring about reciprocation between actors.* Each actor must understand the feelings of his own character, but he may not be highly sensitive to what other characters are doing to him. Sensitive directing is insuring that each actor is hearing the forcings of others, perceptions that will lead to subtle adjustments before action is returned, because only in this way will emotion emerge from a scene. To repeat an important point again, *acting can be described as primarily the process of subtle adjustment:* actors play off one another with strong recognitions and discoveries. Thus, the adjustments may often be more important than the forcings in keeping an audience's attention.

"Hearing" the subtext, then, is at the very core of reciprocation, and the director is the outside person who can be certain that this part of the acting process is fully exploited. Communication to an audience cannot be made by each actor working separately but only when there is high communication between two or more who adjust like the characters they are playing.

A practical example of how an audience reacts when it is deprived of the subtleties of subtext is in the experience with foreign movies where subtitles are printed at the bottom of the screen in English. We are afraid to look at the words for fear of losing the action illustrated in eyes and faces. In English-language movies we have no such problem, if the director has done his job on the subtext, because we can absorb the text and subtext simultaneously.

SPEAKING THE TEXT

As you can now see, "speaking the text" in Realistic plays means conveying the subtext, the "covered-up" text, in very subtle ways. You will see this whole process reversed when you begin dealing with historical drama in Part III because you will find that subtext is much reduced in those plays and the text speaks to the dramatic action directly. However, our attack here is on modern drama, where the actor is required to give both. Too often we take prose dialogue for granted because of its similarity to real life. Yet, only when directors are aware of its subtle complications and its artifice can they bring about the necessary hearing in an audience. If an audience is to hear easily and well, actors must do a great deal of word and line pointing, *textual emphasis,* and the director must be constantly on the alert to be certain they are doing it. Here are a few suggestions:

1. Apply what you have learned in a course in interpretative reading concerning emphasis, contrasts, and echoes (repetitions of words or phrases).

2. As a director, you will insist that all proper nouns (persons and places) be given special emphasis, with perhaps the slightest pause (a caesura) before the word, a technique you often hear good newscasters use. You will do the same thing with verbs because they create the action.

3. You will insist on accuracy in the text, which also means the employment of an author's punctuation, because that discloses what he thinks is the sense as it does in all good writing.

4. You will discourage corruption of the text by such means as substitution of or addition of words because good dialogue is highly economical, with every word selected and necessary. "This is a very difficult line for me to say," says an actor. "Can I change the order or substitute these words. . .?" More than likely he does not yet understand the subtext, or he is emphasizing the wrong words in the text. Since the author heard it, the actor can probably hear it *if you help him find what is underneath the words.* If you learn to spot the emphasis in a line—usually centered around the

verb—you will be able to spot the subtext, and out of that subtext will emerge the meaning of the line which can then be conveyed to an audience *if the right words are stressed.*

5. You will alert the actor to the pauses in the dialogue because they are tied closely to adjustments in the acting process. Their effect is very great, not because they give lifelikeness to speech, but because they *point and emphasize what is spoken.* Do you hear the silences in dialogue? They create the rhythm by punctuating the sound. If the audience is to "hear" the silences, you and the actors must hear them first. Help your actors find them and you will discover new meanings. If properly placed, pauses can sustain attention in an audience more readily than sound because no one knows what will happen next.

6. As you learned in Chapter 5, dialogue is written with the emphasis toward the end of the line, which means that the *line is constructed climactically by placing the emphasis near the end.* Even though actors comprehend the subtext, they may fail to deliver the line with the strength of emphasis intended. *Pitch drop* occurs when an actor loses vocal force before the ending of a word or sentence and drops the pitch, thus destroying the hearing of this part of the line. Actors who are trained in subtextual acting become very self-conscious when a director points to such faults by correcting words or phrases. If it is only an occasional dropping of a word or line, it is better first to look into the subtext for such failures because the actor may be missing the emphasis in the action; but if the failure is frequent, the actor is not fully aware of the climactic construction of dialogue and needs orienting on this point. A rehearsal technique used by some directors is to correct these failures through the use of written notes during the polishing period, when words, phrases, or line corrections can be absorbed readily by an actor because he understands the subtext; the written notes also communicate well because the actor can quietly be alerted to his problem.

The speaking of verse dialogue will be discussed in Part III when the acting of historical drama is considered.

Character Decorum in Speech

In Chapter 6, and again in Chapter 13, we defined decorum as a character's outward show—what he literally looks like to others. This outward show also includes what he *sounds* like. Decorum is always a specific reflection of the given circumstances because environment defines social differences. We easily recognize it in speech, and perhaps with greater force, because characters, like people in real life, may refine their body movements but seldom change their strongly molded environmental speech patterns. A director must give primary attention to such physical verisimilitudes.

A not uncommon practice in playwriting, especially in plays before 1950, was for playwrights to record in writing as accurately as possible the actual sounds of speech they intended for certain characters. Good hearers like Bernard Shaw and John Millington Synge were very successful in this sort of sound transcription, but many writers who could not hear as well went no further than a generalized substandard language. More recently, many writers have not attempted to transcribe at all but have left the sound in the hands of the directors and actors, assuming that their awareness of given circumstances will lead them to the appropriate sounds. Unless a director is fully attuned to the dimension sound can add to production, he will lose one of his most important tools of communication. If he pays attention to this problem, he will know that significant meanings can often be conveyed through sound itself, aside from the words and the subtext.

We are therefore concerned not only with dialects (departures from "General American" as a standard for speech), but with all speech we hear on the stage. Actors may have a full comprehension of the subtext in a Realistic play and yet not be able to convey convincingly the speech-decorum aspects of a character. We simply cannot believe an actor playing a highly refined, urbane, and mannered gentleman who speaks with a distinct country accent; and neither can we believe an actor playing a rough peasant who speaks with the cultured sounds of city refinement. Realistic drama forces this demand on actors and directors, and to sidestep it is to avoid the verisimilitude required by Realism. Nowadays, directors may cast actors on the basis of their speech characteristics alone, preferring to work back into the subtext with the "outward show" in the sound already certain of adequate acceptance, for few actors can handle both refined speech and substandard speech effectively. In the commercial theatre and in the motion-picture industry, rigid casting lines are often observed, with native lower-class urban or country speakers usually employed to do dialect roles and cultivated speakers for refined urban characters. How an actor "sounds" seems to be more important than how he looks.

Of more concern to the director than the special problems of dialects is the level of *good* speech, for it is the only requirement in a wide range of modern drama. The only determining factor in good speech, in the absence of any established American stage standard, would seem to be *an absence of any readily recognizable local dialect*. The vowel structure in good speech would be close to what we recognize as the best urban speech of educated America—the speech we frequently hear from our best national network radio and television newscasters. To go further would rule out the wide range of acceptable American speech.

Speech decorum, in the sense we have been describing it, may actually be more of a casting problem than one that can be remedied during a rehearsal period.[1] However, a director must be thoroughly aware that an actor cannot communicate to and be heard by an audience without distraction unless he can reflect the speech decorum of the character he is trying to represent. All a director can do is to hold an actor to the sound he had in mind during the casting period, although he may be able to improve it extensively by working with the actor on vowel modifications and technical approaches for producing better sounds. A director's best communication to an actor however, may be in his expert conveyance of given circumstances that may stimulate an actor into adjusting his character's speech decorum on his own; but this decorum can be brought about only if an actor has a highly developed hearing capability, a relatively sophisticated talent that can make him sensitive to his own speech and how it can be adjusted. Speech is not changed by telling an actor what he is doing wrong, simply because he cannot hear his own speech unless he has been trained to do so, as actors should be. Good speech, and also good reproduction of dialects, then, can only result from an extraordinarily developed sense of hearing.

Projection

Projection is a very real problem for directors working with young actors because they have not yet realized the level they must achieve in this technique before they can call themselves actors. The professional actor claims his rank as a professional on high performance capability in this aspect of acting; and he may very well continue working for years with voice instructors in an attempt to improve his capabilities. Unfortunately, far too much actor training in America does not insist on intensive work in projection, and too many educational theatre directors take a lax position regarding this aspect of play production. There can be no assumption that, because an actor understands the dramatic action, he will be readily heard, for much prose dialogue can be as difficult for an audience to hear as dialogue in verse.

Projection training is, of course, part of actor training, and we are treating it here only as it concerns production. However, since directors must constantly meet this problem head-on, even though they cannot teach projection in more than a nominal way during a rehearsal period, they must recognize its great importance to the effectiveness of a performance. Projection is a technical problem in communication, and the director provides the listening ear to monitor the actors.

The real problem for the director is bringing a performance to a high level of projection without making the actors so self-conscious of this technical aspect that they lose the high concentration needed in playing the subtext. One approach is to begin the rehearsal period with production techniques by using material other than the text, although it means delay in the work on the actual play in hand. But once the actors are aware of the director's ideas about projection, especially while everyone's ears are free of the text, problems can be met later on because a talking position has been established without fear of upsetting concentration on the subtext. As we have already pointed out in this chapter, an actor who understands the subtext has already greatly improved his projection position. However, there is a great deal more to mastering the problem.

If you listen to first-rate actors in a stage performance or even in recordings of stage plays, you will be most respectful of their technical capabilities. Here are some of them: Articulation, vowel choice, use of regionalisms, pronunciation, relaxation, quality, volume, pitch, a quiet head, energy, and confidence.

Articulation.   Speech is placed forward in the mouth cavity where the articulators—teeth, tongue, lips, and gum ridges—can be exploited fully. Good actors are remarkably energetic in the mechanical employment of their articulators by vigorously moving the jaw, lips, and tongue. Moreover, placing the speech forward overcomes the possibility of sound being buried in the back of the mouth, with a resulting loss of quality. English and German actors, as well as French classical actors, are among the very best in this respect. As a director, you must insist on energetic articulation of sound. Also, avoid run-on or continuant sound, a very great failure since it obscures clear articulation.

Vowel choice.   Except in dialects and substandard speech, the term *vowel choice* pertains to the articulation of the vowels associated with what is considered to be the best American speech, that is, speech without marked regionalism. These vowels are not nazalized, nor are they tense or flat. In the scale of the phonetic alphabet for American English, this means a ''soft'' [æ], or a sound nearer the halfway vowels of New England speech [a] and [ɒ] but not the Italian [ɑ], except in those words employing that vowel in General American speech. Directors must help young actors eliminate characteristic regionalisms, such as the substitution of [ɪ] for [ɛ] in such words as *president*; [æ] for [ɔ] in *water*; a high tense [æ] in *calf*.

Use of regionalisms.   In addition to the vowel problems in the word classes just mentioned, good actors do not employ regionalisms except in the use of dialects. The director should be ever watchful for such characteristics as the Southern dropped ending [n] instead of [ŋ]; the intrusive *r* of New England speech; the added vowels of Southern speech (Bill should not be [biIl] *but* [bIl], and so forth.

Pronunciation.   Good directors, when in doubt, use dictionaries as a guide to correct pronunciation.

Relaxation.   A tense speaker is very hard to hear. Since body relaxation can improve projection tremendously, encourage your actors to relax; a relaxed actor can speak at very low volumes and still be well heard if he has excellent articulation.

Quality.   Relaxation and voice training will improve voice quality, although quality at its base is an inherent *talent* in an actor. In the Realistic theatre, however, the odd-toned voice can be exciting, especially in character roles; on the other hand, straight roles require a better-than-average quality that an audience can tolerate through a full evening. This is a particular demand for women where low-pitched qualities have much to do with good audience hearing.

Volume.   Actors do not reach audiences on the basis of high volumes but on the basis of line sense (subtext) and articulation. Only occasionally is volume actually used as a dramatic technique, and then, above all, the actor must exercise the greatest care to articulate the words, for it is easy to blast the hearability of a word with excessive volume. In general, good actors speak with fair volume, but it always appears easy and unforced; forced volume is a great distraction to an audience because it can hear the actor pushing, as distinct from playing his character. Actors learn to vary volumes because they can convey subtle dramatic meanings by doing so; but they are very careful not to jump in-and-out of volumes in an erratic manner because such sharp contrasts can destroy hearing.

Pitch.   An important factor in hearing an actor is his use of pitch. Good actors do most of their speaking within a surprisingly small range of pitch—perhaps even as narrow as up or down three notes on the musical scale from their median range of pitch. This might at first seem like a monotone to you when you think about it. But listen to a good actor and you will hear that his steadiness and hearability in delivery lie in his narrow range of pitch, which leaves the rest of his range—perhaps as much as three octaves—available for special moments. Thus, he plays a scene primarily in his normal range except for the climactic points when he will extend the range as much as the character-mood-intensity of the action requires. An actor who speaks lines with sharp variations in pitch in the interest of being dramatic is very hard to hear because a listener's ear cannot make pitch adjustments quickly enough to follow the speech. This fault is common in inexperienced actors and is one to which a director must constantly be on the alert.

Quiet head. When he is speaking, a good actor always holds his head as still as possible. This rule is an absolute necessity in being heard. An actor who bobs his head will also ''bob'' the sound; he may also use erratic change in pitch because he wants to be very dramatic. ''Let the speaking do the work in acting'' is the expert advice of the good actor. Use visual illustration when you are not speaking. As a director, you must have faith in the dramatic action and in how well-spoken dialogue can transfer it. Overacting always destroys hearing because it creates distraction.

Energy. The mark of the professional actor is his ability to keep his energy behind his acting at a high level. *Acting is energy transferred to an audience.* This energy is really what the spectator has come to feel, what he wants to experience during an evening whether he knows it or not. Poor speaking betrays poor energy in the actor. As a director, you must try to get your actors to speak with the energy of their entire bodies and not just with voices from their heads alone. A performance is a tiring experience for a good actor because he works with his entire muscular system as well as his nervous system. ''Speaking from the guts'' is no mere expression; it is the essence of projection. Also, keep in mind that rested actors will be much more capable of high energy levels than tired actors, for good voices depend on good health. When playing a series of performances with young actors, you will learn to insist that they have adequate rest.

Confidence. How well an actor is heard depends much on his stage confidence. If he loves to play, if he knows what he is playing (subtext), if he exerts his strong will as an actor, he will probably be heard. *Communication is the desire to reach others;* confidence is akin to command, and good actors command their audiences who hear them.

EXERCISE

The purpose of the few exercises that follow is not in any way intended to do more than the chapter tries to do—to make the director fully aware of his responsibilities in the oral presentation of a play. Separate classes in interpretive reading, voice production, phonetics, and regional speech are so widely offered in training programs that it is expected directors in training will pursue, perhaps extensively, the content of these areas so necessary to their work. Without a full comprehension of voice and speech, a director cannot hope to make an effective production with actors in training.

The following exercises, then, are suggested in the interest of pointing out the ever-recurring problems facing the director in any nonprofessional production. The instructor is urged to use his own range of examples and illustrations to augment an understanding of the often neglected content of this very important chapter. Remember, the most frequent complaint of the audience at amateur productions is: "I couldn't hear the actors." As a director, you must make sure the neglect is not your own fault.

A good collection of recordings is necessary for the following class exercises:

1. Listen to a recording of a Shakespearean play with Laurence Olivier or John Gielgud cast in a leading role. Criticize the articulation and range of pitch.

2. Listen to a recording of a modern play: Eva LeGallienne in *Hedda Gabler* or Michael Redgrave in *The Master Builder* are good ones for exercise, but others made by first-rate actors will do. Criticize the articulation and range of pitch.

3. Now listen again to Miss LeGallienne or Mr. Redgrave and note the perceptive use of subtext.

4. Have two actors who have no previous knowledge of the play read the opening scene of Murray Schisgal's *Luv* to the class. They should characterize the roles only as much as one hour of rehearsal will allow. After hearing them, play the recording made by the first New York cast (Eli Wallach, Anne Jackson, Alan Arkin). Was the sound a surprise? What does the sound mean to a production of this play? Are the actors illustrating the given circumstances of this play? What about the dramatic action?

5. Play the final scene of LeGallienne's *Hedda.* How do the actors play both the text and subtext?

6. Play a recording that employs either an American or an English dialect (Irish, Cockney, Bronx, or Brooklyn speech are good choices). Pick out all the characteristics of the dialect: vowels, pitch lines, substandard English, rhythm structure, national character as expressed in optimistic or pessimistic sound. Repeat with other dialects. What basic elements are present in all the dialects?

7. Play a word-tossing game. One actor says a word with a certain vowel and another replies with the same word and a different possible vowel. ("Possible" means that the word so pronounced must still be acceptable pronunciation for some group.) Can a third actor participate? A fourth? Now try varying the principal vowel in the following sentences: (1) "I have to laugh to see the calf go down the path to take a bath in an hour and a half." (2) "The rains in Spain fall mainly on the plains." Each actor uses the same principal vowel sound in all the appropriate words. How many

possible variations can be made on these lines? What would the use of each vowel mean in a set of given circumstances?

8. Play the dramatic action with a common phrase, with each actor delivering the same phrase with a different action. Try: "I like you," or "I'm going downtown." Have the class identify the dramatic action behind each reading.

9. Devise a dozen word games for class participation. They are fun to play, and they will train your ears to hear sensitively.

MAJOR PROJECT 1A
Scene practice

Here you are: your first major project! Note that it has two parts: the first is directing your own scene; the second is testing your capabilities in communicating with other creative people by requiring you to criticize the work of other directors in this project. Don't fear the second part because the director is a friend, but look at it as a personal challenge all directors must face.

You have worked through Chapters 9 through 18 and have done many of the exercises or similar ones you have devised yourself. Consequently, you should now understand a major approach in this book: the application of the concept of organic communication, the kind of communication that works through the actor with the main purpose of arousing his improvisational sense, and thus his illustrations and activity that will flow from it. You should also be fully aware that the director uses two main areas of communication-stimulation—the visual and the oral—and that only when communication has been achieved through *both* means can it be said that the director has "gotten through". If you, as a director, concentrate on the visual alone or the oral alone, you will quite likely make a poorly balanced playing, for both sides of an actor must be approached if his improvisational sense is to be aroused to the highest degree. The exercises outlined in this chapter, exercises that put together all the things talked about thus far in this book, will give you the opportunity of putting your skills in communication to work.

Getting through to actors, then, is the major problem facing a director. In working it out, you must learn to use *all* the visual and oral tools of communication at your command and not just some of them, and to use them in as many ways as possible, for the frustrations in the directing process result directly from the barrier wall that separates director and actor. You will also discover that student-directed scenes that do not come off usually fail, not because the actors cast in such scenes are weak and ineffectual but because the directors have not broken through the director-actor barriers and reached them with such basic communications as detailed and delineated subtext, reciprocation and adjustment in acting, climactic illustrations of discoveries and adjustments, decorum, articulate conveyance of the text, exploitation of the groundplan, and the many other areas of communication so necessary to make a scene work. *Not until you learn to take the blame yourself for your own failures in getting through,* and do something about them, can you justly criticize actors for their shortcomings. You must learn your own responsibilities first if you are to learn how to lead others.

Director-actor communication, then, will involve the organic use of groundplan, composition, gesture, improvisation with objects, picturization, and movement as the six visual tools for getting through, and speaking the text and projection as the oral tools. Improvisational techniques can be used at all stages, for once you have learned to work with this method of direct communication, you will see how intellectual approaches, such as director-actor discussion, are much less effective ways of breaking barriers. You will also learn that showing an actor how to do it, no matter how exaggerated your illustration may be, is a last resort and not a primary method. After all, *your job is to bring out the creativity in actors* and not to tie them up in the restrictions of mimicry.

THE DIRECTOR AS AUDIENCE

Although the director's primary job of communication is to get through to the actors, you have now reached the point where you should be able to understand the director's second job: to be the eyes and ears for an audience. This second important function of the director is being mentioned only now not because it is less significant than the other but for fear you would see this sort of work as the director's primary job and would, consequently, miss the all-important work of getting through to the actor, or of failing to understand that if you do not recognize the actors as media, you cannot get through to the audience at all. Arousing the appropriate dramatic action in a group of actors is a very difficult process, and you must know thoroughly how that process works before you can judge the quality of what is released to the audience's improvisational sense. Only now are you ready to consider *this second major function of the director: judging the effectiveness of the transfer.*

It is precisely at the point of transfer where the director performs a primary critical function, for now he is not concerned with just getting across the footlights, *but with the appropriateness and effectiveness of the thing being transferred*. Is it the right statement? Is it intensive enough? Is it completely believable? Is the reciprocation between the characters of the desired sort? Is it moving? Or, if the play is a comedy: does it provoke laughter? What is the audience forced to do? Has it been put off balance? Will its curiosity and attention be maintained at a high level? Can it receive the ideas and images as presented? These are only a few of the dozens of critical questions that a director must ask himself of which the sum total will be: *Does it work?* In other words, the director is so much the eyes and ears of an audience that his responses should forecast those of an actual audience. As he responds, so will the audience.

What a terrifying responsibility it is to be the monitor of success for a group of creative people, each one hoping to show himself to his best possible advantage. After being immersed in the enormous detail of rehearsing a play day after day for several weeks, a director must set himself apart, that is, he must become objective about the subjective creation in order to examine what he and the others have made.

So begins the critical function of selection. Some professional directors would say that this is their primary work, that because professional actors know how to act and how to do their homework (bringing in something to look at), the director's job is mostly that of selecting the best that can be provided or of suggesting ways of playing scenes that will improve the selection. However, such a procedure will not work at all with learning actors because so much more must be done to make the acting effective. It is also doubtful that even competent professional actors can find the *appropriate* action in a play without a good deal of director-actor communication regarding the contents of a playscript and the emphasis a director wants to give it. No matter what level of actors a director may be working with, the final question is always the same for a failing scene: Why does it not work?

Here begins the diagnostic process that must be highly developed in every director: discerning why a scene fails, and then, like a doctor, prescribing a remedy. The process goes on continuously throughout a rehearsal period, and particularly in the closing days, the process of judging the product and selecting what works from what does not, and all of this selection based on whether the director responds favorably or not. Somehow, a director must be moved to laughter or to strong feelings in the spirit of whatever a play requires as he watches a run-through; if he does not react so, he will probably find that his potential audience will also respond negatively. This is why the second part of this project—diagnostic criticism—is so important to the learning director.

How to be objective, then, about your own work (the total product you see and hear on the stage) is a state of mind and feeling. *The critic in you* may take a long time to develop, for many young directors cannot make the jump readily from the inner to the outer look. Yet, jump you must if you are to evaluate what you are doing as a director. At best, you are the patient at the same time you are the doctor.

SCENE PRACTICE

Concept

Although you are not yet fully ready to stage a production (the director's function in design will be discussed in Communication 3) you are ready to direct minimally staged scenes with live actors. The approach in this chapter, then, is to bring about a synthesis of all the techniques developed in previous chapters by discussing the director's job with the playscript before rehearsals begin, with actors during a rehearsal period and with "scene critics" after the first performance. Scene practice is the goal you have been preparing for all along, but there are also techniques involved in it that must be carefully followed if you are to accomplish your goal even in a minimal way.

SCENE CHOICE

Scene choice is designated here instead of play choice because it is assumed that young directors can profit most at this point by doing two or three 10-minute scenes from long plays before doing a one-act play. The reasons are very simple. Although a one-act play provides a unity, that is, although it is all about one thing, it will not give you the opportunity to work on play-analysis in depth because the structural elements, particularly dramatic action and characters, are considerably limited. In contrast, the structural elements of major plays, from given circumstances to moods, are fully developed even though a play as a whole may be of inferior quality. In addition, the study of a 10-minute scene from a long play is tantamount to studying the whole play because, for example, you cannot eat a piece of a pie without knowing what the whole pie itself tastes like. By working with long plays, you will learn much about complicated structures, the study of which should greatly increase your respect for the playwright as a craftsman of controlled improvisation. Finally, you will be able to direct one-act plays far better after you have wrestled with parts of longer plays because you will know more about structure and will be able to handle the particular problems they raise. It is commonly assumed that short plays are easier to direct because they are short; however, this assumption is a fallacy you will become aware of when you try one after working in depth on a major play, for a short play is a *tour de force* that requires the most experienced sort of handling to bring it to fruition.

Choose a climactic scene. Every play has a major climactic scene, but each act also has at least one—probably two or three—secondary climactic moments; thus, you have several choices in every play for this project. What distinguishes a climactic from other scenes is *discovery*: an important character, usually the principal one, will discover something new in front of the audience; that is, an important fact will be disclosed to him *through dramatic action* that will decidedly alter his basic course of action. How important a climactic scene is to the play as a whole will depend on the importance of the discovery and the way in which the informant makes information known to the character who receives it. Thus, the playwright excites the audience by the gradual process of building to the moment of discovery; however, the actor caps it for us by the strength, duration, and quality of his adjustment on its reception, a high point in the acting process. *The scene is climactic because the dramatic action has reached a peak in the discovery-adjustment cycle,* leaving the recipient naked, so to speak, for several seconds before the audience while he decides what to do; the audience feels the climax because it is suspended with excitement until it knows what course of action the recipient will take. Thus, a climactic scene is made up of (1) a slow build, sometimes very intricate, with intensive suspense before the release of the discovery; (2) the discovery; (3) the adjustment; and (4) the new course of action taken by the recipient.

You must, therefore, exercise great care in choosing a climactic scene for a project. Other scenes may be effective after a fashion, but they will seem obscure to an audience, whereas a climactic scene will be received with comprehension and high interest because of the strong contrast among its units.

Do not choose a scene with the beginning and ending arbitrarily and formally established by a playwright, for example: Act II, Scene 2, of a play where the curtain (or lights) is raised and lowered at both ends. To all intents and purposes, this scene is a one-act play, and this will not provide you with the learning experience of a 10-minute climactic scene selected from the beginning, middle or end of a continuous act of a play. When you choose a piece of an act, you will find out about the nature of climactic scenes because you will be forced to dig out what leads to a climax, what a climax is, and what leads away from it. Your awareness of unit division will also be intensified because you will learn that a scene choice with only two units will not work, whereas you will have a better chance with three, and an even better one with four or five, for we can see a unit well only when it is placed in contrast with other units.

Do not choose a scene in which two characters discuss a third character who does not appear onstage during the course of the scene. Such scenes are usually transitions in which a principal character uses a secondary character as a confidant. Although the action of the play as a whole is advanced, such scenes do not make interesting choices for beginning directors because they will usually lack the dramatic quality of direct confrontation and, thus, will become very difficult scenes to present successfully.

As a starter, choose a scene with only two characters. You will still have all you can handle. You will also find that 10 minutes with two people in a play will usually rise to a sharp, dramatic climax because the author has intentionally confined his dramatic action, probably to principal characters. This confinement will give you and your actors a tight unity around which to work, for you will need to lead into it (the beginning), bring about the climax itself with its usual big discovery (middle), and bring it to a state of suspension (the end).

The choice should, of course, be from a Realistic play because this is the style of play studied in Chapters 4 through 18.   Other styles will be treated in Part III, but you must first learn to work with Realism as the dominant style of the last hundred years before you try to work with departures from that style. Further, it is suggested that you consider plays falling within the period from 1920 to 1960. You could, of course, go back to Ibsen or Chekhov and still fall within the category of Realism, but their plays are very complex, set as they are in late nineteenth-century Europe. It is also suggested that beginning directors do better in first projects with plays of American authorship because they depict given circumstances closer to their own cultural background. Plays after 1960, although they may have the look of Realism, are not suggested for the first projects in directing because their Realism is deceptive—they look like Ibsen or Chekhov at first glance but they differ radically in many respects. In the 1920 to 1960 period, you must be certain to avoid all the Expressionistic or Symbolistic plays as well as those of the Absurdists. Realism on the stage is *observed* reality, that is, reality that can be easily seen and believed as the appearance of everyday life.

It is suggested that you choose an interior scene—such as a living room, bedroom, or kitchen—or a backyard scene where a groundplan can be arranged much like an interior setting although outdoor furniture is used. Avoid open beach scenes as well as those located in a woods or in any open space because you must first learn how to use occupied space (a groundplan obstacle course) before tackling the complexities of open space groundplans.

The choice should be made from the standard repertoire of plays by well-known authors.   Do you remember Bernard Shaw's quip in the mouth of one of his critics in *Fanny's First Play,* ''If it's by a good author, it's a good play''? This is certainly only the truism Shaw intended; but there is much to be said for the successful, regularly produced author because he has a command over play structure that lesser known or unknown playwrights usually do not have. One of your intentions in doing a scene project is to learn as much as you can about play structure; the best playwrights are the best teachers, so choose their plays.

Limit the length of the scene by the number of units.   A 10-minute scene will usually contain four to six units, all you need if you have selected it properly. You may be in trouble if the scene runs less than 10 minutes because the actions may not have developed quickly and intensively enough to make a satisfactorily unified statement.

Keep your audience in mind when you choose your scene.   Although the primary function of scene practice is, of course, to further your own training in play-analysis and actor communication, you must remember that a play is not a complete form until an audience has received it on its own terms. Do not let audience consideration deter you in any way from choosing plays of high quality because you will discover that such plays can be acted more effectively since they are inventive and rich in dramatic action. Nor do you have to worry about losing your audience because it may think your scene is too obscure, too hidden in the play as a whole. If you have made a solid choice by observing the two basic rules for the number of units (four to six) and climactic action, and if you have expressed it imaginatively and with feeling, any audience will be able to follow the scene. Remember: directing is not book work, but communicating with audiences through actors and staging.

Do Not Edit the Scene Choice

Except possibly for the removal or alteration of a specific word or two that might be distasteful or distracting to your audience, *you must not alter the scene as written in any way.*

If you edit a scene by removing lines, or by removing a character because "he has only two lines, and I don't really need him," you have seriously changed the author's intentions. Young directors, thinking that they can make a better scene of the material, frequently want to edit. You must suppress all such urges! You may really want to remove lines or characters because you do not understand them; that is, you simply do not comprehend why they are there. You can be sure that the author considered all such alternatives when he wrote his play. Have faith in him; he is far more experienced at his trade than you are at yours. When you have had extensive experience as a director you may want to gamble on some editorial adjustments, but at this point you must stick exactly to the script. Furthermore, *do not select edited cuttings of plays for directing projects,* that is, cuttings made by editors who have deleted lines or characters within scenes. In the interest of making plays more appealing to a wider audience, they may have removed crucial dramatic action. Use only fully printed playscripts.

The only sort of editing you should consider is altering distasteful words, such as profanity, or words with overt sexual connotations. You are the judge of what your audience will shy away from, and you must make a decision accordingly about what to leave in and what to find a substitute for. You should not try editing a scene that is strongly marked by the continuous use of such language, since the playwright intended his language to exert great force; therefore, do not choose that scene. An occasional word can usually be readily replaced by a word of less strength. This substitution is done frequently in motion-picture writing because producers cannot take the chance of losing money by offending portions of the potential audience. Isolated words will not reduce dramatic action, nor will their alteration much reduce the strength of a text. The important thing is to remove the distraction these words might cause to your audience. You must not think of such editing as prudish but as good sense in many situations; the world does not live on profanity or other types of abusive language. Furthermore, local audiences may be more conservative than those an author may have had in mind, and if they are shocked, they may fail to hear or see what is truly important in the scene; that is, they may vibrate over a word and become insensitive to the dramatic action.

STAGING A PRACTICE SCENE

Scenes can be performed either in the classroom or on a proscenium stage. The latter will specifically confine the director to a set production form because of its architectural construction. You must not violate the proscenium line by advancing in front of it; always play behind it. That is essential. On the other hand, if you are using a classroom, set the proscenium positions by placing two chairs 24 to 26 feet apart, or the maximum width your space allows (less than 20 feet will cause problems), and then observe rigidly all the laws of the proscenium stage as if you were playing on one. (A good substitute for chair-walls is to use a two-fold screen unit on either side of your stage.)

Use abstract forms for staging. As was suggested in Chapter 11 on the groundplan, you should learn to work with whatever rehearsal-room staging is available. It is far more important to learn how to occupy space with chairs or odd pieces, and to learn the concept of the obstacle course as well as the nature of architectural mass and line, than it is to try to reproduce things exactly as they appear in everyday life. Use chairs as chairs, and tables as tables, of course; but if you and your actors use them properly, you can make them appear to be different sizes, different shapes, different textures, even different styles. You should let stacked chairs represent cabinets, bars, fireplaces, even tables if necessary, and chairs side-by-side represent sofas, etc. Learn to get along on a few items, but *never forget that you are delineating space,* not leaving it empty.

The suggested items in Figure 50 are explicitly designed for a director's rehearsal use because of their wide range of deployment in proscenium staging as well as in other types. Note that they have a neutral quality and do not have to be used as literal representation.

The four screen units are provided to give a variety of wall ideas because walls help directors and actors to know the specific limits of their groundplans. (See Figure 51 for sample illustrations of their simplest use.) Wall units (note the two sizes of the units in the drawing) will also help to enclose all your other pieces, as well as to make your obstacle course specific. The stools, benches, and rocks provide a wide variety of sitting positions. A round table is included in addition to the two square tables because it has different compositional possibilities than square tables. The practical pylons in three sizes open up all kinds of groundplan arrangements; also note they can be used in front (closed) or back (open) positions with different meanings respectively. The platform and step units will encourage the use of levels.

SUGGESTED SCENE-PRACTICE EQUIPMENT

2 REVERSIBLE SCREEN UNITS:
8' HIGH; PANEL #1 = 3' WIDE
PANEL #2 = 2' WIDE

2 REVERSIBLE SCREEN
UNITS, 8' HIGH
PANEL #1 = 1' WIDE
PANEL #2 = 4' WIDE

1-2 STEP UNIT
30" WIDE

2-2 STEP UNITS
3' WIDE

1-2 STEP UNIT
6' WIDE

2 PYLONS
15" SQUARE
4' HIGH

2 PYLONS
15" SQUARE
6' HIGH

2 PYLONS
15" SQUARE
8' HIGH

PLATFORM: 4'X 6'X 12"

ALL PYLONS HAVE ONE PRACTICAL SIDE AND
ARE OPEN ON THE SIDE FACING IT.

1- ROCK   1- STUMP

1- PADDED SOFA-BED
30"X 6'X 16"

2- TABLES
3'X 2'6"X 2'6"

1- WOOD
ARMCHAIR

2- STOOLS

10- STEEL
FOLDING
CHAIRS

2- BENCHES
1-3' WIDE
1-4½' WIDE

1- TABLE, ROUND
3'6" DIA.
2'6" HIGH

FIGURE 50

SAMPLE GROUND PLANS USING SCENE-PRACTICE EQUIPMENT

FIGURE 51

A note about the color of these materials: all the items in this rehearsal set *should be painted a neutral color,* perhaps a pearl gray, so that no single item has any particular emphasis through color value. You may at first think gray is too somber, but you will soon discover that it lends itself equally well to serious plays and to comedies. The intention of using no-color is to reduce the materials to expressions of line and mass without the distractions of particularizing details.

But whether you use classroom furniture or the more elaborate rehearsal-room setup described here and illustrated in Figure 50, you must try to be as ingenious as you can, remembering that a groundplan is a tool of communication to actors and that actors will be only as free as your imagination encourages them to be.

SCENE PREPARATION

Now that you have declared your choice of scene and know the circumstances under which you can produce it, you are ready to begin your scene preparation.

Do the play-analysis specifically as outlined in Chapter 8 (see page 64). *You will need to analyze the play as a whole for most of the preparation.* This point is precisely where many students fail; they think they can do a scene without knowing the entire play very well. Such a view is absolute folly, for a scene is only part of a whole (a piece of the pie) and without an understanding of the whole, a director cannot illuminate the parts. Be sure to study the dramatic action of the scene you have chosen to stage in great detail because all your other ideas will flow out of your understanding of this action.

Now make your promptbook as outlined in Chapter 16 (see page 153). It will contain all your suggestions for visual design, as you presently understand it, from groundplan through composition, picturization, movement, and improvisations with objects.

CASTING

Acting instructors may possibly help you with the casting or arbitrarily provide you with a cast because they know more explicitly what they want their actors-in-training to gain from the experience you are providing. If you do not get such help, you will have to go through a minimum casting procedure with whatever actors are available. Although casting as a procedure will be discussed later in Part III as an intrinsic part of play interpretation, at this point you should be looking for any responsive and cooperative people because your first job is to find out how to get dramatic action adequately rendered and not how to arrive at a delicately poised interpretation. This job will be enough for you to handle. If you are lucky enough to find actors who are able to project some of the decorum and qualities your characters require, you will be ahead in the game. Above all, you should take care not to choose people who are much more advanced in acting than you are in directing, for you need to feel you are in command. You also need to feel free to experiment with all the devices and methods of communication. Actors who can too readily act the scene for you will deprive you of what you must learn about these approaches, and some may even take the scene away from you. You will also probably stand in the way of actors more advanced in their work than you are in yours by restricting rather than freeing them. Consider yourself lucky if you have a cast of two people—whether they have the right qualities or not—who are also eager to learn, eager to experiment, and have strong wills of their own. *Your job is to learn creative leadership*—how to draw out actors and free them to their own imaginations—not the practice of arbitrary totalitarianism. You will also discover that the right qualities are not as important as you may think they are. Actors *act* action and in this way make characters. If you can get the action acted, you will be amazed at how much the particular actor is buried and how much character actually comes across.

REHEARSING

Concepts. Rehearsing a play is putting to work all the concepts and techniques discussed in this book up to this point. The rehearsal is your field of action, and you must give it every bit of imagination and energy you possess, for the success of the performance will depend on what happens here, not in the extensive paperwork preparation you have done. Rehearsing a play is a technique in itself that you must be aware of and learn to do with the greatest care. Your detailed organization here will release both you and the actors to your creative selves, making the rehearsals fun as well as profitable. Putting on a play is like playing a game in which you are the leader and can call the signals. It is also very much like a party at which you are playing host.

Scheduling. A 10-minute scene from a major play requires a minimum of eight hours of rehearsal. Calendar time is very important because an actor needs a good deal of actual time to "try on" and "make comfortable" the strange garments of a character. It is therefore suggested that an hour a day over a two-week period is far better than two hours on one day, skipping the next, three on the third, etc. The time in between the one-hour periods will let both your imagination and that of the actors work on the play. In this way rehearsals actually become experimentation hours based on assessments of the previous day's work and imaginings of what can lie ahead. There is also time to make brief suggestions to actors during the interim period, suggestions that can stimulate new directions or new experiments in the rehearsal itself.

Rehearsal plan. Each rehearsal should be designed to move your scene ahead as rapidly as possible. Here is a possible work plan for each day:

1. Read through the scene. Discuss with your actors the whole play briefly and the structure of the scene. Now tell them how you would like to stage it by setting up the groundplan and letting them "play" in it. Block the scene simply as traffic management so that the actors can "feel" their basic relationships.

2. Repeat the blocking of the first rehearsal. Now begin character development by helping the actors search out some of the dramatic action. Start improvisations now if your actors are capable in this technique. It is better to work on a unit or two than the whole scene.

3. Concentrate on the illustration of dramatic action (organic blocking) in the interest of unfolding the dramatic action and thus the character relationships. Continue improvisations.

4. "Lines off." Improvisation with hand properties can be added to the other communicators, such as composition, picturization, and movement.

5. Run through the scene in order to assess the accomplishment of the dramatic action and thus the character development. Is actor-reciprocation taking place? Is the groundplan working? If not, redo it, paying close attention to the number of acting areas, whether it is a good obstacle course, and whether it can excite the imagination of the actors. Are the *principal* discovery and adjustment in the scene being played with strength and careful pointing?

6. Reblock the scene as needed and work on dramatic action. Is the scene playing in units? Concentrate on actor-reciprocation and on character development.

7. Make clear delineations in unit structure of the scene by working for mood and tempo goals. Concentrate on delivery of the text.

8. Do run-throughs, concentrating on rhythmic beats and pacing.

Note in this rehearsal plan, the director blocks the scene in the first rehearsal in the interest of direct communication. This use of blocking does not in any way rule out improvisational techniques for the purpose of scene discovery (see pp. 188–89), though such techniques can be employed only if the actors and the director are already familiar with their use. If they are, improvisations become the method of direct communication. If not, use *organic blocking*. The purpose, however, is the same: the quick assimilation of the dramatic action by the actors while the scene content is still fresh. The sense of discovery is very important here, for the actors can see more clearly at this point the shape of the scene—the highs, the lows, the erratic points, the discoveries—than they will later when they have become too absorbed in the detail.

Do not go too slowly.   If you are ready with some suggestions of compositions and movements, the actors will respond quickly to the demands of the scene. Your intention in the first rehearsal is to tell the actors *the shape* of the scene through the communicators—groundplan, composition, picturization, movement, and tempos; music played out of rhythm is no music at all.

The lines should be learned by the fourth rehearsal so that the actors can put down the scripts and begin experimenting with illustration *at the same time that they begin listening carefully to each other.* Scene discovery, remember, comes in hearing an action and in making an adjustment. Line learning is this context can be seen as sense-of-the-scene learning, and there is little to be gained by slowing down this process. Find the subtext first, and only then will you be able to start work at pointing the text.

The run-through suggested in the fifth rehearsal is very necessary so that you can see and hear what has been accomplished thus far and where to go next. Do not interrupt the actors in this first run-through, but insist that they play the scene fully as if they were playing it before an audience. Use all your set pieces and properties at this run-through. The assessment that follows is your most important decision-making moment in the rehearsal plan. Is the groundplan working for the actors? Is the shape of the scene fully established in their acting? Is character development (given circumstances plus dramatic action) well underway? Does the scene build climactically through sharp delineation of the units?

Now begin the final work on the scene.   Do not hesitate to find new compositions or movements, or to encourage the actors to find them, in the interest of stimulating new ideas; the actors will tell you instantly whether the new suggestions stimulate them. Shuffle up the groundplan on the same premise: the actors will now show you how to play the scene. Stretch out the scene limits by declaring the peaks and valleys much more dramatically and theatrically. And if the mechanics are stimulating ideas in the action, concentrate on character decorum, character-mood-intensity, unit division, and, above all, on character reciprocation. *This last, remember, is your reason for being:* to help *two* actors find the characters in each other.

The final periods begin with cleaning up the text and in emphasizing the text in the interest of projection. The first obligation of a director is to be certain that a scene is well heard. Apply all the points discussed in Chapter 18. You can reach the actors easily by writing notes as they play the scene, underlining words or phrases in the dialogue that need pointing, and working continuously for the proper emphasis or flavoring of lines or entire speeches. Polish the scene in every way to eliminate distractions. Remember that the actors can now take directions easily and quickly, for they probably know more about the insides of the scene than you do. Insist on high energy and the proper starting points (character-mood-intensities).

Economy in director's suggestions: Do not talk much.   This rule is absolute. The purpose of rehearsal is to let the actors experiment with the acting. If you fill the rehearsal periods with your own chatter, the actors will want to talk too, and the whole thing will turn into a talk-fest shambles. Actors must be kept busy acting, not talking about acting or analyzing the scene. Your directions must, therefore, be economical and explicit, quiet and assured, good-humored and alive. Remember, you are playing a game with the actors, and you, above all, must keep the rehearsal free and comfortable. But you must also insist on what must be done. Honesty is the best policy because students working together will respect one another only on that basis.

Directions are always to individual persons. You must devise your directions always in terms of the individual actors who are playing the roles, never in abstract terms. You must therefore watch your actors carefully, especially if you do not know them well, until you see what kind of suggestions seem to get through. The better you know your actors as creative people, the better you will know how to communicate with them. Some actors will need greatly exaggerated suggestions or images to move them; others will need only the barest suggestions. If an actor is already playing in an oversized fashion, make your images small and delicate. Likewise, revise your approach for the "small" actor. If you need to show an actor what you mean—a last resort—do so in very oversized terms so that he can get the *essence* of what you are suggesting, not the literal reality of that suggestion: your intention is not to have him mimic you but to have him absorb your idea and turn it into his own feeling for illustration on his own terms.

Improvisation in rehearsal. Improvisations are used in rehearsal for the purpose of (1) freeing actors' imaginations, (2) effecting concentration, (3) uncovering dramatic action and character relationships, and (4) bringing about reciprocation between actors. The process is the usual game playing, this time with the material of the playscript before lines are learned or even well established in the minds of the actors. The intention is to draw actors into the given circumtances and subtext of a play by developing in them a high degree of concentration by letting them "feel" their way into close association with each other. Two actors thus make a magic circle of their reciprocal involvement; if such improvisations are done with seriousness and release, actors can literally feel the high-tension rubberband that always ties them together as characters. How much improvisation is actually used in rehearsal will depend on both your knowledge and skill with this sort of communication device and on the needs of the actors: their abilities to concentrate and reciprocate, and how obscure the subtext of the play on which they are working may be to them. This is no place for a detailed discussion of improvisational techniques, but the following is a suggestion of the sort of thing that might be done.

An improvisation plan. One of the main problems with beginning actors is that of releasing themselves to one another on the intimate level, where dramatic actions take place in realistic plays. You must, therefore, design your improvisations with the purpose of breaking down barriers between actors in order to gain intimacy. Remove their self-consciousness by working with them in private. Reducing the light level in the rehearsal room will also help, for actors will feel less self-conscious and be able to throw off their personal facades in semidarkness. Now encourage your actors to sit close to one another on the floor and actually touch one another by holding both hands and looking into one another's eyes. After a communion concentration has been established (this may take several minutes), improvising on the material of the playscript can begin with "number" dialogue (see page 14, Exercise 3) representing the dramatic action. Each participant should "feel" the sensations of *forcing* the other, of *adjusting* when it is his turn to be forced, and of taking his new action on the basis *only* of his adjustment. As the subtext develops in intensity, the two participants should pull or be pulled, never disengaging, and always responding to the pressure (dramatic action) of the other.

The improvisation above can be varied by having the actors sit back-to-back with arms interlinked. Or it can be played by holding hands over a chair, with each actor in his forcing action pulling the other to the edge of his balance (where he is about to fall). Both variations have the same purpose: "feeling" the force of reciprocal action. Such game playing will induce concentration because the participants will become involved in a physical way with each other and feel the intimacy of bodily force.

Once intimacy and the sense of reciprocal forcing has been established, the actors could try improvising the subtext without holding hands or arms. The obstacles in the groundplan can supply the same holding force if you encourage their use. You can also prompt such an improvisation from the sidelines if you want to push the actors into new areas of the subtext. The important thing is to have the actors hold the magic circle of their intimate relationship as long as possible; when it breaks, you will need to start them again.

DIRECTOR'S SELF-CRITICISM

Emphasize the "Big Moment."   Every climactic scene has a big moment that must be set out clearly and climactically. Have you pinpointed the exact moment in the script where it begins? It is your job to see that the actors achieve a high peak at the top of the scene.

Tell yourself the "Long Story."   Go over the entire story of a scene in great detail, *including all action and activity.*

Tell yourself the "Short Story."   Summarize the "long story" in two or three sentences.

"Play" the roles yourself to "feel" it.   When you are alone, use the technique of reading aloud each character *separately* while standing or moving about like an actor playing the role. Do you really "feel" the force of each action? When you have "felt" each part, read them together. Can you "feel" the see-saw battle going on?

Are the characters playing their character-mood-intensities at the appropriate levels?

Is your pacing of the scene in line with the development of the dramatic action? If you try stepping up the tempo of the whole a couple of notches, you will find it can probably move faster than you had previously thought.

Is the violence level accomplished by the actors?   All climactic scenes contain a "violence," sometimes in words but frequently in physical activity. Is the violence freely demonstrated? Have you found the exact word or line when the character makes the climactic discovery and thus begins the violence?

Is reciprocation really taking place?   Can you see the reciprocation? Can you hear it?

Experiment.   In a rehearsal period, nothing must be set in a final way until it works. You must be ingenious, a constant innovator, ready to shift and bend as the need arises. And you must instill this sense of creative adventure in your actors, for they will go beyond themselves if you do. Your job is to make them creative, not to show your own virtuosity. Art is made only in creative circumstances where the imagination can be released. The playscript already provides the springboard; you must provide the swimming pool, the sunshine, the just-right water, and a good deal of the gaiety and laughter.

PERFORMANCE

The audience will tell you very quickly and emphatically whether you have succeeded or not. You must always watch your scenes *with* the audience, listening as closely to it as you do the actors. Scene practice as outlined in this chapter should always be completed by playing for an audience, even if it is only the rest of the class. Introduce your scene quickly and effectively, telling the audience only what it must know to avoid basic confusions. Lengthy recounting of previous action will be meaningless, and will even put the audience off your scene. An audience wants to use its own imagination, its own capabilities, its own resources, not depend on someone else's. It will feel insulted if you tell it (often by overplaying or overemphasizing points) that it is incompetent or insensitive. Reaching an audience is a difficult process, but the actor can do it very quickly and easily if he plays the action intensively and with sensitivity. An audience is not interested in actors per se, but only in the characters they create; they love those actors who arouse character images and strong feelings in them.

Good actors will always listen carefully to audiences before whom they play. This is why the theatre experience is an intimate one: the audience senses the actor, and the actor senses the audience. The gulf of a wide apron, an orchestra pit, or a very large house reduces all of this reciprocal feeling proportionally—the greater the actual distance, the more difficult the reciprocation. An audience seated in the balcony simply does not experience the play at the same level of intensity as those sitting close to the stage. This fact is reflected in the various ticket prices for different parts of a playhouse: you get the kind of play you pay for. A theatre in a democracy, then, really ought to be a small playhouse, not a large one built for the purpose of getting everyone inside who wants to come. We will have more to say about this point of view later.

MAJOR PROJECT 1B
Diagnostic criticism

A diagnostic criticism is a written, and then oral, critical analysis of a scene directed by another director. Its main function is not to make you a book critic, but rather to intensify your skills in oral communication with actors, as well as your own ways of approaching self-criticism, by sharpening your critical faculties under controlled conditions. At first, you may feel uncomfortable about such give-and-take encounter sessions, but if you prepare your written critique well, the oral will go much easier. You will be learning how to listen to others, just as you expect actors and designers to listen to you.

CONCEPT

Although diagnostic criticism is your own analysis of another director's work, it not only gives you additional scenes to study, but it can also develop your capabilities in finding *what went right* or *what went wrong,* simply because at this point you will tend to look more objectively at somebody else's work than your own. "I like it!" or "I don't like it!" are not valid as criticism because they convey only feelings and not objective positions. In one sense, diagnostic criticism is a scene produced in reverse, from final performance back to its origins, with all the significant intervening steps. *Your job is akin to that of a doctor who examines patients who are well and determines why they are well; but you are also the doctor who looks at patients who are ill and tries to find out what has made them ill.* Study of both patients is necessary because you need to recognize easily what works and what does not.

In this view diagnostic criticism is the most positive criticism you can write for other directors as well as receive yourself. Do not fear personal animosities if you are on the receiving end, for the diagnostic critic must prove his points, not merely voice them as newspaper play reviewers too frequently do. Your capability at diagnostic criticism will greatly improve your capability as a practicing director because directing is close seeing and hearing. *Being the eyes and ears for someone else also means looking back upon yourself as a director.*

A PRODUCTION PLAN FOR DIAGNOSTIC CRITICISM

Diagnostic criticism cannot be put to work effectively unless it is incorporated into an organized production plan that allows critics time and opportunity to do their work. It is therefore suggested that the class set up a rehearsal and performance schedule that will give assigned critics (perhaps two or three) copies of a scene several days prior to a performance. Thus, the critics will have time not only to read the entire play but also to consider in detail the particular scene to be performed. In this way, the critics come to the performance with some ideas about the scene and what can be done with it. Although critics should begin their written criticism as soon after a performance as possible, a deadline should be set no later than three days after the performance in order to keep the criticism as fresh as possible, and also to give the experience a few hours of objectivity.

AN OUTLINE FOR DIAGNOSTIC CRITICISM

Here is an outline of what to look for. Study it carefully. Criticisms should follow explicitly the form outlined below. Please use the identical numbering system in writing your analysis.

I.   *Action Summary.* Study carefully a copy of the scene *before* you see the scene performed. Number the units of action and give the action in each unit, *as you analyze it in the playscript,* by showing the reciprocal action in abbreviated sentence form. A (verb) to B, and B (verb) to A. Your awareness and perception of the action, as stated here, is the basis of your criticism, and it will partially inform the director about how you arrived at your conclusions.

II. *Technical Analysis.* Discuss the produced scene under the following headings:
   A.   Groundplan
      1.   Number of acting areas
      2.   Useability
      3.   Ingenuity
   B.   Composition. Discuss the use of areas, planes, levels, body positions, triangles, etc., detailing several examples explicitly.

   C.   Picturization. Detail successful ones particularly noticed.
   D.   Movement. Pick out specific movements and comment.
   E.   Improvisation with objects. Detail objects used and the effective illustration they have made possible. What objects might have been used to better advantage?
III.   *Characterizations.* In this section, discuss the acting of the scene by detailing what each actor has done and estimating the extent of the director-actor communication that has taken place.
   A.   Character *A*
      1.   Comparison of the ideal of the character as drawn in the playscript with the actor's characterization:
         (a) Delineate the character as *you* see it in the playscript.
         (b) Compare how well the actor accomplished this ideal (dramatization, discoveries, violence, etc.).
      2.   Decorum
      3.   Delivery of the text
      4.   Believability
   B.   Character *B*
      1.   Comparison of the ideal in the playscript with the actor's characterization:
         (a) Delineate the character as *you* see it in the playscript.
         (b) Compare how well the actor accomplished this ideal (dramatization, discoveries, violence, etc.).
      2.   Decorum
      3.   Delivery of the text
      4.   Believability
   C.   Repeat *A* and *B* for any additional characters.
   D.   Synthesis: Discuss here the reciprocation—how well the actors played together, their intercommunication.
IV.   *Overall Evaluation*
   A.   Moods created: List here the specific moods created.
   B.   Tone: Enter only *yes* or *no;* make no further comment.
   C.   Qualifications. Qualify *B* here.

WRITTEN CRITICISM PRECEDES ORAL CRITICISM

The reason for written criticism is that it forces you to put into words exactly what you have noticed, both visually and aurally, about a scene, thus giving you specific practice in director communication. Merely "talking" your criticism— that is, doing it in a conversational way in the classroom without first writing it down—encourages looseness of expression as well as muddy thinking. (It will also remove the totally vague and completely empty "I like it!" or "I don't like it!") If you write down your criticism in an organized way, you probably "believe" what you have to say and can support it. Type the criticism and proofread it carefully, for your colleagues will listen to you only if they know you have prepared your criticism with great care.

When the written work has been completed, the criticism should be discussed *orally* in the group. Remember: the instructor will act as adjudacator between you and the director-critic, and will insist on fairness and politeness. So will other members of your class. Oral discussion is the second most important thing you do in this technique (writing down your assessment is first.) *A director must be verbally articulate,* and you can now speak your ideas because you are prepared to discuss them. You should also practice your verbal capability. *The purpose is to get through to another director without so irritating and antagonizing him that you fail to communicate.*

Note that the criticism begins with your own statement of the action. This sort of criticism is based both on your seeing and hearing the scene, and on your study of a copy of the playscript itself. You should know the entire play, and you must be thoroughly familiar with the content of the scene performed. Put down the action carefully, as prescribed in the first section of the form for diagnostic criticism, because all that you have to say can be evaluated explicitly against your concept of the action. If you see the scene before you record the action, you must be doubly careful not to let its presentation of the action sway your own opinion about what is going on. *The secret of good diagnostic criticism lies explicitly in your perception of a scene's action.*

Also pay particular attention to the section on characterization. Again, you must set down what *you think* the playwright prescribes the character to be before you comment on what a particular actor did in making his characterization. A clear analysis here on your part will tell you something about the director-actor communication in the scene: did the director get through to the actors? Other parts of the criticism will soon tell you whether he understood the dramatic action or not. The synthesis in Section III, D of the outline is very important because the effectiveness of the scene will be declared specifically in the level of reciprocation with which the actors play.

Tone is used in Section IV, B to indicate total accomplishment of the aims of the scene. Did the scene work? Did it accomplish its basic intention in the play? Was the audience moved to laughter or to the serious moods intended by the playwright? This sort of statement is, of course, pure opinion, but you know the strength of your own feelings, and you were also aware of how the rest of the audience seemed to respond. *Take a sharp stand on tone, recording "yes" or "no," and then modify your opinion in Section IV, C.*

DIRECTORS ARE HUMAN BEINGS, TOO

In writing this sort of criticism, always remember that you are writing to another human being—a director—who, like an actor, is very sensitive about his creative work. Practice your skill at writing an honest, careful statement without being cruel and arrogant. Do not generalize! Generalities hurt and confuse. Be specific, and be direct, supporting all your points with carefully chosen evidence. The opinionated *are those who speak out of their emotions,* not out of their considered evaluation—a mixture of feeling and mind. Although a director is a person of very strong feelings, he has a mind, and a mind takes care how it talks. Remember that you are making a diagnosis, not writing a diatribe against a production like a professional reviewer with the intention of entertaining casual readers. You are a responsible person who respects the work of others, and your comment will be respected if it is offered with care and precision. But although you must always be honest and say what you think, there is no excuse whatever for cruelty and dishonesty. Look for the best in others to find the best in yourself.

PART TWO
COMMUNICATION 3
The director's design function and the production process

O shows, shows, mighty shows!
The eloquence of masque! What need of prose,
Or verse, or sense, t'express immortal you?
. . . .

Or to make boards to speak! there is a task!
Painting and carpentry are the soul of masque.

Ben Jonson expressing his anger at
designer Inigo Jones for subordinating
the poet's words to scenery

CHAPTER NINETEEN
DIRECTING
IS DESIGNING

Communication 3 is all about how a director "turns on" audiences with play production.

Early in this century, English scene designer Gordon Craig in a brief and very famous essay entitled "The Art of the Theatre" delineated two kinds of directors: the *artist-director* who creates everything, including the playscript, and the *master-craftsman-director* who he defined as a designer-coordinator. Craig's artist-director came to life in movie making where a tradition of writer-directors materialized to become a significant fact of life in that medium, while the master-craftsman became the prototype for the practicing director in the live theatre. As Craig intended, the master-craftsman is an interpreter who keeps a very tight grip on all that happens on the stage from the development of the playscript to the final performance, for in Craig's view only one person could be in charge if the pedestrian was to be avoided. *This is the point of view in this book.*

But before you as a learning director can deal with very personal and individual ways of thinking about a play and expressing it in an exceptional way in production—the subject of Part III—you must fully comprehend the mechanics of the stage: how it can be used as a lively instrument of communication. *It will be how you perceive the options open to you in production that will make the difference between putting an audience to sleep and elevating it to excitement.*

THE DIRECTOR'S RESPONSIBILITY FOR DESIGN

Design is the physicalization of poetic idea.   Consequently, unless a director can control the visual and aural elements that constitute design, he is powerless in making an individual statement—a situation that would put us back in the dark ages of the nineteenth century where the "stage manager" merely gave an order to the Stage Carpenter to have the "Dark Fancy" set, or the "Kitchen" set, or the "Light Fancy" set, or the "Wood" set placed on stage at a given time. That sort of stock scenery, as you can readily see, had no individuality at all in terms of a specific play, but was intended to serve general purposes. Our present convention of making specific scenery for each play may seem terribly expensive and wasteful, but it is part of our theatre aesthetic that demands *individualization.* Therefore, as the principal designer, a director must take the responsibility for the individualized statement. *If he is an artist, he will speak freshly, for art is always a fresh, personal view.*

Directing, then, is not a mere manipulation of the actor and the physical stage; it is *considered* and *appropriate* manipulation, what Eric Bentley calls "the correct presentation of a poem." The concept at its base is simply this: the playscript provides the dramatic action, and the director uses the many tools at his command to illustrate that action—his visual and oral tools with actors which you have already studied, and his scenic production tools, usually with designers, which you will study here. Each group of tools has its techniques and its values. What the director must learn is how to use well all of these tools and not just a few, for the variety and complexity of his production effort will reflect what he knows about them and how well he can use them. Learn the *concept* underlying each technique, and you will then know how to put it to work for you.

The next few chapters in this book, then, will greatly expand the functions of the director, for you are going to look at the director's relationship to the stage machine: the stage area, scenery, properties, lighting, makeup, costumes, and sound effects. The problems connected with using this machine are as complex as those in the director-actor relationship because the stage machine requires a diversity of talents to bring out its highest potentials. When you do the whole job yourself, as you might in a small educational theatre setup or in a one-man, community theatre operation, all you need do is to argue out the designs with yourself and then carry out what your own imagination and your physical resources allow. But a director in this situation is bound by his own limitations, the same sort of limitations he would meet if he tried to act every role in a play himself. Consequently, unless you are totally familiar with all of your options in staging a play, you will not know how to work with designers in synthesizing a production when that time comes. Now is the time for you to examine your options, for you will use them all in Major Project 2 at the end of this section when you design as well as direct your own production.

THE HISTORICAL RELATIONSHIP OF DIRECTION
AND DESIGN

It was the problem of synthesis that brought the director into the theatre in the latter part of the nineteenth century. As has been pointed out frequently elsewhere, the contribution of the twentieth century to the history of the theatre has been artistic play interpretation, an integration process of production in which the director has figured prominently. In this century, we have looked at theatre history not only as a thing in itself but as a highly useful background for production; and it has led us to revivals of both earlier plays and ideas of production on a scale no previous age ever knew. We have tried to make our stage machine adaptable to every period and style, an effort that has led us recently into the trap of multipurpose theatre-building design.

Previous to the late nineteenth century, as was noted earlier in this chapter, stage design was more general than specific, more an appropriate background (and frequently an inappropriate one) for dramatic action than a *participant* in it. This approach directly reflected the concept of a play as a *presentation* in bold, broad lines. The development of science and technology in the nineteenth century found its way directly into the theatre in forms that not only required that scenery appear to be like nature but that it create specific environments for specific plays. This scientific naturalism required much greater control of the stage machine as well as of acting, and it was at this point that the director was brought into the theatre as a much-needed craftsman. The *general* use of the stage soon became the *particular* use of the stage, and out of this was born twentieth-century stage production.

Nevertheless, even though the actor did not actually perform within the stage setting during the seventeenth and most of the eighteenth centuries, we know that some coordination took place, that someone placed the scenery and told the actors where to stand. We usually assume that this coordinator, where there was one, was either the ''stage manager'' or an ''actor-manager,'' but it could just as well have been the stage designer. It was not stretching historical projection out of focus to imagine that when Inigo Jones made his elaborate painted settings for his spectacular masques at the English Court in Shakespeare's day, he also directed the performers to certain positions in relation to scenery which he probably designed with their positioning in mind. Perhaps this ''direction'' is what may have so irritated Ben Jonson and what provoked him to write the lines condemning Jones that appear on the title page of this section of the book (page 196). The designer as stage director has much support when we speculate about the theatre of the past.

But whatever total function designers may have served in past ages, in the late nineteenth century they were brought under the control of directors who could then harmonize their creativity with that of the actors in the interest of making a total theatre experience. And so it remains today.

THE PURPOSE OF THIS BOOK REGARDING DESIGN

It has been generally assumed, largely because of the Stanislavskian wave in actor training, that director training should be primarily in the area of acting, with its subareas of voice, body, and movement. There can be no question that such specialization has its intrinsic values, for who will teach acting if not the director. But this point of view also assumes, unfortunately, that designers will take care of the other aspects of production, that somehow visual design in the theatre is considerably less important than acting design. This assumption is very shortsighted because it overlooks the *concept of total theatre* in which the director as theatrical artist—the point of view of this book—coordinates both the acting and the visual presentation of a play's ideas.

The training of a director in all the areas of design is, therefore, essential, and it should be intensive training, not a haphazard process. Stage designing requires first an artist and second someone who can work within the limitations of the theatre. Stage designing is not the making of an arty background for actors, nor the operation of a technical machine. Instead, it is an organic expression of a high order. Stringent comment on the background and training of prominent stage designers in our century is reflected in the fact that when it comes to writing theatre histories, it is not directors who have made the major contributions but designers.

The program of studies suggested below is therefore set out with the intention of alerting you, as a director-in-training, to the areas of study you should pursue, in whole or in part, if you are to be informed about the design aspect of your work. A well-conceived program would contain much of the following:

A cultural history of specific civilizations (Chinese, Egyptian, Greek, etc.) in order to comprehend the meaning of culture in its social and intellectual aspects

A survey of painting and sculpture; a course in life drawing; an elementary course in painting; an advanced course in art history

Theatre history: theatre buildings, stages, scenery, etc.

Costume history: a history of clothes as well as what was worn on the stage

Elementary drawing for the stage: mechanical, perspective, and free rendition

Scene design and staging materials

Costume design

Lighting design and engineering

Such training may seem extensive to a beginning director, but as you become more familiar with the complex, diverse problems of production in today's art-theatre, you will soon see the need for such a careful step-by-step building of your design capabilities.

THE PURPOSE OF THE EXERCISES
IN COMMUNICATION 3

Since it is assumed that you, as a director-in-training, are simultaneously pursuing some sort of training in design and, consequently, are actively engaged in regularly assigned projects, no exercises in design of the usual sort are suggested here or in the following chapters. Instead, two procedures are used: the first involves working through Chapters 19 through 23 with *a full-length, classroom play* for study as the principal device for emphasizing the director's options in design; and the second involves designing and directing your own live production of a one-act play as a summarizing project for all of Communication 3. These two projects taken together will take you to the second level of directing—coordination and synthesis in play production. The third level—*style*—will be presented in Part III.

Finding a good study play at this point is essential because investigating a director's options in the area of design requires a play with multiple possibilities if you are to see the full range of the problem. Furthermore, a long play is suggested because you not only need to study this form as a contrast to the one-act play, but you will also be able to see the concepts of coordination and synthesis in a large structure because of the scope it allows. Thus, you can make progress on two fronts. Although the class or its instructor can certainly make an independent choice, and may prefer to do so, for purposes of discussion here all the exercises in Communication 3 are focused on Arthur Miller's *The Crucible*. This play offers many advantages because of its undated content, despite the fact that it was written in the early 1950s; its multi-act structure with different locations; its style of Realism that allows a fairly wide scope in staging; and the many problems in coordination and synthesis in design that it presents. Exercises with this play begin immediately at the end of this chapter. They do not attempt to be exhaustive in any way but merely guide you and your class to the sort of questions a director must ask himself.

The main intention of Communication 3 then, is to insure that you comprehend the relationship of the director to visual design by thoroughly understanding the concepts of symbolization, synthesis, and the communication process in design. You will not only need to discuss extensively all of the points in Communication 3 in the classroom, but you are also encouraged to pursue these concepts in discussion with both directing and design students. Here is one place where directors can do a good deal of talking without getting into trouble.

In addition, *you should be certain that you understand one concept before going on to the next.* The material is laid out here in a logical progression, and you can advance only with step-by-step comprehension. Some of the points may seem obvious to you, but dealing with them is just where the difficulties begin; your theatre-going experiences up to this point have probably been quite unoriented toward design and this lack of orientation may have led you to take a very great deal for granted. You will need fresh eyes at this point in order to tear apart the obvious and to discover that the obvious is not obvious at all, for someone has designed what you see and that means that decisions have been made about it. *Always remember that a design is a conceived plan, not an accident.*

You will learn to see well only if you remove your own blindness; no one else can do that for you.

EXERCISE

1. You should begin with your study of *The Crucible* (or other study play) by concentrating on its structure for design purposes. This sort of study is what directors frequently do in making a choice of a play for production; that is, it precedes a major play-analysis but it still enables a director to get a firm grasp of the play in order to make preliminary decisions about it. But you should by no means accept it as a substitute for a full play-analysis, for you simply cannot direct actors without such study. Your first job is to read the play by recording the action in two ways:
   a. Record the *story* of the play by writing down both previous action and dramatic action on sheets of paper with lines drawn vertically to separate the two kinds of action. Record the previous action in red on one side and the dramatic action in black on the other. As you may remember, this exercise was the first one you did in doing a play-analysis. You can do this exercise easily if you make a note about what happens on each page of the playscript, and then carry this note over to your summarizing sheets.
   b. When (a) has been completed, you are ready to go on to a director's scene-analysis. This is done by making a list of all the scenes in the play that are performed by the two or three most important characters. These are consequently the major scenes in the dramatic action because the playwright has deliberately centered the forces of the play around these characters. These scenes are also climactic, thus containing the principal discoveries and consequent adjustments. Analyzing them will give you a quick grasp of the play's structure. (If you choose a study play with only two to five characters, be sure that you select the *principal* climactic scenes since the play will be made up of two- or three-character scenes). In *The Crucible* you will find eight to ten of these scenes. Now write a comment about each scene with attention on two points: the scene's requirements in terms of acting and the scene's requirements in terms of staging.
2. When you have completed the two parts of Exercise 1, you are ready for a class discussion of the play. Proceed in the usual fashion for discussions of play-analysis, but instead of pursuing the seven major elements in detail, concentrate your discussions around specific points, such as:
   a. Why is *The Crucible* not a historical play? Why is it not a costume drama? How is it very contemporary?

b. Who are the protagonist and the antagonist? Be sure you see Danforth's function in the play. Do you see Abigail's function as an instrument to effect the action? How do Proctor and Danforth clash head-on?

c. Characterize Danforth. Can you see him as a politician rather than as a stern judge representing the church?

d. What is the real witchcraft in the play? Should an audience believe in the witchcraft shown on Act I? What should an audience reaction be to this act? Could certain lines possibly produce laughter? Should an audience hold the same view as John Proctor? Why?

e. What role does Reverend Hales play in the action? What are his polar attitudes? Does he change? What are John Proctor's? What are Danforth's?

3. If you have done Exercises 1 and 2 carefully, you should be able to delineate the differences in structure between a long play and a short one. What does the long play allow in the way of character development? How many major characters are developed in *The Crucible?* How complex is the action? How many plots are there in *The Crucible? (Plot* means "separate lines of action:" Abigail and the girls, Abigail and Proctor, etc.)

4. Read Gordon Craig's essay, "The Art of the Theatre." Discuss its contents in class.

CHAPTER TWENTY
THE DIRECTOR
AND THE
STAGE MACHINE
Symbolization
and synthesis

This chapter is mostly about theatre aesthetics, the concepts behind all the practical work you do in the theatre. It will challenge your patience, your attention, your mind, your image of yourself as a creative artist.

We have become so accustomed in this day of science and machines to seeing things around us only in external ways—that is, in terms of what is useful or functional—that we find it very difficult indeed to recapture the other kind of seeing we knew as small children but somehow lost when subjected to the controls and conformaties of adult life. Yet, this must be done if we are to discover what art is all about. Wordsworth's "The child is father of the man" has very special meaning from an artistic point of view because it epitomizes the very nature of the artist who must relearn or recapture the freedom and simplicity of childhood vision. The employment in actor training of improvisation and games has as its goal the freeing of the individual from rigid behavioral patterns and releasing the imagination as an active, living force. The same thing must be done for the learning designer or director. *In the art world, to see things eccentrically is to see them normally and freshly.* Without this free imagination, one is forever tied to accepted and prosaic realities.

Motion pictures prior to the 1960s and most television from its beginnings to the 1970s had enormous influence on this restriction in seeing because they largely assumed that what we see literally and see quickly is all that there is.

However, our vision has again been opened to the mainstream of the history of art forms by many works in both mediums that have penetrated surface realities to take hard looks underneath. Films, in particular, have won favor with adult audiences, not because of their sexual content but because of their mature themes and complex perceptions. And these films have had an effect on the theatre by helping to force the theatre back into the mainstream of dramatic literature where revelation and poetic insights are a way of life.

SYMBOLIZATION IS THEATRE

Symbolization allows us to see life more clearly, more perceptively, by sensing it through the recognizable essences of things. This definition does not in any way rule out the use on the stage of what we regard as real objects. What it does force us to do as director-designers is to use objects in *appropriate* and *contextual* ways so that their full values can be exploited artistically and our vision amplified. When used in these ways, the stage machine becomes organic: not only do we show scenery, properties, lights, or costumes for what they are in themselves, but we greatly extend their life and vitality, their image-making powers, through actors who reveal their essences.

As a director, then, *you must learn the fine art of symbolization if you are to use the stage machine with any degree of sophistication.* You will find that you can reach audiences excitingly and with direct contact through symbolization where you have failed with the mere use of surface realities. *Design, therefore, is not decoration but organic symbolization.*

Stage Convention

A *stage convention* is a contrivance with symbolic values. Continuous use of a contrivance so firmly establishes it in the feelings of audiences that they accept it as part of familiar stage form without any effort whatsoever. They perceive its symbolic meanings and take it for granted. Conventions thus become deeply rooted, so much so, in fact, that artistic revolts are often needed to overthrow them. The raised platform is just such a form. So are the proscenium arch, painted scenery, the architectural stone wall of the Greek theatre, and the Shakespearian stage that projects into the house. The late nineteenth century went through a revolt in its attack on Romantic staging, replacing it with illusionistic conventions (like observed realities); and the twentieth century is going through a similar revolt against the illusory theatre in its attempt to break away from the conventions of Realism.

A director must grasp the concept of stage convention and the force it exerts on popular audience feelings and comprehension. This perception is also a basis for understanding design.

Why Study Theatre History

This book cannot possibly examine, except in a general way, everything a director must know about theatre architecture, the stage place, scenery, costuming, makeup, lighting, and sound. Each is a specialized study in itself and should be pursued with specialized intentions. What needs to be pointed out here is the nature of change in the design function throughout the history of theatre, and the necessity for a director's understanding of it.

An important point: *The form of theatre does not change but only the conventions and symbolizations within that form.*

Changes are clearly marked by shifts in conventions, but *the constant factor behind all the changes is symbolism: each age finds a characteristic symbolism for projecting its ideas through its stage machine.* Imaginative theatre historians, such as George Kernodle and Richard Southern, have pursued these changes in great detail, and you should study their books for specific illumination of the subject.

Consequently, what follows is a brief résumé of the interrelationships of the staging tools. They are set out at this point in the interest of showing what the director must study of theatre history if he is to comprehend the theatre machine and thus have a sophisticated view of all his options.

Theatre architecture.   The study of theatre architecture deals with the relationship between the playing space and the audience. Such study leads to a comprehension of the "size" of plays and what this has to do with the arrangement of audiences; an awareness of the effects of physical distance on the relationship of actors and audience; an understanding of how visual and aural comprehension by an audience depend not only on this distance but also on the height levels of audience positions in relation to the playing space; a comprehension of the problems of acoustics and of an actor's projection arc (the maximum arc—from side to side—that a speaking actor can use and still be heard); and an understanding, of the nature of stage lighting vis-a-vis architecture—daylight or artificial devices in space.

Playing space.   This area of study is concerned with what is commonly referred to as "the stage." But since that term is so often confused with a raised platform, the broader, more conceptual, term is used here. Any historical study of playing space would certainly reveal that actors have played on the ground level with the audience on the same level; on the gorund level with the audience raised in graduated steps; on both ground level and raised platforms simultaneously; on raised platforms of varying levels, with the audience below or on various levels above; in circular, square, rectangular, or triangular arrangements.

Scenery.   In the broadest sense, scenery delineates the backing of the playing space or the occupation of the space itself, and is so used in discussion of theatre history. Thus, it includes permanent architectural facades, moveable backing pieces, permanent or moveable objects, platforms, and other devices within the playing space. Study of theatre history shows a wide variety of uses, from the architectural facades with moveable pieces in the playing space that we know to-day, to the latest devices of projected scenery, either stationary or moving behind the actor.

Costuming and makeup. The actor has always worn something to declare his difference from members of the audience, although, as in the case of modern Realism, this difference is so subtle as to be almost imperceptible. Yet difference there surely is, because costume, like all the other tools in the stage machine, must symbolize. Costumes, as we notice through a study of theatre history, can make an actor look larger than a human being by raising him on stilts or increasing the height of his head with extended headdress; they can make him look wider, and thus more imposing, by extensions of shoulders and arm garments. The actor's face and head can be changed into all sorts of shapes and meanings through the use of masks, wigs, and false hair or through its pale descendant, painted makeup. Some periods of theatre history used what was regarded as the best court dress; some have used archeological and historical reproduction; and some have worn practically no costume at all in an effort to find a neutral body.

Lighting. The history of lighting in the theatre is not as extensive a study as is, for instance, scenery and costuming, but the director must be fully aware of what was done in order to more fully comprehend dramatic literature and historical stage production. The fact that audiences of the Greek theatre, the Roman theatre of Plautus and Terence, the Medieval street theatre, and the Elizabethan public playhouse all saw plays in daylight tells us much about the workings of the plays and their productions. Likewise, to see the Renaissance drama in candlelight as did Shakespeare's audiences at Blackfriars theatre (one of the first indoor playhouses in England), or at the Teatro Olimpico, or at Drury Lane in Garrick's day, is to help us understand intimacy, confinement, and how "soft" lighting can create a rare beauty of its own. And to be aware of the gas lighting of the nineteenth century is also to comprehend the enormous revolution in lighting when theatres shifted to electrical power and control. To view lighting only as it is used today is to miss its historical significance as a theatrical device and a manipulator of audience perceptions. Why burn torches in midday as was done in street theatre in the fifteenth and sixteenth centuries? In order to get to the "guts" of a play of any era, a director must study how lighting or other effects were used at that time.

Sound. The reed and stringed instruments of the Greeks; Shakespeare's live musicians above the stage and on the stage as actors; the Drottningholm's cannonball track above the stage to make thunder; the nineteenth-century's orchestral background to the melo- (music) drama—all these are design ideas, some so thoroughly embedded that they become conventions plays could not do without. We are so accustomed to hearing music as part of a movie sound track that we take it for granted as a convention and we are startled to hear a film deliberately designed without such a score. Can you hear the sound of an actor's voice in a huge Greek amphitheatre? From a Roman platform in the context of a fair? From a scaffold erected on a street for the commedia dell'arte? From the intimate forestage of a 600-seat Georgian theatre? From the stage of an enormous 3000-seat nineteenth-century stage? The motion picture is largely a visual experience: we watch the face and eyes of a character through close-ups, and in this way we come to know him intimately. *In contrast, the stage is largely an aural experience, for we are moved intensely by the live human voice and less so by what we see.*

The study of theatre history, then, as distinct from the study of dramatic literature, is the study of variations in the use of staging concepts—variations that have been extensive. Thus, a director who is not also a student of theatre history can have only a superficial understanding of the major tools through which he makes his creative statements. You can readily see that this knowledge is necessary for the staging of historical drama, but you must also be aware that it is of enormous value in the staging of modern drama simply because your knowledge of *what is possible* in making theatre can be greatly extended.

SYNTHESIS

General Design Versus Specific Design

Stage design means making something for the stage *by intention* rather than leaving the effect to accident. This definition implies that stage design is an art form, and consequently must have unity, coherence, proportion, arrangement, selection, economy, grace, and rhythm. A director's visual sense, like a costumer's or a scenic artist's, must be highly refined in order to be capable of perceiving the essential elements of form that contribute to the making of symbolic representations.

Design, therefore, is always a *specific thing,* though a particular design may be stated so simply that it appears to have a general quality. But if what is placed on a stage is too loose, too free, if it lacks an interesting arrangement of line and mass, we cannot, as audience, perceive it at all. Thus, if a director-designer simply places materials on the stage without conceiving their effect, he will not make a statement we can call design, for they will have no relationship to other aspects of the context.

As previously mentioned, the director's role in the theatre in the twentieth century is *to bring about a synthesis in design: to place actors in relationship not just to each other but to the materials on the stage* in a coordinated design that could make the meanings of a play not only much clearer but much more exciting. In the latter part of the nineteenth century, Appia and Craig had developed the concept of synthesis, that is, one person should do all the physical designs of scenery, costuming, and lighting. But what also became clear was that if he were to control the physical production completely, he would also have to control the actors. Thus, the concept of the director as a master-designer was born. Since then, although the one-man autocrat has been rare in practice, the concept of synthesis has been well established, for it is the only way specific design can be controlled.

Balance and Imbalance in Synthesis

Balance is at the heart of the concept of synthesis. *Without balance in the media brought together, without the most careful joining of playscript, actors, and designs, there can be no synthesis.* This statement does not at all imply that a production must have these in equal parts, and must look like a product of a vegetable juice blender— an undefined reddish mixture. Instead, a production should be more like a well-conducted symphony in which the conductor brings out at appropriate times, and with appropriate strengths, the various components of his orchestra—now the violins, now the horns, now the cellos, now the woodwinds—while he is blending the whole into a sensitive, harmonic, and absorbing complex.

It is easier to see the nature of balance by looking at imbalance in production. Among the factors that contribute to imbalance, the following occur so frequently that they are worth pointing out as production traps: (1) self-conscious directing; (2) underdesign; (3) overdesign.

Self-conscious directing. When we watch a production, if we are too aware of the mechanics, *too aware of a striving for effect,* we are watching self-conscious directing. Instead of being drawn into the inner story-line and receiving the production with unbroken empathy on the level of our imaginations, we are disconcerted and distracted by a director who lays a production onto a playscript rather than *pulls it out of* the playscript. Thus, his blocking may be mechanically contrived rather than organically embedded in dramatic action, or the designs may be too self-conscious, drawing audience attention away from the actors. It can be said that directing is the art of reducing distraction in the imaginations of viewers in order to leave those imaginations free to do their own work. By pushing too hard for effect in the wrong way, the effect is lost. The focus of an audience must always be placed on the human values deriving from the playscript and not on the mechanics of projecting those values.

Underdesign. When a director is not thoroughly aware of what part visual design plays in play production, *he may settle for a much less effective statement than a play needs for its best fulfillment.* When this happens, such a production will lack vitality or enough symbolization to project the play into the imaginations of an audience. Theatre as distinct from drama means the actual live presentation of a play before an audience through *theatrical* means; it is not merely a play read for an audience. The values are very different. Some critics of modern Shakespearian productions maintain that far too many are overproduced, that they cannot "hear" the play because there is too much scenic enhancement. What they are probably saying is that they do not like theatre very much as a production art but are enamored of the text as a piece of literature that must be preserved at all cost. If we, as audience, get hung up over Shakespearian wordage, it may not be at all because of the elaborateness of the production but more likely because of the difficulty with an archaic language. Underdesign may perhaps make a Shakespearian production more easily heard, but it may lose the very essence of what is most Shakespearian about it which only the "vulgarity" of theatre can reproduce. Underdesign and simplicity of design are not the same thing. *Simple design can be highly organic and can intensely arouse imagination.* The director's goal is to release imagination in an audience, and he must find the necessary symbols for doing that with each play he produces.

Overdesign.   The greatest danger that occurs when a director can work with skilled designers is *doing too much.* Each designer, as a matter of course, wants to make his own design as effective as possible; and when a costumer, a scene designer, and a lighting designer are also involved, the whole problem of balance is intensified. *The principal danger is that of overwhelming the actors* who have difficulty enough in holding their own against the dynamics of visual effects. It is in controlling this situation, like controlling the balance in acting, that the director exerts a primary force on production. But the great problem is that, as with actors, he must work through the imaginations of others (the designers); and it is in guiding these imaginations, not in dictating their direction, where his primary work as a director-designer is done. *Overdesign can be ruinous because it stultifies audience imagination by depriving it of focus on the intrinsic values of a play.* An audience can all too easily be swept away by spectacle, with the consequent loss of the play as a total theatrical experience.

Counterpoint in Synthesis of Design

At first glance, it would seem possible for a director to achieve synthesis in the areas of visual design—set, costume, and light—by bringing the designers to the same point of view regarding the emphasis to be made in a production; that all a director would need to do would be to declare the emphatic points. Such a procedure, however, not only does not exploit the design possibilities, but it may actually stultify audience imagination and cause distraction by too obvious overloading at the points of emphasis.

Although a director and his designers must have a mutual understanding of a basic common direction, *full exploitation of visual effects lies not in the likeness of the designs but in their difference.* You will understand this idea better after the discussion of the design process in Major Project 3, but at this point you should appreciate the fact that *arousal of imagination frequently depends on clash and conflict in the visual effects, not on repetitive or seemingly harmonious statements. As characters clash in a play, so must the various elements of visual design.*

A simple example of how *counterpoint* can work is in a production of a historical play that uses an abstract setting, realistic costumes based on clothing of the period, and lighting with strongly contrasted highlights and shadows—all to the accompaniment of modern jazz as musical background. As you can see, an audience will be disconcerted by the lack of expected harmony, with the consequent awakening of fresh imagery of all sorts. If the acting is strong and very much alive, this theatrical experience can be a truly exciting one.

The theatre is an attack on the senses as well as on the mind, and without sense-awakening approaches to design, the basic nature of theatre is lost.

Counterpoint as a design approach does not in any way imply that all production must be highly melodramatic and theatrical; it merely suggests that different areas of design can do different things, and that *it is the total effect the director must work for—an effect that is disconcerting rather than restful.*

Counterpoint is, therefore, an important principle in design. The director who does his own designing must give intensive consideration to this point because he is a ready victim to the obvious in design. When he may think he is moving his audience with intensive design emphasis, he may merely be hitting an idea on the head with a sledgehammer and thus driving it away from imaginative audience reception. *Do not wallow in design emphasis; "counterpoint" it.*

EXERCISE

1. If you have not already done so, read Richard Southern's *The Seven Ages of Theatre.* This will give you an excellent idea of the concepts of symbolization and convention in various historical periods and in cultures very different from our own.
2. Apply "symbolization" and "stage convention" to *The Crucible* in a class discussion.
   a. Why is *The Crucible* not an everyday reality, but a symbol in play form?
   b. List as many symbols from the play as you can find.
   c. How is the title of *The Crucible* symbolic?
   d. What are the conventions in staging that can be used for this play?
   e. How would *The Crucible* have been staged in Shakespeare's day? Is that sort of production still valid?
3. How can *The Crucible* be overdesigned? If you read the review's of the first production in New York, you would know why Arthur Miller restaged it in a much simpler way. What do you think he accomplished by doing so? Is underdesign of this play quite possible?
4. What counterpoints would you propose in staging *The Crucible?*
5. Discuss "symbolization" as a concept.

CHAPTER TWENTY-ONE
DIRECTOR'S OPTIONS 1
Choice of the stage

Although the goal of Communication 3 is the mastering of the coordination-synthesis process in designing a production, you must, before you can approach the designer—either the designer in yourself or persons other than yourself—be keenly aware of the full range of possibilities and options open to you as a director. Many students study the areas of design through specialty courses without actually seeing how these courses overlap, and how they may be similar in approach and arrive at similar concepts. But since the concept advocated here is counterpoint in design, the director must penetrate as deeply as he can into the differences in options available to him. The range is great, and when to use which ones is an important part of a director's decision making.

What follows in this chapter is a detailed examination of options in the choice of the stage. As you will note, this option, as well as those in the following chapters, is developed here in close relationship to the historical backgrounds outlined in the last chapter. The intention now is to show you not only how you can apply theatre history to the designing process, but also to give you an active idea of how your imagination must work if you are to preside as the leader in the process of coordination.

One rule is necessary in approaching this and the following two chapters. *Do not take anything for granted, but argue it with yourself and with others* until you have declared solid positions of your own on each of the many options open to the director.

THE TWENTIETH-CENTURY STAGE MACHINE

No age has ever had such a highly developed stage machine as our own. Many of our recently built theatre plans, both for professional purposes as well as for educational training, not only have flexible stages where the architectural form of the stage can actually be changed, but they also have two or three theatres of different shapes and sizes where different sets of aesthetic values prevail. However, today's problem does not lie in the flexibility of the machine but in the same old indecipherable question: "How can audience imagination be excited?"

The stage as a tool of production in today's theatre has probably undergone the greatest shift in concept of all the areas of design. Whereas past ages had fixed stages on which to mount productions, our age is characterized by its concept of flexibility; that is, it is now assumed that no one stage form can do the work for all the historical and modern drama being produced. Consequently, a major set of options open to a director lies in his choice of a specific stage form for a particular play. This fact does not imply that the theatre in which he works does not have a permanent stage form built into the structure, for it probably does (usually proscenium in style); but if a director is to follow recent methods of production, he will find himself altering the stage form to meet the requirements of the other options, or finding a place to play outside his established theatre.

Four distinctive architectural stages merit discussion here: (1) proscenium, (2) arena, (3) open-thrust, and (4) forestage-proscenium. The order of discussion does not indicate any preference but has been deteremined by logical progression. The term *found space* might have been added to this list because it is still in use these days, born as it was in the 1960s, to describe whatever audience-actor relationship a director decides to use, whether it is a theatre, a church, a hall, a garage, etc. It is not discussed here, however, because the use of such space, no matter what label may be attached to it, probably falls into one of the four major categories.

Proscenium Stage

Although the dominant hold of the *proscenium stage* as the principal convention for presenting plays in our time has weakened a good deal since the mid-1950s, especially in college theatre productions, it is still very much with us and probably will be for some time to come. As a matter of record, new theatres are still being built with this stage as the architectural form. Because you are already familiar with many of its workings from your previous study in this book, it is being discussed here first.

To repeat, *if you comprehend the theory behind this stage, you will be better able to see the workings of the other stages* discussed later in the chapter. Do not take the proscenium stage for granted because it is familiar to you, but read the following material carefully, checking it against your present knowledge of this stage.

The proscenium stage as a convention is basically *illusory;* that is, it has the inherent capacity of creating the illusion of the real world we see every day. We sit in front of it and are expected to believe that what we see taking place through that rectangular hole cut in the stage wall is so close to an imitation of life that we can forget we are in a theatre. This illusion is heightened because we cannot see any changes of scenery made since *"the wall"* intentionally hides all the machinery, and either a curtain is closed or the lights are extinguished so that we will not be distracted. Furthermore, to reinforce the sense of illusion, the lights in the auditorium are turned off while a performance is in progress, so that we cannot see other members of the audience except for the backs of their heads as we sit behind them. In this sense, *the experience is something like reading a novel, something we do alone;* but by hearing responses from other members of the audience, we still feel part of a group.

This experience of the darkened, picture-frame theatre has been confiscated by motion pictures, which in many ways do a much better job because they can use unlimited scenic backgrounds, can employ the close-up (thus bringing the actor far closer visually to an audience), and can amplify sound so that hearing, even in delicate nuance, is never a problem. Movies can also maintain audience attention at a very high level through the techniques of moving the camera and making instantaneous changes of scene. *As an illusory device, the proscenium stage is now a poor cousin to the motion picture.*

Because of this competition with the movies, the proscenium stage in the twentieth century has been much pressured by other forms. The first attack came in the development of new scenic approaches that since mid-century have all but removed the nineteenth-century box-setting convention and replaced it with fragmentary walls, set pieces, and even projected scenery. Thus, this trend has altered an aesthetic that requires actual reproduction of places and has moved us toward a new one based on *suggestion* of those places, all in the interest of exciting audience imagination by forcing it to complete what has been left out. Architectural units—platforms, steps, etc.—have come into wide use in an attempt to create verticality on the stage and, in this way, to overcome its flatness—flatness because everyone in the audience sees the same dimensions from its frontal position. So many alterations in the use of scenic materials on the proscenium stage have been made in recent decades that we must accept the fact that the proscenium stage has outlived its day, and that designers have been doing everything they can to overcome this stage convention while still using it as the established form.

Nevertheless, because painted cloth on frames can still excite audiences, it is hard to believe that other forms can completely replace this device that took over 300 years to perfect.

Perhaps one manifestation of the movement away from the proscenium is the building of small playhouses—university theatres, for example—which seat only 400 to 600 spectators. Even though such houses may be built in the proscenium style, there is a question as to how conscious most of the audience actually is of the proscenium. The opening, though it may be of standard dimensions (32' × 18'), is so large in this small theatre in relation to the audience area that the arch effect literally does not exist for most of the audience. Broadway play reviewers, a group that has not pushed the new concepts, have probably seldom truly experienced the closed, framed effect of the proscenium stage because, by sitting so close to the stage, they have literally been "within" the frame. It might be said that in the twentieth century only the back-of-the-house or the balcony viewer has had much of a proscenium-arch experience—the "removed" illusory experience. That theatre-goers attending "thrust" theatres still prefer to sit facing the front of such stages, rather than on the sides, indicates the hold of the old proscenium convention.

Blocking suggestions.   Both composition and movement on the proscenium stage have been discussed extensively in Communication 1, where it was assumed that if the learning director understood the concept of the proscenium, he could easily move to other forms. In brief, the concept of composition and movement on the proscenium stage is illusory; that is, it must *appear* to be lifelike, although some very definite conventions must be observed.

Thus, as noted above, compositions on this stage are largely open to the audience, with the apex usually placed upstage. Actors can, of course, turn their backs to an audience, but such positions must be momentary simply because an audience wants to watch the frontal actor in order to follow his reactions and because it cannot hear very well the lines that may be thrown upstage. Just as furniture pieces are placed in open positions, so must the actor place himself in positions of that sort as often as possible. But this opening front also necessitates deemphasis, which can be brought about by back positions, using the weak upstage corners, standing behind furniture, etc.

One rule, however, seems to dominate the use of this stage: *no actor must appear to violate the proscenium plane by walking through it toward the audience or appear to be outside the prescribed lifelike lines of the setting.* This rules does not mean that actors cannot look directly toward an audience or face that way, but it does suggest that compositions should be arranged (with downstage placement of secondary actors, for instance) so that they will not appear to be in violation of proscenium logic. It does suggest that an actor who takes a position at either corner of the stage gazing out into space makes a poor composition because it implies that the actor is facing a wall (the imaginary proscenium wall) and is thus doing an eccentric rather than a lifelike thing.

The convention of the proscenium stage, is, therefore, *an appearance of reality,* not reality itself. No matter how lifelike a play may seem on this stage, *it is never life itself.*

Arena Stage

Although theatre-in-the-round or the *arena stage,* in which the audience tightly surrounds the acting area, has never been established as a major stage, it has had a popular life, not only in community and educational theatres but in some professional circumstances as well, especially "dinner" theatres. Like the proscenium stage, it was first seen as an illusionistic stage in its conventions; but recent users have greatly extended its possibilities, perhaps associating it more closely with the night club or cafe presentational stage to which it is definitely related.

This stage came into use in the late 1930s out of a desire to produce plays on low budgets during the years of economic depression. Since scenery was eliminated, it appeared, in its earliest uses to be even more lifelike than the proscenium stage—like a play in someone's living room.

But another convention operates in arena staging that tends to break down its illusory elements: members of an audience can fully see and watch many other members of an audience. This "panavision" creates the paradox of an audience watching lifelikeness of a very subtle sort take place in front of them at the same time it is participating in an obvious *communal* experience. When an audience surrounds a play, it is performing one of the oldest rituals of mankind: the tribe standing or sitting in a circle around its ritual dancers, its medicine man, its heroes who move around the fire in the center.

Thus, *the intimacy of arena staging is its prime convention,* for the audience can sense the actor in a very personal way: his breathing, his perspiration, his body sounds, even the shower of his spittle when he speaks vigorously. It is a kind of motion picture in live stage form. Yet the experience actually goes beyond that of the movie because it has no such barrier as the lifeless projection screen and can exhibit the flesh-and-blood actor in close-up to the voyeurism of an audience. The participatory-theatre experimentation of the 1960s greatly depended on this "touching" possibility of actors and members of the audience.

But how real is it all? Again, *arena staging gives only the appearance of reality.* The room created in the acting area may look like a real room, the food consumed by the actors may be real food, the costumes worn may be genuine clothes, the speeches the audience hears spoken in low tones and even whispered may seem realistic in the extreme. Yet all this is not life itself, for a play is always an artificial thing that involves selection and exaggeration (less than life as well as more). One of the techniques in arena style is for the actors to begin playing at a low level—as close to reality as possible—in order to draw the audience into the illusion, and then to raise the level gradually in size and proportion until the acting resembles what is seen on the proscenium stage. *Theatre-in-the-round is not for the inexperienced amateur but for the capable and trained actor.*

Another convention that the director must be aware of in using this form is the specific location of the acting area. Should the actors stand on the same level as the first row of the audience? Should they be at least six inches or more below? Should they be a foot or more above the floor level of the first row? Such a decision is crucial because the separation of the stage from the audience, which lowering or raising can accomplish, will subtly modify the convention. The raised stage may so set him apart from the audience that the result is a *platform stage,* which may no longer be considered intimate or illusory. In this instance, the actor will loom over the members of the audience, part of whom will now look up at him. From this view, he may no longer appear to be just another member of the audience going through a dramatic experience but may now be viewed as a kind of *superbeing—an actor.* By raising the stage, the theatre-in-the-round may be converted from an illusory aesthetic to a nonillusory one in which the audience's experience can be very different. The circular location of the audience is the first convention of the arena stage, to be sure, *but the second is surely the level of the stage.* The director must be aware of the changing aesthetics when he manipulates the playing area.

Moreover, the fact that an audience sits on four sides is no reason to limit set design to furniture alone. You should think of this stage as having all the potentials of a circus arena, with vertical exploitation one of its important extension possibilities. Thus, this stage, just as with the proscenium, becomes a cube which can be occupied dramatically and theatrically not only by actors but *also by look-through scenery.* Anything goes as long as it stays within the logic of its aesthetic. Placing covered scenery on this stage would certainly obscure audience vision, but when skeletal frames are introduced you have both good vision and the suggestion of Baroque scenery. Looking through such frames is no problem at all for audiences, for we actually see much in real life through interrupted views. You must learn to exploit this stage in every possible way, for the communal theatre has great potential for our times because it is quite different from motion pictures or television.

Blocking suggestions.   It should now be apparent to you why we emphasized organic blocking (using the tools of illustration for purposes of communication from director to actor) over the pictorial in our discussions on composition, movement, etc., in Communication 1. If you understand the organic concept, you will have little difficulty in arranging on the arena stage everything from the groundplan to composition and movement. The basic principle is still the same: *By arousing the imagination of the actor through insuring his understanding of and sensitivity to given circumstances and dramatic action, the imagination of the audience can be stimulated to strong empathic action.*

The pictorial requirements in arena staging are fairly obvious. The four-sided audience demands a four-sided look by the director. Or better still: *forget* the one-sided view of the proscenium stage and direct the actors into intense character-action relationships and the compositions will largely take care of themselves. Two principles of all good composition should be kept in mind: (1) play the limits of the stage on an obstacle course, avoiding climactic compositions as much as possible; and (2) play a cat-and-mouse game in composition; now one character pursues and the other retreats, and vice versa. Actors will frequently turn outward toward one section or another of an audience as the most natural thing to do in getting away.

If the center point of the stage is thought of as the center of a clock, variety in composition is infinite (see Figure 52). A groundplan can readily be designed that will fan out from the center (see Figure 53). The use of a center object approachable from all sides will avoid the deadlines of a cleared space and will provide the obstacle course so necessary in a dynamic groundplan.

FIGURE 52   FIGURE 53

Note that Figure 53 has four major stage areas. By using the areas in combinations with only occasional use of one area, a dynamic interlocking of the stage will result, and all four audiences will see the play equally well. An actor's back facing one part of the audience is an accepted convention of this stage; but this rather extreme body position can be kept at a minimum by frequent shiftings to other body positions. When back positions must be used as the best illustration of a dramatic action, the *neutral corners* (entrances to the stage where no audience is seated) can be employed effectively. The problem of quick entrances and exits on the arena stage is always difficult because of the distance through the audience that must be traversed, but this problem can often be solved by occasional use of entrance-walkways as acting areas: an actor starts speaking on the way in, or stops halfway out to give an exit line; or through the use of *vomitories*—entrance-ways underneath audience seating—where actors can enter the acting area directly without being seen.

Again, it must be emphasized that the purposes of organic blocking, as stressed in Communication 1, is to *free the dramatic action. If the actors understand their intense relationships to one another, good blocking cannot help but materialize.* This blocking can then be modified to meet the demands of pictorial necessity and variety.

Open-Thrust Stage

Open-thrust is used here to describe a theatre setup in which audiences are seated on three sides of a raised stage, with *the stage backed by a wall on the fourth.* It is open because no portion of the stage is concealed from the audience (like the arena); that is, everything must take place *before the audience;* it is "thrust" because it juts out from a concealing wall *into* the audience area.

This is the classical stage, the oldest form we know. A version of it was used by the Greeks in the fifth century B. C., and it was also the stage of Shakespeare and of classical Chinese opera. Its revival in the twentieth century has come about in part because of the increased emphasis on the production of historical drama that had been written for this convention. But there is good reason to believe that it has won acceptance in recent years more as a reaction against the two-dimensionality and illusory quality of both the proscenium stage and the electronics—the "shadow" projections of movies and television. In the 1960s it became part of the search for a viable ritual-stage that could express our age.

The dynamics of the open-thrust convention lie in its plastic, sculpturelike capabilities, for the actor is three-dimensional in every way. The theatre experience is thus greatly heightened in contrast to the proscenium style, for *it puts the live actor back on the stage in full force where his energy and radiance are dynamic realities and are not withdrawn or are merely behavioristic experiences.* The open-thrust stage could have the same illusory aesthetic as is possible in arena staging when the actors and audience are arranged on the same floor level; but its *basic concept is that of a raised stage.* Thus, *the intention is not representational but presentational.*

Presentational is a term commonly used to describe the nonillusory theatre experience. This aesthetic—the oldest in the history of the theatre—makes no attempt to fool audiences into believing that they are looking at the real thing. "This is the theatre," it says, "and here is a stage, here are actors, and here is an audience, and what you see and hear takes place *only* in this theatre; it resembles life, yes, but it is definitely *not* life." Consequently, this stage is in sharp contrast to the concept of the proscenium stage where life and what happens in the theatre have been confused. *Theatre as a pure art form distinct from life and stated in obvious theatre conventions is at the basis of the concept.* The audience may become involved in a play, but it can never forget it is in a theatre—a place where one watches play-making and not a peep show for a slice-of-life.

The treatment of the back wall of the stage is an important aspect of the open-thrust stage because it provides the background against which the play is seen. This wall may be designed as permanent architecture when the theatre is built, as in Greek and Elizabethan theatres; it may be partly architectural and partly painted, as in Chinese classical opera or in Japanese Noh staging; or it may be even a curtained wall, as in the extant drawings of early Renaissance playings of Seneca and Plautus. But *whatever form it may take, it provides a more or less permanent facade against which the play is performed.* Whatever alterations that may be made from play to play are made in the acting area with the use of temporary materials either carried on by actors or placed before the play begins.

The open-thrust convention places full responsibility on the playscript and on the actors and, in a sense, frees both from the confines of the visual statement of exact place. Thus, the "stageplace" can be anything the actors with their costumes and properties declare it to be. The suggestion made by some early twentieth-century scholars that signs were needed on Shakespeare's stage to tell audiences where scenes were taking place can easily be seen as nonsense today because we know through the use of this stage that audiences can move quickly from one imagined place to another with only the slightest suggestion—that being either an opening line, a property such as a military banner, or an explicit costume such as armor. Modern plays present no more difficulties about place than do historical dramas, and, as a result, *we have begun to question the validity of exact place: Does it confine, more than release, an audience's imagination?*

Lighting has become an important convention in the use of this stage, particularly with modern plays, as we have not yet given up the convention of the rising and falling stage curtain in the proscenium theatre to mark interruptions in the stage action. Consequently, plays are still being written with this dramatic cutoff in mind. On the open-thrust stage, as well as on the arena stage, light control is presently used to function as the curtain, with actors entering and taking places in the dark and departing in the same way. When plays are written for it—and the experiments of the 1960s turned up a few—characters will probably be given reasons for entering the scene and leaving at its end, as in historical drama, and with this technique the lighting conventions could change radically.

Another modern convention that has been used occasionally with this stage is the vomitory as described in the discussion above on the arena stage. Before the introduction of this convention, actors either entered at the rear of the stage or approached the stage through the audience as in arena staging. The vomitory solved the problem of quick entrances because a large number of actors could be "vomited" onto the stage area very quickly and then disappear at the end of a scene within a few seconds. The entrance and exit tempos of the proscenium stage were thus preserved almost intact.

The old convention of "scenes above," as in Shakespeare's theatre, has been retained with only minor modifications through the use of backwall structures that permit actors to appear above the stage on scaffolding or through windows in the stage wall. *Vertical playing space thus becomes an inherent convention in this stage form.* Even modern plays with their simultaneous use of upstairs and downstairs can be satisfactorily accommodated through skeletal look-through structures placed in the acting area.

Blocking suggestions.   Composition and movement on this stage follow the same usage as in arena staging, with one major exception: *the neutral rear wall permits positions similar to those used on the proscenium stage—a pitfall for the inexperienced director because he too readily assumes he is working on a proscenium stage and encourages his actors to take much too frequent frontal positions.* This is catastrophic because it nullifies the function of this type of stage as a fully participative audience ritual and instead assumes the objective-observation function of the proscenium stage. "Spin the wheel" and "face out from the center" are the major suggestions here. You must learn to see the acting from all three sides and to encourage actors to open up their illustrations to all three audiences and not to just one. If you follow the principles of organic blocking, as outlined in Communication 1, you will have little difficulty in showing a play to a multiple audience.

The placing of steps around the perimeter of this stage will aid greatly in achieving variety in stage levels, particularly if two or three steps are employed. Lower steps can be used to deemphasize secondary characters and higher steps to focus strong emphasis on the principals. The center of the stage becomes the strongest position since it is equidistant from all parts of an audience. And you must learn to play the full limits of the stage space in order to enhance the climactic compositions when characters are finally brought together.

Forestage-Proscenium

Although other terms might be used to describe this stage, *forestage-proscenium* is used here because it tells us the way in which it has come about in recent years through joining proscenium conventions with those of the open-thrust stage. Nominally, it is a raised proscenium stage with a forestage erected in front of it—the same stage that was used in seventeenth, eighteenth, and nineteenth-century theatres when the pure proscenium stage was in its making. For this reason *forestage-proscenium* might be regarded as a return to the past because it again moves the primary playing area forward of the proscenium line after nearly 300 years of watching the play gradually retreat behind that line. However, it is closer to the fact to see it as a natural evolution from the pure proscenium stage.

As a modified proscenium stage, then, audiences will sit in the frontal position, although the side areas of ovular proscenium auditoriums now are given better sightlines than they ever enjoyed with the pure proscenium stage. The *forestage-proscenium* is an adapted form because it is neither fish nor fowl but tries to be both. It has undoubtedly come back into use in an attempt to modernize the proscenium theatre.

The conventions on this stage are therefore obvious: the proscenium wall conceals the use of stage rigging for the spectacle of painted scenery, while at the same time actors, who in this convention play largely on the forestage, appear to be more plastic, more three-dimensional to audiences. The proscenium arch itself is much reduced in value and may, by the judicious use of masking scenic pieces, appear to be blocked off entirely. A stage that seems to be very deep can thus be achieved, similar in kind although not in dimension to those of the late eighteenth and early nineteenth centuries, such as New York's Bowery Theatre with a phenomenal depth of 128 feet. The Baroque scenic tradition can thus continue in full force on this stage, and the acting can be done both behind the arch and in front of it, allowing a director to greatly expand or contract his stage as he may see fit.

If the forestage is deep enough, this stage can also be brought close to the open-thrust aesthetic, for architectural backwalls and curtained walls can shut off the upstage area. The only problem is the largely frontal audience. The use of additional projections from the forestage, which places the actor farther out in the audience, an help to remedy this situation, although such a stage can never achieve the same feeling provided by the pure open-thrust form.

Blocking suggestions.   Proscenium and open-thrust blocking procedures must both be employed on this stage because of its combination of frontal and circular presentation depending on which areas of the stage are in use. Proscenium blocking tends to work better in upstage positions because of the hearability factor which must enter into any consideration of such a large stage space. Low volumes can be employed in extreme downstage positions but may not work at all when a scene is played upstage. Rather than create distorted hearing by raising volumes in the upstage positions and lowering them in downstage positions, the director can adjust the upstage or downstage blocking to meet the needs for volume, thus allowing the actor to concentrate on the dramatic action without worrying about oral projection.

As has been suggested above, the spectacle and dramatic value of a full use of the stage space can be very great. The director must, therefore, learn to use the extremes of the stage from far upstage to far downstage, from far right to far left. The actual physical distance between actors can take on significant meaning when used judiciously. In contrast, the director will also learn to exploit the intimacy of far-downstage positions, which can be collected and tightened by selected lighting for effective presentation of intense dramatic ideas.

EXERCISE

1. *The Crucible* has been played in various productions on several different types of stages, possibly all four discussed in this chapter. Discuss the following:
   a. Why does this play seem to be open to flexible staging? Do you think Miller conceived of it as a proscenium-style play, or did he deliberately open the structure to other staging possibilities?
   b. What are the advantages and disadvantages of playing *The Crucible* on (1) an arena stage, (2) an open-thrust stage, (3) a forestage-proscenium?
   c. How would you approach the blocking of *The Crucible* on any of the stages mentioned in (b)?
   d. Which of the four stages would you choose? Why?
2. How can you vary the arrangement of the open-thrust stage? What would happen if you thrust the stage too far into the audience by making it much deeper than it is wide? If the stage were made 20 by 20 feet and you could vary the height of each of the four 10 × 10 foot sections, what would happen in projecting a play? Can you think of a play that would conform to such a stage?
3. Discuss the differences in the effect the following arena stages would have:
   a. One that is six inches below the first audience row
   b. One that is two feet below the first audience row
   c. One that is on the level of the first audience row

4. Can you identify the stages represented in Figure 54? Note that each one is part of a circle with the degree markings representing the size of the audience areas.

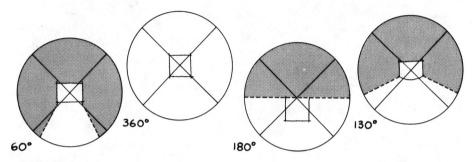

FIGURE 54

GAME OF VISUAL PERCEPTION 3: CHOICE OF STAGE
(See pages 77-78)

For each photograph answer the following:
a. What is the type of stage and the position of the audience?
b. How does the three-dimensionality required on the proscenium stage differ from that on the thrust?
c. How is "intimacy" gained in each staging represented in the photographs?
d. Does the thrust stage "say something" to audiences in these stagings?

PHOTO 27   *Children of a Lesser God* (Medoff)

PHOTO 28   *Come Back, Little Sheba* (Inge)

PHOTO 29 *Resurrection of Jackie Cramer* (Gagliano)

PHOTO 30 *The Creation of the World. . .* (Miller)

PHOTO 31   *LaRonde* (Schnitzler)

PHOTO 32   *Alice in Wonderland* (Becker, Thomas)

PHOTO 33 *Child's Play* (Marasco)

PHOTO 33a *Stuck* (Shank)

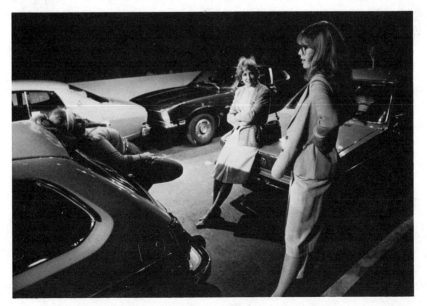

CHAPTER TWENTY-TWO
DIRECTOR'S OPTIONS 2
Scenery, properties, and lighting

Now that you can see how the director's design function requires some very important decisions about what sort of stage to use in presenting certain plays, you are ready to look at the options open to you in deciding what kind of scenic materials to put on the stage you choose and how to light those materials. It should now be obvious that you can exert important leadership in shaping the direction of a play's physical production.

Again, you must keep in mind that the content of these chapters is not intended to substitute for extensive training in design, but only to point out to you the many paths open in staging a play. The more you know about what can be done, the more inventive and adventurous you will be in producing plays, since reaching audiences with fresh imagery depends on knowing thoroughly the tools with which you work.

OPTIONS IN STAGE SCENERY

As can readily be seen from the previous discussion on stages, if we think of scenery only as painted flats and drops, we can apply the term only to the pure proscenium stage and the forestage-proscenium. However, nowadays this meaning is too narrow because the open-thrust and the arena can both use staging pieces that modify acting areas; and although these modifications may be simple, they are nevertheless scenic in concept. The word *scenery* is actually derived from the Greek *skene* and Roman *scaena,* both of which stages had permanent architectural facades before which the actors performed. *We can define scenery, then, as any device which makes a change in a stage, starting with the stage floor.*

From this point of view, it is obvious that the director and the designer will approach each stage form in terms of its own concept and conventions. *Scenic design is, thus, both architecture and painting* and may be both at the same time. Five distinct types of scenery are delineated in the following pages: (1) painted, (2) architectural, (3) painted-architectural, (4) projected, and (5) fractionated.

Painted Scenery

You are probably most familiar with painted scenery, which dates in its continuous use from the sixteenth century. It consists of painted cloth mounted on frames, the type we still see in wing-and-drop settings, box settings, and set pieces (flats, ground rows, etc.) placed at any point on the stage. In its *commonest usage* it is *illusory* in concept with the intention of making such scenery appear to represent what we see in real life. Thus, it can be either *painted* architecture (interiors and exteriors), *painted* nature (wood scenes, etc.), or combinations of such content. In this sense, painted scenery is two-dimensional, like easel painting; but it is cut into many pieces and placed on the stage in such a way that it gives an audience an illusion of three dimensions, with depth as well as height and width. To heighten this three-dimensional effect, in its early usage the stage floor was raked upward from front to rear, thus forcing the perspective. As you can obviously see, such scenery required stage machinery (lines, pulleys, etc.) both for hanging it and moving it. Consequently, we have the changeable scenery associated with the proscenium stage where *the proscenium wall is used to conceal all the machinery* necessary to make quick and effective shifts from one represented reality to another.

The fact that this convention would have such a long life in the theatre—a life unbroken until the twentieth century—is not difficult to understand. The development of drama from the sixteenth to the twentieth centuries was a gradual approach toward photographic reproduction, an approach which reached its peak in the latter part of the nineteenth century, and in this development the statement of more and more exact places became part of the stage aesthetic. The new staging, that is, the staging as it has evolved in the last half century, has been a revolt against photographic reproduction of exact places, a revolt that has led to new stages and new scenic concepts.

The nineteenth and twentieth-century box-setting is, thus, painted scenery carried to the extreme of representation: the photographic reproduction of an interior. The painted walls and ceiling are made to look like the real thing in both color and texture; and the actual placement of the flats and jogs, slanted walls, slanted ceilings, exterior views placed outside windows and doors, etc. are all intended to increase the architectural illusion to a point where it is difficult to believe that one is not looking into a real room. Yet, of course, it is all make-believe, with the intention of fooling an audience. The adding of architectural pieces to these painted flats, such as real window frames, door frames and doors, wood molding, and wood-beam ceilings, increases the illusion of reality.

If the director is thoroughly aware of the history of this tradition and of its full exploitative possibilities he can understand more readily the departures from this convention, and he will also have a clearer idea of how and when to use such scenery in designing productions.

Architectural Scenery

Architectural scenery, as defined here, includes not only permanently built structures, such as the rear wall of an open-thrust stage, but also all structures that move upward from the flat stage floor and create a three-dimensional mass.

As pointed out above in the discussion on open-thrust stages, the rear wall of such stages *may be* part of the permanent architecture, like the altars in many churches, and arranged in such a way that it can serve a large body of plays as did the Elizabethan rear wall. It does not need to be a flat surface, but can be projected onto the stage, since the sides are open to the side audiences, as in Tanya Moiseiwitsch's design for the stage at the Stratford (Ontario) Festival Theatre. Thus, the wall may contain not only doors for entrances but also raised portions and approaching steps. The wall is, nevertheless, a permanent facade. Although a few theatres have been built in this manner, it is unlikely that it will become the common stage device in this century. However, the learning director must become fully aware of its concept and exploitative possibilities if he is to understand the nature of flexible stages.

Equally important as a concept is creating architecture through the use of platforms and steps. The Baroque scenic tradition developed the concept of moveable wings and drops and, later, walls and ceilings; the "new" staging of the twentieth century added the development of the stage floor, not as a painted or raked plane which had been a convention for 300 years, but *as an architectural mass.* Platforms and steps are always fabricated with hollow interiors; but the fact remains that they occupy real space, which makes them architectural in every sense of the word. The new concept, then, is of a three-dimensional stage with the capability of making the actor *visible to the audience at any level* within the rectangular prism or cube that composes the stage area. To know the values of such dramatic capabilities is to extend tremendously the director's use of the stage.

Painted-Architectural Scenery

Much of today's staging is a combination of both painted and architectural scenery. This combination has probably come about because today's theatre is transitional with no single established form. Thus, we use what is effective in both types of scenery, rarely using pure forms. However, only through understanding the pure form can the director decide how to best exploit a particular play. A spectator's imagination usually is easily aroused by fresh, dynamic impulses, but it can also be stultified by a too self-conscious use of scenic materials. The process is, as it always is in art, one of selection.

Projected Scenery

Projected scenery has evolved out of the twentieth century's development of electric light and its projection. Designers are still finding new ways of making statements after many years of experimentation, a fact which indicates that its full range of uses is yet unknown.

Among other things, we have learned that:

1. Projected scenery can take the place of both architectural and moveable scenery as a backing for a scene;
2. It can be used simultaneously in direct coordination with moveable or architectural scenery when projected on a screen either built into other scenery or mounted in front of it;
3. Moving picture projection as scenery with actors moving in front of it can provide unusual theatrical effects. Some uses have coordinated the actor and such moving scenery, producing the effect of the actor walking into and out of the projected, moving scene;
4. Projected scenery can be changed instantly, and multiple quick changes of location, as in moving pictures, are possible as they never have been previously;
5. Projected scenery lends itself readily to abstractions, increasing the symbolic uses of backgrounds. When multiple, simultaneous projections are used, a montage effect is possible; thus, it can be idea-building;
6. Projected scenery is comparatively very inexpensive to use.

From the preceding list, it would seem that projected scenery has an active future ahead. However, one of the drawbacks is that it imitates too readily the motion picture, and this imitation takes the theatre closer to a form it is trying to escape. Yet, in trying too hard to escape, the theatre may be only bypassing its own destiny, for the future may depend on an even closer liaison between these two forms. Whatever its future may be, a director must be fully aware of the freshness of this scenic option and must learn how and where it can be appropriately employed.

Fractionated Scenery

Fractionated scenery is used here for want of a better term to describe a popular form of staging that deploys several types of scenic pieces, some connected and some unconnected, with the intention of suggesting a room or other place with a minimum of scenic materials. Thus, such staging may use flats, cut flats (a piece of a wall), screens, platforms, step units, curtains, hanging drapes, suspended flat pieces of practical window frames, ground rows, selected rear backings, skeletal framings, or any other scenic devices.

A procedure used fairly frequently is to place whatever is used against a skycloth in order to convey a sense of greater space or to give the impression of seeing inside and outside simultaneously. *Fractionated scenery is, therefore, a direct move away from the representational effect of the box setting and a move toward simplified and abstract staging.*

There is no question about the advantages of this sort of scenic statement, since fractionated scenery possesses the power of releasing audience imagination by forcing it to complete necessary but omitted lines or to interpret and put to use any inherent symbolism that may reside in such fractionations. Therefore, the justification for such staging goes far beyond the practical limits of low-cost production or easy moveability of such settings in a multiscene play. Simplified realism of this sort can release the poetry in a play by giving the audience a free-flight experience instead of confining it to prosaic realities.

Fractionated staging can, thus, employ all the previous scenic options: painted, architectural, painted-architectural, and projected. Its free form may well account for its frequent use in contemporary scenic design.

Combining Scenery and Stage Choice

This section would not be complete without brief mention of the random options in scenery available to a director on the various stages. Thus, arena and open-thrust stages can use look-through scenery set upon the stage floor as well as architectural steps and platforms. Painted cloths (drops) can also be stretched *above* these stages to achieve effects similar to the "heavens" in the Elizabethan public theatres, actually the painted underside of the penthouse structure. Drapes or structural materials cannot only be suspended from above but may be pulled up from the stage floor, thus employing Baroque scenery but placing it in a different context than on the proscenium stage. Trap doors can be employed advantageously on these stages as well as on the proscenium and forestage-proscenium arrangements to lend a further dimension by implying other "places" beneath the stage. Moving scenery on turntables or tracks parallel to the curtain line can also be employed on the proscenium and forestage-proscenium setups to give the illusion of the actor moving great distances or of changing places in transit.

The intention here is by no means to make an exhaustive list of possibilities in the use of scenic ideas on these stages but rather to suggest the scope of designing activity in which a director must become involved. Part III will again consider these options in the discussion on individualization in stage production, but you should keep in mind that the stage as a machine can do anything you want it to do as long as you thoroughly know its limitations. Scenic design as a fresh statement can grow only out of your imaginative use of the broad range of materials available to you. You must study set design in depth if you are to become an effective director.

EXERCISE

1. *The Crucible* has been played on the proscenium stage with (a) highly developed, illusionistic box settings and (b) fractionated scenery made of curtains and screen units. Discuss the effect of each production. Which would you prefer? Why?
2. What colors and textures would you use on painted scenery for *The Crucible?*
3. If you were to stage *The Crucible* with projected scenery, what would you choose for the projections? What would be the effect of such a production?
4. If you were to stage *The Crucible* in an illusionistic manner, what sort of research would be needed to locate the appropriate set properties?
5. Would you use look-through scenery for staging *The Crucible* in arena style?
6. Could you stage *The Crucible* on either the open-thrust or arena stages with set properties made of plain, box-like cubes two feet high, wide, and deep? What would be the effect? What other geometric forms could be used and what would be their dimensions?

GAME OF VISUAL PERCEPTION 4: SCENERY
(See pages 77-78)

1. What is the function of the scenery in each photograph?
2. Why is "pictorial" scenery used less frequently in contemporary plays?
3. Can you "see" the following scenery in the photographs: architectural? painted? fractionated?
4. Can you "see" the three-dimentionality of the scenic devices?
5. Which production used a revolving stage?

PHOTO 34   *Undiscovered Country* (Schnitzler)

PHOTO 35   *Peer Gynt* (Ibsen)

PHOTO 36 *The Price* (Miller)

PHOTO 37 *Indians* (Kopit)

PHOTO 38   *Rosencrantz and Guildenstern Are Dead* (Stoppard)

PHOTO 39   *Servant of Two Masters* (Goldoni)

OPTIONS IN STAGE PROPERTIES

Definition

As Chapter 13 has already pointed out in some detail, there are two kinds of properties used on the stage: (1) set properties, associated closely with the definition of acting space and scenic ideas; and (2) hand properties, actually held in the hand by actors or capable of being held in the hand. Both are extremely important tools for the director because they can determine in a primary way how actors will find their illustrations of dramatic action. To repeat again the premise: *Imaginative use of properties, both set and hand, permits the actors to project sense imagery directly to an audience who then puts that imagery to work in its own imagination.* Because properties are used in such personal and individual ways, the director even more than the designer must give the most careful attention to their selection.

Set Properties

If you have studied this book from the beginning, you will remember that in Chapter 11, on the groundplan, it was emphasized that set properties occupy space and therefore determine a very great deal of what happens in the visible acting areas. The actual selection of a specific set property may be the designer's decision but not before the director and designer have decided *together* how much space such a property will occupy and what its nature, and thus its usability, will be. Carefully selected set properties will delineate the specifics of an obstacle course, which will, in turn, declare emphases in compositions and the nature and kinds of movements. Set properties are often handled by actors because they sit on them, lean over them or against them, walk around them, or sometimes actually move them. They also become animate in certain compositions, and their mass and shape are always factors in this animation. Reread the groundplan section and you will appreciate even more, at this point, why the director must make set properties a primary part of his designing vision.

In brief, the obvious functions of set properties are to delineate given circumstances and to provide common uses. In Realistic plays they are invaluable in showing subtle gradations in environments, and in most other plays they provide similar information although not on such a refined scale. Set properties are functional in their common uses as chairs, tables, beds, desks, benches, stools, cabinets, etc., but above all, as has already been suggested, they serve as obstacles in a groundplan to keep characters apart and to make it more difficult for them to reach one another, thus creating activity and illustration. Well-selected properties can greatly stimulate an actor's ideas about illustration.

The options open to a director, then, would consist of quantity (the number of set properties that can actually be used effectively), size, shape, mobility (can they be moved on the stage by an actor, or do they contain inherent movement?). A director also has a choice of real (archaeologically accurate) objects or abstract objects such as geometric forms. Whatever a director decides to do, he will probably select set properties in coordination with the scenery chosen for a particular play, since the design of one will tend to enhance the other.

Hand Properties

Hand properties as an element in design have also been treated extensively in Chapter 13, and little that is new can be added here. To reiterate: *Hand properties are the extension of the actor's arms and hands;* they are, thus, subtle tools of illustration because they possess capabilities of sensory illustration that the hands alone cannot provide. Any director who does not give primary attention to the selection of hand properties is merely ignoring one of the actor's principal tools of illustration.

For this reason, *the final selection is not a designer's decision but a director's oftentimes in consultation with his actors.* Hand properties can be modified and even changed as actors use them during a rehearsal period, and they should, therefore, not be set permanently before rehearsals begin. Furthermore, they should be selected in terms of the particular actor who is to use them. Remember: there are no *general* properties, only *specific* ones. A designer cannot possibly be as aware of this fact as can a director, who should regard the choice of such properties as his own particular province and look to their actual selection with the greatest care. Be meticulous! No one else can be except the actor.

In summary, hand properties are occasionally functional in their common uses, provide specific reflections of the given circumstances of the play, enhance the individual actor as an instrument by giving opportunities for fresh illustration other than through the use of the hands, are capable of making light (candles, flashlights) and sound (snapping a book shut), and have inherent mobility (visible liquids, eyeglasses, telephones, automatic weapons, books, flags, fans, etc.). The options open to a director concern type (size, weight, and shape), mobility, archaeological accuracy, and abstraction (use of a stick for a gun, a cane for a sword, etc.)

EXERCISE

Make a list of hand properties for use in Act II of *The Crucible.* What items did you add to the list beyond those specifically called for, such as the doll, chains to tie Proctor, whip, etc.? What can be done with hand properties associated with the fireplace?

GAME OF VISUAL PERCEPTION 5: PROPERTIES
(See pages 77-78)

1. What properties are actually required?
2. How can the hand properties be used to illustrate dramatic actions?

3. How do the environmental properties create moods?
4. Do the properties "help" the actors communicate dramatic actions?
5. Which properties are symbolic of place and which ones are symbolic of characters? Do any seem to be intrusions or "laid on"?

PHOTO 40 *Orpheus Descending* (Williams)

PHOTO 41 *The Philanthropist* (Hampton)

PHOTO 42
The Effect of Gamma Rays...
(Zindel)

PHOTO 43 *The Lady From the Sea* (Ibsen)

OPTIONS IN STAGE LIGHTING

Director-Designer Relationship

As with the design of properties, a director has a primary and personal concern for what happens with stage lighting because light has the greatest capability of giving an edge to the final statement of a scene's mood. If what is designed differs markedly from a director's intention with that mood, both the statement by the actor and the statement in the lighting will fight strongly against each other. *Stage lighting is not mere illumination but specific illustration of a very subtle sort, the sort that can reach an audience's imagination more quickly and more subliminally than an actor often can.*

In everyday life we know that light can stimulate delicate psychological feelings that affect us strongly; consequently, light in the theatre can affect us even more intensely because it has been intentionally selected. The director-designer relationship must, therefore, be a very close one, because *lighting design is the actual extension of the director's most sensitive and most personal vision.*

The director's training in stage lighting should be extensive because he should not only be able to visualize the scope of lighting but also have a firm technical knowledge of how to achieve what he wants. Lighting designers can, of course, add greatly to the possibilities in any one situation, but unless a director knows this tool firsthand, he will not be able to communicate to a designer what he feels and sees in a play.

Variables in the Problem of Design

However a director goes about acquiring his training in stage lighting, he will most certainly learn a great deal about the following options.

Illumination. The basic function of stage lighting is, of course, to make the actor visible to an audience. At first, this remark may seem to you a simpleminded statement, one that anyone could take for granted. However, such is not the case, for good illumination on the stage today means not only a large quantity of lighting equipment but also expert use of that equipment to heighten the effects of the actors *in movement.*

The problem is historical. When the English theatre moved indoors at the beginning of the seventeenth century, both actors and audiences were illuminated with the same light provided by overhead and sidewall candelabra. Subsequent development in the use of the stage, along with the increased emphasis on illusion in the stage picture, brought about not only a gradual separation of the stage from the house, with separate lighting provided for each, but also eventually the convention of the darkened house. The control of light became increasingly important as candlelight was superceded by oil lamps, which, in turn, were pushed aside in the nineteenth century in favor of gas, which finally gave way to the incandescent lamp. The unusually minute possibilities for control afforded by electricity revolutionized stage lighting practice and provided us with the theories under which we are presently working. However, the basic intention has always been the same—to make the actor readily visible to the audience.

Greater control of light on the stage, however, has not necessarily meant a better theatre experience. *"Hearability"* (an audience's capability of hearing actors), for instance, has a great deal to do with visibility. We have learned that when low lighting is used to achieve certain effects of mood, *the capability of hearing is reduced.* It is not that an audience lip reads what actors are saying, but more probably that feelings created by such light tend to cloud the hearing (a psychological problem). From another point of view, we know that too much light, now entirely possible because of improved lighting instruments and quantitative control, can reduce visibility; we lose contour in the faces of actors and, thus, we not only reduce hearing but also facial projection. Color has been long used in stage lighting as a technical convention, but we have discovered that it can be very tiring on the eyes, thus reducing both hearing and seeing. From the above, it should be clear that good illumination is not just a matter of turning on lights; it is the result of careful design for the appropriate circumstances of a play. *Selective visibility* is a good phrase for it.

Source considered. One of the remarkable coincidences in the development of the theatre is the invention of the incandescent lamp at approximately the same time as the shift in playwriting to the new style of Naturalism. Naturalism, of course, means strict verisimilitude to nature, and in the theatre it meant photographic reproduction. Only electric light made this goal possible. Lifelike sunsets and dawns were now realizable on the stage, and interior rooms could be lighted with accurate window effects, shadowed corners and ceilings, lamp effects, and lighted entranceways. When wall switches were turned on, rooms were immediately flooded with light. Chandeliers, wall brackets, lamps, fires flickering in fireplaces, and sunlight and moonlight were the motivating sources of the light, and audiences looked at an appearance of reality and accepted all the logic of the sources within its own sight. Any violations of the logic could be quickly detected and could, therefore, become distractions. If the lighting design was logical, the audience accepted the *source considered* and took it for granted. In the representational theatre, then, lighting must have all the appearances of accepted motivation because we are familiar with what we see and we believe in its reality.

Source not considered. The wave of Naturalism temporarily sidetracked *the oldest theory of lighting from a nonconsidered source.* Again, at first you may think this theory means merely turning on the lights without specific motivation from lamps, sunlight, etc., but it can mean much more than that. In contrast to representational light from a source considered, *nonconsidered source* is *presentational light,* or *light as it exists only in the theatre.* A spotlight that obviously comes from a projection booth at the rear of the house and is thrown on an actor is the most obvious example, but in general use it means that a motivating source for light is unimportant and, thus, is not considered.

Such light can come from above the actor, with the instrument concealed from the audience and with the intention of providing an illusory effect; but since the light is not motivated from any logical source it becomes purely conventional. *The actors are merely gathered in the light.* As an audience, we do not worry about where the light comes from—it just comes and we find other values to concern us.

Source not considered is the lighting used on open-thrust and arena stages and frequently on the forestage-proscenium convention, because parts of the stage picture can be selected from the total possible picture for certain scenes, with the light areas changing from one location to another as various parts of a stage are used. Thus, large stage areas can be cut into small stage areas, and grand scenes and intimate scenes can be played in sequence. The audience accepts the convention and focuses its attention on the dramatic action and not on the appearances of reality.

Composition in lighting.   Since stage lighting in modern theory and practice is provided by specific instruments and is not a general illumination from massive sources, the director-designer must be fully aware of the three-dimensional capability of lighting control. Actors and objects can be made highly plastic, with their depth emphasized. You will remember from the experiments in your lighting class that light thrown from the front tends to flatten faces, and that side light and back light, especially if unbalanced in quantity and color, will reveal their three-dimensional qualities. By manipulating intensity, direction, and color, the masses on the stage can be made more dynamic and more alive, simply by emphasizing their lines. Good lighting, therefore, has enormous architectural values.

Color or noncolor.   Although there is always a certain amount of color in the electric light emitted from an incandescent lamp or other light sources, the consideration here is whether light should be projected through color media (gelatin or other filtering material) or left in its original state. The American theatre, in contrast to the European theatre, has tended to use color media much more extensively; however, the growing development in repertory programming in the United States (as opposed to the fixed staging of one particular production) has introduced, perhaps out of necessity as it certainly has in European repertory theatres, the nonmedia approach. Since the intention in this chapter is only to show the range of possible exploitation, which direction you go is immaterial as long as you understand the values of both methods of lighting the stage, so that either can be used in designing productions.

The **color-media approach.**   As you have already learned in your lighting classes, white light is composed of red, green, and blue light. It is thus possible to give an appearance of natural light by throwing a combination of these colors, usually highly modified, on the actor. The usual procedure is to create a "living" quality by producing highlights and shadows—warm gelatins from one side, cool ones from the other. As you may know, blending light made of the same color components is often used, usually from the front by means of striplights or soft-light instruments, to soften the mechanical lines of the angular light but not in any way to destroy its effect.

Since the range of possible warm and cool colors can vary greatly, now the director enters directly into the decision making because the light can strongly affect the pigmentary colors in costumes and painted settings. A good lighting designer will, of course, consider what will happen when he sets up such a design. Unless the director is thoroughly aware of his coordinating function in this respect, he may lose the values of the other designs he has carefully nurtured. The worst that can happen is the graying out of pigmentation. Color media create many problems which necessitate an extensive knowledge of light on the part of the director if they are to be met head-on.

Color in light is also a matter of taste, as color choice is in scene design and costuming, because it possesses highly sensuous values. We can see this obviously in motion pictures and television when we contrast the effect produced on us by color film with that of the "black and white" convention. Color can greatly excite the audience, for it works on us much as any sensuous excitation—we vibrate in psychological response.

Perhaps light has played a larger part in declaring the style of Broadway theatre than any other element of design, for much of it has been erotic and sensual in its usage of gold, brown, orange, and amber light, sharply contrasted with heavy blues and purples. Whatever may have brought this usage about, it is apparent that heavy mood effects can be created entirely by the use of light alone and that the mood is in the color. A director must be thoroughly aware of the potential of color media if he is to control not only the values in lighting but also the values in pigmentation of scenery and costumes.

The *noncolor approach.* This approach seems to provide more ready control over design as a whole than does the use of color. Although it allows close-to-true colors of costumes and painted scenery to emerge, there is a certain brightness, a certain coolness about unfiltered light that can reduce somewhat the psychological grip of actor-audience contact. Much can be said for the days of candlelight on stage, or even gaslight, because those media were soft light sources that tended to soften actors' faces and bodies. Unfiltered electric light, even with the use of properly adjusted makeup, has a flat, unrelieved quality.

A possible compromise lies in the careful use of softening filters—frosts or filters with a light tinge of pink or amber—or noncolor light softened with border striplights and back lighting. If instruments are properly placed to produce excellent compositions, the light can be increased or decreased through these softening filters and the whole design can be brought into harmony.

Movement. In the same sense that we talk about *changeable scenery* meaning the creation of new places through the shifting of flats, drapes, borders, wings, wagons, and other elements, sometimes directly before the eyes of an audience, so may we consider *changeable lighting,* for lighting is the most flexible of all the elements of design in production with the same capability for instantaneous change we find in movies. Lighting can, therefore, be said to have movement—akin to music in its inherent rhythm and sequence.

The obvious examples are in those lighting designs that incorporate sunsets or dawns: we actually see the light move in changing patterns and we realize that what we are watching is not simply a verisimilitude to nature but an artistic representation of natural phenomena. What is less obvious is our acceptance of changeable light to "open up" or "close down" scenes. *Controlled light has spatial properties that permit the declaration of infinite spatial relationships.* Thus, within the same scene, we can create different emphases through the use of lights, moving from one point on the stage to another, from one intensity to another, and from one dominant color to another.

The fade-out and fade-in of lighting provide the same function as the act curtain, although the speed of such changes can be adjusted dramatically with much more diversity than can be arranged with a curtain. We can also crossfade, moving from one light pattern to another, a convention similar to the wipe of a motion picture. We can follow the actor with a follow spot, thus seeming to move his scenery with him, and we can isolate him completely from others around him and then have him seem to join the group again.

This inherent characteristic of movement in light can provide many theatrical moments, but when improperly used it can be both self-conscious and distracting. Good stage lighting must seem to happen and must be exactly right for any given moment.

Moods. It is obvious from the previous discussion that light has a very great capability of arousing moods (strong feelings). Moods in lighting are *consequences of light,* the goals of the director-designer. Light can create the bright, happy moods of comedy or the cool, shadowed, dislocated light of the serious and troubled. It can draw us into the illusory world of representation, it can arouse images of the world of fantasy, or it can make us accept explicitly that we are only in a theatre and that what we see can only take place there. We can be plunged into strange feelings of darkness or inebriated with great quantities of light. We can feel the enormous shock of symbolic color—red is blood, yellow is sunshine, blue is night, brown-orange is heat, etc. Through the use of projections, we are allowed to sense much more strongly the idea of place without seeing its actual, three-dimensional reality. Light is not just seeing; it is feeling. *As the light goes, so go our feelings.*

A director is a maker of moods and light is one of his strongest allies in the making.

EXERCISE

1. What would be the effects if *The Crucible* were staged with each of the two approaches to lighting, that is: (a) color, and (b) noncolor?

2. Is *source* considered a necessary concept in staging *The Crucible?* What sort of instrumentation would you use for an open-thrust staging of this play? What would happen to the flow of the play if you used area lighting, raising and lowering it in various areas as they became dominant acting areas?

GAME OF VISUAL PERCEPTION 6: LIGHT (See pages 77–78)

1. What is the dramatic force of the well-lighted character in each photograph when contrasted with the low-lighted character? What happens beyond emphasis?
2. How is mood created through light in each photograph? Picturization?
3. Can you find a photograph elsewhere in the book that illustrates the difference in lighting for a comedy from that for a serious play?
4. Do you see how light actually controls space in each photograph? Does the designer light the place or the space?

PHOTO 44 *The Council of Love* (Panizza)

PHOTO 45 *Summer and Smoke* (Williams)

PHOTO 46 *Cabaret* (Masterhoff/Kander/Ebb)

PHOTO 47 *Misalliance* (Shaw)

PHOTO 48   *The Collection* (Pinter)

PHOTO 48a
Arsenals (Lawrence)

CHAPTER TWENTY-THREE
DIRECTOR'S OPTIONS 3
Costume, makeup, and sound effects

Because costume is associated with the moving actor, it is the most dynamic and "living" of all the visual designs. With this in mind, the director can be much more certain about how he can bring counterpoint into the total design if he first makes choices among the options outlined in Chapters 21 and 22. He will then know how close the costumes will be to the audience, what kind of scenery will be used, what color plan is intended for the settings, and what the lighting potential may be. The director can then make the major decision about how far to stretch or contract any or all of the designs, and costume in particular. The *makeup design* will, of course, have to wait for costume decisions, for it is inherently part of costume and should be designed in close coordination with it. The following discussion of the director's options in these two areas will follow that order.

The final decision that must be made in design coordination is what to do about *sound effects,* including the use of music. Because of their very important mood-inducing characteristics, sound effects must wait until the director knows what can be achieved through visual effects. Consequently, the last section of this chapter will be devoted to the director's options in the use of sound.

OPTIONS IN COSTUME

Definition

We are so accustomed to thinking of costume as period dress—actors dressing up in clothing much removed from our own time—that we are apt to misinterpret the basic concept of costume. Although it may be defined in several ways, one of the best is to see *costume as live scenery worn by an actor in a particular role in a particular play.* Acting is impersonation, not reality; so is costume, for it is the exterior reflection of the actor's impersonation which assumes that the person portrayed is someone other than the actor himself. Just as the playscript is an artificial device because it involves specific selection and arrangement, so also is costume: The designer (or the actor in other eras) has to choose the particular and appropriate dress for a particular circumstance. Costume is, therefore, an integral part of production design, and the director must pay the most careful attention to it.

How strange you feel when you try on someone else's clothing—a jacket, a coat; and you feel even more self-conscious the more personal the items of clothing actually are because they may actually bear the scent of the owner. What you are feeling is the strength and individuality of the person to whom the clothing belongs. In this sense, costumes *belong* to other people, and the actor's job in his process of impersonation is to make "the dress" belong to the character he creates.

As with the other tools of production, the intention here is to discuss costume, not as training in depth, but only as one of the director's possibilities in production—how a director looks at costume and what his options are in applying it to stage plays. It must be assumed that your overall training will involve an intensive study of clothing as well as costume design and its construction, for only in such a study can you really comprehend the range of this complex craft. Without knowledge, you will be forced to rely entirely on the work of others, an approach that can be disastrous as far as production idea and unity are concerned.

Capabilities of Costume

A director should not only be fully aware of the nature of costume but also of its capabilities as a tool of production. What follows is a summary of the main ways in which costume can directly affect production.

Given circumstances. Because costume is "scenery on the move," it has the inerent capability of locating the time and place of a play with some accuracy. Thus, it is quite possible to reflect economic circumstances as well as social, political, religious, and climatic aspects of a given environment. In particular, it can bring onto the stage all the rituals in a given circumstance: the synagogue or the church, the evening dress of the military or the diplomatic corps, the pomp and circumstance of court ritual, or the decorations of a country wedding. Dress can tell us immediately where we are and can provide much of the detail affecting a particular environment.

Characer and dramatic action.   Costume particularizes and individualizes because dress moves with the characterization being made by an actor. Since the personal choice of clothing is a suitable reflection of the individual who wears it—"he feels like his costume"—the director-designer must always look for the specific idea, rather than the general. Costume design involves more than ordering dress from a rental agency where the materials are assembled as general items with very little regard paid to individuality since they are to be used over and over again in different ways. Rather, it is the result of the particularization of character, usually with a specific actor who is to play the role in mind. Using the general design of a costume house may be a quick way out of a tight circumstance; but the loss of individuality—of character as it is perceived by the director and designer—is the usual result. The same failure in design is also possible when dress is pulled from a stock wardrobe unless the director and costumer undertake the crucial and time-consuming problem of design—the search for fresh and individual statements.

What does clothing say? Does it say it in the specific terms of the dramatic action embedded in the playscript? What do the appearances of a character have to do with the actions he takes at the strongest moments of forcing? Does he look different on the outside from what he really is on the inside? These are the questions about the dramatic action that must concern the director. In real life, we find much concealment, much covering up; so, it is logical that we find the same types of concealment in plays. A brutal king might be an elegant dresser, but he also might be a careless one. The convention of dark clothing on a nineteenth-century villain might become light and colorful dress on a twentieth-century character. *Since dramatic action frequently deals with the opposites of appearances, the intention of costume design may often be simply to surprise an audience into unexpected revelation.* In Edward Albee's *Everything in the Garden,* for example, the suburbanites, who dress casually in disarming sportswear that reflects excellent taste, are also capable of murder when the secrecy of their lives is endangered. *Costume is character* and thus shocks audiences.

Color, texture, and form.   Form in costume means silhouette or shape. It is the sum total of the lines of a costume, and it is thus the most basic aspect of a design. The lines may follow the contours of the body; or they may create artificial lines related to the body but nevertheless distinct from body lines; and they may do both at the same time. Thus, we have the changing aspects of the fashion—the relationship of the physical contour of the body to materials in order to alter the exterior line. Because form is basic, it is more general than either color or texture; but without the basic architecture there would be nothing on which to build specifics. Costume begins with form.

As we have already pointed out in the discussion on scenery and lighting, color has strong sensuous, even sensual, values: we find it exciting, often erotic, and in some way theatrical. As we move in color in real life, so also we move on the stage where there has been no possibility of passing through a black-and-white convention as in movies and television. The director who misses the option of using color knowledgeably in costuming is simply missing an important emphasis in design.

The same can be said of the *texture* of materials, for without texture and color we cannot see contrasts or find emphasis. Texture gives boldness and clear statement by providing the necessary exaggeration that makes possible the projection of ideas from the stage. Cloth can vibrate: it can seem to stretch or hold rigid positions; it can lie in soft folds or be pressed in such a way as to seem firm and unyielding; it can have great bulk or be nothing at all. We see and feel texture, just as we see and feel color.

Movement.   As has already been pointed out, costumes are not static but, by their nature as coverings for human beings, dynamic and moveable. Only the few items that seem to be arbitrarily fixed—tights, corsets, metal armor—violate this characteristic. And because costumes move, they convey to viewers the many images inherent in flexibility, images that range from stiffness to complete freedom and flow. In this sense, *a costume lives if the actor inside it is fully aware of how the costume ought to move.*

For this reason, matching footwear to the style of a costume is so important. A body moves as its feet move since the whole body structure depends on what happens from the ground up. An actor cannot make a costume move in its inherent logic unless he can "walk" the costume properly. A director must have a full awareness of the capabilities of costumes (and this awareness includes wigs and hats), if he is to exploit them, that is, to create the appearance of logical and living clothing on his actors. *Part of his job is to show actors how to wear their dress in the appropriate way.*

Composition.   Since costumes are seldom seen alone on the stage, the art of costume design is to foresee all the possible compositions (actor groupings) that might turn up in the staging of a play. The problem is much more complex than arranging scenery because costume is always dynamic—it can move with the actor to any position on the stage—and yet, it must always do its most effective work no matter where it is. *To the costume designer, the effect of the ensemble is as important as the individual costume; it should also be of prime consideration to the director because his compositions that reveal the basic action of a play can literally be destroyed, or at least greatly weakened, if the costume ensemble is not properly designed.* This is why the director and costumer must work very closely together.

Composition in its simplest form means placing the strong costumes—those striking in color, mass, line, texture—on the dominant characters and designing the dress of the secondary characters to recede away from the primaries, with those of third and fourth importance definitely placed on the fringe of the design. Since color is so powerful as a centering force in composition, it is usually made the springboard in design, with the other design elements following closely on its heels. The color palette—the arrangement of the entire ensemble in gradations of color—thus becomes a significant principle in the technique of costume design.

It is for these reasons that the director must be absolutely certain that his costume designer sees the play as closely to his own vision as possible, since the costume designer, like the lighting designer, is an alter ego of the director. Without this parallel viewing the director has no control over the subtle physicalization of the moves a character makes because an audience will actually see most gesture and all movement *through* a costume; thus it should not be a barrier but must be a helpful illuminator. Yet, the relationship of the director to the costumer must be a free and fully creative one for the costumer.

Mood. Because costume is worn by the moving actor, it is a more intensive and continuous conveyor of mood than either setting or lighting. Our feelings as members of an audience are definitely aroused by costume, even though we are not conscious of how the effect is made as we should not be. Again, we can see that costume *is* character, for we are led away from the actor and toward charcter through the particularizing aspects of good costume design; in the end, it is character that moves us. If a costume is stronger than an actor, however, it can readily seem self-conscious and be distracting, a condition that definitely reduces mood possibilities. Costume must be an aid to feeling and not an inhibitor. *Every aspect of costume design can evoke mood: color, line, mass, texture, movement.*

Some Suggested Options in Costume Selection

Overdressing versus underdressing. It should now be clear that the line between overdressing and underdressing is a subtle and delicate one. If a costume is "right," it can do an enormous job in helping an actor; but if it varies too far on either side of the scale, an actor must work *against* his clothes. Finding the right balance depends on successful communication between director and designer.

Neutral dress. This term means literally *no seeming costume effect at all*—a very difficult possibility in design since any clothing an actor wears takes on some meaning. Perhaps the dress that would be closest to neutral is the leotard—the thinnest sort of cover for the actor's body. It can be said to be neutral because it has no movement of mass in itself—what moves is the actor alone; and if all actors in an ensemble wear the same color of leotards, color will not be an individualizing factor in the composition. The actor is thus left free to express his "body idea" without assistance from the amplifying and illusionary effects of costume.

Archeological clothing. This term refers to stage dress that comes very close to the reproduction of the real clothing of any period. At its poorest and least communicative, such dress is actual reproduction; *at its best it is modified and artistically conceived, although it is still closely related to the basic historical design.* Clothing worn in modern Realistic plays is usually archeological, since reproduction or the use of real clothing is one way of gaining verisimilitude. Yet, a director and a designer quickly learn that photographic reproduction will not stimulate imagination in an audience unless such clothing is most carefully selected in terms of its overtones or symbolic values. Modern dress, because it is more sublte than that of other periods, is therefore among the most difficult designs in costume to achieve. When the clothing is well-selected and arranged, thus becoming costume, it can perform the same function for a modern character as historical costume can for a character in a play of another era. In this sense, Realism is an enemy of costume design because the tendency is for directors to accept reproduction rather than design.

Ritual and rite.   Many plays contain actions that revolve around formal ceremonies or deal with characters closely associated with such ceremonies—gods, priests, hangmen, lawyers, warriors, etc. Since such characters are symbols in everyday life, they must be treated as such on the stage. Just as a director would be extremely careful in reproducing a religious ritual, so he must also exercise expert judgment and care in the design of the dress that illustrates such rituals. In the imaginations of a general audience, the dress becomes the ritual itself.

Abstract.   In one meaning of the word, all costume is abstract because it is not reality; but here *abstract* refers to that class of plays in which dress must be invented. What do the devils look like in *Doctor Faustus?* What will man wear in the twenty-first century? What do the fairies wear in *Midsummer Night's Dream?* What does the Man from Outer Space look like? Children's plays are full of this sort of costume requirement, and many adult plays include abstractions. Without a lively imagination about such costuming, a director cannot make the points he sees in a play. Can he help a designer without doing a design? This question is a real problem.

Summary of costume options.   From the preceding discussion, it should now be clear that the director can move in multiple directions in making decisions about design. But instead of searching for historical accuracy he will probably follow the usual route of adapting historical clothing by finding and reproducing its essence; or he may dress his play in *contemporary modern*—another way of saying modern dress; or he may use the fashions of a period quite different from the one associated with the play. If none of these options seem to fit the bill, he may turn to neutral dress or abstract form. The intention will always be the same, however: to reveal the interior meanings of a play through the outward show.

Rehearsal Techniques

Approaching costume.   The rehearsal period is the time of experimentation when an actor searches for and hopefully discovers the character he is trying to play. One of the best aids to his imagination is the "feeling" of a character's dress because it can show him how the character moves, how he gesticulates, and often, in a detailed way, how he feels. An actor can discover these things because the restrictions of a character's dress may differ sharply from what the actor normally wears in everyday life. *Clothing is the shell of a character, and the actor must discover the qualities and the nature of that shell.*

Rehearsing in portions of the final costume that an actor is to wear can be very helpful, for it is director-actor communication in a very real sense. If you, as director, do not know explicitly how a costume should move, enlist the aid of the costume designer to help you instruct the actors.

Shoes.   Since a character's body movement is declared by his feet (how he stands and moves), appropriate foot gear worn in rehearsal is of specific help to an actor in devising his characterization. An actor in a Wycherley or Molière comedy should wear the high-heeled shoes he will wear in performance; or, if he is to wear boots or heavy shoes, he should work in them as early as possible. Women should wear high heels if the costume will eventually require them, or sandals if they are the requirement. The actor who feels the effect of the footwear, who lets it work on his imagination, is telling himself much about the person he is trying to play. At first, the footwear will seem awkward and unfamiliar, but this is precisely why it is the very best moment for an actor to discover the new things the footwear does to him and to his characterization. If he makes imaginative discoveries, an actor will forget the difference from his everyday wear because he will have incorporated ideas about how his feet move into his moving character. *"As the shoes go, so goes the body."*

Other dress.   Period plays should be rehearsed as soon as possible in the basic costume which may amount to no more than long skirts, coats, flowing shirts, or head wear. Underpinnings are very important because costumes move on the basis of what is worn beneath them. Restrictions of any kind—an amplified stomach, armor, corsets, tight vests, stiffened garments, etc.—will tell the actor much about how his character will move. Directors who do not insist on this kind of help early in rehearsals will face actors at dress rehearsals and performance who have not absorbed ideas about the clothing: the actors move, but the clothing does not, or vice versa. Communication is a subtle process and the director must use every device to help his actors find their characters. Costume is one such device.

EXERCISE

1. If you were to stage *The Crucible* in "archeological clothing," what would be the symbolic meaning of the play? What would it be if you used highly simplified dress, that is, if you followed the lines of historical dress but reduced all decoration to a minimum? What sort of dress would you choose for arena staging? For open-thrust? Would nearness to an audience make a difference?

2. Why would a low-key color palette be a design idea for *The Crucible?* Would you decide to go in that direction? Would there be any difference in this choice when considering proscenium-style or arena-style productions?

3. How would you dress Danforth? How would his dress differ from the other clergy? Would he be more urbane, more sophisticated, more vain? What could you tell us specifically about him through the dress that he wears?

4. How would you dress Proctor in Act IV? What would Elizabeth wear in the same act? What about Tituba? What could you show beyond the specific images of physical torture and deprivation?

5. If you dressed *The Crucible* in dress approaching the "archeological," would your men need wigs? If you decided on a much simpler dress, would Danforth still wear one? What would be the minimum treatment of hair styles?

GAME OF VISUAL PERCEPTION 7: COSTUME
(See pages 77-78)

1. Can you see the line (silhouette) of each costume shown in the photographs? The texture of the materials employed? The possibilities for animation of the costume?

2. Can you see character-illustration in each costume?

3. Pick out one costume and describe its inherent capabilities for enhancing dramatic moment.

4. Can you see the difference between serious and comic dress?

PHOTO 49   *The Matchmaker* (Wilder)

PHOTO 50   *The Wonderful Wizard of Oz* (Skotnicki)

PHOTO 51
You Never Can Tell (Shaw)

PHOTO 52   *The Imaginary Invalid* (Molière)

OPTIONS IN STAGE MAKEUP

In today's stage practice, makeup has two significant functions: (1) to assist the statement of an actor's characterization and (2) to counterbalance the effects of stage lighting. Both of these functions fall into the director's hands because the first is closely tied to how he thinks an actor can best illustrate a character, and the second is closely related to the lighting problem. The costume designer is also much interested in makeup because of the good and bad effects that hair styles (both head and face) as well as facial coloration have on a costume as a whole; and the lighting designer is interested because the colors and textures of makeup can either complement or seriously hamper his design. Thus, it is up to the director to coordinate all three specific interests as well as those of the actors who will not only be wearing the makeup but will be executing the actual agreed-upon design.

Stage makeup means the appropriate application of color—pigmentary color, the same as is used in scene painting and costuming—on an actor's skin with the *intention of exaggerating the facial features in order to make them appear specific and emphatic.* The actual design of a makeup depends on how the directional light is used in a particular setup—where it comes from, its color, its intensity. Good makeup is never noticeable to an audience except in those plays where it is used as an obviously stylized device, for it is part of the actor's face and is therefore part of his reality. Consequently, makeup cannot be a laid-on stage tool but must be organic in that it expresses the actor's characterization in the context of the stage lighting. Since it is the director's job to coordinate makeup on a technical level with costume and lighting, the usual procedure is for the director, in consultation with the costume and lighting designers, to design for each character a facial mask—what he looks like—so that this problem is considered systematically. Actors can then execute their own makeup and can be confident of their adjustment in a specific design.

Good makeup exploits given circumstances as a matter of course (time, place, social level, etc.) because they are the outward visual show of a character. "What do I look like?" is the question the actor asks himself. And this is also the director's question because *makeup can tell an audience—especially through the use of hair— about the degree of character conformity or nonconformity, about his vanity and his awareness of others, about his sense of personal style.* Makeup provides an audience with its primitive visual idea of a character, the frame of reference from which the dramatic action can emerge. In this sense, *makeup bridges the gap between a character's costume and the physical character in the body of an actor.*

A director's options in makeup design, then, rest primarily on what happens in the lighting and costume designs. The more he understands about lighting, particularly about the specific effects of light-colors on pigmentation-colors, the easier it will be for him to effect the appropriate coordination. Exercises in a laboratory lighting situation where makeup can be introduced should be of great benefit. Likewise, the more he knows about hair styles and styling, the better he will be able to coordinate costume effect with character expression: you will, therefore, need to study hair in its relationship to costume, including basic knowledge of how wigs are constructed and worn effectively.

Good stage makeup is the result of a director's specific seeing, for many possible effects are lost by young directors who look at makeup as a general tool instead of a specific one. Learn to plan designs with the greatest care and with an eye toward theatrical possibilities. We have lost the art of makeup in the modern theatre, not only out of disuse but also out of negligence. With no one usually assigned to design this area of expression, it has been left in the hands of actors who simply cannot see themselves, or with a director who does not assume it is one of his primary coordinating responsibilities.

In brief, makeup expresses character, complements lighting, exaggerates, emphasizes, or distorts facial structure (through the use of putty or other structural additives). The director can call for historical accuracy in terms of hair fashions, for abstractions such as the use of symbolic colors or designs, for no makeup at all, or for the use of masks. The latter are as much employed in our theatre today as they have been in any theatre of the past with the exception of the Classical Greek (where they were used exclusively), for we have found them extremely useful in expressing symbolic ideas.

EXERCISE

1. What would you suggest for makeup on a proscenium stage for Act IV of *The Crucible* to assist the costumes you devised in Exercise 4 following the section on costumes? On an arena stage?
2. What kind of hairdos would the girls wear in Act I?

GAME OF VISUAL PERCEPTION 8: MAKEUP
(See pages 77–78)

1. What is the function of the masks in each of the two productions shown?
2. Can you see makeup as masklike?
3. Why are masks so dramatic? Can they "create" mood?
4. Look at other photographs for "straight" makeups you think are effective.
5. What is the function of makeup in the production of *Jack or the Submission?*

PHOTO 53 *The Adding Machine* (Rice)

PHOTO 54 *Yerma* (Lorca)

PHOTO 55   *The Effect of Gamma Rays. . .* (Zindel)

PHOTO 56   *The Effect of Gamma Rays. . .* (Zindel)

OPTIONS IN SOUND EFFECTS

The point has been made several times in this book that the theatre is more of an experience in sound than in sight, for it is the actor's voice that finally moves us, wrenched as it is from the heart and the body. We are, of course, easily excited by the visual, particularly because of its sensual, erotic capabilities, but we are not apt to be so deeply moved by what we see, except in an actor's spontaneous use of gesture and movement in support of vocal sound.

It is not at all surprising, therefore, to find that supplementary sound has been used throughout the history of the theatre. Music has always played a part, sometimes accompanying the actor's voice either directly when he sings or indirectly as background to his speaking—a convention employed on the stage for 2500 years before it was adopted by motion pictures as one of its primary conventions. The other use of sound—sound effects—has been developed extensively in the Realistic theatre, although certain effects such as thunder or cannon have been in use since Elizabethan times or before.

The director who is thoroughly aware of how to exploit sound is well on the way to making total theatre.

Music

The director is usually his own sound designer because most theatre setups do not include a musician as part of the permanent staff of designers. And even if they did, the coordination would have to be as close as that of the director and lighting designer because *music is as personal and as delicately sensitive in its capacities for arousal of the imagination as is stage light.* Music can often be a distraction and not an intensification as it ought to be. A most meticulous approach is therefore necessary if it is to be used as a helping tool.

Music in the play.   Many plays are written with a specific musical requirement—a song, a dance, an instrument—which necessitates its performance on the stage in front of the audience. The problem is a double one: to find the music itself, if none is specifically provided; and to work out a way in which it can be done, either by the performers onstage or by the subterfuge of a substitute offstage. Finding appropriate music is often very difficult, a problem that can frequently be solved only by having the music composed especially for the production in hand. *The latter approach has the merits of free flight on the part of the director because he can work closely in a stimulative way with the composer,* accepting or rejecting what seems right or inappropriate as he would do with a lighting designer. But this approach also has its own inherent problems if it is not to be a distraction. Music within a play must somehow catch the beat of the particular moment of its use, because the playwright, if he is a good one and not just a maker of entertainments, has included it not as a decorative device but as organic material intended to heighten, intensify, or fill a gap where spoken words cannot do the work. Often the words of a song will be the key to the musical line the playwright hears; or he may have suggested titles of specific songs, in which case the director must search them out in order to hear their ideas and rhythms, although he may decide for a number of reasons, including the capability of his actors who are to perform them, to have *similar* music written. But whether he uses something from the music library or has it composed, *the director must be constantly alert to the fact that such insertions in a play are dramatic actions in themselves and must produce the same effect as actions in the dialogue of the play. Music has subtext as well as text.*

The performer, if he is actually to perform the music "live" onstage, is often the key to what can be done, for his talents will determine how far the music can go and still be effective. Actors frequently have musical talents; but whereas an individual's acting capability may be particularly suited to a particular casting, his musical talents may lie far afield from the necessary requirements. To work around this situation, it has been frequent practice to place a live piano or other instrument offstage with the actor dubbing onstage; or to have an actor speak the words of a song, or half speak or half sing them. But these substitutions are poor seconds, for a live musician onstage can provide fine moments if he is truly an actor; however, if he is not, he can be a genuine distraction. Insertions of music into a play are difficult to perform successfully unless the director has solved all the attendant problems.

Background music.   This is the mood music used as background to acting with which you are so familiar in motion pictures and television. In those media it is firmly established as a convention. But it has not been so used in the theatre since the passing of nineteenth-century melodrama (drama with music) early in the century. Perhaps it lost force when the motion picture took over as the popular entertainment. But more likely it had served a purpose in the theatre of another age and was abandoned when other conventions for obtaining mood effects were developed—lighting, for instance. Nowadays it is occasionally used and then usually with a logical offstage source of motivation. In this instance, music may emanate from an offstage band or orchestra that is related to the action in some way or from a single instrument played by one of the characters in the play. *Good dialogue, because it is also good sound, does not need musical support to enhance its mood qualities,* whereas in film-script writing, where dialogue is often secondary to visual effect, the work is done partly by spoken words, partly by the music, and mostly by visual storytelling. *The theatre is a place for sound, but the legitimate play is not musical theatre; its own inherent sound values must be carefully discovered and preserved.*

Music between scenes.   This convention has continued in the theatre since Shakespeare's day because it can provide the mood-bridge from one major action to another. *Such bridges can tie diverse sections of plays together, especially when changes of location are involved.* A few seconds' wait while the scene is changed is a very long time in the theatre, and music can help to pass this time by bridging, in the imagination of an audience, the closing mood of one scene and the opening mood of another. One technique used is the overlap: beginning the bridge music a few seconds before the end of one scene and continuing it for a few seconds after the start of the next. Used in this way, the music not only helps the work of transition, but it also acts as a relief from the spoken play—a resting moment for the audience. In addition, it gives a sense of quick passage of time. The theatres of the seventeenth and eighteenth centuries, and even much of the nineteenth, used these bridges to cover the changing of the scenery before the eyes of the audience. But with the use of the act curtain and the darkened theatre as devices for separation between scenes, the convention was continued in the interest of occupying the audience. The use of this convention is, however, a matter of the director's interest and taste, for some directors prefer a ''clear'' play—one that stands alone on its own organic sound. The strongest argument in favor of bridge music is that the theatre is a sound experience, and the assault on the human ear can be more complex, more arresting, than it can be with only the actor's voice.

The problem of finding appropriate bridge music is as difficult as finding appropriate musical settings for songs in a play, for *the bridges must reflect the beat of the play.* This requirement does not mean that the bridge must be the same beat, for *effective bridges are often counterpoints to a completed scene or even to the play as a whole.* It is the search for less counterpoints that encourages the use of modern jazz or other modern music as bridge music in productions of classical drama. The counterpoint is what the director is after, for he wants to shift the audience's mood quickly from one emphasis to another; he may even want his audience to think and feel modern though the material of the play may belong to another age and time. By using classical jazz in Christopher Marlowe's *Doctor Faustus* or a Bach chorale in jazz style in Shaw's *Saint Joan,* an audience can partially sense the modern quality and meaning of each play and be divorced from any preconceptions about it, for the music has been used to jolt it out of its expected responses and to give it a sense of present context.

The possibility of distraction with bridge music can be great. The director must therefore exert every care to be certain he has found the appropriate bridges in terms of the meaning of the production as a whole. Sound is as subtle as light and can easily throw an audience in a wrong direction.

Sound Effects

The use of offstage sound effects, with the exception of thunder and fire arms, is largely a convention of the modern Realistic stage. Such effects are an extension of onstage illusion because they give weight and quality to offstage places, even though such places can exist only in the imaginations of an audience. The development of radio broadcasting in the 1920s and 1930s as a total assault on the ear undoubtedly had a good deal to do with the development of sound effects on the stage because the theory was the same: excite the imagination through the use of familiar sounds. Thus, productions of Realistic plays often require the arrival or the departure of wagons, horses, cars; rain and thunder effects; crickets and night sounds; sirens, airplane engines, bombs, guns, blasting, cock crowing, clocks, bells, etc. Closely tied to this use of offstage sound is the use of onstage radios and television sets with their voices and sounds from elsewhere, and the use of onstage telephones which allow audiences to imagine what the caller has said while the visible actor speaks his part of the communication.

These conventions are still effectively in use, as productions of such plays as Ionesco's *Rhinoceros,* with its terror-arousing sound of offstage rhinoceri, can attest. The imagination of an audience knows no limits in the hands of a director alert to sound possibilities in the theatre.

Although not nearly as sensitive as music in the effect it will have on an audience, sound effects must be carefully selected in order to evoke clear and precise imagery. Bells of different pitch and volume have differnt symbolic meanings; the age and style of automobiles can be pictured by the proper selection of sounds; the mood effects of a storm in contrast to a rain can be very different. The problem is one of appropriate selection. The careful director will enhance a production, but the careless one will merely add distraction.

Again, a play production is an experience in sound as well as in sight.

Electronic Equipment

The director must be thoroughly familiar with the use of all sorts of sound equipment. He may actually "cut" his own tape—that is, make a cue tape for a production. He should know how to copy, how to cut and splice, how to set up a cue tape with leader insertions, how to set up instantaneous cues on the tape deck. He should also be familiar with the capabilities of speakers and their offstage or onstage placement to achieve the best effects. Finally, he must always supervise the setting of the volumes himself in order to bring the electronic sound into balance with actors' voices. The fidelity of sound reproduction is an essential in the theatre of our time when excellent equipment is readily available.

EXERCISE

1. One of the ways to set the different locations (time and place) of *The Crucible* and to tie the four acts tightly together in idea is by using a narrator. The usual approach is to record the narration on tape because the resulting sound would be distinctly different from the live voices of the actors on the stage. How would you go about making such a tape on a portable recording machine? Discuss methods of cutting, splicing, and setting up cues.

2. Would the use of bridge music increase the effect of the play? If so, what would you choose as music?

3. What sound effects are needed for *The Crucible?* Would you use live or recorded sound?

MAJOR PROJECT 2
Designing and directing your own production

You are now ready to undertake the difficult process of making a synthesis—*something new*. It will be "new" because it goes beyond simple coordination of the parts and involves *your personal selection* of the pieces in *appropriate amounts*.

In working out this project, *you will do all the designs completely by yourself, because every learning director must discover firsthand the complex problems facing designers in the various areas.* Later, at the end of Part III, you will learn how to work with designers. But at this point you must learn all you can about the processes of design. In addition, as you do this project, you will be debating with yourself the procedures you would use if you had designers. You must learn how to free the design part of yourself, which is subjective by nature, so that you can take an objective view of what you are putting together in your synthesis. *You must free yourself before you can free others!*

It should now be clear to you that *a director's primary field of action is communication,* first to his actors and designers, and then, through the imagery they create and he helps to select, to his audience. *The actors and designers are his media,* for only through them will his ideas about a play take form and be able to reach others. Once again, here is the process: *a playwright imagines an improvisation and gives it form through his use of given circumstances, dialogue, dramatic action, characters, idea, moods, tempos; a director then reimagines and recaptures the improvisation; he then helps the actors and designers to discover the improvisation he sees and feels in the way he sees and feels it, and to recreate it through themselves, thus giving it intensive personal life. If the images they create are strong enough and appropriate enough, the improvisation will be projected in such a way that viewers can receive it and act on it by reimprovising what they have seen and heard in their own terms (vicarious experience).*

Thus, a play is not an object transferred in a direct way but a series of improvisations capable of producing images and, consequently, strong feelings. In this sense, it can be said that a *play hovers in space between the stage* (playwright, director, actors, designers) *and the audience,* with the latter receiving it only if it has been released in terms the audience can understand (see Figure 55).

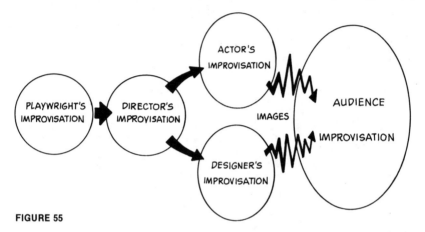

FIGURE 55

PRACTICING FULLY DESIGNED PLAY PRODUCTION

If you have had sufficient formal training in all the design areas, as you should have had by now if that training has accompanied your instruction in directing, and if you have done many of the exercises in Part II on *The Crucible* or another study play, you should be in a good position to undertake a directing-design project *on your own.* As was suggested at the beginning of this chapter, although you may sooner or later work with designers, *a director-in-training must go through the full process of design a few times by himself; that is, he must do all the designs in order to understand the concept of synthesis.* The content of this brief section, then, is devoted to a step-by-step process of designing your own production.

PROJECT A: SELF-EVALUATION
IN THE DESIGN PROCESS

1. Before you begin work on a live production, you should practice coordination and synthesis in visual design and in sound design by doing a project specifically with that focus. A one-act study play (the same one studied in Part I would be an excellent choice. You and your fellow students should observe the following rules for this production game:

    a. You must do all your work alone and without advice or consultation of any kind. Remember that this project is a test of your imagination and skills.

    b. Follow the procedures outlined in the previous sections concerning coordination.

    c. Prepare your designs with a specific proscenium stage in mind, for that is the type of stage you should understand best through your work in Part II.

    d. Do only Realistic design—that is, designs extracted directly from what you see about you in everyday life, although you may use fractionated scenery rather than a box setting if you prefer to do so.

    e. Make design plots in all six areas: (1) setting, including groundplan and an elevation sketch *in color;* (2) properties, both set and hand; (3) lighting; (4) makeup; (5) costume; and (6) sound. Make all set drawings to scale and do renderings of costumes, makeup, etc., in color. Make complete lists of all materials required.

    f. Be accurate, be neat, and be comprehensive.

2. When Exercise 1 has been completed, you are ready to make a class evaluation of what has been accomplished. Compare the projects and note specific differences. Each area of design should at first be treated separately but always with an eye to how it relates to other areas. The focus of the discussion should be placed on two primary points: freshness of the ideas presented in the designs and the problems of coordination. Group designing of the same play has the definite advantage of showing you where you stand in the development of your capabilities in designing. Therefore, each member of the class should evaluate the following:

    a. What is my present capability as a designer in each design area?

    b. How can I develop my skills in each of the weak areas?

    c. What is my comprehension of the principles of coordination and synthesis?

3. The class should now *review the entire process of production in as detailed a way as possible, including all of the concepts and approaches outlined in this book up to now.* You should give particular emphasis to the functions of play-analysis and to the relationship between the director and actors. Intensive discussions of acting are most valuable at this point, particularly if the emphasis is placed on methods of communication. The problem of design can also be given emphasis by encouraging students in the class who are specializing in design to discuss the ways in which they work and the kinds of communication that get through to them.

PROJECT B: YOUR OWN PRODUCTION

1. You are now ready to do the major project: designing and staging (with the help of your cast) a Realistic one-act play of your own choice. A one-act play is suggested because it will still provide you enormous oppor-

tunities without getting mired in the difficulties of a long play. And Realism should still be the style of your choice because you have not yet studied the problems of departures from Realism as discussed in Part III. Perhaps you may wish to undertake a "new" play written by one of your fellow students. Much can be learned from such collaborations that will prepare you for the big project at the end of Part III. But be certain the play is Realistic in style.

2. The production should also be confined to the Realistic style, although you may now wish to experiment on a thrust or arena stage. *Minimum staging* provides the full opportunity of handling actors in the unity of a complete play without introducing the complications of full settings and costumes. If possible for this project, minimum lighting and sound equipment should be employed, thus giving you the opportunity of putting to work your lighting, sound, and makeup designs. If hand-property substitutes can be found, this design can also be fully used. Costumes should be whatever the actors can provide after close consultation with you. Minimum staging permits a good basic production experience without the complications of set and costume building.

3. A detailed preparation, including the *play-analysis and all the designs, together with the list of materials needed,* should be submitted for approval in advance of the rehearsals. You should then cast your own play, if possible, and proceed with production.

EVALUATION

After the completion of Project B, a thorough evaluation of your work should be made, considering the following points:

1. The Playscript
    a. Comprehension of the dramatic action
    b. Understanding of unit divisions as illustrated in the playing
    c. Sensitivity to moods and tempos
2. Design Areas
    a. Validity of design ideas, with each design examined separately
    b. Ingenuity in the designs
    c. Skill in execution (shop experience in technical skills)
    d. Leadership ability in handling a work crew
3. Acting Area
    a. Achievement of an exciting choreographic pattern (composition, picturization, movement)
    b. Skill in communication (achievement of reciprocation)
    c. Development of characterization
    d. Achievement of "violence level" and climaxes
    e. Performance of the text (the "oral" play)
4. Tone Achievement
    a. Accomplishment of mood goal

PART THREE
INTERPRETATION
A matter of style

I told you my belief in the Renaissance of the Art of
the Theatre was based in my belief in the Renaissance
of the stage-director, and that when he had understood
the right use of actors, scene, costume, lighting, and
dance, and by means of these had mastered the crafts
of interpretation, he would then gradually acquire the
mastery of the action, line, colour, rhythm, and
words, this last strength developing out of all the
rest. . . .
Then I said the Art of the Theatre would have won
back its right, and its work would stand selfreliant as
a creative art, and no longer as an interpretative craft.

Gordon Craig
in "The Art of the Theatre"

CHAPTER TWENTY-FOUR
THE DIRECTOR
AS CRITIC

So, you've decided to become a director! That's why you are starting to read this part of the book. It is going to be difficult going in some sections because it's all about following the director at work in his personal creativity and commitment. And that's a big challenge.

When New York's Theatre Guild was first being put together back in the early 1920s, the people who set it up—Lawrence Langner (businessman), Philip Moeller (director), Augustin Duncan (director), Lee Simonson (designer), Helen Westley (actor), Rollo Peters (actor), and very shortly thereafter, Theresa Helburn (manager, playreader, director)—saw their primary mission as that of making "plays that mattered" into first-rate entertainments. In other words, they saw the paradox of theatre: it is intended to entertain, but it is also intended to move men's minds and feelings. To them, this was what was new and refreshing about their plan, because they saw an audience "out there" who were starved for good theatre. As the years went by, they proved their premise many times over, not only changing the face of the theatre on Broadway, but setting a pattern for educational theatre in the colleges and universities across America.

"Theatre that matters" is the premise of this book. Moving audiences is partly leading them with significant plays into paths and levels they have either not previously experienced or recently explored. Theatre may be a "big laugh," but it can also be a chuckle or a smile, and, on the other hand, a deep concern, an ache, a tear, a gasp, so deeply satisfying one never forgets the experience but keeps it on the edge of memory like a dream that will never fade.

This part of the book is all about how to do this, all about producing plays that matter. And further, how to make them "your own."

FORM AND CONTENT

Up to this point, the discussions of play-analysis and staging have concentrated on the two basic elements of all the arts, namely form and content. *Form* is the shape and structure of something, while *content* is the material being shaped. These terms were not used in previous discussions because we preferred to define *structure* and *material* in a more interwined way without drawing hard lines of distinction or attaching labels. Moreover, it was assumed that the learning director would only be baffled by this labeling and could best discover their meanings in the process of doing. You now have enough background to differentiate the meanings of these words and to see how they apply to directing. Understanding them is very important in defining the concept of style.

The study of play structure in Part I examined the *form* of a playscript, and to do so, we broke the play-analysis into six pieces: given circumstances, dialogue, dramatic action, character, idea, and rhythmic beats (tempos and moods). In this way, we could be certain that we were examining the entire *dramatic content* of the play. The content was thus revealed through an analysis of form. Likewise, when we studied the process of stage production, we examined the form of staging through the six visual tools: groundplan, composition, gesture, picturization, improvisation with objects, and movement; the oral tools: speaking the subtext, speaking the text, decorum in speech, and projection; and the stage tools: the stage, scenery, properties, lighting, costume, makeup, and sound. When all of these elements of form in staging are employed appropriately, we also have a *theatrical content*. Thus, we have form and content in staging as well as in the written play.

The major point about form is that although content cannot be revealed without it, form is still *general*, rather than a specific statement of content.

STYLE

Style is what makes form individual and specific.

The purpose of Part III is to help you specifically pin down style in your awareness so that you can see the possibilities in both playscripts and their production on an entirely new and different level. You probably remember high school performances that were dull and boring although you may have responded favorably, as did the parents present, out of loyalty and a sense of belonging. Occasionally something clicked and held your attention. That something was probably brought about through style. The college productions you see are apt to hold your attention more continuously because many directors and designers working at that level know how to present plays with style and have the actors and staging resources to make it possible. Successful professional productions are marked by their individuality, their style, and it is the style that is discussed by everyone when they talk about such productions, whether they know what style is or not.

Audiences always respond to individualization because subtleties move them, where general statements do not.

The main problem, therefore, is how to elevate the generality of form into the individuality of style. Part III undertakes to answer this problem by first showing you how to *recognize style in a playscript* and then how to *make a style-analysis*. The discussion then turns to production with the intention of showing you how the director is a stylist and how he makes style in play production. Exercises are included in some of the following chapters, some of them based on historical drama, all leading to Major Project 3: Directing a Full-length Play with Designers.

As you will note, many of the examples of Part III are drawn from significant historical and modern plays on the assumption that at this point you have a fairly good background of dramatic literature. You should view Part III, therefore, as advanced study in directing, although you will be able to comprehend the content if you have worked through Parts I and II with attention and care and if you have accumulated some experience from the live directing projects suggested in Part II.

Here the hard work begins. Many young directors do not progress much beyond the directing level of Part II because they are too eager to get into play production and do not realize that there is still much preparatory work to be done. You will note that Part III ranges much more widely than the previous parts of this book, and you will thus need to do a great deal of thinking and talking about it. *If you want to be a good director instead of a merely adequate one*, you will have to give close attention to the many special studies outlined in the following chapters since *successful directors are stylists who make things of their own.*

WHAT IS STYLE?

It is easy to recognize form, but style is much more difficult to delineate because we perceive it on an emotional level without being conscious of what we are really seeing until we *make* it conscious. In addition, our recognition of a style often depends on comparison, namely, experience with many different objects in the same category. We all know what an automobile is when we see one because that is form; we can easily tell the obvious differences among motor vehicles, trains, airplanes, and boats because we know the differences in their forms and functions. Even a young child with several of these objects as playthings can categorize them as modes of transportation, even to the extent of pointing out their obvious differences in form. Moreover, when the field is narrowed to motor vehicles, for instance, there is still little problem for most people in noting differences among passenger cars, pick-up trucks, trailer-trucks, and motorcycles. When we further reduce the field, most people begin to encounter difficulties in recognition. Because you in particular may be interested in cars and have looked closely, when you discount the differences in engineering performance, can you delineate the differences, for example, in sedan models among (1) Fords and Chevrolets, or (2) Buicks, Oldsmobiles, Dodges, and Pontiacs? Note that there are two groups mentioned. Can you separate the differences in the models in each group? If you can, you are involved in differences in style or *styling*, as the automobile manufacturers say.

Yet, this example will not do for objects of art. Commercial design, whether of a toothpaste carton or a package of cigarettes, involves a certain amount of style because manufacturers want you to recognize an individual item on a crowded shelf, although the style is intended for reproduction in thousands, sometimes millions, of the same item. Yet, despite the quantity of reproduction, such items have an individual look and can be delineated readily from other items in the same form.

In art, we are concerned with extremely narrow categories, usually only a handful of items with the same individualized look. Thus, we can talk about Cézanne's style as differing from Van Gogh's, about Brahms' symphonies differing from Tchaikovsky's, about Ibsen's plays differing from Strindberg's, about Arthur Miller's plays differing from Tennessee Williams', about a Sam Shepard play or a William Albee play. We also have seen differences in stage productions by directors Bill Ball and Alan Schneider and in movie productions by Ingmar Bergman and Francis Coppola.

Four points can be made about the preceding pairs of artists. First, each pair represents the same art form. This fact is important to our understanding of style because we can understand this concept—much better if we stay within specific categories. Second, notice that the two people in each category are contemporaries—they did their work or are doing it in approximately the same period. The important thing about dating art is that each age (an age can vary from twenty to fifty years) establishes its own variations and refinements of form by setting up something that can be recognized as the *style of the period*, the individualization of that age. Thus, we can speak of Elizabethan style, French Classical style, Romantic style, Realistic style, etc. When we consider drama, we note that each period has made general modifications that all dramatists of that period use; by noting these characteristics, we can delineate the style of a period. We can also do the same for production by labeling the styles Elizabethan platform staging, seventeenth-century Italianate, nineteenth-century Romantic, or twentieth-century Realistic. By these designations we may take a different look at each one, no matter whose individual work we may be examining.

Third, notice in the pairs listed that names of people have been used because this is the only way we can delineate the most subtle aspects of style. "Style is the man," goes the old adage. This saying means that every creative artist will make individual alterations within the general style of his age, individualizations that people who look closely at art will recognize as unique in the artist—truly *his signature to the work.* Style may have broad meaning referred to historical periods, but it can also have a very specific meaning referring to the unique work of individuals. In its most refined sense, style is the significant aspect in the definition of art itself, that is, something unique and highly individualized.

Finally, notice that each pair of artists differs in how it makes contact with spectators or audiences. Cézanne and Van Gogh make direct contact through direct showings of their work in museum galleries. However, Brahms and Tchaikovsky as well as Ibsen and Strindberg and Miller and Williams must depend on interpreters to present their works because the forms in which their works appear are incomplete *without audience performances.* Ball and Schneider are interpreters of playwrights like Ibsen and Strindberg through the medium of theatre, but they can overlay plays with their own individual styles. Bergman and Coppola are part creative writers and part interpreters, because they usually create both the form and content of their movie scripts, and go on to interpret them through the form of cinematic staging. Although their work is in movies, both Bergman and Coppola are examples of Gordon Craig's artist-director, while stage directors Ball and Schneider are what Craig labeled master craftsman directors, that is, directors who act as interpreters of the work of others. However, no matter what the relationship may be between the creative and the interpretive, all the people mentioned here have developed a recognizable style all their own. To clarify this point, we have given examples of various art forms along with categorical differences in style for each pair of artists, with the implication that each artist will make his own personal and individual statement.

Style, then, is both the individualization of art form and the way of moving spectators (those who only look) *and audiences* (those who both hear and look).

INTERPRETATION IS CRITICISM

Interpretation is the director's goal because, as a master craftsman-director, he *interprets* the work of the playwright rather than creates the playscript himself. To carry out this function, he becomes the primary critic in the theatre. To understand his work better it is most useful to compare him with the other "interpreters" who work in and around the theatre, namely the newspaper reviewer and the dramatic critic. All three are essential to a vigorous and active theatre, but each has a distinctively prescribed job to do.

The Newspaper Reviewer

Most of the comment about the theatre we read in newspapers and periodicals is not criticism at all in the strict sense of the word. Rather, it may be better labeled "reviewing," because its primary function is to look at a produced play in its final form and in its natural habitat—the theatre—and then judge its merits and failures. Consequently, the 500- to 800-word review we read in a newspaper shortly after a first performance of a play is the opinion of a trained and experienced viewer who is reporting his reactions to the play, the acting, and the directing to a waiting public, who in turn, enjoys the reviewer as an entertaining writer and often listens closely to his advice on whether to spend money and time on a particular play.

Such brief and personal news reporting serves the theatre by spreading word about a produced play. But such reporting also harms the theatre when the reviewer sets himself up as the primary interpreter by substituting his own opinions about what he thinks a production should have been for the one he is seeing. Instead of holding the eye of his reader on what is there, he may focus on what he thinks should have been there. When the reviewer does this he moves into the director's realm of interpretation, and thus becomes an armchair director.

The Dramatic Critic

Another level of critism is closer to the function of the director. Although dramatic criticism has appeared more or less regularly throughout the history of the theatre, it has never been so much in vogue as it is today. Dramatic criticism is essay-length interpretation, usually of one play, although comparisons are often made with others based on inherent, internal structure. Dramatic criticism is similar to the process outlined in Part I of this book, where the intention is to illuminate the content of a play and what ties it together. When this sort of criticism becomes too literary (pursuit of the structure of dialogue alone), its use to the director is limited; but when it adheres to those basic elements of structure that have clear theatrical values, it can be most helpful.

A dramatic critic is not an armchair director because he is not concerned with a play's production. A playscript's inner, often hidden, workings interest a dramatic critic because he is looking at the evidence that lies entirely in the play's structure itself. This approach recognizes that plays are poetry and that playwrights are poets who communicate to others through metaphor, symbol, and other types of direct communication and not merely through exterior dialogue.

A learning director should cultivate the habit of reading dramatic criticism as a way of developing his own sense of what to look for and how to find it. However, when he does so, he will also find that dramatic criticism has shortcomings. Because its primary intention is to illuminate the mysteries of drama, it too often turns out to be just another interpretation. The critic has looked intensively at the play to support his own ideas about the structure and meanings and he has shown textual proof to validate his views. However, he can easily be led astray by placing too much emphasis on what he has taken for proof. Unveiling the mysteries of poetic experience requires exceptional vision indeed; such vision is rare and so are good dramatic critics.

The Director as Primary Critic

Despite the presence of the reviewer and dramatic critic, *the director is the primary critic in the theatre.* The function of criticism is to interpret and illuminate a work—a perfect description of the director's job. In comparison, the dramatic critic works only with the playscript, which in itself cannot be complete since by its nature it requires actors and production to give it full life; the reviewer works with the finished production and *provides a criticism of the director's interpretation* while at the same time he tries to fulfill the nominal responsibilities of a dramatic critic by examining the playscript. *Only the director works in a firsthand way with both the playscript and the production.*

This function is nowhere better delineated than in T.S. Eliot's essay "The Function of Criticism." In that work the celebrated poet-playwright-critic is talking about literary criticism, but it can be just as readily applied to directing. In it he draws a sharp line between two major approaches to criticism. The first, the intuitive approach, he labels *whiggery*, that is, what proceeds without principles from the "inner voice."

> "If I like a thing, that is all I want," so the argument goes; "and if enough of us, shouting all together, like it, that should be all that you (who don't like it) ought to want. The law of art . . . is all case law. And we cannot only like whatever we like to like but we can like it for any reason we choose."

Such practitioners, Eliot maintains, are not concerned with literary perfection but only with momentary and personal values. The second approach (to Eliot, the only valid one) *is more analytical, more conscious criticism,* the sort a superior writer must apply to his own work, for the critical activity finds its highest, true fulfillment in a kind of "unison with creation in the labour of the artist."

At one time, Eliot took the position that the only critics worth reading were the critics who "practiced, and practiced well, the art of which they wrote." Later, he modified this view in the interest of finding a more inclusive frame and he then concluded that the most important qualification for a critic was a *"highly developed sense of fact."* This allowed him to permit inclusion of critics who write about the works of others but he points out the rarity of good practitioners: "For every success in this type of writing there are thousands of impostures. Instead of insight you get a fiction." *The best critic is one who sees a work of art steadily and sees it as a whole.*

In applying this distinction to the director, whiggery would seem to be as unacceptable an approach to directing as it is to criticism. How a director feels about a play will certainly affect his treatment of it because he is dealing with art and not science, with intuition and not scientific fact, which must be explicitly and fully explained, with the behavior of human beings as set out by the playwright and not with puppets. Nevertheless, *a predominantly subjective approach to directing is incompatible with the director's function* of finding unity and order in the playscript, in acting, and in design because he must constantly exercise his objective, analytical, critical view in order to control his media, which are subject to constant variations. As a stimulator of ideas, the director is involved in getting from the playwright the strongest play, if it is a new one and he can control its development; and in arousing the actor to his best performance and the designer to his highest level of creativity. The director's success is also tempered by his mastery of the physical materials of the stage. Among artists, he might be compared in some respects to the architect, who is also concerned with the limitation of materials and the ability of the craftsman on whom he must depend for the execution of his ideas.

In summary, since the master craftsman-director is the subject of this discussion, you must assume that *the director's function is largely one of interpretation*, that his primary concern is *about* something that someone else has already created (the playscript), or, as in the case of the actor and designer, something that someone else is about to create.

SOMETHING TO SAY

Since the primary job of the director is *interpreting* what has already been set out for him in a playscript, how can he make an individual statement that can be classified as style without violating the integrity of the playscript especially when *the temptation of not telling the truth is always there.*

The answer is relatively simple although the achievement of style is not. The assumption is that a director will be in command of a production, both of the actors and designers, and that he fully comprehends the *form* of the playscript and its *style*. *A director's style will be stated in the individual qualities and emphases he gives to the form, content, and individual style of a playscript through the production elements at his command.* The director's statement of style evolves as he makes decisions about which direction he will take with a play. Here are a few of the basic questions that will have to be faced, and out of the answers will come his style:

What is the dominant idea in the play?

Whose (which character's) play is it? *(This is a very important decision about character emphasis.)*

What *actions* should be given the most telling emphasis?

Is the production to emphasize text or subtext, and in what balance?

How can the given circumstances be individualized?

What dominant moods can emerge?

Who shall be cast? (texture and balance.)

How shall the design be stated? (as Realism or as a departure from Realism)

When it comes down to the fine points in a play there is no absolute interpretation. Its ideas will fall within a narrow range, but it is just that narrow range that is left open to the director and out of which will come his individual statement, that is, his style.

Style is beyond form and content; it is something personal to say.

STYLE IS TODAY'S STATEMENT

To reproduce an historical play exactly as it was first presented is impossible. Even if all the information were available, we would not want to do such stagings because audiences simply would not understand them. When we read a play by Shakespeare, we are immediately conscious of all the "odd" words and phrases because we see them in print. If we were to see a historical reproduction of a Globe theatre performance, it might very well look and sound much the same way, just as odd and peculiar to our eyes and ears. Since the pronunciation of English has undergone extensive change in the 400 years since Shakespeare's day, the play would probably sound foreign to our ears. If you have seen motion picture revivals of 50 and 60 years ago (Sarah Bernhardt as Queen Elizabeth, for instance) you will remember how the audience probably laughed at what looked like odd, elaborate behavior of the actors and at the overly exotic qualities of the settings and costuming. *You were watching acting and design styles of another age,* and the audience was not able to reconcile it with its own prejudiced, highly indoctrinated, well-conditioned conception of style.

STYLE IS THE PRIMARY MEANS OF IMMEDIATE COMMUNICATION

No age has ever been more aware of the necessity of making today's statement than our own, a fact that we can blame on the pressure of our highly developed communications media because photography has made it possible for us to see more clearly than ever before how quickly styles can change. From the 1980s we look back at photographs of the styles of the 1960s and 1970s and find them old-fashioned, just as people from the 1960s regarded the 1950s, and so on. Style says something to us quickly and easily. This characteristic is readily illustrated in dress, where new styles quickly become old styles in a continuously changing, arbitrarily forced world of industrial design. A designer makes a new-look dress; other designers more or less copy the creation to set the fashion, and when others follow in numbers a fad is declared. A style remains in fashion only as long as it is not replaced by a newer style with more ready communication.

Avant-gardists are the makers of new styles because they are always in search of a fresh means of communication, a new way of saying something. The speed of present-day electronic communications—radio, television (photography), motion pictures (photography)—has reduced the length of time a style can stay in fashion. Not long ago style seemed to last for several years, perhaps as much as one or two decades; now the "new" is given such quick circulation that a style's lifetime seems to be markedly reduced. Last year's avant-garde in the popular music field (the latest strange sounds, rhythms, and words) will be superseded this year by another style that will soon become the craze or the rage, words that to you may sound quite out of style.

An awareness of the immediacy of style, that is, its quality of being contemporary, is most important to the director. His job is to get through to an audience no matter when the play he is producing was written. The problem is always one of communication through style. The director not only has something to say because he sees it vividly in the context of his own time, but if he is to communicate to an audience, he must also say it in the immediate terms most understandable to his audience.

It is the living, breathing immediacy of style that makes it one of the director's primary tools of communication. Although the *adaptation* of historical styles will be treated in a later chapter, it is necessary to note here that no matter how an adaptation is made, *if the style is too unfamiliar to an audience it will not be very effective* because *the theatre demands group recognition.* There is no harder demand on any artist than this because the tendency is to play it safe, to be conventional and not to strive for the new.

Thus, the range of style for the director is an extremely narrow one since he must constantly fight the paradox of *reaching an audience on the level at which it can understand him* while at the same time trying to find new and exciting ways of communicating. As a popular art form, theatre in the past usually lagged as much as a generation behind the other forms while it was waiting for the general audience to catch up. Today this is no longer the case because with urban culture and its "mirror" television constantly before us, the new quickly becomes old.

CHAPTER TWENTY-FIVE
STYLE IN
PLAYSCRIPTS 1
General characteristics

The purpose of this chapter is to pull together many of the ideas and bits of information you may have garnered from your courses in dramatic literature. To some of you this may look familiar, and thus redundant. But if you will read it through carefully, you will see that it's about the special way a director looks at plays and playwriting in order to put them to work for him. This will challenge the critic in you.

The *form* of drama in Western civilization, as distinct from theatre, has always contained the same basic elements since its beginnings in the fifth century B.C.: given circumstances, dramatic action, characters, idea, dialogue, tempos, and moods. What has made drama seem different over its 2500-year history is the rearrangement in value and emphasis of these basic structural elements. One age, from Ibsen to 1960, for instance, gives great prominence to given circumstances, with detailed emphasis thrown on previous action; whereas another, such as the Elizabethan Age, ignores this aspect almost completely. Dramatic action is relatively simple in some periods (Greek) but complex and extensive in others (Jacobean). Characters are largely primal types in some periods (Greek) but intricate and highly detailed in others (Ibsenite-Chekhovian-Strindbergian Realism). Dialogue is in verse form in some, with emphasis on variety in meters (Spanish Classical), and in prose, sometimes quite elaborate, in others (English Restoration Comedy).

These variations in the basic elements of dramatic form are what distinguish the drama of one period from the drama of another. The student should remember, however, that categorizing is only a general sorting of the thousands of plays we wish to know better. The only way he can be sure of what he has in hand is to take a particular look at a specific play through play-analysis. Playwrights, we like to think, are free improvisers like other artists, and only at certain times have they been expected to conform to established rules prescribed through one sort of pressure or another (as in Neo-Classical). We are so accustomed in modern times to think of playwrights as free spirits that we seldom realize how many restrictions on form and "community style" actually bind them. Like entrenched governments, revolutions by playwrights or theatre people, sometimes physical ones, are necessary to overthrow overused forms. Victor Hugo's revolt with *Hernani*, J.M. Synge's and the Abbey Theatre's with *Playboy of the Western World*, and Ibsen's and Strindberg's with their shocking sex drama are obvious examples.

EMPHASIS IN CONTENT:
TRAGEDY, COMEDY, AND OTHER TYPES

One of the oldest ways of specifying differences in the content of drama is type designation. Ever since Greek Classical times, drama has been divided into categories as a way of grouping plays of like intent and similar structures. Although tragedy and comedy (the two major types) had different origins in the ancient Greek world, with separate heritages of rituals and mythology, by the fifth century B.C. they were brought together within the same *general* form, with both employing dramatic action, characters, idea, dialogue, choral groups, music, and spectacle; both types were performed in the same religious-theatrical temple as well—the Dionysian theatre.

The difference between these two major designations lay in how the basic elements of dramatic form were used and the kinds of emphasis given to each element. This method of play description has been so useful that present-day dramatic critics wrestle with the same basic problems that faced Aristotle: what makes each type work? What kind of emphasis must be given to each element in each of the two structures to achieve the total composite effect required by each structure? Consequently, an extensive literature has developed around the theory of drama in the attempt by each age to define these composite types. Critics know that the types work in the theatre, and the theoretical discussion is directed toward penetrating their poetic mysteries.

A learning director cannot advance very far into the realm of style unless he comprehends a good deal about these composite types. *What makes an audience laugh?* or *What can move it deeply?* are most important questions a director must answer for himself. An extensive knowledge of the composite types may not only unlock historical drama for you in a very direct way but give you the key to modern drama as well. With a strong awareness of types, you can then proceed to unfold for yourself the ways in which each individual playwright attacks his problem—what the playwright's style is all about.

The intention here is not to provide a theoretical study of the composite types but merely to describe these types in a general way in order to alert you to basic differences. Your course work in dramatic literature will help you develop your understanding in depth, and you will add greatly to this understanding through regular practice in play-analysis.

Again, you must remember that each age has made its own description, sometimes *pre*scription, of these composite types. It is, therefore, impossible to treat them briefly without including points that some ages would take strong exception to. Nevertheless, here are some general statements.

Tragedy

"Tragedy is. . . ." whatever each age had thought it to be, for it has had the most intensive treatment of all the composite types. But, in general, all ages and cultures have seemed to agree that it is serious throughout; that it deals with man's relationship to forces outside his petty, domestic world; that it is about a better than average man, frequently highly placed in society, who makes a discovery that brings about a great change in his life, usually resulting in his death. Further, that he *usually*, but not always, comes to a knowledge about himself in relation to the outside forces; what happens as a result of the discovery affects all that he holds most dear in his life, but he has the great courage and strength to face his destiny. And very important, that a member of an audience may be greatly moved to pity him for his suffering and, at the same time, may fear that the same thing could happen to him. Finally, the language in which these plays are written is heightened beyond that of everyday speech and frequently is set down in verse.

Tragedy is about violence and suffering. These aspects are what make it so compelling in the theatre, for they can take us to the periphery, to the very brink of life's experience. During a lifetime we all go through a certain amount of suffering and may even have an experience approaching violence, but few of us ever experience life even near the level of the tragic hero. Yet, we recognize that it could happen, that it is possible; and it is just this possibility that makes tragedy so utterly believable.

Isolating the violence is a key to understanding such plays, for it allows working backward from the climactic peaks in order to discover more readily what led to them. *As a director, you will want to give violence great prominence, because through the very force of its presentation an audience can experience the intense emotions of the aftermath. Great drama is always about the great passions in life where the desire to maintain integrity supersedes all other desires.* Consequently, producing tragic feeling on the stage is a very difficult matter even when you understand what violence is and what precedes and follows it.

Today we have many problems in defining our drama as tragedy because emphases differ from those of the classical forms. "Serious drama" or "a play" seem to be more apt descriptions because they exhibit no pretentions about the contents and may include some humor. While they show the principal character in conflict only with other men or with groups in the society, and not with forces beyond earthbound human contacts, as did the Greeks, and may not end in the hero's coming to know his own weaknesses, they contain the same basic elements of all tragedy: fierce integrity on the part of the hero which leads him to a do-or-die position, and the violence he must undergo when he makes his principal discovery. *Only when you make an exhaustive play-analysis of a serious play can you see why it is truly serious and what the consequences will be to an audience that views it.* Your directing skill will be marked by your perception of tragedy and the intensity with which you show it on the stage, for tragedy presents great intellectual and emotional challenges to any director who undertakes it.

EXERCISE

1. Apply the basic description of tragedy just discussed to the following plays:
   a. *Oedipus the King* (Sophocles)
   b. *Macbeth* or *King Lear* (Shakespeare)
   c. *Doctor Faustus* (Marlowe)
   d. *Phaedra* (Racine)
   e. *The Master Builder* (Ibsen)
   f. *The Crucible* (Miller)
   g. *Riders to the Sea* (Synge)
   How do these plays differ in structure and how are they alike? Examine and specifically compare their endings.
2. Is Ibsen's *Ghosts* a tragedy?
3. What is a tragic hero?
4. Since discussions of tragedy can be most profitable, the class should devote as much time to thrashing out its complexities as students' backgrounds and time allow. If possible, each student should do an analysis of a tragedy of his own choosing, with the focus on what makes it tragic.
5. If the students in the class are prepared with background for advanced study and time is available, Aristotle's *Poetics* should be read and discussed at this point, with emphasis given to separating Aristotle's delineation of *general* play form from his *specific delineation of tragic form.* The advanced student can also benefit greatly from reading Maxwell Anderson's "The Essence of Tragedy" and Joseph Wood Krutch's "The Tragic Fallacy." Additional readings can be added as background and time permit. But no readings can be a substitute for the analysis suggested in Exercise 4.

Melodrama

This word has been used for nearly two centuries to describe those plays in which theatrical "activities" dominate the dramatic action. These activities tend to make the action superficial, which, in turn, reduces the development of character. Such plays live in large part on their external excitements, resulting in the capabilities of holding audiences in firm grip because their danger levels are both high and obvious. The word *melodrama,* since its earliest usage, has meant "drama supported and enhanced by exciting music," a perfect description of today's detective and police thrillers on television. Classical tragedy also had music, but it was used in support of choral songs and not merely to excite the emotions *behind* stage activities.

To see melodrama only in the light of those travesties of nineteenth-century *"mellers"* where the villain operates the buzz saw while the heroine advances toward it on the log rollers, or in terms of twentieth-century TV spy films with delicately turned bank robberies behind the Iron Curtain, is seriously to malign it as a composite form of drama. We frequently use the term *character melodrama* not only to denote the stature of the better plays but also to describe an entire range of dramas that cannot fall into the category of serious play or tragedy even though the moods of such dramas are indeed serious. They do not qualify as tragedies because their actions are always man-versus-man in his dealings in everyday life: the protagonist must overcome his antagonist as in tragedy but for superficial gains—money, property, upholding the law, and others. Although such plays deal with psychological aspects of character, they do not penetrate deeply enough to be intensive perceptions of life. Instead, they play on our sense of personal security, on our prejudices (we tend to destroy those things we do not understand), our morbid curiosity, our moral codes, and on our personal search for excitement to relieve ourselves from the boredom of everyday life.

A director must learn the sensitive skills of staging melodrama if he is to learn how to direct the intensive activity, often melodramatic, in the serious drama. In one sense, all directing is finding the best external means of communicating dramatic action, and a director should therefore get into the habit of looking at all plays as melodramas if only to see how the excitements in them are created and what levels they reach. Without this skill of expressing external dangers, a director will never know how to project the quiet, interior dangers more deeply and subtly embedded in serious drama. The rhythms and tonal pitches of melodrama are the best possible avenues to learning what the term *theatrical* means in the theatre—a high sense of personal (audience) danger. You should direct melodramas, then, before you try to direct highly serious plays.

We tend to laugh at the melodrama of the nineteenth century without recognizing that no age has produced more melodrama than our own, especially in the popular forms of movies and television. Melodrama is the stuff of popular theatre because it provides theatrical thrills without requiring serious work on the part of an audience, and thus its specific external look is shifted as prevailing activities become too obvious because of their overuse. *However, the basic emphases in this composite form always remain the same: intensive action, highly dramatic characters, moral tone, strong moods and tempos, and emphasis on external, and thus on theatrical, illustration.*

EXERCISE

1. What is the difference in structure between *Oedipus the King* and *Night Must Fall* or *The Little Foxes?* Why can the last two be called "character melodramas?"
2. *Hedda Gabler* is sometimes labeled a melodrama. Why? Be very careful not to belittle characterizations in that play.
3. Why can *Macbeth* be labeled, as it sometimes is, a tragedy with melodramatic overtones?
4. What is melodramatic about the following plays:
   a. *The Dutchess of Malfi* (Webster)
   b. *Woyzeck* (Büchner)
   c. *Camille* (Dumas)
   d. *An Enemy of the People* (Ibsen)
   e. *The Little Foxes* (Hellman)
   f. *The Homecoming* or *The Birthday Party* (Pinter)
   g. *The Glass Menagerie* (Williams)
   h. *The Curse of the Starving Class* (Shepard)
5. Do a written analysis of a melodrama of your own choice, and prove that it is a melodrama or how it compromises the form. Here are some suggestions of categories: *Ladies in Retirement; The Cat and the Canary; Rhinoceros; The Zoo Story.*

Comedy

The most difficult of all the composite forms for a young director to understand is comedy. Tragedy is more a matter of feeling than of mind, and both the young director and the young actor can comprehend that form on the basis of their past emotional experiences in everyday life, though perception in depth requires experiences in depth. *In contrast, comedy is more a matter of the mind than of the feelings.* To find a joke funny one must perceive the incongruities that are presented in the joke: it amuses precisely because *A* is not congruent with *B*; but we must know both *A* and *B* intimately in order to note their incongruities.

The director is constantly confronted with the fact that *if he and his actors are to make an audience laugh, they must first understand the jokes themselves.* In this sense, comedy may seem to require greater maturity not only on the part of the director and the actors but also on the part of the audience, although the actors may have great capacities to communicate comic ideas and thus simplify comprehension on the part of the audience. What may be obscure on the printed page can appear both obvious and funny in the hands of comic actors—the instruments through which the incongruities are conveyed.

Although there are many levels of comedy that range from humor (the audience *likes* the trapped character and laughs with him) to satire (the audience looks objectively and closely at the trapped character, usually disliking him and laughing at him), comedy as a composite type has specific, identifiable emphases within the basic elements of dramatic form. A good comedy throws a strong emphasis on a character who is simplified in such a way that we can readily see the distortions that have made him a fool in other men's eyes; we can see them, that is, if we understand what is considered normal behavior in the society reflected in the comedy. Norms are, therefore, very important in comprehending comedy. Thus, the action in comedy consists of a string of incidents that reveal the fool in situation after situation where he always shows the same distortions, the same variations from what is considered normal behavior. Consequently, the fun of a comedy usually consists of the reactions of the other characters to the continuing stupidities of the principal character until he finally sees how distorted he is, or, more usually, the others decide that it would be heartless to make him face his realities. In this sense, comedy is a social leveler because it shows average or less-than-average people caught in their own foolishness. It is based on the principle that no man knows what he is, that he cannot see his real mirror image but only what he wants to see.

Comedy thus produces laughter on the basis of distortion in character—a blind spot in the character's own view of his actions. Comedy can be gentle if the audience is led to sympathize with the behavior of the character, but it can be very cruel when a character gets no such sympathy and is laughed at.

The ideas behind this category of plays all concern man's adjustment to the social patterns in which he lives. They are literally plays of man against man. Given circumstances play an important part in setting up a comedy, for what may be funny in the context of restrictions of one social group may not be funny in another context at all. It also follows that the given circumstances place men and women on a fairly equal basis, for many of the ideas in comedy concern the struggle between the sexes, the age-old battle that never wants for an audience. Women are rarely the fools in comedy; it is the men who are the distorted ones in a world largely of their own making. Women are usually seen as creatures of common sense, while men are the creatures of nonsense in their confusion with what seems to them perfectly logical and so right that it can be taken for granted.

Dialogue is also given significant emphasis in comedy. In high comedy, we have conversation at its cleverest, its wittiest. Thus, language is not just a conveyor of action, but a delight, an entertainment, in itself. We love word play because we all use language, but we all do not have the capability of putting it together in amusing ways. However, though the young director must be highly aware of the text in a comedy, he must also pay the most careful attention to the subtext because what is truly funny will be there. As with the other forms, comedy is still a matter of dramatic action.

A knowledge of comedy from a theoretical point of view is invaluable to a director, for he will sooner or later tangle with this composite type. Among the valuable principles he will learn is the one that always causes trouble if he does not know it: *characters in comedy are all deadly serious about their points of view, and the principal fool is the most serious of them all.* We laugh at characters in a comedy because they take themselves so seriously. The young director will learn that comedians do not pretend to be funny, but that they are so caught up in the distortions they are playing that they are absolutely convincing in every aspect of those distortions. Good comedians are thus not laughing at the characters they are playing but are being those characters, a fact that makes us laugh all the more. An actor who plays a comic role in such a way as to show that he finds the character funny is seldom funny to an audience.

Directing comedy, then, involves knowing what is funny and then playing the action very intensively. Life is comic when we perceive the incongruities, and so it is on the stage. Comedy is all joke-telling of an elaborate sort.

EXERCISE

1. Apply the basic description of comedy discussed here to some of the following plays by citing how each play differs in structure but how they are generally alike:
   a. *The Frogs* (Aristophanes)
   b. *The Brothers* (Terence)
   c. *Volpone* (Johnson)
   d. *Tartuffe* (Molière)
   e. *The Way of the World* (Congreve)
   f. *The School for Scandal* or *The Rivals* (Sheridan)
   g. *The Contrast* (Tyler)
   h. *Man and Superman* (Shaw)
   i. *The Show-Off* (Kelly)
   j. *The Circle* (Maugham)
   k. *Everything in the Garden* (Albee)
2. What is a comic fool? Cite specific examples from the plays in Exercise 1.
3. Analyze a recent joke you have heard. Exactly what makes it funny?
4. Do a detailed analysis of a comedy of your own choosing by citing all the points that prove it to be a comedy.
5. If the students in the class are prepared with background for advanced study, and if time is available, the following should be read, studied, and discussed comparatively: George Meredith's *An Essay on Comedy* and Henri Bergson's *Laughter*. Additional readings, such as Northrup Frye's "The Mythos of Spring: Comedy," from *The Anatomy of Criticism* (Princeton, N.J.: Princeton University Press, 1957, pp. 163–86) can be most illuminating.

Farce

Just as melodrama is a diluted form of the serious play, so farce is a diluted form of comedy. Again, as in melodrama, the basic elements of the master type have been simplified and the emphasis placed on the external aspects. In addition, just as tragedies may contain some scenes where melodrama takes over in the interest of intensive physical illustration (Shakespeare's *Macbeth* is a good example), so comedies may contain scenes where farce is used to intensify the illustration.

Farces are usually packed with laugh-getting situations and business, for the emphasis is thrown on simplified characters, ingenious involvements, and physical illustrations. In television such plays are often labeled "sitcoms" (situation comedies). Although the characters are close to the realm of comedy by being distortions of life, they are meaner, more superficial, more puppetlike. It is precisely because they take life so seriously and can see no other avenues but their own that we find them funny. Excellent examples of farce are the motion picture reels of Laurel and Hardy where both characters have below average intelligence, both are clumsy and awkward, both are sober and serious, both work industriously with failure courting their every move. We can see ourselves in their farcical antics because we all have a certain amount of the same problems in everyday life; but at the same time, we can laugh at them not only because they are below average ("meaner") men, which brings out our own feeling of superiority, but also because we are distanced in a very specific way and made to see only certain things.

Farce takes on the look of exaggeration because of its simplified structural elements, but we can also see and easily recognize the incongruities in characters and actions because the actors hold them out to us in very clear ways. Although tragedy and comedy can be read from the printed page with a certain amount of reward, farces require acting to give them specific life because the funniest moments may be involvements with stage properties or machines or physical contact among the characters. Only occasionally do we have farces that depend on language as one of the major emphases, and in these cases the fun is still in the acting, for it is the actor's sense of timing in line delivery that will provoke the laugh.

Good farce on the stage is rare in our day because movies and television are more capable of presenting the contrivances of farce. But however a director picks up his knowledge of the dramatic values in farce, if he understands this composite type well, *he will be able to augment his sense of illustration in directing the higher form*—comedy. Fools are fools, and in working with comedy, a significant moment of farce that is still in taste and in line with character can often bring audiences to a clear understanding of the blocks in characters. Farce may be a lesser form of comedy, but it has the greater capacity of arousing audiences to explicit laughter by bringing them into the peculiar realm of fantasy that surrounds a farcical moment. An audience is simply lifted out of its sense of reality and led to believe in, if only for a few moments, the rarified world in which the farcical characters live.

EXERCISE

1. What is farcical in the following plays:
    a. *The Comedy of Errors* (Shakespeare)
    b. *The Doctor in Spite of Himself* (Molière)

    c. *She Stoops to Conquer* (Goldsmith): Is this play a comedy or a farce?
    d. *Box and Cox* (Morton)
    e. *The Importance of Being Ernest* (Wilde): Is this play a comedy or a farce?
    f. *Misalliance* (Shaw)
    g. *Boy Meets Girl* (Spewack)
    h. *The Bald Soprano* (Ionesco)
    i. *Luv* (Schisgal)
2. Why is the play of "Pyramus and Thisbe" in *A Midsummer Night's Dream* a farce?
3. Is Beckett's *Happy Days* a farce?
4. Do a written analysis of a farce of your own choice by proving from the structure that it is a farce.

Other Composite Forms

Although there are a number of labels in use to describe other composite forms (tragicomedy, absurdist comedy, for instance), what they tend to do is cross the lines of the major ones described above, thus delineating new composites by rearranging the emphases. At best, such labels are merely descriptive. Once the director understands the nature of composite types and how the principal ones are composed, he will realize that the game of close identification can be infinite, simply because there are so many possible arrangements of the pure composites (see Polonius's speech in *Hamlet*, Act II, Scene 2). Serious plays, for instance, may contain comic moments just as comedies may contain serious moments. *All labeling will, therefore, contain a certain amount of readjustment to this mingling of emphases, for few plays precisely conform to the strict definitions of the pure forms.* If you keep in mind that the director always deals with specific plays, and that the major categories are abstractions, you will not get caught in the dangerous game of labeling plays, thinking that you have a better understanding of them because you have assigned them to categories. You must also keep in mind that changes in drama come about when playwrights break the narrow prescriptions of composite types.

EXERCISE

1. How would you describe the following composite types? Try to use specific labels although they may be made by combining some of the four composite types already delineated.
    a. *The Bacchae* (Euripides)
    b. *The Second Shepherds' Play* (Anonymous)
    c. *Much Ado About Nothing* (Shakespeare)
    d. *The Misanthrope* (Molière)
    e. *A Month in the Country* (Turgeniev)
    f. *The Three Sisters* or *Uncle Vanya* (Chekhov)
    g. *The Plough and the Stars* (O'Casey)
    h. *Idiot's Delight* (Sherwood)

    i.   *A Man for All Seasons* (Bolt)
    j.   *The Boys in the Band* (Crowley)
    k. *Rhinoceros* (Ionesco)
    l.   *The Shadow Box* (Cristofer)

2. Make a list of as many plays from the modern repertoire you can think of that seem to cross the lines of the pure types. Why do we have so many today?

CHAPTER TWENTY-SIX
STYLE IN PLAYSCRIPTS 2
The playwright considered

It is dangerous to rely on historical sources in an attempt to understand those many plays that deal with history, simply because playwrights do not write history but use it only as background. Nevertheless, a knowledge of history—and this knowledge includes backgrounds in our own time—is an essential director's tool.

A well-known American dramatic critic recently remarked that he could not see how directors could direct or critics could write about plays since 1920 without having a lively understanding of Marxist philosophy and all of the forces working out of it. Although he was no Marxist himself, he felt that political ideas involving either favorable attitudes toward it or condemnations of it were everywhere in modern drama, and a director or critic could easily miss them unless he was politically oriented. What this critic implied by his statement was that a director cannot modify or adapt historical drama to our own time and tastes without knowing a good deal about the historical background out of which the plays of that period were written; knowing an author's bias or lack of bias toward what he took as historical fact can tell us much about the individual direction he may have taken in a play.

A director, then, must also be scholar, though he may think that label too pretentious. But whatever he calls himself, he certainly must do a great deal of probing into backgrounds if he is to understand the drama with which he works. If a playwright is still living and willing to offer assistance, conversation with him can easily solve the problems about background; but if this is not possible, a director will need to do a lot of spade work. To know an author and his sense of history as well as to know the historical background of his plays, is to understand the circumstances in which the author's style took shape.

Biography and history are therefore essential working tools in directing.

BIOGRAPHY AS SOURCE MATERIAL

Since playwrights tend to write about the things they feel strongest about, biographical research can often turn up parallels in an author's own life to the content in his plays. Understanding the playwright in Jean Genet also requires comprehension of Genet as a thief, as a convicted and sentenced criminal, as a hunted and haunted man, and as a homosexual. The same necessity for inside awareness applies to Sartre, to Shaw, to O'Casey, to Brecht, to Saroyan, to O'Neill, to Hellman, to Albee, to Shepard, and to any other playwright whose works a director wants to produce.

Certainly, we can be misled fairly easily by biography because at its base it is only an interpretation of someone's life, what the biographer thought it to be. And autobiographies are usually even more risky as dependable sources. But by reading such background materials carefully and by exercising your own sense of logic against the myth-making or image-making that may go on in any particular study, you can sift out significant points. More recent biographers have turned away from mere reporting of incidents and toward a sort of literary psychoanalysis. But the traps in this approach may be more frequent because the projections are more speculative, though the insight is keener and more revealing, and thus more illuminating to a director.

What is perhaps most directly useful about biography is the context out of which a particular playwright works. If a biographer has done his job, not only do the social, economic, political, and religious worlds in which an author lives and works stand revealed, but also the way he may have participated directly in dealings outside of his life in the theatre. Playwrights are public personages, and, as such, they become involved in human relationships and commitments that reveal them as individuals. Consequently, what they write about for the theatre may be very closely tied to their everyday behavior and social participation. This interrelationship has been particularly true among twentieth-century dramatists; but as we learn more and more about historical figures—Molière or Lope de Vega, for instance—we can see how they too were motivated in their writings out of the personal and public contexts in which they lived.

To be a director is to be highly curious about human beings. It follows that a director is not merely interested in the imaginary characters in the plays he mounts on the stage but is intensively sensitive to the revealing moments in the lives of the people with whom he works most closely, particularly his blood brothers— the playwrights.

HISTORY AS SOURCE MATERIAL

Again, it is necessary to point out that a director's pursuit of the historical background out of which a play is written can be very misleading, but with the exercise of great care, it can tell the director a good deal about a play.

Two aspects of historical review must be considered and clearly separated by a director. One is what the director accepts as historical fact *today*, and the other is what the playwright accepted as historical fact *in his day*. These two points of view may be in complete disagreement, and the director must keep them distinctly apart. We have been so influenced by nineteenth- and twentieth-century interpretations of history, many of them based on new scholarly discoveries, that we are all too ready to apply them to the thinking in other ages.

The safest approach to the study of historical backgrounds is to read contemporary (contemporary with the playwright) or earlier accounts of events used in plays that might have been available to the authors who wrote them. In this way, a director more easily can see what led to a playwright's interpretations of the events, and the resulting prejudices can stand revealed. Understanding Goldsmith's *She Stoops to Conquer*, for instance, can be much more lively if a director understands Goldsmith's immediate sense of history, his feelings about the new changes taking place in the late eighteenth-century society he wrote about—a class society confronted by humanist influences stemming from the revolutionary ideas associated with a slowly emerging philosophy of democracy. There are many lines in this play that must be interpreted in the light of eighteenth-century thought and feeling if they are to get through to twentieth-century audiences with force, clarity, and good humor. Likewise, you will know a great deal more about Lope de Vega's *Fuente Ovejuna* if you try to discover why the play seems to be filled with what we take to be democratic sentiments. Or about Marlowe's *Doctor Faustus* if you ask yourself: Why was he so angry at the Roman Church? or Why was he so angry? Or about Shaw's *Man and Superman* if you ask: What is the difference between Jack Tanner's political philosophy and Straker's? Or about Brecht's *Mother Courage* if you ask: Did he warp historical fact to make his play apply to the war-torn Europe of the 1940s? Or about John Osborne's *Look Back in Anger* if you ask: What was Osborne so mad about when he wrote the play in the mid-1950s? Or about Shakespeare's *Henry VI* if you ask: What did he know about Joan of Arc beyond hearsay?

Wherever the search may lead a director, he must always keep in mind that his intention is not to infuse a play with his own interpretation of history but to better understand an author's sense of what he was using as background. *The intention is not to uncover an author's errors in historical fact,* although that may be quite revealing, *but to see fully what the author found dramatic and exciting in his vision of humanity placed in the historical context in which he told his story.* Plays are largely about a *peripheral* situation surrounding historical events, but to see the periphery more clearly you must comprehend the core.

A director is not a historian or an archeologist in a technical sense, but he must have a lively feeling for history and how it works in plays.

OTHER WORKS BY A PLAYWRIGHT
AS SOURCE MATERIAL

In the study of one particular play for production, if a director studies three or four additional plays by the same playwright—plays written in approximately the same time period—*he will usually turn up most of the essential characteristics of that playwright's style.* This is not to say that playwrights repeat themselves in content, although this can occasionally happen even with the better ones, but it does suggest that because style is a very personal thing it can become inherent in a whole body of work.

Thus, we talk about an "an Ibsen play," "a Chekhov play," "a Shaw play," "a Williams play," "an Albee play," a "Shepard play," a "Henley play," and by these designations mean a characteristic style associated with each writer. We mean that

> each playwright probably chooses his themes from a certain range;
> the dramatic actions he devises are probably either serious or comic, or perhaps both;
> the given circumstances he arranges probably deal with people from a certain class who hold attitudes inherent to that class, and with much previous action or little previous action, depending on the emphasis he, as a playwright, gives to environmental control;
> the characters he draws in detail are scaled to the action;
> the dialogue he sets down has certain specific and individual markings because dialogue is the expression of his subconscious self, despite his conscious use of techniques in its composition;
> the moods and tempos he pulls out of all this particular usage will be individually marked in as positive and identifiable a way as the works of a musical composer.

By looking closely in this manner at a playwright's individual characteristics, the examination of several of his plays *written in approximately the same time period* can establish the general style associated with his work; and from this general description the director can move to specific elements in the particular play he wants to produce. *Comparative analysis is one of the surest ways of pinpointing style,* for what goes for one play probably goes for another *if their time of writing is fairly close together.*

The period of composition, then, is a very important consideration because the works of some writers span several decades during which time their style changes. If we are to understand changing style in a playwright, *we must compare works from different periods of his writing.* Ibsen's playwriting, for instance, spanned half a century. To understand the body of his work and be able to place any one play, we must know that his earliest plays can be loosely characterized as romantic-historical dramas; that he followed this style with the allegorical dramatic poems of *Brand* and *Peer Gynt;* and that he followed these in turn with the Realistic plays dealing with the contemporary society he knew. Later, the style of this middle period gave way in the late 1880s to a new one in which symbolism played a dramatic role, and finally in the last plays to what some critics have termed Expressionistic. Thus, it would be quite wrong to define Ibsen's style only in terms of *A Doll's House* or *An Enemy of the People.* We can, perhaps, group all of Chekhov's plays together because they were written within a much narrower time span, although perceptive students of his dramas usually see differences between the early and the late plays.

Do playwrights consciously look for new ways and thus new styles to express themselves? Like the rest of us, they are strongly influenced by the real world, and it would be strange, indeed, if they did not move with the times. *In one sense, this is what art means: the fresh revelation of man in the context of his times.* When we say that the plays of a certain author mirror his society, we mean that he found an individual way—his style—of telling his audiences about themselves that they could see clearly what they were compelled, involuntarily, to watch and listen to; and with study, we too can see that society clearly.

A director must be aware, then, of the shifts in style in a playwright's work, for in this way he may discover points of style that run throughout the body of his plays as a whole. In addition, the more he knows about a playwright's other works—his poetry or fiction—the more easily his style can be detected and pinpointed. Of particular value are his theories of drama and the practice of playwriting. Like most working artists, playwrights resist telling us how they make plays because they recognize that creative art is subjective, and that revealing the creative process in oneself is an extremely difficult, if not impossible, business. Yet, when they do write critical comment, as have Jonson, Lope de Vega, Molière, Hugo, Shaw, Chekhov, Maugham, Anderson, Miller, Williams, and many others, they must be listened to with great attention, for what they have to say may be of great import to their plays when you contemplate production.

STYLE IN TRANSLATIONS AND ADAPTATIONS

Strictly defined, a *translation is a literal and literary carry-over of a playscript* from one language to another, with the translator paying strict attention to accurate word or phrase duplication. *An adaptation is a loose carry-over of a playscript in an attempt to recapture its spirit and feeling* in language inherently possessing the capability of reaching audiences for which it is intended. In an adaptation, scene and line alteration is entirely possible because the intention is to transfer a play, not as a piece of literature, but *as a piece of theatre.* It is readily apparent that these two processes are very different in their intentions and thus in their final products. *The director's problem is to be able to perceive the quality of the transfer, no matter what method is used.*

Whether you are dealing with a translation or an adaptation is a most important consideration in perceiving style, for you will be entirely at the mercy of those who carry over plays written in languages with which you do not have a firsthand acquaintance. Since style is the inherent individuality in a work, how can you, as a director, possibly know what that individuality is unless you have either a firsthand command of the language in which a play is written or great faith in the capabilities of a translator or adaptor. Much attention has been given to this aspect of play production in recent years.

As the world has grown closer together and as we have found great value and interest in one another's plays, *theatre people have recognized that foreign-language plays do not transfer on the stage through words alone, but that far more intensive revelations of the works are necessary if the characteristic styles of the playwrights are to be captured.* The trend in the American theatre has been away from translation and toward free adaptation, not only of contemporary works but also of Greek drama and of French classical drama, on the premise that translators are usually only "language-oriented" and adaptors are "playwrights" who are not only able to comprehend dramatic action and its theatricalities first, but are also able to find the appropriate language of the theatre to cover them. But there may be poor adaptors, just as there are poor translators. In fact, some adaptors treat works in such a loose manner that the original work may be quite mutilated.

The process of adaptation is a most difficult one. After Lillian Hellman had adapted Jean Anouilh's *L'Alouette* for the American stage under the title of *The Lark*, she said she would never tackle an adaptation again because it was the most difficult dramatic composition she had ever done, with none of the compensations of free creativity. To understand the kind of work she did, you will have to compare her version with Christopher Fry's "translation" of the same work for London production. You should also note that the New York production was a success, whereas the London production failed. Can you see why?

For a good look at what has been done with ancient Greek drama, you should compare a recent adaptation by William Arrowsmith with one by Gilbert Murray, also an adaptor; and compare both of these against a standard translation by Jebb, Coleridge, or Trevelyan.

The search for style, then, in foreign-language plays depends a very great deal on what a particular translator or adaptor has discerned about the style of the original. If either is both a perceptive playwright and a critic with the capability of looking closely and "telling the truth," a director may find the style close to the original; if either does not know how to make the transfer, the director who uses such translations or adaptations, in T. S. Eliot's disparaging phrase, will "make a fiction" of the original work.

In approaching foreign-language plays, then, a director should examine closely all of the translations and adaptations available to him as well as a text in the original language. This means careful comparison, sometimes of several works. Translations are frequently helpful because, although they may not be readily playable on the stage, they provide clues to what adaptors have left out or changed. If possible, the director should work with a language consultant who can make fresh translations of contested passages or explain why translators or adaptors have chosen the language they use. In some cases a new adaptation will result because the director sees in a playscript dramatic possibilities that other translators or adaptors have completely missed. At the very least, out of this comparative examination a director will learn the strength of the playscript with which he is dealing, and he will be able to penetrate the stylistic characteristics much more readily. Style is the man. *And with foreign-language dramas, the director plays the role of detective even more than he does with plays in his own language.*

A word should also be said here about what to some people seems to be the curious phenomenon of plays written for the London stage, in English of course, which do not succeed with American audiences and vice versa. The difficulties, encountered in this exchange of plays in the same language points all too clearly to the very real problems in transferring drama from other languages. Failures in transfer can be explained only from the viewpoint that plays are deeply embedded cultural mirrors that require sensitive understanding of the culture out of which they are written if they are to be fully comprehended.

In particular, because contemporary drama looks so closely at cultural environments in its attempts to unravel psychological problems, unless an audience can feel the environment of the play through its own parallel and sympathetic environments, it remains insensitive to the dramatic action in a play except on a superficial level. This failure to feel environments has also happened to the European politically-oriented drama of commitment since 1920, such as that of Brecht, which escapes many American theatregoers because they cannot sense the dark intensity of the environment out of which these plays appeared. Similarly, the changes in English society, including the breakdown in the class structure, are unfamiliar and not well understood by American audiences. English audiences are similarly subject to miscomprehension when it comes to looking at American plays. If you read the reviews of the London production of Arthur Miller's *Death of a Salesman*, reviews which obviously show a poor perception of intense American concerns, you will know more about the problems of cultural transfer.

EXERCISE

1. Compare available translations and/or adaptations of the following: *The Bacchae, The Trojan Women, Oedipus Rex, The Frogs, Medea.*
2. Compare the "A" text with the "B" text of Marlowe's *Doctor Faustus.* See W. W. Greg's parallel text published by Oxford, 1950. Note the very great difference in content.
3. Compare several editions of Farquahar's *The Beaux' Strategem.* Note particularly the nineteenth-century acting edition.
4. Compare translations and/or adaptations of the following:
   a. Ibsen: *A Doll's House, The Lady from the Sea, The Master Builder, An Enemy of the People*

b. Chekhov: *The Sea Gull, The Cherry Orchard*
c. Strindberg: *The Father, The Ghost Sonata*
d. Pirandello: *Six Characters in Search of an Author*
e. Williams: *The Glass Menagerie* (variant versions in this instance).
f. Anouilh: *The Lark*
g. Albee: *Everything in the Garden* (Should this be viewed as an adaptation of an English play?)

CHAPTER TWENTY-SEVEN
STYLE IN PLAYSCRIPTS 3
Inherent individuality

Now that you are more aware of the nature of style as the *individual emphasis in form*, you should be able to do a much more intensive play-analysis, what amounts to an analysis on a higher level. In Part I, the intention of the discussion about play-analysis was to make you aware of the basic essentials that comprise dramaturgical form and their relationships to content, with the focus placed on the Realistic style. In the chapters immediately preceding this one, we showed much more specifically how form and content are related to each other and how they relate directly to style. Further, we discussed the types of plays (tragedy, comedy, etc.) in order to show the options open to a playwright in the interest of revealing how he can begin to individualize a play's action by treating it in a certain way. And finally, we pointed out how a director can get inside a playwright's style through working with biography, history, close study of other works, and study of translations or adaptations.

At this point, we can go to the crux of this discussion: how to do a style-analysis. Once you have learned how to do this, you will no longer approach plays in a general way but will always look for the specifics of individualization. You will learn to characterize the plays of a certain author as you would characterize one of the persons he may draw in a play. And further, you will learn to separate one play from another in the body of his work because you will be looking very closely at their specific characteristics. His plays will become personalities to you as readily identifiable from each other as are your close friends. *Once again, a director always directs a specific play, never a general play.*

WHAT TO LOOK FOR IN ANALYZING STYLE

Style-analysis as a technique is based on play analysis; this implies that you should not undertake it until you have completed an intensive analysis of the form and content of a play—a play-analysis—in the usual manner. You will be tempted to try to do both analyses, the play-analysis and the style-analysis, simultaneously, but if you do, you will miss significant information about the play. If you think of the first analysis (the one outlined in Part I) as *play description* and the new one outlined here as *style-analysis,* you will better understand why the first analysis must be done before undertaking the second.

What follows is a list of suggestions about what to look for in making a style-analysis. Many of them have been discussed in detail in the two previous chapters, so this can serve as a summary review. But there are many new suggestions that may at first glance have the look of play-analysis but go far deeper into the individualities of a play. Be sensitive to their difference if you are to understand the level on which you are now working.

Near the end of this chapter you will find a work sheet for style-analysis that you should add to the form for play-analysis at the end of Chapter 8. Used together, these two outlines cover all the major points of a play's form, content, and style.

Looking Outside the Play: Sources and Backgrounds

1. Date the play both in its general historical period in relation to other plays and in the body of work by the specific author under consideration.
2. Study the author's background through biographical sources. Try to relate him to his time, and try to see him as an individual working in a general cultural and aesthetic pattern. Probe his personal life for reasons why he should write the sort of play he does.
3. Study at least three or four other plays closely associated in time to the principal play under study. If the playwright's career has been a long one, examine other plays separated by at least a decade or more before and/or after the principal play. Study other works by the playwright, such as his poems, novels, short stories, essays, and, if available, any dramatic criticisms he may have written either about the work of other playwrights or about his own. Criticisms of this sort are invaluable since they may illuminate the playwright's specific intentions in writing his plays and whether he carried them out or not, or they may defend his work in a most revealing way. Introductions to plays often contain such inside views.
4. Carefully examine all available editions, or, if a play derives from a foreign language, study the available translations and/or adaptations. Read any commentaries that accompany them in the attempt to understand what a particular editor, translator, or adaptor had in mind when he undertook the editing or the transfer of a work. These introductory essays frequently contain valuable insights into various aspects of play structure which, after your own study, you may accept or disregard for good reason.

The translations and/or adaptations *should be studied for their actability in terms of the playwriting craftsmanship exercised in the transfer.* Compare lines and speeches for economy in word usage, imagery and poetic value, and simple craftsmanship in technical details, such as building to the ends of lines and speeches. Examine comparatively the available translations or adaptations for mood values, theatricality, and for all the dramatic values you think are commensurate with the play.

If a historical play in English is under consideration, you should look at all published editions, or if available, at unpublished manuscripts. Not only do playwrights change their own work before publication, but editors often make extensive changes depending on where they obtained the work for publication. Many plays have been published—historical as well as modern—as acting editions; that is, they are versions used by acting companies in actual stage productions, and they consequently reveal any additions or cuttings that may have been made in mounting a specific play. Such acting versions appear throughout English drama, from Marlowe's *Doctor Faustus* to Farquhar's *Beaux' Stratagem* to Williams' *The Glass Menagerie.* Only by careful examination of all available editions can you really know what sort of playscript you have under study. This may leave you in some confusion as to what to do, but at least you will be making your own decisions affecting style and are not so apt to be misled by others.

5.   Study the historical context of the specific play's setting. Where did the author get his material? Are the sources available, as is Arthur Miller's for *The Crucible?* If so, read the sources and, while doing so, try to decide why he selected the material he did and why he treated it as he did. Bernard Shaw's *St. Joan* and Jean Anouilh's *The Lark* are both about Joan of Arc and both draw largely from the same sources, yet each is different. Shaw's play, by his own confession, is a direct interpretation of history. Anouilh is not very interested in history but is greatly concerned with recapturing the poetic nature of the mythology surrounding Joan and her spirit as a French symbol in the context of a confused France following World War II. Lillian Hellman, in adapting Anouilh's play, made a third version—a melodrama that tells us more about her feelings concerning the Spanish Civil War of the 1930s than it does about the context of Anouilh's play or about the historical fifteenth-century context of Joan. What would you decide after reading the historical backgrounds?

Remember that you are not going to write your own notions of history into a play. The sole purpose of such study is to understand as thoroughly as possible what an author thinks and feels about any background material he may have used. Your own study must be pointed toward revealing a playwright's awareness of history and how he approached his use of it.

Historical-sociological research may also be of immense value in working with all kinds of plays, including fairly recent ones. How did people live? What were the mores in real life which the author mirrors, and how did they guide their actions and behavior? What is the play's context in which the author places his action? *Note that the dramatic actions of many plays depend on revolt against a society's existing requirements for behavior.* If a director has a more lively understanding of moral, religious, and social patterns, he will be better able to see the rigidities that must be overthrown. And with comedy, how will a director know what is funny unless he is knowledgeable about the patterns that make a character so ridiculous in the eyes of his contemporaries?

6.   Finally, when you have completed your other studies, you should study the dramatic criticisms written about a play—what others have said about it. This study should wait until you have made your own play-analysis so that those criticisms don't interfere with your own critical views. But sooner or later you must make comparisons, if only to pit your own conclusions against other interpretations. Instead of weakening your own ideas, countercriticisms should actually strengthen them because you

will then have a critical "audience" to fight with. Directing is setting out one's own interpretation with strength and decision. It cannot help but advance on firm ground if weak and vague comprehensions are thrown out in the "critical battle" and the strong ones are given purpose and direction. A strong director—the nature of his job says that he must be strong—is also a strong critic because he has faith in and has made a decision about his own interpretations or critical statements.

Looking Inside the Play: Inherent Style-Analysis

Again you must keep in mind that what follows is only a list of suggestions for helping to discover the *emphasis* a playwright may give to the basic elements in play-analysis. *His style will be defined by his particular use of the elements he considers most expressive of his ideas.* All plays will have all the elements, but individuality will reside in the particular use of those elements.

Given Circumstances

1. *Environmental Facts.* What level of society does he write about—lower, middle, or upper? Does the author show strong interests in political or religious backgrounds? What are the mores issuing from these environmental factors, and how strongly does the writer impose them on his characters? Is environment assumed (the royal court in *Hamlet*), or does the writer specifically and intentionally set out a mass of detail (small-town life in *Ghosts*)?

2. *Previous Action.* Does the author use a minimum of previous action to tell his story (*Macbeth, Delicate Balance, The Homecoming*), or is a great deal necessary (*Hedda Gabler*)? Where does the playwright begin his story: near the beginning so that he can show all the incidents (*Hamlet*)? or toward the end, just before the final major discovery (*Oedipus, Who's Afraid of Virginia Woolf, Cat on a Hot Tin Roof*)? More recent plays (since 1960) seem to have reduced previous action to a minimum in comparison to the way Ibsen and those who followed his techniques handled it. Departures from Realism tend to treat previous action only fragmentarily because the intention is not psychological development in depth but the unfolding of the action of the moment (*The Adding Machine, Our Town*).

3. *Polar Attitudes.* This is a most important stylistic declaration because *the points of view a playwright's characters will take toward the environment will, in turn, tell us what that particular writer considers important in the society he mirrors, and from that will come the actions of the play.* All plays are about revolt of some sort, about a character's overthrow of or submission to the restrictions that have fenced him in. Thus, as was shown in Chapter 5, the attitudes toward the environment at the opening of a play set up the initial pole in the major character (or characters if two are under consideration), which will be changed during the course of the action, resulting in a new attitude and thus a new pole at the end of the play. Plays take place between these two poles. *The style may be declared,* then, *by what sort of poles an author sets up* and, particularly by how he has individualized them so that they are fresh and therefore have the potential to move audiences. We are seldom moved by the trite; much of a writer's capability will lie in his devising of the polar structure. Since the initial pole will initiate the action, what sort of pole an author chooses will declare a point of style.

Dialogue

The way a writer handles dialogue can certainly declare the outward appearances of style; since dialogue also contains the action, the most careful scrutiny of this basic element is absolutely necessary.

Along with the usual study outlined in Part I, the director should *pay particular attention to those idiosyncracies in line development that bear the personal touch:*

1. Look for specific choice of words, with close attention to repeated words that may contain strong moods or even symbolic values.
2. Look for choice in phrases, especially if the play is in the Realistic style and the speech is intended to reproduce folk idiom. Does the playwright use key phrases to set off the speech of certain characters in idiomatic fashion?
3. Look for poetic overtones in word and phrase choice declared by the use of imagery. How elaborate are the images? How frequently do they occur?
4. Is the dialogue *economic* as a container of the action? How much room does it allow for acting? Does it tend toward the literary?
5. Does the playwright intend textual dominance or does the play exist more on intensive illustration of the subtext (Shaw versus Saroyan)?
6. If the lines are in verse form, what is intended in the way of rhythm delivery? Eliot, Fry, and Anderson, as well as recent versions of Greek plays and plays by Molière, among others, all require special handling because of the verse forms. Are you sensitive to the styles?
7. Reread and restudy "Dialogue: The Facade of the Playscript" in Chapter 5 to insure that you are aware of the nature of dialogue.

Dramatic Action

Again you should be certain that you understand the basic characteristics of dramatic action set down in Chapter 6 before you proceed. Now look carefully for the following:

1. How complex is the action? Is it (in Aristotle's definition) simple or complex (*Hamlet* versus *Mother Courage*)? Has the playwright written his play around a very simple unity of action, or does he have a multiplicity of incidents affecting two groups of people (double plot) only casually related but who must be brought together in a final synthesis (*Henry IV, Part 1*)?
2. How are time and place handled?
3. Whose play is it? Only by an intensive analysis can you sometimes determine this question in plays where two or three people seem to play very strong roles. *One character, however, must dominate.* Therefore, it is essential that you decide which one, for the author's style will be exhibited in the subtlety with which he handles such characters and the care with which he delineates them.
4. What is the *type* of the action? Here is a basic declaration of style. What sort of serious play or comedy does the author write? If you can describe it, you are describing a point of style. If the category is comedy, does he specialize in dialogue? In situations? In irony? In youthful caprice or in mature foolery? Is he a satirist? If you categorize him by the type of drama he writes, you will be able to pinpoint his style more clearly because you can compare his treatment of that type to that of other playwrights.
5. A major aspect of style lies in the sort of actions a playwright chooses to show on the stage. We say that drama is the showing of the strange, the unusual, the extraordinary, but what we mean by these words can differ greatly. We tend to regard as extraordinary those actions in real life in which we do not all participate: murder or violence, torture, sadistic cruelty, family destruction, and so forth. And it is possible

to bring any or all of these onto the stage, although in some historical periods they were banned. But are they the extraordinary?

Much modern drama converts peripheral action into the extraordinary—not the obvious we can all observe but the subtle, marginal action we seldom pay attention to in moments of great stress. Thus, when we see an automobile accident in the street, a normal person's attention is apt to be caught up in the details at the center: the injured, the ambulance personnel, the police, the wrecked cars. *Peripheral action in this instance would be the actions outside but near the core of the accident*: someone in the crowd who reacts out of mental recall or guilt; someone not associated at all with the accident who reacts in a certain significant way. These are what good playwrights are apt to find most interesting. Thus, we do not usually need to see hard violence on stage because the truly exciting moments, the real violence, is on the edge of the violent activity, and it is this marginal activity that holds our attention in the theatre. Here is the point: Authors declare themselves stylistically through the sort of actions they choose to record in the theatre.

6. How does the playwright make discoveries in the action? What characterizes the climaxes? Is the playwright truly theatrical?

7. Try to find the rhythm of the action. Here is a subtle delineation of style that is inherent in an author's work, something that can be very revealing of an author's individuality. If you can find his rhythm, you have pinned him down.

Character

A playwright is frequently known (his style) by the sort of characters he draws. One of the common truisms about Bernard Shaw is that his characters all sound alike, that they all seem to be talking as Shaw talked. This is a generalization to describe a point of Shavian style, for with few exceptions, the characters in Shaw's plays, no matter what level of society they come from, all talk in a dynamic, articulate way; there are no dunderheads, no inarticulate people, no low-energy types. Here is a point of style that a director must not only be aware of but learn to utilize to full advantage. In contrast, although Tennessee Williams' women might be grouped together as psychoneurotics—a point of style—the problem in style-analysis comes in trying to separate them to discover their special and distinctive psychoneurotic qualities. Like Ibsen, Williams has specialized largely in drawing female characters, but the life of each play will rest on the delicate shadings he gives to each character. Note Ibsen's specific attack. To describe his women as suffragettes or "new" women is to fail at delineating their differences. It is true that many of them are in revolt against the hard, Victorian, conformist world made by men, but you will find that they differ extensively once you examine them in depth. Ibsen's approach to playwriting often led him into drawing antipathies: Once he had developed a woman from one point of view in one play, he would follow it from just the opposite in another. Although they both drive men to their deaths, Hedda Gabler and Hilda Wangel (*The Master Builder*) are very different.

Style in characters, then, lies in the sort of people a playwright is interested in and wants to say something about. He does not select his people at random and by accident but chooses them from among those he knows best, those he has studied in real life and can see clearly. In this respect, there is no gap between William Congreve and Somerset Maugham, both of whom wrote comedies of manners about English society, because each wrote about the sort of people he saw about him. To hold our attention, plays must reveal humanity; thus, it is the particular eyesight a playwright possesses that will or will not open up life to us. We are not talking about photographic reproduction here but about perception. *Style results in perceiving clearly*, first by the playwright and later by the director, *for the clearly perceived statement can be singled out from what is generalized and poorly observed.*

What often holds our attention in the theatre is not the people we know but those we do not. The new have something of an exposé quality about them, and for this reason, new playwrights are always finding their way into the theatre; they are able to show us new people, new in the sense that they are freshly perceived. The interest in folk plays in America during the 1920s and 1930s may have come about as a reaction against middle-class drama. Was the middle-class audience that primarily supported the theatre bored with looking at its own kind? Did it find in the simpler life of the lower class something that was not only absorbing but also revealing? But look what happened when playwrights began to tell the truth about the lower class: that it was poverty-ridden; that poverty could be totally destructive; that the middle class was an actual enemy because it shut itself off from the lower class and forced its continuance. Here was the shock drama of the 1930s and again in the 1960s, that took seriously the characters caught in these given circumstances. The movement of audiences away from such truth telling is a matter of theatre history.

Here are some things to look for that concern style in character drawing:

1. Does the style lie in the *desires* of the characters—*what they want?*
2. Does the playwright deal with eccentric or rarely seen characters who hold audiences with great fascination (Genet in *The Balcony, The Blacks, The Maids*; Mart Crowley with homosexuals in *The Boys in the Band*; Gerome Ragni and James Rado with the hippies in *Hair*)?
3. Is it possible, in controversion of Aristotle's *Poetics* and Maxwell Anderson's "The Essence of Tragedy," to write successful tragedies about evil people? Who declares what evil is? And once we see "evil people" in explained circumstances—what makes them think and behave in the way they do—can we then see them in any other light but as human beings who may not agree with the way the majority thinks and feels? Are gangsters like Bonnie and Clyde the evil ones, or is it the society that made them the villains? The classical definition of evil seems to have altered, for in recent times there seems to be no fence between good and evil. Humanity can be anything, and absolute goods become only what the majority at any one time says they are.

Thus, *the problem of human values can become a matter of style.* Playwrights in revolt will give their characters those values necessary to achieve their ends. Consequently, the theatre in our time often holds our attention because age-old values people have long believed to be true are debated and even discarded. *Our most energetic modern theatre concerns characters who are caught in this revolution in value judgments.*

Idea

One of the crucial points about style in drama is that ideas in plays *become lost in time*. When we lose the context of a period, we also have great difficulty in reestablishing the ideas that made the plays of that period live in their day. Until fairly recently, the production of historical drama was approached only as storytelling drama with no other purpose than to show human motives and actions. In this sense, they were dead plays, because they were far removed from the heat and conflict of our own day—the quality in present-day drama that holds our attention. Nowadays, many directors approach the old drama quite differently because they have come to believe that such drama can also exist on the idea level if the ideas can somehow be pulled out of them; and also, that these plays are no different from modern plays but only seem so because we cannot "feel" the ideas easily. At the basis of this approach is the concept that plays always have underlying ideas and that plays are written out of an assumed context which its audience takes for granted. Thus, in this view, it is not that the historical dramas lacked ideas, but that *we have lost the contexts in which they were written*; and if directors can only discover the contexts, they can find out what made them vivid and living experiences to the audiences who saw them, and consequently, bring them alive for audiences today.

Therefore, the point of style—whether one is considering modern *or* historical plays—is what the playwright chooses to write about. *What are the ideas in an author's plays that make him distinct from other playwrights?*

The implication here is that no matter when a play was written, a director must search for the idea at its core if he is to fully comprehend that play. In today's approach to production it is not the updating of plays that interests directors but why they were written in the first place. To discover the idea behind a play is to discover the need for producing it. Productions that lack this purpose will be diffuse and vague.

It is also true that many plays are unified primarily by idea, especially contemporary drama. *Hair*, the rock musical of the 1960s, for example, is not held together by its story but by its theme or concept. Often such plays do not have characters in the usual sense; that is, the actors do not pretend to be someone else. Instead, they are agents of the play, and thus of the idea. Expressionistic, Brechtian, and Absurdist plays are also idea-unified in a similar way.

Here are some suggestions about style in ideas:

1. If you want to understand Ibsen, read a play from each of his four periods and compare the ideas in each.
2. Perform a similar experiment with Chekhov, although you will find that his plays are written over a shorter time span. Why are the ideas in each of his plays harder to separate?
3. Now look at the ideas Edward Albee uses. How do they differ from Harold Pinter's? from Samuel Beckett's? from Bertolt Brecht's? from Eugene Ionesco's? from Sam Shepard's? (Note that each playwright in this group is characterized stylistically by the ideas each develops in his plays.)

4. What is the idea in Euripides' *The Bacchae?* Read some recent criticism of this play to compare with your own ideas about it. Do you have any comprehension of what Shakespeare wanted to do with *Henry IV, Part I?* with *Othello?* with *As You Like It?* What was Molière's idea in *Les Précieuses Ridicules?*

5. Study the ideas in Brecht's *Mother Courage* and *The Good Woman of Setzuan.* How do they specifically mark his style?

Moods and Tempos

Although moods and tempos derive from the more basic elements of action and characters, they can explicitly mark style. The making of moods is the goal of the playwrights, as it is also that of the directors. Some playwrights—Chekhov, Saroyan, and Williams, for instance—have such lyrical capabilities that the moods they create tend to dominate their plays, and we characterize them explicitly as mood dramatists. By this designation we mean that their most prominent mark of style *lies in the quality of the moods* they make. But all plays reach and hold audiences through the power of the moods they are able to evoke, with one fact quite clear: moods must be inherent in the playscript, for they cannot be overlaid during production.

The first good reading of a play should tell you about its moods. Now is the time to note whether they are unusual and vigorous enough to declare a point of style. Later, after you have studied the play, you may find it more difficult to decide.

Tempos can be treated in the same way—by early discovery. Writers are characterized by their sense of rhythm in the same way we distinguish composers of music. Can you recognize anything distinctive in a play you presently have under consideration? Do you sense the strong variations in tempos? Is your playwright musically minded? What can be played very rapidly? What must move very slowly? Are there strongly marked differences in contrast throughout? Does the author have a marked sense of pause?

If you can detect the moods and tempos in several plays by the same author, you have probably found his basic rhythms. Some directors specialize in staging the plays of certain authors simply because they feel themselves in close harmony with an author's rhythms. But finding such rhythm is no easy matter. Because moods and tempos are more subjective than the other elements, it is often difficult to know, as a director, whether you have caught the style-rhythm of the author or are merely showing your own style-rhythm. A director has as many problems with letting his own personality show at the expense of a playwright as an actor has in trying to create a characterization.

SYNTHESIS OF STYLE

It is obvious that by summarizing all the points of style you have collected in this advanced level of play-analysis, you will be making not only a style-analysis of a playwright's work in general but also a style-analysis of a particular play. One point is very important: Work on this summary statement *must be done in stylistic terms* and *not* in terms of basic play-analysis. In other words, style-analysis *assumes* a knowledge of form and content; if you have made a form-content description first (basic play-analysis), doing a style-analysis will be relatively easy. Therefore, always study the play first in terms of form-content analysis before trying to set out the style-analysis. *If you do not work in this order, you will miss important aspects of style because you will not understand the content well enough to collect all the elements.*

The study of style in a particular play, then, is the study of its individuality. Before you write a job recommendation for a person, you first have to know a good deal about him; *a style-analysis is a personal recommendation of a play in the most specific and heartfelt terms.* "Style is the man," and you know the man well.

What follows is a suggested procedure for making a style-analysis. As you will note, it is a summary of the content of this chapter. Therefore, the purpose of the following work sheet is to help you discover a play's style by pinning down its individuality. When you have acquired experience in style-analysis in depth, much of what you will find difficult to do here you will later do very easily and quickly. But now is the time to teach yourself efficient procedures for the careful scrutinizing that discovery of style requires.

STYLE-ANALYSIS WORK SHEET

I. *Introduction*

  A. A style analysis should not be made until a play-analysis, as outlined on pages 64–65, has been completed because the content of this second analysis must be based on the accumulated content of the first. If you do a careful indepth play-analysis, you will have the facts necessary for answering the questions introduced here.

  B. Never force your play-analysis when you are looking for answers to the questions on style. *If your proof is not readily available, it may not be in the text of this play.* Be honest with both yourself and the play. Remember that the style of a playscript is based explicitly on what is there, not on what you imagine is there, although you may have to use your imagination extensively to pin down the explicit.

  C. The order of development of a style-analysis is the same as for play-analysis. Stay with that order and you will better understand the relationships of the basic structural elements in a play.

  D. Your intention in a style-analysis *is to look for the individualities* in a playscript. But remember that your author will have some of the same aspects of style as his contemporaries. These aspects are part of the statement of style and should be recorded as such. This approach is particularly essential in defining Realism, where you will too easily take many stylistic devices for granted because they seem to fall within common usage. Therefore, be certain to look closely for variations in that usage.

  E. The form of the style-analysis work sheet is arranged to cover the seven basic elements of play structure. The questions in each section are intended as suggestions and reminders of what to look for. The actual completion of such a work sheet should take the form of essay answers, but they must be brief, clear, and exactly stated. Do not use the questions as ends in themselves, but rather as springboards to guide you to your own perception.

II. *Given Circumstances*

    A. *Environmental Facts.* Is specific emphasis placed on any one of the categories? (Your answer here may well tell you the particular socio-political bent of your playwright and the play you are dealing with.)

    B. *Previous Action.* How much is used? Is there a specific emphasis on a certain kind of previous action? How is it inserted into the play: all in the first part or sprinkled throughout? How expert is the author in presenting previous action through present dramatic action? Where does the dramatic action begin in relation to the previous action: near the beginning with a minimal previous action or near the end with much previous action? What sort of thing is recalled: situations, character delineations, psychological flavorings?

    C. *Polar Attitudes.* What sort of poles has the playwright set up? Are they fresh? Are they obvious? Is the principal character readily declared through your analysis of the poles? How many characters are given polar positions (potential for change)?

III. *Dialogue*

What is distinctive? Has the playwright a "listening" ear? Does he use words in an individual way? Beyond the basic dramatic actions, what marks the speeches? Does he use characterizing phrases and repeat them? Does he use monologues (Chekhov, O'Neill, Osborne, Shepard)? What marks the length of the speeches? Is he witty? Of what does his wit consist? If it is other than prose, what characterizes the verse form? Does the playwright have a genuine ability for using verse forms, or are they laid on? If a line were to be quoted, what would declare its individuality? Does the playwright have a poetic quality, a sense of mystery, in his dialogue? How obvious is the dialogue?

IV. *Dramatic Action*

    A. *Unities.* Does the author observe or violate the unity of time? Of place? Of action? How tight is the unity of action and what makes it so? Does observance of the unities give the play an artificial or a natural flavor? How far-ranging is the action? Are there many minor plots or only a few? How tightly are the minor plots connected with the main plot or with each other?

    B. *Type.* What is the type of action? How can you support this emphasis from the detailed action? If it is tragic, what specifically makes it so? If it is comic, what specifically makes it so? If the emphasis is divided, how is this division done? Why? Does the action declare the play a melodrama or is the action only melodramatic? Why? Is the action farcical or comedic with farcical moments? Why? If the action is tragic, how does it stand up against Aristotle's definition in the *Poetics*? If it is comic, how does it stand up against Henri Bergson's definition? against George Meredith's? If you label the play serious, why?

    C. *The Ending.* How is the ending of the action handled? Do the characters make discoveries about themselves? Is a *deus ex machina* used?

    D. *Technical Development.* How are the *climaxes* handled? Are the methods of discovery logical and exciting? How quickly does the first action begin? How would you describe the surges in the play?

V. *Characters*

    A. *Choice.* What sort of people does the author write about? Why is the author interested in these people? How conventional are the characters? Are they conformist or relatively free? Are there any fantastic or allegorical characters? Why are they used?

B. *Development.* How finely drawn are the characters? Are they types or individuals? Why?

C. *Values.* What motivates the author in drawing his characters? Does he let them go free? Are they positive or negative people? Why or why not? If the play contains a hero (tragedy), what makes him one? If it contains a fool (comedy), what makes him one?

VI. *Idea*

A. *Choice.* In comparing this play with others by the same author, what sort of ideas does he like to treat? Is the idea in this play fresh or worn? Why?

B. *Validity.* Is the author an original thinker in any way? Does the idea have validity today? Why or why not? Is the author moralistic in the presentation of his idea or purely objective?

C. *Motivation.* Does the author seem to care strongly about the idea in his play?

D. *Quality.* Is the idea poetic? Is it purely practical? What is the potential of the idea for surviving?

VII. *Tempos*

Does the author have a musical sense? How can you prove the answer from the playscript? How sharp are the variations in tempo? Does the author tend to use erratic tempos, fast tempos, or are they slow and stately? What kind of music does the playscript suggest to you? How individual, how original is the author's musical sense? Is the rhythm of this play typical among the author's works? Can you describe his rhythm?

VIII. *Moods*

Is the play a *"mood"* play; that is, is it distinctly marked by mood dominance? Do moods tend to dominate logic? How do the mood-arousing techniques used by this author differ from those of another? How much does word choice have to do with mood arousal? Does the author use theatricality or business for mood arousal or does he generate the moods directly from clashes in the dramatic action? Are the moods odd or relatively usual?

IX. *Summary of Style*

You should now make a summary statement of the style by noting the points in your analysis that you think have the greatest emphasis. If you can integrate them in a conclusive statement of this sort, you will pin down your play as an individuality, for the summary is the epitome of your style-analysis.

EXERCISE

You will have to practice style-analysis extensively until you see clearly what must be done and why you are doing it. The tendency at first will be to revert to the content of play-analysis because it is easier to deal with content readily perceived than to deal with it in an overview. But with practice you will learn to separate the two levels of analysis and become much more articulate at the higher level.

The exercises that follow are intended to enrich your experience in style-analysis by leading you into divergent areas of play structure, beginning with the plays more familiar to you and progressing to the more difficult and removed ones. As you will note, the exercises are presented more as challenges than as specific problems to be completed.

You will remember that although the exercises begin at the style-analysis level, it is expected that you will first complete a play-analysis before beginning at the second level.

1. Do a style-analysis of *Riders to the Sea*. Can you see it as a play about three women instead of Maurya alone? Is the play a tragedy? If so, how does Synge get his tragic effect?

2. Do a style-analysis of *Ghosts*. Is this a romantic story about the sins of a father or is it an attack on a blind, middle-class morality upheld by a confused and weak clergy? Is Pastor Manders a villain or a comic fool?

3. Do a style-analysis of Chekhov's *Uncle Vanya*. Is it a comedy or a tragedy? How can some critics say that there is very little dramatic action when every page seems crammed with it? How does Chekhov handle dialogue? How does he handle mood values?

4. Do a style-analysis of Shaw's *Man and Superman*. How does Shaw handle dramatic action? Why is there so little of it? Is there great activity in the dialogue? What sort of characters does Shaw deal with here? Why? Is the play all "Shaw-talk," or are distinctive characters developed? Why is the play a comedy?

5. Do a style-analysis of Pirandello's *Six Characters in Search of an Author*. How does Pirandello tear apart the premises behind Realistic psychological drama? Is the play structurally classical in its use of the unities and denouement?

6. Do a style-analysis of Elmer Rice's *Adding Machine*. Why is it categorized as an Expressionist play? What is the play's intention? How are dialogue and character handled? Is the play a comedy?

7. Do a style-analysis of Bertolt Brecht's *Mother Courage*. Why does the dramatic action seem to have no climax but seem to be joined end-to-end? What is the function of the songs? How does Brecht use given circumstances to make his play meaningful today?

8. Do a style-analysis of Ionesco's *The Bald Soprano*. Can you see it as a conventional, classical comedy with a well-developed, logical action, conventional character types, climax, and denouement? How can you be easily misled by the dialogue?

9. Do a style-analysis of Marlowe's *Doctor Faustus*, using the B text with the comic scenes. How did Marlowe violate classical notions of a tragedy? What characterizes Marlowe's poetic line? Did Marlowe intend an allegory on his own times, an attack on his own political confinement?

10. Do a style-analysis of Molière's *Les Présieuses Ridicules*. How does the translation or version you are using present Molière's style in comparison with that found in other versions? Why is this play a comedy? What was Molière's motivation in writing it? Does it have present-day meanings?

11. Do a style-analysis of Farquhar's *The Beaux' Strategem*. What does Farquhar intend beyond a simple story of high jinks? What can get through to an audience today? How does Farquhar devise dramatic action in this play? What characterizes Farquhar's style in dialogue?

12. Do a style-analysis of Goldsmith's *She Stoops to Conquer*. What characterizes Goldsmith's handling of dramatic action? Does the play contain satire? Why? How is it easy to dismiss this play today as only shenanigans? What are its strongest eighteenth-century qualities?

CHAPTER TWENTY-EIGHT
STYLE IN PRODUCTION 1
General characteristics

Now that you are much more aware of style in playscripts and can identify a playwright's individualization, you are ready to attack your own problems of making style. *The goal is to make something you can call your own while maintaining the integrity of the play and the playwright.*

When applied to play production, *form* means the *general* shape of the staging, as opposed to *specific* shape. This definition implies that a playscript has been physicalized on an available stage, that it has been given some sort of scenic investiture, that it has been costumed and lighted (perhaps only with daylight), and that it has been acted at least in a minimal way. All staged plays have form because they observe the basic premise that makes the theatre a live ritual and different from the other arts, namely that a play is a story devised for presentation on a stage by actors before an audience. As pointed out earlier, basic form in production has remained unchanged since the fifth century B.C.; it is production *style* that has changed.

Style in production, as in playscripts, means *specific individuality*, a major step beyond form. As discussed earlier, style is defined as *both the general characteristics of staging in any particular age and specific characteristics of an individual production*, general characteristics being those conventions in staging that each age has developed and kept in use for a period of time (Elizabethan style; Restoration style, etc.) and specific characteristics as what a director implements in staging a particular play.

Today's director, then, serves as more than just a coordinator in play production. Instead, he is a stylist, an individualist. However, at the same time, because the theatre has always been and always will be a group art, he must learn how to lead his fellow craftsmen to creativity beyond themselves if he is to make the unique production he envisions. Are you both "a dreamer" and "an adventurous leader?"

PRODUCTION STYLE AND THE CHOICE
OF DRAMATIC EMPHASIS

The crucial point in style-making comes at the very beginning, when the director makes a firm, basic decision concerning the kind of statement he wants to make about a play. Every other move in this complex "chess game" will hinge on this decision. The director must, therefore, do his homework thoroughly so that he does not discover later in the rehearsal period, when it may be too late to redesign the production, that he has gotten off on the wrong track. As pointed out in Chapter 27, a thorough play-analysis topped by a style-analysis can lead to sensitive decision making because what your dramatic imagination may see in a play can be quite different from what someone else sees. *Your individual perception will be the basis of your style.*

Two basic decisions must be made: (1) Whose play is it, that is, which character is dominant? (2) What is the spine of the action?

Before we are aware of style, we are apt to assume that plays have limited basic meanings and that the principal characters are always declared. Thus, *Antigone* is about Antigone; *Macbeth* is about Macbeth; *Tartuffe* is about Tartuffe; and *Ghosts* is about Mrs. Alving. This assumption may be true up to a point, but beyond that, individual opinion comes into play because we make the play we see and feel. All we must do is place a very strong actor in what appears to be the second role and we literally see a new play. Why can't Cassius, instead of Brutus, dominate Shakespeare's *Julius Caesar*? Or Mark Anthony? Can't Creon become the principal role in *Antigone*, Lady Macbeth in *Macbeth*, Orgon in *Tartuffe*, Oswald Alving or Pastor Manders in *Ghosts*? Is Anouilh's *Becket or the Honor of God* about Becket or about the King? (Remember that Laurence Olivier switched from Becket to King Henry after playing the first role for many performances.)

Plays, you may argue, are about both the protagonist and the antagonist and both must be given equal positions. However, doing precisely that may weaken a play's structure. It will be better to settle on one character and give him prominence in every way. This will prevent begging the issue and will present a clear point of view. You may be prejudiced, but audiences can either argue with your view or see something new in it. When Tyrone Guthrie cast a black actor as Horatio in his Minneapolis production of *Hamlet* in 1963, he greatly changed the significance of this supporting role and, along with it, the usual concept of Hamlet as a character. What would you make of the play on those terms?

Characters are, of course, *the result* of the action in a play, for we see what they are primarily on the basis of what they do. Therefore, character and action are intertwined in such a way that one declares the other. Once a character has been established, he cannot be artificially manipulated; that is, he cannot be made to do things in violation of his character without stretching our sense of logic to the breaking point. (Have you read Robert Ardrey's *Thunder Rock*, in which one character, a writer, tries to manipulate a set of characters he has imagined only to find out that it is impossible?) Yet, it is possible to let actions lead our imagination in certain directions by building up evidence in those directions.

When Olivier made his film of *Hamlet*, he shocked critics and audiences alike with his strong emphasis on the Freudian aspects of the characters. Is Hamlet in love with his mother? Through a succession of scenes in which his camera probed Hamlet's subjective self, he placed major emphasis on this point. When the same actor played Othello as a full-blooded African Negro, with emphasis on Negroid physical features in face and body, he created a fresh view of a character in action—a fully declared style for the play. In an age when many people fear but at the same time are intensely curious about miscegenation, he played on the full value of that fear-curiosity and thus startled his audiences into new vision. *Romeo and Juliet* played by teenagers instead of mature actors as it was in Zeferelli's Old Vic production in 1961 and his movie version in 1969 gave audiences quite a new experience with the play.

What can be done with *Hedda Gabler*? Is there only one way to treat it or are there several possibilities? What happens with a production if:

1. Hedda is played as a Medea-like woman who revels in her dominance of others whom she craftily destroys?
2. Hedda is played as a nyphomaniac who brings about destruction of others because of the sexual denial of her marriage and the restrictions society has placed on her?
3. Hedda is played as a woman, perhaps homosexual, who hates and despises men because she considers them inferior and who goes under only when she finally meets an equal in Judge Brack?
4. Hedda is played as a masochist, as a suicidal paranoiac, who destroys everything about her, including a possible child before birth?
5. Hedda is played as a selfish, self-centered virgin who cannot stand violation of herself in any possible way?
6. Hedda is played as a "good" woman?

All these are options open to a director in his decision-making role. What his individual decision turns out to be will determine the style of his production.

Up to this point, serious plays have been under discussion, but you must be aware that decisions about comedies and farces may be even more difficult to make because the director must decide what is really funny in a play and how he can convey that joke to an audience. Comedy exists in the theatre only when a director and actor understand the incongruities; only then will they know how to reach audiences with the fun of a play.

Deciding whose play it is and, accordingly, making gradations in the comedy are absolutely essential if a production is to have stylistic unity. Feydeau's *A Flea in Her Ear* cannot exist on its second-act chase scene alone but must be carefully constructed as both a comedy of manners and a comedy of character in the first and third acts. *She Stoops to Conquer* is not just about Tony Lumpkin's high jinks but must also be about Mrs. Hardcastle's pretensions, Mr. Hardcastle's puritanism, and Marlow's impotence with well-bred women. If young Marlow is played straight, that is, as only a bashful young man, the principal comedy may not come through nearly as well as when he is played as an experienced London rake who moves unerringly among servant girls or the demimonde but turns to rubber when confronted with middle-class "goodness."

If a director does not discover how to make *The Way of the World* or *The Importance of Being Earnest* "talk well," he might better delay production until he does, since both plays depend extensively on their verbal wit. Is Sheridan's *School for Scandal* about Joseph Surface? If he is made the central fool in a slippery, falsely pious way not only can he be drolly amusing like Tartuffe, but he can also cause the other fools to stand out clearly. Without solid building of character based on decision making about character, comedy can never work because we are amused primarily by the incongruities in human behavior and not by the situations in which characters are caught.

"Whose play is it, then?" is a decision of major importance, and you can make this decision only by making the most personal and intensive examination of the action in a playscript and the characters that grow out of it. Once you know who will dominate and why, you can determine the specific line of action you want to emphasize and in this way declare the *spine* of your production. Each character will relate to this spine of action exactly as you intend him to relate to the principal character. You will now have a specific and personal way to tell the story of the play on the stage as you see it.

Although the Stanislavskian technique of declaring the spine by using the infinitive form of the verb is rather involved (see the essay by Elia Kazan, "Notebook for *A Streetcar Named Desire*," in *Directors on Directing*, ed. Toby Cole and Helen Chinoy, Indianapolis: Bobbs-Merrill, 1963), you may find it useful to reduce your decision on the action to this highly abbreviated form of summarizing. *Whatever method you use, the purpose will be to crystallize your own personal vision of the action* so you can easily hold onto this central drive that will declare at the base your style of production.

PRODUCTION STYLE AND CASTING

The style of a production will depend significantly on how a play is cast. Strong actors, appropriately cast, can declare the emphasis you have in mind. However, if they are inappropriately cast they can warp it. Casting is the basis of interpretation and it plays an intrinsic part in making style. Whoever plays a role will endow it with his specific personality, no matter how carefully the chosen actor works within the confines of the actions since, by nature, actors possess radiance and that radiance will suffuse the action. Who the director selects will declare the overall style more than any other factor.

Casting is such a delicate matching of weights and qualities, partly subjective and partly objective, that there can be no sure way to go about it. *Casting projects the future of a production*, a gambling process in which a director tries to foresee what will happen by balancing certain actors with clearly defined qualities against other actors with different qualities equally well defined. It is all weights and measures.

However, if the director has done his homework and if he has a fair choice of actors from whom to select, the style he envisions has a good chance of emerging. Success in this aspect of production can come about only if a director has a firm idea in mind of what he wants; haphazard casting can only lead to confusion.

The following are suggestions for the casting process, all of which affect style in one way or another.

Orchestrate Voices

A cast with a variety of pitch differences will not only increase the hearability level but will readily declare character qualities. We take for granted that characters in operas are written for certain voices—tenors, sopranos, bassos, etc.— but we are apt to forget that characters in plays have similar pitch requirements, although the range when compared to opera castings can be much greater and is not as stereotyped. Hear the play "in concert" during a final casting session by *not looking at the actors but only by listening to them* if you want to know what it is apt to sound like four weeks hence.

Size-and-Shape Type Casting versus Antitype Casting

Style in production often depends on the *unexpected*. Visual stereotypes may be necessary in some roles, particularly those that exert no particular force on the action and act as instruments to the main action. However, individualization in casting major roles may turn a worn play or a worn idea into a fresh and vitalizing experience. Antitype casting is casting against what seems to be prescribed type. From modern psychological drama we have learned one important principle that pertains to all drama: What people look like on the outside does not at all prescribe what they are like within. Consequently, in casting historical drama as well as modern plays, directors have turned away from nineteenth-century type casting and more toward antitype casting.

Where does the truth lie? Bertolt Brecht in describing the sorts of actors he would like to play his roles specifies "potato faces" for his women. He is suggesting that it is impossible to portray the peasantry who populate his plays with conventional types, and that truth lies in the rugged edges actors bring to a play rather than in their physical attractiveness. Julian Beck in his Living Theatre productions took the same position: Truth, and therefore beauty, lies in the spiritual values one holds and not in the visible physical realities; therefore, what we take for physical ugliness may possess inherent beauty. Further, it is possible that only by being "turned off" by unsympathetic exteriors can we begin to see the beauty behind those exteriors. Whether or not you agree with Brecht or Beck, you will discover that a high potential for production style lies in antitype casting just as you will find that certain plays (Feydeau's or Oscar Wilde's, for instance) cannot do at all without conventional beauty in its women as well as its men.

Special Qualities Reveal Action

The previous discussion declares the necessity for a director to cast a play in such a way that it can augment what he believes to be the emphatic action. Only then can he ensure that his point of style will be preserved. A large variety of actors can play a specific dramatic action fairly convincingly, but only a few will possess those essential qualities that will endow the action with moving overtones. Leading actors in the professional theatre know this fact, and they avoid roles they feel they cannot fulfill in this special way. In the amateur theatre where the director has a great deal of control, he can usually cast the actor who can best illuminate the emphasis he has in mind.

The search for special qualities, then, is the major attack in the casting process. Actual selection may revolve around whether a role should be played by a "cool" or by a "warm" actor since these qualities cannot be acted but will be inherent projections. Some actors can project more intellectuality than others; some project pure animality and nothing else. Some actors have natural decorum in voice and gesture for projecting upper-class roles, whereas others simply cannot reflect such conformist qualities of behavior.

What can be achieved in style will depend on what a director can project of his action-emphasis through the actors he selects in casting.

Overcoming Blocks

What stands between a director and adventurous, more exceptional casting and thus clear declaration of style are the blocks of (1) playing safe, (2) forming preconceptions about certain actors, (3) seeing and hearing too many actors in casting sessions, which results in a sort of blindness and deafness, (4) failing to make objective assessments before final decisions are made.

To help you overcome your blocks you need to develop specific techniques that will lead you away from subjective viewing and toward objective assessment. Get yourself into the habit of making a new tryout card for each actor on which you can record his voice quality and speech pattern, his sense of the dramatic and the theatrical, his capability at improvisation, his dominant qualities as you can see them on the surface, and his capability as an actor in general. Read each actor in several roles, particularly at the outset the one you think him least qualified for, and then make specific comments on his card. Use closed tryouts (one actor at a time) in the interest of keeping him from copying others reading for the same roles, and of relaxing him sufficiently so that he can show you who he is. After this initial assessment has been made you can hold group readings or improvisational sessions. You also must arrange your early tryout plan in such a way that you are always seeing actors as individuals; later when you see and hear them in groups, you will be able to see how each actor affects the balance in the group—what he can contribute that will be individual and, therefore, partly declarative of style.

A highly useful technique for sorting your actors is casting sheets on which you can list in numbered columns (1) the characters in the playscript (men and women collected separately), (2) a brief physical description of each character along with any special qualities essential to the role, (3) names of all actors who can possibly play each role, (4) tentative decision one, (5) tentative decision two, (6) tentative decision three, and (7) final decision. You should gather all this information on two or three sheets of paper so that you can look at the entire situation easily and comparatively. Items 4 through 6 will indicate each reassessment you make as you progress through the casting period. Before you make a tentative decision take a long, hard look at your choices: Are they fresh in qualities and ideas? Can you hear their voices in your mind's ear and are they the right ones? Are you being adventurous in leading young actors away from their tired stereotypes and toward sensitive and individual statements? Are the protagonist and antagonist in strong contrast? Are there possibilities for development of each actor as an actor during the rehearsal period?

The intention of all of these questions is to make you aware of what lies ahead, what an audience will eventually see and hear. Above all, if you want to declare individuality in your productions (that is, make style) you must be as adventurous in casting them as circumstances will permit because fresh statements are always the ones that communicate most easily to audiences.

PRODUCTION STYLE AND POINTING
THE DRAMATIC MOMENTS

Now that you have cast the play and moved into the rehearsal period, you are faced with many new decisions in effecting the dynamics of the play as you see it, and, consequently, the style that will emerge.

Violence, Size, and Energy

A distinct mark of style in play production is the *violence level*. Most young directors are afraid to open all the stops for fear such a procedure will result in overplaying and thus make the illustrations appear stagey. You should take just the opposite point of view while recognizing at the same time that opening the stops does not necessarily mean playing at high volumes but often just the opposite. *Good actors move audiences precisely through the intense level of illustrations they give to the violent moments—the climactic peaks of a play.* At these peaks they expend enormous energy by using their bodies as great and powerful instruments of communication. If we watch them closely, we also note that gesture has either increased or decreased markedly, for illustrations of violence require size in acting.

How you show violence on the stage will reveal your sense of style. You must never fear overplaying; it can happen only if the actors do not believe their dramatic action or fail to act reciprocally. Conversely, you should not underplay because it will never move an audience beyond itself or carry it into the astounding mysteries of the passions of life. Nor must you think that violence, energy, and size apply only to great drama. These elements must be used in all drama, serious or comic. *Audiences come to the theatre to feel energy vicariously;* this identification is what actually thrills them because it makes them perceive that such energy is also possible in their own lives. If you miss this inherent point about the need for acting, you will never touch audiences.

To make the "theatrical moment," make it in big, bold strokes (high volumes or low volumes, big movements or practically no movement at all). In your study of the playscript you should mark (in red pencil) the big moments in three stages: (1) *how* they are approached; (2) the exact points of climax; (3) how the characters move away from them. Then, in rehearsal you can help your actors see their great importance and can find the violence levels they require. Some professional directors use this power as the core of their work with the actors because it "phrases" a play and "paces" it through *contrast.*

The Light Touch

Style is also revealed by getting a play acted with a "light touch." Can you project violence fully and still do it with a light hand? This is the paradox. A light touch depends partly on directing techniques but much more on a director's natural sense of *taste.* It does not at all mean a withdrawal from intensive dramatic moments or a backing away in any sense from the fact that the theatre is a robust, knockabout business. What it does mean is that audiences are neither deeply moved nor made to laugh in the theatre if the acting is too heavy, stolid, or predictable. Theatre is an art form that dances and sings and is full of surprises; it is not sluggish battle between fighters, but a sparring match between boxers. *A light touch means a seeming lack of effort that permits the audience to relax into the play.* Poorly performed plays never let you relax because they always seem in danger of going awry.

Building imagination depends on a director's sense of taste, a quality that can be cultivated if he has an inclination to find out what it means. *Good theatre always has taste, since acting at its best is not reality but ideality.* Because selection and emphasis are possible in theatre art, what can be *suggested* is usually more powerful than what we encounter in much of everyday life. A director who plays music and lets his actors dance, both seriously and joyously, can make his points of style with clarity and feeling.

Tempos (Pacing)

Finding the appropriate tempos for a production is to discover an inherent way to project style. Tempos are always a matter of feeling and are deeply embedded in the personal nature of style. How a production moves will declare its style because rhythm is the basis of comprehension; we vibrate emphatically if we catch the rhythm and only then do we believe a dramatic action to be right and true.

Actors are frequently excellent musicians, but the primary job of determining tempos lies with the director because only he can control multiple-actor situations. As noted in Chapter 7 in the basic discussion of tempos, a play has a surging effect in its structure of action, like surf rolling in on a seashore where the waves grow larger and larger until they finally culminate in a climactic wave, which is then followed by a relative calm before the next surging begins. The director's job is the find these surges and to pinpoint their beginnings and endings.

The emergence of style depends on whether a director can build the surges accumulatively with variations in tempos, pauses, and climaxes in such a way that a performance becomes a rhythmic whole. Each performance must achieve this effect or the style will be lost. This is why plays that have long runs must be frequently redirected, with redirection actually the process of rediscovering the rhythm that has been lost. Top-flight baseball players, for example, lose their batting rhythm from time to time, sometimes for weeks or months, and go into a slump. Their recovery depends on again finding the split-timing (the inherent rhythm) that first established them at the top of their trade. So it is with actors in an ensemble: Once the rhythm is lost it must be rediscovered or audience concentration will be lost.

Style and the Amount of Actor Illustration

If you were to see a production of Racine or Corneille at the Comédie Francaise in Paris, you would be struck by the quietude with which the actors perform their roles. This quietude is a point of style because it assumes that French classical drama gains its greatest effects from line delivery and not visual spectacle. Some plays like *Le Cid* may be spoken in a hushed sound, only a few steps up from whispering, with the actors making very few movements or gestures. Such a style results in a dynamic and exciting theatrical experience because the verbal delivery is so unusual in the context of minimum visual illustration. Only at the Comédie will you hear a performance like this and you will be struck by its unique quality of style.

How much a director gives an actor to do or encourages him to develop will be a major point of style. American directors tend toward relatively heavy visual illustration, keeping the stage constantly busy. English directors do somewhat less, with a leaning toward economy and sparseness. French directors do least of all, in comedies as well as in serious plays, preferring their classical emphasis on the spoken play, whether modern or historical. How much visual illustration you use will depend on your inherent sense of rhythm and what you think your particular audience needs to keep its attention and concentration at a high level. Overillustration may make a play seem choppy and insecure, whereas underillustration my make it seem vague and undeclared. The only way out of this dilemma is to use *appropriate* illustration. Therefore, each play will have its own rhythm of illustration built into it, and the director must find this quality and develop it in his own terms and in those of his expected audience. For the most part, learning directors tend to underillustrate or to emphasize small, detailed movements at the expense of larger, more dynamic surges. You will, of course, discover how to handle illustration only through experience, but you must recognize at this point that style will emerge only when you use appropriate illustration.

Style will depend on the kind, quality, and quantity of illustration your production contains. You must learn to compose a play's illustrations so that there is always room for the "bigger and better" ahead. Quiet beginnings can lead to dynamic endings, whereas the reverse may result in boredom. Learn to build climactically; much of the secret of audience control will lie in this capability.

PRODUCTION STYLE AND THE CHOICE OF THE DESIGNS

The Metaphor

Many directors and designers build productions around metaphors because these images are, at the base, style-oriented. If the metaphor is a good one, it can have continuous application with many overtones throughout the areas of design or will at least work well in one area. The production style can, therefore, flow from such an image.

If the playscript of *The Beaux' Stratagem,* for example, is thought of as a clever chess game, with scene after scene of subtle maneuvering, it can be carried into production with a painted floorcloth made to look like a chessboard. Scenic pieces can then be whisked on and off like moves in the game, with each new setup forcing a new play by the characters involved, and so on. A metaphoric approach of this sort certainly has limitations, but it is possible for an exciting stylistic production to emerge. However, a director should never force a designer to work in this way unless he has been so trained. It is better for the director to create such an image for himself and then use it as he can.

Dominance in Scheme-Making

Production style depends greatly on physical production—what it looks like and how it works. Since a play is always seen as a fluid progression, a tight interrelationship in the choice of stage, scenery, properties, light, costumes, makeup, and sound is absolutely necessary if a style is to emerge. What the director must bring about is a production scheme that works because it enhances the actor as the principal instrument in the storytelling. It is the director's job to decide what should be dominant in a production scheme and then to tie in the other designs to that dominance.

The Mermaid Theatre's 1969 production of Henry Fielding's *Lock Up Your Daughters* used a marvelous stage machine, a high platform raised on a pedestal with two swinging arms, each having platforms and steps, and the entire structure mounted on a turntable. This machine not only allowed multiple locations both on the stage level, steps, and above on the moveable platform, but it also provided extensive possibilities for movement in a lively and vigorously busy play. *She Stoops to Conquer* (London, 1969) was played on a modified Elizabethan stage with a sharply raked forestage, side entrances, inner-below entrances, above positions, and a neutral area surrounding the whole as a place for the garden scene. By avoiding the usual eighteenth-century arrangement of wings and backdrops, the play was seen in a fresh way on what amounted to an Elizabethan stage.

Mart Crowley's *The Boys in the Band* (1968) was also staged on a modified Elizabethan stage with the scene "above" (the bedroom) approached by means of a curving staircase. Even more stylistic was the use of a Serlian adaptation: real furniture was placed against wall units covered with photographic murals of real rooms with furniture. The effect was super-Realism. Equally radical was the production of *Hadrian VII* (1969), which was staged in curtains with the exception of one interior scene (the attic). *Hair* (1968) revolutionized the American musical by not using conventional scenery at all except for a small scaffolding at the rear of a huge stage space and a few carry-on pieces. An unusually complex lighting design "in space" declared the style.

Many more examples of style can be given to illustrate how various directors and designers have seen plays in action and what they have chosen to dominate the physicalization. In the constant search for style, a new convention has appeared: *the more limited the scenic investiture, the more important the lighting becomes as emphatic design.* This convention in turn as forced changes in what to do with the lighting. Should it be full of color or should it be primarily white light? Should back lighting be employed as a basic principle? Should the quantity of light be an important factor in the style? All these questions directors will have to answer for themselves as each production is undertaken. In costume design, we are beginning to relearn earlier ways as we tackle the problems presented by the open stage with its strong sculptural demands.

The significant point in this discussion is to show once again the necessity of seeing interrelationships in design and how a director can make something fresh out of old theatrical devices. We no longer seem to be content in the theatre with the aesthetic of "peeking in" on humanity. Audiences now seem to want a theatrical theatre of high image-making potential in which it can more directly participate.

Counterpoint in Scheme-Making

It is important at this point to reread carefully the section on the *counterpoint principle* discussed in Chapter 20 to see how counterpoint is essential in the development of a production style. Designs that proceed from a single impetus will lack contrast and even necessary conflict. A director must see that each design fulfills its particular values in a production and that it exerts the force of its own individuality, its contributing point of style.

Results of Good Scheme-Making

A production must move. This is a basic fact about the theatre, a fact that no director can ignore. *Pacing a play also means pacing the scheme of production* because style will be the rhythm of the whole. In multiple stagings, where several sets are used, the quick change, perhaps in front of the audience, is an absolute necessity. In this sense, we are back to the seventeenth-century masque tradition and its influence on moveable scenery: We want the change as part of the theatrical experience. To lower the curtain and take an intermission for changing scenery (the practice of the theatre of illusion) is no longer feasible in a theatre that places a great deal of emphasis on things happening in a spirited tempo. *Style will depend on a workable production scheme.*

Tempo. Can all the designs be moved with the necessary speed to provide the appropriate tempo necessary to convey the style? The director must decide what the overall tempo should be and then see that designing is done in accordance with it. A clearly defined tempo in a production scheme will give an audience both a sense of security and rhythm of the whole. Waiting for scene changes reduces audience attention and concentration because once a production is set in motion it must continue to move rhythmically. If changes are made on a darkened stage, they must be made in a matter of seconds because waiting in the dark brings an audience back to its own reality, making it self-conscious. The major problem usually is scenery; but costume, light, and sound also require careful designing if the scheme is to work.

Effortless scheme-making. Graceful scene changes, if they are visible, are as essential in production as effortless acting. Whatever is done, and this includes visible actors or stage hands making changes, must seem right and inevitable since *the danger lies in making an audience overly aware of the staging effects,* a situation that will reduce their attention and concentration on dramatic action and character. Rhythmic changes tend to enhance the feeling of style because they have been made part of the overall rhythm of the play and are integrally associated with it.

The theatricality of change. Is the change interesting in itself? Without drawing attention to it, does the change provide the dramatic effect of suddenly presenting a new scene, costume, or light? The purpose of scene change is to provide new locales and new time settings and thus new action. However, does the change contain the element of surprise? The style of your production may depend on it. What is the mood contrast in the scene change? Can the dramatic difference be clearly pointed up with dynamic effect? Therein may lie declarations of the production style.

CHAPTER TWENTY-NINE
STYLE IN PRODUCTION 2
Modern plays

The general treatment in this chapter may disappoint you if you are looking for quick answers about how to effect production style with recent plays, the ones you are probably most interested in. Yet, you should now be well aware that finding style is entirely up to you, that it must grow out of your sensitivity and imagination, and a great deal of hard work.

All that can be done here is to alert you to the problems and some possibilities for solving them. You must do the rest. And if you do it well you will see how style in drama shifts from one tack to another, and how, consequently, style in production must also shift to keep abreast of it.

MODERN DESIGNATIONS OF STYLE

Although theatre historians and dramatic critics have categorized theatre history in accord with national development or historical eras (for example, Greek, Roman, Medieval, English, Renaissance, Jacobean, Restoration, French classical, etc.), when designating modern production styles they have tended to use labels often associated with other modern art forms—Naturalism, Realism, Simplified Realism, Surrealism, Symbolism, Expressionism, Formalism, Theatricalism, Inner Realism, Absurdism and others—as a means of grouping plays and productions on the basis of their likenesses in style. And rather confusingly, these forms have been applied to playscripts, as well as scenic investiture, lighting, costumes, makeup, and occasionally acting, although acting cannot easily be forced into formalistic patterns without being self-conscious or stripped of its human qualities.

For all practical purposes, however, there are only two major stylistic designations for modern drama and production that concern the director: (1) Realism and (2) departures from Realism. *These designations assume that Realism is the foundation from which other modern styles depart.* Once you grasp this concept, you will have little difficulty dealing with the jargon that accompanies modern stylistic descriptions since 1870. Nor will you need to join the labelers of style at this time but can devote your energies to making descriptions in your own language on the basis of what you see and hear and thus what you comprehend.

That labeling serves the function of separating differences is, of course, recognized, but the label alone will do no more than provide a general view. Specific designations must be based on analysis. By dividing all modern drama and production, then, into the two major groups of Realism and departures from Realism, you can proceed to specific labeling as you accumulate knowledgeable experience, not only through the actual process of directing plays but also through diverse theatregoing experiences and through looking at photographs of productions. Do not let yourself be confused by the labeling, or the categorizing; learn to make style-analyses by yourself and leave the labeling to others. Eventually, you should become familiar with the labels attached to departures from Realism since they are so widely used and can be confused with each other.

The intention in this chapter is not to undertake a detailed breakdown of the differences in modern styles but to plant an approach to the problem so that you may pursue it and grow with it at your own speed. Of very great help are two major discussions on the subject you should read: Mordecai Gorelik's *New Theatres for Old* and John Gassner's *Form and Idea*. Style is a complicated subject for the learning director, and only through study can you begin to formulate your own ideas about it. You may already have a strong, natural sense of style, but you *can learn how to exploit it only by becoming aware of what options are open to you* as a director. Makers of style lead the way and others follow; but no stylist ever works in a vacuum.

Realism

The range of Realism has been so wide during the hundred years of its history that we cannot describe it easily as one style. But simply stated, it moves from an exact copy of life (Naturalism, or reproducing nature exactly as it is seen with the eye) to a form so simplified that many aspects are only suggested (in production, painted molding is used in place of real molding). Whatever the gradation may be, the intention is to show life as it actually appears to be. *Realism is therefore a style to describe appearances.* Because human beings live their lives surrounded by these appearances, it is assumed that we can understand them as individuals if we can see them in the midst of their specific, viewable surroundings.

That this point of view (aesthetic) is seriously open to question is revealed in the fact that no sooner had Realism been established as a style in the 1890s, than the new stylists damned it as unpoetic, noncommunicative, inartistic, and as simply untrue to life. From that point on, we have had a steady stream of "departures from Realism," though Realism itself, in one modification or another, still remains the dominant style.

Departures From Realism

As the phrase implies, *"departures from Realism" includes all drama and production that moves away from the literal appearances of things. The basic intention of these styles is to communicate through essence rather than through appearance.*

The audience is given the feeling of something, and consequently, it is able to receive the communication in direct terms. This aesthetic approach assumes that observed realities do not communicate well because they are so familiar that most people do not perceive them, and thus cannot feel them. Reality is thus given a high degree of symbolization, frequently in abstract terms. And on the stage the designer creates lines and masses that contain essences of real objects, and we are able to *feel* them directly without the distractions of familiarity and everyday use. As viewers, we find these exciting and illuminating, not only because of their direct communication, but also because we may actually be "perceiving" the objects for the first time in our lives, not just "seeing" them. Art is an emotional experience and not an intellectual one.

One of the principal points about using such a label as *departures from Realism* for production designation is that it readily parallels departures from Realism in playwriting. We can see the two moving side by side since the 1890s. *But it does not necessarily follow that the departures from Realism in plays will all require departure from Realism in production.* Here is a crucial question about modern style: When can departures in production be used most effectively?

In the 1950s and 1960s, after several decades that thought dramaturgical style should be supported by the same sort of production style—that is, Realistic plays should have Realistic settings, and departure plays should have departure settings—what seemed to be thoroughly accepted has given way to a new style. *Today, we have no confining rules about style because anything goes that will work with audiences.* This flexibility means that Realistic plays can be effectively produced using departure approaches. Thus, dramatic writing and production style are recognized as two separate and distinct areas of theatre as far as style is concerned.

ADVENTURE AND EXPERIMENT—DIRECTOR'S STYLE

How much of an artistic gambler are you? Unless you are willing to venture as an "idea man" in the theatre, as a "maker of visions," you will never become a stylist and thus will never fulfill your total function as a director. It should be perfectly clear to you by now that taking risks is not done for adventure's sake but out of the strongest integrity and the highest regard for limitations in the theatre. Yet, even with these apparent restrictions, you can move out alone and make something that can be called style.

A director's statement of style is the physicalization of a play in such a way that an audience is lifted into a fresh and exciting perception of that play. Production style excites because it communicates emotionally; it can never be dull because it is a very personal, very intimate statement.

EARLY REALISM (1870-1915)

Since much of this book has been concerned with the Realistic style before 1960, further discussion of its general characteristics would be redundant. *But watch out! There are changes within that loosely defined style you must discover for yourself.* And these you can become aware of only through the most careful reading and analysis of the dramatic literature written in this style. Have you read a dozen plays by Ibsen? Another dozen by Bernard Shaw written before 1925? All of Chekhov's and Strindberg's? These are the Early Realists; and to know them well is to make yourself aware of the changes that follow their work, including today's plays.

When it comes to production, you will have many options to consider. Perhaps the biggest problem is that there are so few limitations in producing modern plays, for we are passing through an age that has more diversified staging than any previous period. The problem lies in finding what will work best. This has become increasingly evident as we try to bring the Realistic plays written before 1920 into clearer focus for present-day audiences because their dramaturgical techniques appear dated to us now. We certainly produce them, as some directors do, in the style of their first performances. But we may very well prefer to look at them in the same way we look at historical drama and to treat them as such.

This means that *a wide range of stylistic possibilities are open to a director in search of fresh meanings,* possibilities that may take him far from the box settings in which most of these plays were originally played. Like the American playwright-adaptors who have worked at transferring the plays of Ibsen, Chekhov, and Strindberg— Arthur Miller (*An Enemy of the People*), Thornton Wilder (*A Doll's House*), Stark Young (*The Cherry Orchard*), and Eva Le Gallienne (*much of Ibsen*)—American directors feel the pressure for finding fresh stagings. The "historical approach" is a good one because it recognizes that the major problem is audience communication. It is important to remember that these plays appeared on the heels of a Romantic theatre in which acting style by present standards was flamboyant and fully declared. Although the dramaturgy changed noticeably in style from that of Romantic drama, this does not imply that the acting style playwrights had in mind followed the same pattern. An acting statement may, therefore, lie somewhere between the large, flamboyant acting style of the Romantic theatre and the small, behavioristic pattern of post-World War I Realism. If you look for a larger, more dynamic style for the acting (perhaps something like that in early silent movies) in contrast to what playscripts seem to literally suggest, you may find that these plays can grip audience attention where a more sedate, a more naturalistic style will not.

Another acting problem with these early Realistic plays is finding the decorum of the characters represented. After all, the characters who populate these plays, whether they are Norwegians, Russians, or Frenchmen, are close kin to middle-class Victorians or Edwardians; and since the style is "observed Realism," *a director and his actors must find that outer facade that allows such plays to work. You must never forget that an important part of the style of "observed Realism" is showing a facade that covers up the interiors*—the skeletons in the closet—a game of hide-and-seek. You must, therefore, learn to build facades of manners just as you would for a seventeenth- or eighteenth-century comedy of manners, for you cannot break through them dramatically if they are not demonstrated. How actors walk, sit, stand, talk, laugh, greet others, wear their "clothing-costumes," dress their hair, handle objects, and so on, thus becomes very important. The post-1920 American lower- to middle-class folk drama has so disarmed us about a society in which class distinctions are taken for granted that young directors overlook the necessity of showing the mannered facades of the people in early Realism. *These plays are about environment and how it forces action.* You must, therefore, give intensive study when producing such plays to how you can reveal given circumstances with the greatest strength.

MORE RECENT PLAYWRITING (SINCE 1915)

The problem facing the young director is always to force himself into a fresh approach for each play he undertakes. We tend to take many plays written in the 1960s and '70s, for instance, too much for granted by assuming that because they look like Early Realism on the outside, they must belong to that familiar category. You will, therefore, need to search out the difference between "outer" Realism and "inner" Realism. Once again, *a director must always do a detailed style-analysis of every play he considers seriously for production, for only through this process can he be sure of a play's potential and thus be able to find a style that would give it life on the stage.*

You must also make your own intensive structural examination of the wide range of *departures from Realism* written since 1915. You should be able to pinpoint the styles of Wedekind, Toller, Andreyev, Kaiser, Ghelderode, Ansky, Cocteau, Lenormand, Capek, Jarry, and particularly Pirandello. Similarly, you should know O'Neill's departure drama and what characterizes his style in such plays as *The Emperor Jones, The Hairy Ape, The Great God Brown,* and *Strange Interlude,* as well as his more Realistic style in *Desire Under the Elms, Mourning Becomes Electra, The Iceman Cometh,* and *The Long Day's Journey Into Night.* You must also know the Americans—Odets, Rice, Sherwood, Behrman, Hellman, Saroyan, Howard,

Wilder, Williams, Miller, Albee, and Shepard—as well as or better than O'Casey, Synge, Maugham, Osborne, Bolt, Behan, and Pinter. The Brechtian style will attract you but you will need to give it a hard look to see how it works, just as you will need to study Sartre, Ionesco, Genet, Adamov, Beckett, and other European playwrights such as Frisch, Shafer, Dürrenmatt, and Betti. In other words, *you must study all we consider the best of modern drama. You must know the differences in order to see the likenesses.* But above all, you must become aware of the nature of individuality, the nature of style in playwriting, so that you have points of departure for making style in production.

Your biggest problem, however, may be controlling production, not finding what to exploit in it. Flight must assuredly take place; but to a young director flight in production too often means making the audience self-consciously aware of the clever staging—an approach that can obliterate the text and all that flows from it.

Departures from Realism (notably the Expressionist drama of 1910 to 1930, and the drama of the 1960s and early 1970s), are particularly prone to such treatment because they look so eccentric, so "out," that an inexperienced director goes all "out" in emphasizing eccentric aspects. You must learn, therefore, to recognize these plays for what they are: structured drama and not "odd happenings." Poetic prose or verse form must be delivered carefully and with great attention to line dynamics. Character "types" (types in contrast to the individuals in Realistic drama) need much more than obvious demonstration of why they are. Dramatic action needs the fullest sort of illustration to bring out the basic conflicts. Political and social points of view need careful pointing in lines and character demonstration. Moods and tempos must vary radically from those of Realism.

You must learn to avoid gimmickry in setting out these plays, for if you fall victim to such methods, it undoubtedly means you have not uncovered the inner recesses and the potentials of these unusual plays. *Departures from Realism as a category is the modern theatre's poetic drama,* and you can let it live only by treating it with integrity in production. Let it fly, let it excite and thrill with its physicality, but *let it come through on its own terms* and not through gimmickry you may devise because you think that it is the only way you can help it survive.

STAGE LIMITATIONS AND AVAILABLE OPTIONS

The options in staging discussed in Chapters 21 and 23 of this book are the basis for all modern production. Although these options allow very great freedom, a director may find himself physically bound by the limitations of a proscenium theatre in which he must produce. However, where this single form has been amplified or replaced in favor of multiple forms, as it has in some educational and nonprofit theatre plants, directors have found new ways of meeting the problem of modern communication. Multiple-production approaches are now possible as never before because we are overcoming the retrictions of theatre architecture and can think more and more in terms of stage-audience relationships and what they can do. Staging has thus become a matter of control of space, with its focus on intensive communication—reaching out and touching. The new freedom has given directors more possibilities for creating dynamic and varied theatre experience than any age has ever had. Whether or not the director can use it wisely and with sensitive imagination will probably declare his future need in the theatre.

As was noted in Chapter 22, the movement away from the proscenium has also given lighting a new dimension, as the problem is now that of *defining space* in a dramatic way. Although no similar declaration is apparent yet in costuming, the fact that costumes are often meant to be seen on many stages "in-the-round," more as sculpture, than they ever have been before, makes it quite possible that stage wear may undergo pressures that will move it away from the representationalism that has largely confined it since the nineteenth century.

ACTING STYLE OF RECENT DRAMA

A major assumption of this book is that the prevailing acting style in America, inspired by Stanislavski, has placed its primary emphasis on the subtext and its conveyance to audiences with extensively detailed illustration. But by comparison with the "behavioristic" acting of the 1930s and 1940s, there has been an increase in the size and deliberateness of illustration. More recently, greater emphasis has been placed on "delivering" the text, undoubtedly under the pressure of the English tradition and the common necessity for actors to perform in historical drama where concentration on the text is necessary. Thus, this more highly developed process of intensively illustrating the subtext and delivering the text expertly has brought us closer to the historical line of acting as we have watched it shift and change over the period of 300 years.

The acting style for recent drama, then, could be defined as highly illustrated psychological projection of both subtext and text. This style demands the focus of primary attention on character-mood-intensity to bring about "violence levels" in appropriate tempos. The director's best instruction in acting, beyond his own active experimentation as an actor himself, lies in watching the best of contemporary acting—the prevailing general style—for only then will he begin to see how particular actors differ in the way they do things. Eventually, he will be able to answer for himself why the best actors are the most effective with audiences, that is, what makes them stylists in their acting.

DIRECTOR'S STYLE

The emphasis up to this point has been on how to bring out the individual work of others. We have thus defined director's style as the individual product he assembles out of this exploitation—what we defined earlier as theatrical art. It should now be clear to you that *a director can only be what he is as a person:* the strength of his artistic perception and taste; the strength of his capabilities in being a leader; the strength of his skills in theatre techniques; and above all, the strength of his quiet, unassuming communication. The individual thing that he wants—the style of his production—can only emerge out of these qualities. Talent in a director, then, means innate possession of some part of each of these qualities; he must then build on his talents extensively through hard work and imagination.

EXERCISE

1. Concentration on plays from early Realism can accomplish a good deal for you simply because it will enable you to see the variations in Realism as a style and why the departures from Realism were necessary. You should, therefore, direct a scene from Ibsen, Chekhov, Strindberg, or early Shaw—stay with the masters to learn the most. Study the structures of their plays and isolate their individualities. Scenes from these plays done on the proscenium stage not only will tell you much about them as plays, but will give you motivations for moving to other stages with later plays.
2. Similarly, concentration on departures from Realism will give you a grasp of these styles. Direct a scene from Wedekind, Pirandello, the German or American Expressionists, Brecht, Saroyan. Save the "absurdists" until you have done the earlier playwrights. And save Pinter, Albee, and Shepard until after you understand the others.
3. After you have directed the projects suggested in Exercises 1 and 2, you should try a scene from a play written after 1963 that "looks like Realism." Be certain to note *the shift away from much previous action and the increased allegorical values of the action.* Are the departures still Ibsenite types? Or are they more abstract? Is the emphasis in your play on idea? What is "dark comedy?"

GAME OF VISUAL PERCEPTION 9: STYLE IN MODERN PLAYS

1. What is "theatrical" in each photograph? What would attract audience attention?
2. Can you contrast the style of production of *Delicate Balance* and *Pantagleize*? Also *Dear Liar* and *Cowboy Mouth*?
3. Can you see the symbolism in *The Flashing Light Bulb*?

PHOTO 57
Delicate Balance (Albee)

PHOTO 58 *Crimes of the Heart* (Henley)

PHOTO 59
Dear Liar (Kilty)

PHOTO 60 *South Pacific* (Rodgers, Hammerstein, Logan)

PHOTO 61   *The Flashing Light Bulb* (Allen)

PHOTO 62   *Suicide in B^b* (Shepard)

PHOTO 63 *Cowboy Mouth* (Shepard)

PHOTO 64 *Pantagleize* (deGhelderode)

PHOTO 65
The Visit (Dürrenmatt)

PHOTO 66   *Sunday in the Park with George* (Sondheim, Lapine)

PHOTO 67 *Evita* (Webber)

PHOTO 68 *End Game* (Beckett)

PHOTO 69 *The Doctor's Dilemma* (Shaw)

PHOTO 69a *Godspell* (Schwartz)

CHAPTER THIRTY
STYLE IN
PRODUCTION 3
New plays, musicals,
operas

Although this book is not the place to treat the directing of new plays, musicals, and operas in any detail since each is the subject of a book-length study in itself, some mention is needed because every director, sooner or later, will tackle one of these forms. He may have little specialized background for dealing with them, but it is nonetheless assumed that he can handle them as part of his job.

A young director can feel relatively secure with much of modern drama and even some of the historical, but brand new plays are in a class by themselves because they usually require extensive rewriting in cooperation with a playwright, a complicated objective/subjective process the director may not be ready for. Doing musicals and operas are also off his usual track in presenting him with the problems of "How much do I know about music? About dance? About singing, either solo or group? About leading actors, dancers, and singers in unfamiliar forms? About coordinating a staff of talented assistant directors in these areas?"

The contents of this brief chapter are therefore limited to the pitfalls you may encounter in dealing with any one of them. Still, caution never stops the adventurous director but waves him on like a red cape does a bull. But don't do your bullfighting without learning how to make the bull do your bidding instead of the other way around.

NEW PLAYS

In one sense all plays you direct are new plays since they are new to you. But as the preceding chapters have shown, there are specific ways to identify their contents and note their individualities. Your strength as a director would be indicated by how well you did these jobs of play-analysis and style-analysis.

A completely new and untried play can be approached in exactly the same way. Here the crux of the matter will become clear to you. When Shaw kiddingly says through one of his character critics in *Fanny's First Play,* "If it's by a good author, it's a good play!", he is not really kidding because he knows that experienced playwrights know how to make plays, that is, how to construct them in such a way that they will work with live actors on a stage before an audience; and these writers have lists of successful plays as proof.

A novice playwright is exactly like a novice director: Look in the mirror for his image, because he, too, will be striving for exactly the same goals you are—holding an audience tightly with theatrical matter that will move it to laughter or tears, or both. When he makes his original improvisation—his scenario—and shows it to you, he is holding his capabilities up for your examination and criticism. Are you sensitive to his fears of what you, as a director, will think of it? Further, what will you do with his delicately devised creation? Will you cut it up, axe parts of it, give it the death blow? Or will you let it live, breathe life into it, and make it fly? Or at least help him do so?

So, your quest in dealing with a new play and its playwright is the same as the one you have learned in dealing with actors and designers: working with this fellow-creator in such a way that his great effort is enhanced and not derogated. "As the objective 'outsider,' can I help him rework his improvisation to give it the strongest theatrical values it will allow? I am supposed to know how these values work in the theatre, yet am I really more sensitive to them than he is? Have I really examined his vision closely enough to make a judgement, or do I just want to turn his play into what I would like to make of it? Am I poaching or thieving?"

As you can see, these are subjective questions the director must ask of himself before he reaches out to the playwright. Only then will he be able to deal on a one-to-one level, and perhaps enhance the play. Such relationships are tender and must be full of understanding on your part, for without closeness and sensitivity, what you intended for help may well turn into confusion and "the director's play," not the playwright's. Look before you leap.

Although there is a great deal more that makes a play work than its structure—for example, its imagery, its mood values, its peaks, its understanding of life—the structure is one place to begin your study of the playscript. Since most novice playwrights may not yet be aware of the inner workings of dramatic action and its relationship to character development but tend to see a play more as a literary display through dialogue, you can focus your critical awareness in the usual manner of play-analysis by asking all the necessary questions about workable structure. Do the scene units serve direct functions? Are they sufficient in scope and dynamics to tell the story? Do they move in climactic order from a beginning to a middle to an end? Do they show a change in the principal character; that is, has the character come to any new knowledge and thus declared new directions?

Once you have perceived the weaknesses and *strengths* (this is very important) in the structure, you can then do a style-analysis in the usual manner to see what individualizes the play and really makes it work.

By following these objective procedures you will not only know a great deal about the play at firsthand, but you will have specific points for your talks with the playwright. When you begin these, there is an absolute caution: *you are not the author of this play* but an informed critic who supposedly knows how plays work in the theatre. *Listen! Listen!* to the playwright. Try to discover what he has in mind, for this may reveal to you qualities you may have missed as well as give you jumping-off points in your talk. Your prime action is to communicate, not dominate, for the object is to help the playwright improve his play and not that of shaping it to your own mold.

Plays are not just written; they are rewritten. You can help this process if you go about your work as critic with the same caution and care you give to the creative efforts of actors and designers. Skins in the theatre, no matter how tough they look in public, are very thin indeed. Be a "head's up director," not a know-it-all.

MUSICALS

Music in the American theatre comes down to us from the eighteenth century, when the convention of a theatre-orchestra playing "airs" and accompanying songs in plays as well as entracte singing and dancing was in full sway. Later, in the nineteenth, the orchestra began providing background music to onstage dramatic action, a convention that was continued through the era of the silent movies, and with the advent of electronic sound down to the present. The nineteenth century also saw the expansion of songs in plays, especially those with native American comedians, and then singing and dancing in great quantity in the minstrel shows.

In our century, with George M. Cohan leading the way, the theatre musical came into its own, first in the skit/song/dance and production numbers of musical revues, then with *Oklahoma!* and its counterparts in the highly integrated form of musical comedy, with its story told in dialogue, in songs, in production numbers, in elaborate scenery, costumes, and lighting, and with a big orchestra in the pit. The "big musical" of the 1950s had arrived, and with it the strong need for the stage director. But what sort of director could do the best job became the question.

An important point to remember: Many of the new musicals were adaptations of regular stage plays: *Oklahoma!* from Lynn Riggs's *Green Grow the Lilacs; Carousel* from Molnar's *Liliom; Kiss Me Kate* from Shakespeare's *Taming of the Shrew;*

My Fair Lady from Shaw's *Pygmalion; Cabaret* from Van Druten's *I Am A Camera.* Stage directors thus found a place because the new form needed acting, careful scenic development, and coordinated staging. But since the performers were also required to sing and dance, the director would either have to be proficient in one of these areas (Gower Champion and Bob Fosse in dance) or serve as a stage director-coordinator (George Abbott). Subsequently, when the "big musical" gave way because of its enormous expense to the "intimate theatre" of *I Do! I Do!, The Fantasticks, Chorus line, A Little Night Music, Take me Along, Sweeney Todd, Edwin Drood,* and their kind, the stage director was assured of a place, especially because the singing-dancing chorus was gone and the weight of a show now fell on the performance capabilities of the principals in acting, singing, and dancing.

"What sort of musical can I do?", then, becomes the question a director must ask himself.

In the big musicals the director is largely a coordinator, and as such he participates in every aspect of the production, from designing to execution. The structure is already firmly established through the book and music, and he will do well not to tamper with it until he understands the relationships of certain songs to dramatic moments and scene changes. Instead, he exercises his ingenuity by talking music with the conductor, discussing dancing with the choreographer, working out staging with the set, lighting, and costume designers, and closely coordinating his plans for use of the stage in "getting out the book" with anyone concerned. Finally, the director will bring it all together—this enormous pattern of dramatic scenes, songs, and production numbers with their dancing and scene changes; and he will set the rhythm and pace of the show.

With the intimate musical, the director may participate directly in all aspects of development. So, the questions now become, "How much do I know about musical form? About dance? About combining them with dramatic moments? About learning how to respect the creativity of the people in music and dance? These will declare the director's range and scope in the planning and execution. If you can work partly in all of these areas, and know how they contribute to the story line and dramatic action—the dominant thing the audience desires and expects—you will know how to raise your creative partners to greater achievement.

The handling of musicals is thus very much like staging plays: the more you understand about style and how it can work for you, the more you will see what you can do. Remember: Music has been a part of the theatre since the days of the Greeks, and its place in today's theatre as a way of communicating form and feeling differs little in function from its ancient forebears. To understand the American Dream of success, as presented in *42nd Street*, is to understand how each age has always found a way of showing its mythologies and mysteries on the stage, and how it has aroused audiences to high spirits, even exultations, in doing so. Musicals are very much a part of our time and our feelings about life in America.

Doing musicals is truly a venturing out. It will challenge all your skills in coordinating and finding rhythms in a conglomerate of music, songs, dance, and dramatic moments.

OPERA

Opera, no matter how it is staged, is always a musical event, and it is the conductor who is in charge of the total production.

Yet this does not mean that a stage director cannot make a genuine contribution, despite the fact that opera has long been caught in the mesh of tradition that makes it seem more rigid than it actually is. Until recently, the physical production was in the hands of opera stage managers who knew the scores, the scenic investitures, the stage business, the movements of the choruses, and much more. But after the middle of this century, stage directors were often employed in hopes of updating the opera stage in line with twentieth-century stage conventions. With the growth of opera production in the universities, this became the general rule at that level. After all, opera in its first appearance at the Teatro Olimpico in Vicenza at the end of the sixteenth-century was thought to be a close representation of classical Greek drama—the singing actor in significant dramatic actions. So it should be no surprise to find directors at work on opera production today as primary assistants to musical conductors.

The realistic operas of Puccini and other composers of his day seem almost as real to us nowadays as straight plays, that is, if they have been staged with full awareness of their romantic and lyrical intent. And though Wagnerian opera is far removed from the seemingly real street events of Puccini, Wagner believed his work was music-drama and assiduously blocked the staging in great detail with poetic imagination and the full use of the theatrical conventions then available to him.

However, in universities, or even some secondary school situations, most young directors are far more likely to be called on to stage operettas like *The Student Prince* or *The Mikado*. In a very real sense these types are as much plays as musical events, with their prescribed dramatic actions and fully defined characters that need acting and activities beyond the music to give them full life on the stage. In working with these pieces, the imaginative director can readily see the difference between traditional business and what he can devise to illustrate it.

Whether you direct operettas or opera, your sense of style will be a primary take-off point, as well as your awareness of musical form and how it dictates stage behavior. At any rate, your homework of play-analysis, then style-analysis, will lead you to what must be done. Only then will you be able to talk to the music people and begin the intense process of production with designers and the singer-actors. Help yourself by closely observing the work of other directors with these forms, for they will show you how they have found relationships of musical patterns to stage movement, as well as how to resolve the necessity of the singer's eye on the conductor's beat—the face-front in its most inflexible form. The main problems will center around developing units of action, though character-mood-intensities have been well-prescribed by the music. You will learn that you must make climactic illustrations strong enough to match the music and thus capture the overall intent.

In the 1980s, we seem to have passed the age of assuming that opera is *entirely* music. Consequently, other factors have come into play. In Italy, Italian opera glistens with excitement because audiences hear the language and understand what is happening. In America, television productions of opera *with captions in English* have done much to distinguish the first-rate singing-actors from the others, simply because audiences can now be the judge of the total experience. No longer are we being told what we should be "seeing" through the cloud of music delivered in a foreign tongue, but we can actually see and hear what is happening (or not happening) firsthand.

Therefore, much more pressure has been thrown on conductors, and their stage directors, to insure clarification of action through meaningful and dynamic illustration. When opera singers in the old tradition learned a role, they learned the traditional stage business attached to it, and this has continued to a certain extent. Nevertheless, singers as well as conductors, especially in university situations, are more open to fresh ideas that will help the total communication. The sensitive director is thus in a good position to enhance that communication with blocking suggestions and other organically conceived ideas. Have respect for tradition, but be adventurous too.

Intimate opera in the arena style or on a small projecting stage with one or two pianos has found some favor in recent years, but it is not without problems. *Be inventive with opera, but take great care not to destroy its main function as a form of music.* The meaning of "grand" in grand opera might conceivably derive from the unusual scenic investiture so usual in preceding centuries, but in its basic sense it refers to the grand scale of the music and the use of serious themes. Reducing such pieces to "the play's the thing" can subvert their inner cores as musical form. Yet stage directors can participate in the modern resurgence and public interest in this old form of theatre, now spread across America in opera companies in several major cities, if they approach it with the utmost respect and learn to talk with music people in their own language.

CHAPTER THIRTY-ONE
STYLE IN PRODUCTION 4
Historical drama

THE ADVENTUROUS DIRECTOR

No young director should tackle historical drama until he has a backlog of experience in modern play production; nor should he venture into this most difficult realm of staging until he has a lively concept of styles in both playwriting and production. Historical play production is not for the novice but for the experienced director simply because, as the previous chapters have pointed out, a mature understanding of play-analysis, together with a strong sense of what composes individual expression (style) are basic requirements.

Yet, the peculiar paradox is that venturing into historical play production is one of the best ways to learn about the modern theatre, because historical perspective lets us see much more clearly the changes and distinctions in modern styles in both playwriting and production.

This book, therefore, takes the position that although period play production *for a public audience* should wait until a director has accumulated some experience with modern plays, *training in directing cannot be complete without experimentation with historical drama.*

Thus, laboratory production exercises that can be readily combined with critical discussions are suggested, for a very great deal is to be learned through personal discovery. Like the other arts, play production is discovered in the doing and not in talking about it. Even though such experimentation may turn out poorly, the conscientious student will learn how to use his imagination as well as how to restrict himself.

It follows without question, however, that all such production experience must proceed in the pattern suggested in Part III; first, a style-analysis of the play, then, and only then, a stylistic approach to production. In this sort of laboratory experience, the use of scenery, lighting, and costumes would not usually be available. Yet, much can be done even with these limitations, for you still can decide on an appropriate stage, determine minimum lighting, design a groundplan, and, above all, *work with actors*.

You must learn how to handle essentials before adding other determinants of style. It is quite enough to wrestle with the ideas in an antique play; with what translations or adaptations may be available; with the problems of verse forms; with acting problems of all sorts, including the all-important one of intensive work on delivering the text; with the choice of stage; and with the necessary choreography. Visual designs can wait until later when you will have much better ideas about their use. Actors like to experiment too; so, learn all you can from them.

THE RANGE OF CHOICE

The body of historical drama, as defined here, includes all plays before 1875. This date is, of course, an arbitrary one, but it is used here as it is in most modern drama studies in order to mark the beginnings of Ibsenite Realism which closely relates to the dramaturgical patterns still dominating our stage.

Although the range of drama throughout the 2400 years before 1875 is extensive, the actual repertoire of such plays actively produced in America would probably be less than 100, of which only about half are produced regularly, and the other half sporadically. European theatres range more widely because of their national dramas and state theatres, and therefore do much better.

The following list will give you some idea of the scope of producible historical drama. In looking at this list, however, you must keep in mind that many historical plays are given individual productions when directors discover unexpected pertinence in them, and that this list contains only the most frequently produced plays.

Historical Plays Produced in America in Educational Theatres and Occasionally by Nonprofit Professional Theatres

FAIRLY FREQUENTLY	OCCASIONALLY
Oedipus Rex	*The Agamemnon*
Antigone	*The Choephori*
Medea	*The Eumenides*
The Trojan Women	*Electra* (Sophocles)
The Bacchae	*Prometheus Bound*

Lysistrata
The Birds
Shakespeare: fifteen of his most
popular plays

Hippolytus
Hecuba
The Frogs
The Menaechmi

LESS FREQUENTLY

The Second Shepherds' Play
Everyman
Doctor Faustus
The Shoemaker's Holiday
Volpone
The Alchemist
The Beaux' Stratagem
The Country Wife
The Imaginary Invalid
The Bourgeois Gentleman
Tartuffe
The Doctor in Spite of Himself
The Highbrow Ladies
She Stoops to Conquer
The Rivals
The Mistress of the Inn
The Servant of Two Masters
The Inspector General
Wozeck
A Month in the Country

OCCASIONALLY

The York or Chester Cycles
Gammer Gurton's Needle
Shakespeare: ten of his less popular
plays
The Duchess of Malfi
The White Devil
'Tis Pity She's a Whore
Fuente Ovejuna
Cervantes: Short plays
All for Love
The Way of the World
Love for Love
The Misanthrope
The School for Wives
Maria Stuart
Faust I
The Contrast
The Critic
The School for Scandal
Fashion
Uncle Tom's Cabin
Ten Nights in a Barroom
Across the Country
Rip Van Winkle

Additional Plays Produced Occasionally in Europe but Rarely in America

Classical Greek plays other than those noted above (in Greece)
Sencea (Italy)
Mandragola (Italy)
Shakespeare: all other plays (England)
The Jew of Malta (England)
Edward II (England)
de Vega and Cervantes (Spain)
Molière: all other plays (France)
Corneille, Racine, Marivaux, and Beaumarchais (France)
Goldoni (Italy)
Goethe and Schiller (Germany)
Nathan der Weise (Germany)
Hugo and de Musset (France)
von Kleist (Germany)

You should note from this list that France and Germany regularly produce a number of native playwrights whose works are little seen elsewhere; Italy and Spain occasionally revive plays by Goldoni and de Vega, respectively; Greece presents frequent revivals of the ancient Greek dramas; and England stages a variety of English plays. Only America has no regular productions of native historical drama. Except for *The Contrast, Fashion,* and *Uncle Tom's Cabin,* very few nineteenth-century American plays are staged except in the distorted form of travesties *(Ten Nights in a Barroom; The Drunkard,* etc.).

As a result, *America, more than any other nation, is heavily involved in producing the classics from the European repertoire.* This is particularly so in educational theatres, where even Japanese Kabuki plays have been attempted. Thus, in search of tradition wherever they can find it, Americans borrow heavily from the English drama and make regular forays into the French, the German, the Italian, the Spanish, the Russian, and the ancient Greek. Shakespeare and Jonson are as much produced in America as in England, although their minor plays are less frequently tackled. Jacobean and Restoration dramas are not often produced, for in many ways these plays are deeply embedded in English culture and are thus more difficult to transfer. The English comedies of the eighteenth century are not infrequently produced, although not without the attendant problems of separated cultures. To see *Lock Up Your Daughters* or *The School for Scandal* in London where one is surrounded by architectural and historical reminders of the eighteenth century is quite a different matter from seeing these plays in New York or Chicago. Nevertheless, the body of producible plays is still a fairly large one, and the director's problems stem mainly from finding ways to tackle each national drama.

THE DIRECTOR MUST HAVE SOMETHING TO SAY

Producing a historical play without having something specific to say can only result in vagueness and lack of meaning. Audiences turn away from such productions because they look like dead museum pieces caught up in costume and staging display. To make a historical play meaningful to an audience, a director *must first find and pin down a core idea that is meaningful to him.*

Having "something to say," however, does not mean overlaying a play with a director's own ideas, for his intention is not to act as a collaborative playwright but as an interpreter who wants to bring alive from the printed page what he feels to be moving or amusing in a play's content. *The director's intention, then, is to put on an entertainment that a modern audience can respond to,* and to do it in such a way that that audience will be able to feel and think about what the director has felt and thought about in his association with the play.

This challenge is very great because historical drama is truly inert drama— remote in ideas, archaic in language, even obscure in many actions—until someone comes along with a sensitive perception and a gift for style-making to breathe life into it. "Something to say" in this sense becomes a personal conviction, and out of such a conviction can come clarity and unity.

But once you feel strongly about a play, you must submit yourself to the next personal challenge: Will my ideas mean anything to average theatregoers who have not studied the play carefully? This is a rigorous, direct question because a director can easily be trapped, once he studies a play, by the historical context within that play and what surrounds its writing. *The challenge is to say something for now and thus to place the play in a present-day context.*

Perhaps the challenge will be only that of revealing the blind spots in our present-day way of looking at things. But more than likely, if a director searches deeply enough into a play, an idea can be found that can disturb us into new thinking about the world we live in. Great plays have the capability of revival because, somehow, they manage to say things about mankind that have been true in all ages. How to present those ideas so that they can be readily perceived by audiences today is the problem in production.

Here a director's acute sensitivity to his own times becomes a necessity, for he must find in these old plays those things that his audiences feel and know about their own culture. Of one thing he can be certain: Playwrights throughout the history of the theatre have been writing about human beings for audiences who have been intensely interested in the dilemmas of other men and how they were either trapped by them or escaped them.

The form of drama as human spectacle has not changed, but only the immediate contexts in which such actions take place. A director's study of a particular historical drama, then, must proceed on the closest examination of the dramatic action in the context of the given circumstances. Once you comprehend this close relationship, the inner values of the play will become much more apparent to you.

In the 1960s, for instance, audiences could better understand violence and revolution in historical drama because of their own similar dilemmas. Not only was that decade actively making new plays that contained these feelings, but it revived a number of old plays that "came into meanings" not previously apparent. Jacobean drama, some of Greek drama, and even Shakespeare can be cited, along with productions of such plays as *The Dutchess of Malfi, The Bacchae, The Trojan Women, Prometheus Bound,* and even Shakespeare's history plays, including *Henry VI* and *Coriolanus.*

These plays seemed to find audience comprehension on the level of feeling because directors found ways to make them speak the *"rhythm"* of the 1960s. *The premise that historical drama is acceptable to modern audiences whenever the rhythms are closely parallel to modern feelings makes excellent sense.* Such a theory implies that the dramatic actions in such plays are recognizable and meaningful on the subjective, emotional level.

But no matter how a play is reasserted with present-day meaning, *a director must believe in that meaning as strongly as he would in that of a recent play based in his own context.* Finding something to say is finding the first point of style on which all other production points will depend.

ARTS-AND-CRAFTS HISTORIES AND ARCHAEOLOGY
AS BACKGROUND STUDIES FOR STAGING

Because a great deal of a production style is expressed in visual languages, whether or not a director deals with modern or historical plays, he must have a sensitive and detailed knowledge of the past. When objects or dress are new, the people who make them use them naturally and freely because they have discerned their need and can take their functionalism for granted. But when we use historical objects or historical dress, if we are to prevent them from "using" the actors (a situation that never fails to draw attention to the objects or dress and away from the dramatic action) someone—and the someone is usually the director—*must know their original need and thus their proper use.* The same thinking applies explicitly to set design, whether it is a wall treatment, a furniture piece, a door, or a stairway that is being considered. Guessing is no substitute for knowing what is right.

This approach has never been more important than it is today when we frequently abstract historical places. The style of presentation may only suggest a specific locale; yet, the design must start from a reality since all true abstractions are firmly rooted in real-life usage. Conversely, side-by-side with the "theatre of suggestion" is the "theatre of realistic reproduction," a style that may continue for many decades, as we continue to live in an age of science where we are very much interested in explicit circumstances. Some settings we see on the stage today are almost as exact in their photographic realism as any that Antoine brought onto the stage in the 1890s during the height of Naturalism. The style of Realism as we have known it during the twentieth century is far from dead, and the director must be thoroughly familiar with real places if he is to exercise any control over the design of a production.

Of equal importance with scenic investiture is costume. *The history of clothes is required knowledge,* not only for designing stage wear but also for acting in such wear, because real clothes had and have movement of their own making. If you visit the Smithsonian Institute in Washington, D.C., you can see nearly 200 years of women's evening dress in the wax museum of former Presidents' wives. The fun in viewing this collection lies in imagining how the flowing skirts of the earlier periods moved in contrast to the confined dresses of the 1920s and 1930s. Such knowledge of dress can tell one much about decorum; and since decorum is style, directors can be sure to bring style onto the stage if their awareness of clothing is highly developed. A comedy by Feydeau or Oscar Wilde, for example, would be very poor without such awareness. Actors expect directors to have this information at hand, although they may pursue the subject on their own.

A background for the making of style, then, is the study of archaeology, within which the study of portrait painting, which mirrors the past, may be most rewarding. Everyday crafts also tell us much, as do studies of music and architecture. *A director is constantly on the museum route because his job often requires him to mirror past ages.* He is also an avid reader of social, economic, and cultural history because he must know what a playwright of another age takes for granted that his audiences will bring to the theatre without his explicit mention in the play. The actual style of production may well be far from exact *re*production, but such stagings all begin with a keen awareness of what real places and real clothes looked like.

THE HISTORY OF PRODUCTION AS BACKGROUND

Approach and Uses

Historical play production as a term means the production of plays in their *original context* insofar as that context can be determined. Awareness of theatre architecture and how plays were produced is invaluable simply because playwrights have always taken for granted the stage machine for which they were writing, since they were making skeletons to be fleshed out and clothed by production. The study of the artifacts of theatre history can tell us much about the buildings and the productions in them.

Historical stage costume is much more difficult to ascertain accurately because few records exist to tell us explicitly what was worn. Until well into the nineteenth century, actors wore what they considered appropriate out of their own wardrobes because coordination in design had not been established as a premise in staging, as it is today, except in court masques. But it is the rarity of visual historical records that makes this study fascinating. As you continue with directing, you will learn to look everywhere for hints—at paintings of actors (not very reliable), at line drawings and etchings, at brief descriptions some viewer thought worth setting down. *Your eye for such detail needs careful exercising. Too many students regard theatre history as a peripheral rather than as a central study in their work, a point of view you simply cannot hold if you are to be a director.*

What to Look For in Historical Play Production

Since the production style of each period will differ in what it emphasizes in form, the study of any particular period will revolve around the basics of all production form: (1) stage shape and audience position, (2) scenic investiture, (3) properties, (4) costuming, (5) lighting, (6) makeup, (7) sound, and (8) acting conventions. The following check sheet of what to look for points out the range of your necessary study, because you can apply these questions to any period in theatre history. As a continuation of the material included in Chapter 20, this list encourages you to search out theatre history as explicitly as you can in the interest of discovering the nature of production style. You will certainly add to the list of questions here as you continue to make detailed historical studies on your own.

EXERCISE: CHECK SHEET FOR HISTORICAL PLAY PRODUCTION

It is suggested that the question sheet be applied to at least two different periods of theatre history so that the production style of each can be seen in contrast. The general assignment can be broken down further by alloting each of the primary areas to a few students who will then pursue the search in detail and report their findings to the class. Make a list of new questions raised in the general discussion.

1. *Stage*
   Where does the audience sit or stand in relationship to the stage? How close?
   Is the stage raised above the audience or lowered below it?
   Is the stage raked? How much?
   Is the stage roofed? If so, what purpose does the roof serve?
   What is the exact shape of the stage? Is there an apron?
   Is the stage floor trapped? Why?

2. *Scenery*
   Is the scenery a permanent architectural facade? If so, why? What purpose does such a facade serve? What does it do in terms of line and mass? How do actors gain entrance to the stage? How do entranceways affect the speed of entrance and the relationship to action already going on? Is the scenery fabricated and changeable? If so, what are the active functions of such scenery? What is done with line, mass, and color? How real is such scenery? How much of the stage is occupied by scenic investiture? Are the stage spaces above the usual acting areas used? What are the acting areas and how effective are they?

3. *Properties*
   What is the quantity and extent of the set properties? If none are used, why not?
   How real are they?
   Are they carried onto the stage or previously set?
   How often do actors use hand properties in acting? (Confine your answer to historical use, not what you would do as a director.) What kind of properties do they use?

4. *Costuming*
   Why are costumes used?
   Is what is worn costume or clothes?
   How are the line, mass, and color employed?
   What is their potential for movement?
   What is the silhouette for both men and women?

5. *Lighting*
   Is daylight or artificial light used? What would daylight accomplish? If artificial, what is the method? What effects can be achieved?
   Where does the light originate?
   Is the audience lighted with the same light as the actors? Why?

6. *Makeup*
   What function does makeup serve?
   What techniques are used? How widely do they range?
7. *Sound*
   What kind of sound effects are used?
   How are sound effects made?
   Are they live sounds or mechanically reproduced?
   Is music used? How?
8. *Acting*
   How is movement employed?
   What is the size and the scope of gesture?
   What sorts of compositions are used? Is the full stage used or only a portion of it?
   How well is the actor heard? How does he probably project his voice?
   Is speaking the primary theatricality? Why?

REACHING AUDIENCES

Style in Staging

Once you have found a modern meaning for a historical play you are considering, you are in a position to decide on the physicalization. The problem is the same one confronting the director in finding something to say about a play: *the physical staging must somehow convey modern feelings if the play is to come alive on today's stage.* Archaeological reproduction, as we have pointed out, is a dead end, and finding other ways is quite necessary. Here are a few possibilities:

Adaptations of historical stages. One approach to the design problem is to devise a modern staging that uses the basic elements of the historical stage for which a particular play was written. With this approach, a director has the possibility of finding the inherent physical rhythm of a play because its production can proceed from its historical environment. Although playwrights have always written for a specific stage, it does not at all mean that they did so consciously, for they probably took the popular stage form for granted; yet, *it is precisely this subconscious assumption of stage "place" that will make the patterns of the play vibrate with life and vitality.* By adapting a stage to incorporate modern feeling in a direct way, a director can meet the inherent demands of a play in its original context, and, at the same time, can reach his audience directly because it will "feel" the stage subconsciously as a part of its own world.

Such staging will involve the use of mass, line, and color in such a way that it will be in keeping with modern rhythms. Thus, the production will look very modern without the playscript actually being so. The use of modern lighting procedures can aid greatly in such staging.

Relocation of a play in an entirely different historical context. Another approach in trying to reach modern audiences is to mount a play with settings and costumes in a completely different period from both the time in which it was first produced and from our own. When the American Shakespeare Festival staged *Troilus and Cressida* in Civil War costumes back in the 1960s, the intention was to place the play in a context American audiences could understand, not that of their own day but that of America's past history. The New York Shakespeare Festival took a similar approach with *Much Ado About Nothing* in the 1970s by staging it in an American context of 1900. Such relocating has definite advantages, since it is possible for an audience to see a play imaginatively through its personal feelings about past historical associations. The "something to say" is thus historically placed; but because of the symbolism and mythology surrounding such history, an emotional reaction on the part of the audience becomes possible. (Note how Bertolt Brecht has used something very like this approach in his retelling, with modern overtones, of John Gay's eighteenth-century *The Beggar's Opera* under the title *The Three Penny Opera,* and Farquhar's *The Recruiting Officer* under the title *Fife and Drums.*)

Even though costumes and scenic pieces of the relocated period are used, modern lighting effects can still give the production a sense of belonging to the here and now. The challenge in this sort of symbolic transfer is to find an appropriate historical period that will reveal the play; but the director must remember that if he forces such a context, it can be both distracting and confusing.

The use of a neutral stage.   Another stylistic approach is an adaptation of a form of staging introduced by Jacques Copeau at the Vieux Colombier in Paris nearly a century ago. His idea was basically architectural, for it required a single unit setting that could be rearranged via a system of interlocking platforms and steps to become locations for scenes without "representing" them in a realistic way. All recent architectural stages proceed on the same principle: a stage machine that can be easily manipulated.

The neutral stage has many advantages since it leaves the audience's imagination free to create its own places. Because this stage is functional, it offers extensive opportunities for variety in movement and scenic locations. Period costumes on this stage are very effective because they provide "scenery" in a modern, dynamic way. Modern principles of stage lighting can also be used effectively to give a seeming modernity to a production.

Modern dress production.   This style can be very effective with highly selected historical plays. The intention is, of course, *to make the play belong directly to us by giving it the look of contemporary life.* Thus, the choice of stage is modern (perhaps open staging); the properties and costumes are of recent fashion; and the lighting and sound are what we would expect in a contemporary play. Such stagings are not easily accomplished in America because of the difficulties in finding gradations in dress to readily delineate class differences that audiences will easily recognize, particularly those of royalty. But even if parallels in dress can be found, forcing plays into this kind of staging does not always help communication. It has worked for *Julius Caesar, Hamlet, Coriolanus,* and *As You Like It,* but *Othello* or *A Midsummer Night's Dream* might suffer badly, although some directors will try anything in the interest of more direct communication.

Acting Styles

As we have already pointed out in previous discussions, one approach to acting (the usual one) is to take the given circumstances of a play literally—that is, to reproduce the exterior decorum we would expect the characters in the play to show us. Thus, an actor would illustrate the literal appearances of the social level of his character through his gesture, movement, speech, and use of his costume. And since decorum can mean either control or the lack of it, the actor would move through the action of a play with the literal range of the decorum specified by appearances. Our believability would in this way be satisfied on the basis of appearances. Those plays dealing with nobility would thus have a look of formality, with controlled gestures and movement; and other plays, particularly seventeenth- and eighteenth-century middle and upper-class comedies, would have varied decorums but would still be near the formal pattern. But no matter how formal or informal the decorum might turn out to be, *we would accept it as Realistic in style* as we would accept Ibsenite drama because the appearances would be all of a piece. Thus, what has been called Realistic acting would support a Realistic interpretation of a play.

But quite a different approach to acting historical drama is to overlay the given circumstances, and thus the decorum, with *psychological* acting, which means that the gesture, movement, and so on would be expressive of the inner character and would not merely show the appearance of the literal decorum-character. This approach would allow a great increase in the range of illustration, for control or lack of control would not be determined by the decorum of social level but much more by motivation of the dramatic action. Consequently, another level of Realism in the acting would result, the level on which modern plays are now seen and heard—*Inner Realism.* Thus, the actors of the roles of Romeo and Juliet would not be bound by the decorum of the historical social level but would be free spirits in today's society. Or Hamlet would not be a "prince" first and a man with intense feelings second, but vice-versa. As you can readily see, quite a different play can result from the use of this style.

Consequently, we cannot say that historical drama is acted Realistically on our contemporary stage without defining the levels of Realistic style. You should be aware, however, that audiences have become so firmly rooted in expecting representational appearances in historical drama that any other stylistic approach may seem a defamation of Shakespeare or of the Greek dramatists. But there is no question that the "modern acting" approach has genuine validity and may be the only way the old plays will continue to find audiences. Your decision on style here is a very crucial matter.

SPEAKING THE PLAY

But whichever acting style you choose, you must not forget the absolute necessity for finding the violence level in the playing. Historical drama is written largely in verse forms in order to allow direct and intense expression of emotions. Character-mood-intensity thus becomes a matter of very great importance, for the *poetic drama sings, surges, and reaches peaks we seldom find in plays written in prose.* You must learn to exploit poetic forms and not to fight them.

Although you may learn fairly easily how to draw the subtext out of actors, *getting out the text* is quite another matter because so much emphasis has usually been placed in modern actor training on "getting across" the subtext. As a result, young actors tend to fight the verse line instead of recognizing that it is their best tool for reaching audiences. A director may need to reorient himself as well as the actors by emphasizing that *the action in such plays lies directly and literally in the lines and not in the subtext* as in a modern psychological drama. At first, this may seem like a betrayal of modern approaches to acting; but you will soon see how effectively audiences can be held in tension by the force of the spoken word alone. That is how they will experience it if you really believe it yourself and sell it to them.

Careful study of verse structure by a director is, therefore, essential if he is to get the most from his actors. Neglect of this technical approach can only result in a ragged production for telling the subtext in verse plays is not nearly sufficient; it is the "way" it is told—*the style of the spoken language*—that makes the difference.

A director's training must therefore include a concentration on the study of verse dialogue and how to exploit it with actors. Such study will make a director aware that his first obligation to an audience is *letting them hear such dialogue with ease and without distraction.* If he does not, its effect and thus much of the action in a play will be entirely lost.

This is a big order because verse dialogue, such as Shakespeare's or Marlowe's, often clouds our hearing with archaic words and phrases, lost allusions, inverted sentence structure, and frequent poetic imagery that cannot be received until the previous problems have been navigated. A director does not try to circumvent these problems by removing difficult lines from a playscript, but he faces them head on by paying close attention to the mechanics of verse structure, such as punctuation, emphatic words or phrases and where they fall in a line, placement of the caesura, cohesion within a single line or within several lines through proper breathing and the elimination of false pauses, and above all to the meter.

This last point is important, for the discovery of a line's meaning by an audience may lie much more in its inherent rhythm *when properly delivered* than in its denotative word meanings. To convey to young actors a sense of meter is often like trying to teach tone-deaf people how to sing. But without such a sense, an actor cannot deliver verse dialogue with meaning and excitement. Do you sense the musical form of such verse dialogue yourself? If you can "hear" it, you may be able to teach "hearing" to others.

Good verse delivery also means careful physical control by actors. As a director, you will learn to insist that actors keep their heads quite still when speaking; that they place the articulated sound as far forward in the mouth as possible; that they do not try to move across the stage when they are delivering a line; that they do not blast into lines with excessive volume, thus producing an in-and-out volume effect; that they keep fairly narrow ranges in pitch variation; that they relax the body and thus the voice to allow easy projection of the lines; that they articulate with great care; that they use pleasing vowel structure; and that they place caesuras where they belong and do not include false pauses.

Because verse plays contain high passions that tempt actors to "out-Herod Herod," *you will also learn to insist that textual delivery must take precedence over all subtextual and visual illustrations,* for a passage unheard is a passage that bores an audience and prevents its comprehension of a play.

EXERCISE

As was suggested earlier, learning directors should direct scenes from historical drama as a necessary part of their training, for the perception of modern drama and the scope of modern production can be greatly increased with this essential background. The student should, therefore, undertake the production of several ten- to fifteen-minute scenes chosen from the standard repertoire of historical drama. Preparation and production procedures should follow those prescribed at the ends of Part I, Part II, and Chapter 27 (style-analysis).

One way to start is with a scene from a Greek play, for it will give you an excellent basis for comparison with other period plays in a chronological order. But if scenes from several period plays can be directed, much can be learned by working backwards: Do a scene from Ibsen first, then move to the eighteenth, seventeenth, and sixteenth centuries and Medieval, Roman, and Greek periods in that order. You will then see the relationship of modern drama to all the rest.

Make your choices wisely. Remember that historical drama *requires focus on the text,* which means the most extensive use of actors' voices. Learn all you can about the power of big volume, energy behind acting, and the physical demands on the actor's body.

Your designs for staging a scene from a historical play will give you a far better idea of how to get it acted. Do it with imagination and inventiveness. Remember that you must study the original forms of production in order to understand the playscript fully; but your obligation now is to an audience. "What can you do to make these old plays exciting now?" is the question that must be foremost on your mind.

GAME OF VISUAL PERCEPTION 10: STYLE IN
HISTORICAL DRAMA (See pages 77-78)

1. Can you pick out the elements of style in each photograph? Which element is given the most emphasis?
2. How does the style of each production close the time-gap between the historical date of each play and a modern audience?
3. How does each of the two productions of *Earnest* "say" the same thing in a different way?
4. Can you delineate the variety in Shakespearean production by contrasting the illustrations shown here?
5. How would you stage each play? Can you individualize each one?

PHOTO 70
Love's Labour's Lost (Shakespeare)

PHOTO 71   *School for Scandal* (Sheridan)

PHOTO 72
Titus Andronicus (Shakespeare)

PHOTO 73
The Imaginary Invalid (Molière)

PHOTO 74 *The Cherry Orchard* (Chekhov)

PHOTO 75 *The Importance of Being Earnest* (Wilde)

PHOTO 76   *The Importance of Being Earnest* (Wilde)

PHOTO 76a   *The War of the Roses* (Shakespeare)

MAJOR PROJECT 3
Directing
with designers

THE INTENTION OF THE FINAL PROJECT

You are ready to undertake the final project in this study: the directing of a long play. The intention throughout this book has been to guide you step by step to this project where you can demonstrate your mastery of the directing process.

To recapitulate, Major Project 1 provided you the opportunity to work closely with actors in scenes from long plays and Major Project 2 encouraged you to completely *design* as well as direct a one-act play. Since then you have navigated the complexities of style and you should now have a good idea of how to give a produciton your own stamp while also revealing the individualities of the playscript and actors. You are now ready to work with designers, and learn how you can free them in bringing about total synthesis.

PLAY-ANALYSIS/STYLE-ANALYSIS AS THE SOURCE
OF DIRECTOR-DESIGNER COMMUNICATION

Just as directors read a playscript visually, that is, with active imagery of what it might look like on the stage, so do designers. In fact, many designers firmly believe that their first impressions are the strongest ones and that their early images, because of their strength and intensity, are those an audience will respond to imaginatively. Consequently, they feel that pursuing a play further in an analytical way will reduce their ability to design freely, and there is much to support this attitude because designing is largely a subjective process, reflecting how one feels about a play. However, the danger lies in the fact that the images a designer sees, like those seen by an actor assigned to a specific role, may not only be confined to his own area of design but they may also stem from a reading of a play that is quite different from what you the director may have in mind.

Since the main problem in synthesis is to find a total visual statement that will also coordinate with the statement the actors are making, a director's view of a play must be multidirectional and truly comprehensive. In this sense, a director does a total design of a production in his imagination—how he sees it in its entirety. However, as you will read in the next section on director-designer communication, *if a director tries to inflict his own specific images on the minds and feelings of his designers,* he may directly inhibit their creative capabilities just as he would those of his actors. Therefore, he must learn how to listen; and further, how to adjust to their needs.

The best approach to director-designer communication is, of course, the director's homework on play-analysis and style-analysis because they are more objective and more idea-including than any subjective imagery you may try to convey to a designer. It is also the long way around, but short cuts can be destructive and *the purpose is to free the designer* (just as you free your actors), not to bind him. The problem in this approach depends on what a designer is capable of in the way of play-analysis and style-analysis. If he understands and works from this position, as some designers do, communication between you and your designer may be relatively easy. If he does not, you may have to work with him on a subjective level, which can be more difficult. Whatever the method, the intention is always the same: to find *neutral* ground that both you and your designer can till together.

WORKING WITH DESIGNERS: THE PROCESS OF DESIGN

Understanding the Playscript: The First Discussion

Since the director's intention is to convey *his vision* of a play, a certain amount of controlled discussion with his *group* of designers is absolutely necessary. This means bringing the play to a conscious surface, which is something of a risk with designers, but it must be done if a multiheaded production is to be avoided and only one idea is to prevail, namely the director's.

The problem is how to bring about this mutual understanding without reducing a play to a mere mass of intellectuality that could stultify designers. Yet, the risk must be taken if the neutral-ground approach is to work at all. Too much intellectualizing can be prevented if the director keeps the discussion moving along the storyline with concentration on the dramatic action and human elements of character. He can work similarly to the way he handles actors, revealing the action as simply as possible in the interest of arousing spontaneous and inspired illustration. By carefully pointing the emphasis in his storytelling, a director can plant unit ideas and, finally, the main idea itself.

A certain amount of challenging by designers of the director's perception of the action at this point is useful for sharpening emphases and clarifying their necessity. However, the detailed refinement of idea should be carried on in the next major step (separate discussion with each designer) in the interest of preventing overdesign, as delineated in Chapter 20.

The director's procedure in this first group discussion should also be focused on conveying both his own perception of the style of the playscript, and the general style of the production he wants to bring about. You should therefore try to convey to the designers the point of style *in the playscript* you think can be developed and emphasized, stylistic points about dramatic action, characters, ideas, dialogue, mood values, tempos, and given circumstances. Only when designers comprehend fully what you see as individual and different in a playscript can they begin to move along the lines of the production style you intend. It must be emphasized again that *overdiscussion of these points by the group can stultify individual designers. The primary emphasis must be on the skillful handling of the storyline and the human values in a playscript.*

Individualizing Design: The Second Discussion

After the first general discussion the director should work separately with each designer, if he has more than one, in order to prevent duplication of emphasis and to bring about desirable counterpoints in design. This procedure recognizes the individuality of each designer and that each has his own way of approaching design as well as an individuality of expression. The second discussion(s) must, therefore, take the directions desired by each designer.

A designer may want more play-analysis, more explanation of stylistic emphases declared in the first discussion. Therefore, your intention should be the same: to leave the designer as free as possible in forming his visual images while you make certain he understands the playscript as you do. Once this understanding has been achieved, it is possible for you and the designer to discuss his actual images or at least to discuss directions those images may take. You can also present certain images of your own, images that are perhaps highly exaggerated or generalized with the intention of conveying a broad idea of your conception without pinning the designer down to a specific, confusing image, if you exercise extreme care about intruding on the designer.

Some scene designers have been trained to approach the design of a particular play by looking for an overall metaphor (a total visual image) as a way of finding production unity. Now is the time to discuss the metaphor the designer may have in mind and for you to understand thoroughly all of its implications.

This understanding can become a basic position of discussion, another neutral ground, because it is a broad imaginative statement of a play. Since the metaphor provides the unusual opportunity of visual projection, both the designer and you can come much closer in communicating with each other.

Other designers do not work from this sort of unity-making device but see design directly in terms of mass, line, color, and physical materials. They are not working from limitations, but they want to imagine the range of expression possible with the ideas of the play in mind. Again, the director can discuss expression of the play through this approach; but he must be careful not to commit himself on specifics but help the designer find the *general* range of illustration.

Ideas About Design: The Third Discussion

With a mutual understanding of the play as you see it now in hand, the designer presents some specific design ideas. The third discussion is much like your meeting the actor in a rehearsal and the actor acting out his own understanding of a play while you look on and then respond as a critic to the actor's efforts. In the case of designers, your criticism is aimed at the design's ability to reflect accurately and imaginatively your own perception of the play. If it does, agreement is easy. If it does not, or does so only partially, further discussion is necessary, even acting out a portion of the play for the designer. You are now working closely with the designer and the result is a collaboration on the designer's visual images.

This is a crucial point in discussion because both director and designer must be tolerant of each other's creative capabilities. If a director does not thoroughly project within his own imagination the ideas of the designer and if he does not perceive how they differ from his own visual conception, he may be discarding adequate, even exciting statements because of his own prejudice. On the other hand, if a designer does not give his work freely for inspection with some expectation of modification, no meeting of the two is possible. *All is based on mutual trust and the give-and-take of responsible, creative people.* Without this mutual effort the creative process in the theatre is impossible.

You can now test the proposed designs in terms of what could happen. In the case of scene design, you would test the compositions and patterns of movement as they could be projected out of the obstacle course proposed by the designer. Some designers work directly from inherent movement principles; that is, in their view good design proceeds from strong compositions and effective ideas about movement. In this sense a design is organic. If you work with such a designer, you must analyze a design very carefully to be certain you understand the principles of movement and can readily see their exploitation possibilities. If a designer is not oriented in this approach, you must work out in your own imagination how you can build the inevitable compositions and movements directly into the designs.

Similar *testing* of costume and lighting must also be made, with the utmost attention given to their exploitative possibilities. Discussion with the costume and lighting designers about imagined compositions at the principal climaxes in a play will ensure the types of emphases needed from each medium at those points, resulting in designs that can be "raised" or "lowered" to coincide with those emphases.

It is at this point that you can exercise your strongest control over the counterpoint principle discussed in Chapter 20, since you can strengthen or weaken designs as you see fit, whereas later when they are constructed, changes would be impossible. Only lighting design, as compared to scenic and costume design, has ready flexibility and can be shifted even in the final rehearsal period. However, the discussion period is the time for planning the number and location of instruments because later shifts are difficult and time consuming.

The Decision: The Fourth Discussion

Unlike the director's work with actors, transpiring as it does over many hours of regular daily meetings, which brings about a gradual process of mutual understanding, work with designers must be concluded early in a production period. This may involve only a few hours of actual director-designer contact. Furthermore, irrevocable decisions must be made because design deals with costly materials and hours of labor, the results of which cannot actually be seen until they are built in their final forms. Modifications in acting can take place through the final rehearsals, but not so with most designs. The director must, therefore, be able to project fully in his imagination the effect of the designs he may see only on paper or, at best, in scale models. Like all designers, he must be capable of full visualization in his imagination. The strength of his production will be reflected in the degree to which he can exercise this capability.

The *final testing* now takes place. Will the designs work? Does the director thoroughly understand their exploitative possibilities? *Has a synthesis in counterpoint actually occurred as far as the director can now project in his imagination?* Will the dramatic action in the playscript actually be enhanced by the designs so that moods will be clear and strong? Will the actors be able to dominate the designs?

Once the commitments to designs are made, the director must believe in them with full knowledge that he cannot change them except for minor details. Fully aware of how he can best make the designs organic in the production, he can then move forward in his rehearsals.

Keeping the Designer Free

The most important aspect in design approach is for the director to free his designers and not to entrap them within his own specifically imagined designs. This capability takes a strong director because a clash in design ideas is as likely as a clash with strong actors over dramatic action and its illustration. *The approach to both designers and actors is identical, since the director's intention is to carry them, through inspiration, beyond themselves.* Any director who fails to see that design exploitation is a major part of his work does not understand the nature of theatre. A play can live with actors alone, but a life of that sort will be anemic without the trappings of theatre. The major problem is the appropriate control of those trappings. Only with that control can an artistic whole emerge.

EXERCISE

Direct a play of your own choosing with the specific help of a designer(s). The preliminary words of advice are contained in preceding chapters, but here are a few warnings:

1. Choose a play of quality by a well-established playwright. He will teach you about structure and style.
2. Choose a play commensurate with your production circumstances, with prime attention to the availability of actors and the size of production that can be undertaken. A small cast, one-set play is enough to tackle at this point.
3. Choose a play within the scope of your perception and capabilities as a director as well as the capabilities of your actors and designer(s).
4. In doing your homework, first reread the chapters on style in Part III and then do a style-analysis and make a production scheme before talking with your designer(s).
5. Work with your designer(s) as you would with your actors. Remember that you will fly with a play only as you let your actors and designer(s) fly.

EPILOGUE
ON THE ROAD
Your future
as a director

"How do I fit into all this? Can I get a job as a director?"

Every student wants to know what lies ahead. However, if you expect now that you have completed your training in directing that you will be entering a plentiful job market, you have not yet faced the realities of trying to work in the highly independent and truly creative world of an art form where everything is pretty much touch-and-go.

You should also be aware that young people go into directing, just as they do acting, with little or no formal training and go on to successful careers as full competitors. The theatre has no barriers to talent. The only advantage your training has provided is time and place to try your wings in order to uncover your artistic talents and your capabilities in leadership. Beyond that, you should also be able to see the scope of the field of directing and the opportunities for finding your way. You are now on your own, as all artists are, and what you make of it will depend on yourself.

What sort of director do you want to be? That is the question you must now face, for there are many routes to travel. Some of these overlap, and it is quite possible that you may be working in two areas simultaneously, and over a period of years you may navigate all of them.

Descriptions of the various areas of employment open to you are given in the following section. For purposes of discussion they have been gathered together under six headings: The Professional Director, The Managing Artistic Director, The Academic Director, The Community Director, The Managing Director, and The Experimental Director.

THE PROFESSIONAL DIRECTOR

Professional directing heads the list of job possibilities because it is the most demanding and most difficult to achieve. All directors who earn their living directing plays as part of their work are, of course, professionals, but the rarer breed are those who work full-time with full-time professional actors and designers in what remains of the "private-profit" commercial theatre. This, of course, means on and off Broadway, as well as its close relatives—dinner theatres and East coast summer theatres. But since the 1960s with the growth of regional, nonprofit (government-supported) theatres located in major cities across the United States, opportunities have greatly increased. "I'm going to New York" may still be the goal of some, but in the 1980s there are other places where professional directors can earn livelihoods.

What you would find most challenging about these jobs is, of course, their special demand: "Everyone you would work with knows his job and expects to be creative in his own way. The content of this book has tried to lead you toward this goal, for the process of the director's tasks in production is always the same—freeing artistic talent, no matter what the level. What is different about the professional director's job is that (1) he must have exceptional capability in handling new plays and their playwrights, or in devising new ways for presenting old ones, and (2) he must work creatively with talented actors and designers who will expect independence in their own creativity. This is obviously not a job for a beginner. Experience is a basic requirement for entering the competition at this level, experience that has placed as much emphasis on how to communicate with mature actors as on theatrical schemes and rhythm awareness in presenting plays. Part III of this book lays the groundwork. However, from that point on if you enter this field you will soon discover that a "talented" professional director is defined largely in terms of his personal attributes as a creative human being who can reach other highly poised creative talents in achieving professional qualities and standards. This is the major league.

Pursuing a career in today's art theatre will make enormous demands on your energies and creativity. This is why, if you intend to go this route, you must direct, direct, direct, whenever you can. Remuneration is unimportant; experience is all. You will become aware that there are many kinds of nonprofit theatres where you could be invited to work. (See *Theater Communications Group* publications.) Some mainly offer programs of revivals and musicals, while others work with new plays entirely or as part of the overall program. Some are pointed toward children's theatre, and some toward ethnic groups. The range is extensive. Whatever you decide to aim for at the professional level of directing, you must be aware that relatively few jobs exist and that getting one of them may not depend on your talent but "knowing someone" as well as being in the right place at the right time. Age is no barrier, for youth is much in demand in the new theatres that developed in the 1960s and 1970s. What you believe in and how committed you want to become may very well determine your status as a potential director in a group that is motivated by a strong central purpose. "Theatre is commitment," you will discover, has a very special meaning.

One avenue to professional directing is stage managing where you can watch professional directors at work. You can also learn much about the business aspects of producing plays and the dynamics of pacing, intensity, contrasts, and other theatrical pointings. Good commercial theatre is difficult to achieve, and audiences have a right to expect something of quality in return for their money.

THE MANAGING ARTISTIC DIRECTOR

A new job for the professional theatre director that came into being with the regional nonprofits is that of Artistic Director. This job was declared explicitly because such theatres could not survive without one, and it is still the order of the day. As the "producer" in these theatres, and usually also a primary stage director, an artistic director can formulate policies; arrange programming; hire actors, designers, and other stage directors; declare the image of the theatre in the public view; and establish activities seminal to the growth of the theatre. He usually works closely in concert with a Managing Director as his primary advisor on budgetary matters, marketing, public relations, box-office procedures, audience perquisites, rentals and peripheral money-raising activities, financial drives, etc.; but his autonomy is explicit and necessary, with only his governing board who can hire and fire him to answer to. Otherwise, a theatre is his to command, including its audience because he understands its needs and desires. This last does not in any way imply following the easiest route, but instead means genuine leadership because it will be through his eyes and visions that audiences will grow in capabilities as well as numbers.

THE ACADEMIC DIRECTOR

Although there are relatively few jobs open to full-time professional directors, perhaps no more than 200 to 300, there are hundreds in the academic world. Although most directors work only with actors in training, they can claim the "professional" designation in the sense that they earn their living by producing plays and teaching others how to do so. When secondary and primary school activities are added to those in colleges and universities, the annual number of productions is in the thousands, and their audiences in the millions. Academic theatre is the single largest employer of expert theatre personnel in this country.

Although the description of job possibilities in this section is confined to colleges and universities, this does not imply that a well-trained director works only at that level. Directing is directing and the same processes outlined in Parts I, II, and III of this book are carried out at all levels. Intensive work on Part III can open up new vistas and approaches for everyone. In colleges and universities the approaches in Part III are absolutely necessary because excellent theatre plants are everywhere and the onus is on the director to produce a wide variety of plays, both modern and historical, in varying styles of production. He is the composite leader: the organizer, producer, publicist, primary critic, scholar, theorist, adventurer, teacher of acting, directing, and other theatre courses, and the prime mover and inspirational force. In fact, so much is expected of directors at the college/university level that it is no wonder good ones are scarce and superior ones as rare as in the commercial/professional theatre.

What attracts many people to this area of directing is not just the availability of jobs but the prospects of a career of varying interests and intensities. There is always the climb up the production from simple to highly complex plays, including the historical drama; but there is also the intellectual and spirit-satisfying compensation of classroom teaching where the process of developing young talent can become an end in itself. "There are just many more opportunities to express yourself," one hears; or "I'd rather see a young talent unfolding his wings anytime than work with pros."

The top group of academic theatres is now as well-poised for production in both equipment and design personnel as most professional repertory theatres anywhere in the United States or Europe. That is why the pressure is on directors to work with originality and style. Some not only have graduate student actors to ensure, in the view of some directors, more satisfying casting, but also companies which include one or more professional actors, either as members of the teaching staff or performers hired for particular plays or a season. In these situations the stakes are high because with so many resources on hand a director, like a football or basketball coach, must succeed with the public. The emphasis on "winning" (the commercial goal) may supersede the primary objective of training students in theatre crafts. Consequently, many directors prefer to work in less demanding situations where adventure is possible because "failure" is not demeaning and may even be productive as a learning experience.

THE COMMUNITY DIRECTOR

The "new" community theatre is a product of the increasing emphasis that cities across the United States have placed on recreational facilities since the 1960s. For some, the motivation was sociological, a means of meeting inner-city problems with a recreational resource. With federal grants-in-aid to help some cities increase local funding, theatre participation was now looked at as a way of satisfying the needs of the new community groups that had become clearly identified in the 1960s and '70s as never before, including Blacks, Chicanos and other ethnic groups, senior citizens, etc. The old community theatre, the one that since the 1920s had satisfied the artistic and social needs of local adult amateurs, was now changed in direction and number, with special emphasis on children's theatre and creative dramatics.

The community theatre director in the 1980s is now identified at several levels. He may be a specialist with ethnic groups, senior citizens, children, or adult art-theatre. In the number of jobs available, this area now holds second place to academic theatre, and it shows a remarkable holding power. In some instances, enough funds are available to employ not only a director but a designer and technical director as well.

The primary function of recreation, however, does not imply shoddy, amateurish production. The adventurous director can move as he will. Every opportunity to make something the group can be proud of will depend on the vitality and skill of his leadership. Community theatre is still largely unexploited because until recent years it has not had institutional security of the same sort as college/university theatre. However, its potential is great for the enterprising director. Theatre is a sociological institution, and the community is the proper base for its activities.

If you want to work as a community director you will need to augment your theatre training with exposure to sociology and community dynamics and financial and business management because success in this area combines artistic talent and sound production sense. In most instances, at least early on, you will be more of a producer than director; your growth will lie in your ability to do both effectively. You will also be a teacher in the academic sense, for you will be a developer of talent as well as good community relations.

THE EXPERIMENTAL DIRECTOR

It is perhaps stretching the point to label *improvisational theatre* for audiences "experimental" since it has been around in its present form since the early 1960s. Yet, it is rooted so deeply in the nature of theatre ("two boards and a passion") and has such a noble lineage in the Commedia 'dell Arte, that it is not at all surprising to find it still moderately healthy in the 1980s. This is a director's theatre, for he alone is responsible for its life, its energy, its content, its artistic product, and its overall meaning. However, the word *director,* as defined throughout this book, must be modified because in practice improvisational theatricals involve group improvisations, and such improvisations are not the product of one man's imagination although that man may lead others into the improvisations and influence their shape. What is made is that which emerges from interchanges within the group. A much better designation is "artist-leader," simply because it implies both a strong artistic background in theatre as well as exceptional leadership capabilities.

Although improvisational theatricals are group-made, they still have unusual capabilities of conveying intensive dramatic ideas through the elements of visual and aural theatricality, through the variations and unexpected possibilities inherent in improvisation, and through a minimum of improvised words that may or may not employ the interchanges of dialogue. Consequently, such theatricals are not open to "interpretation" by other directors and actors outside of the group because they are the improvised and unique products of the group and its leader who stamp them with the only possible interpretation—the one *they* reveal to an audience. Since all the rules of improvisation apply, the participants are not actors in the traditional sense, nor is the staging in any way restricted to the conventions of established forms.

The intention here is not to discuss the techniques of making improvisational theatricals because any techniques used in the process can be evolved only by a group itself in the process of effecting its own artistic goals. Therefore, they cannot be readily catalogued as can interpretive techniques. Furthermore, introducing present means when the range of possibilities can be very great would only confuse what is really important for a director-in-training to understand as clearly as possible: how the artist-leader differs in his work from the master-craftsman interpretive director.

There is no question that leadership of a very definite sort is involved. In its earliest declarations this leadership was based in a commitment to social, political, or religious ideas, or all three at the same time. Thus, it was not just the leader's knowledge of the art and craft of the theatre that made him a leader but his belief in a view of life coupled with a dedication approaching that of a reformist—a dedication demanding that he reach and influence people with his ideas and points of view. His intention, therefore, was not to propagate other people's ideas, such as the interpretive director does with the work of the playwrights he produces, but to arouse through a group statement the specific point of view he wants to inculcate. His leadership necessarily involved collecting around him a group that sees eye to eye with his ideas and has a similar desire to propagate them.

"Who is this sort of theatre for?" is a question you will have to decide if you elect this form of work. Is it primarily for the benefit of the actors who participate in it or for the audience that is also encouraged to participate in it? Expression of audience opinion has been so curtailed in the twentieth century from the general participatory noise of the nineteenth and preceding centuries that more involvement seems possible. And what will the spectators be expected to do? Will they no longer be spectators but actors in the improvisation itself? Will a new audience be found for it, a primarily youthful audience in contrast to the mature, middle-class audience of the established theatre? Will the new audience demand immediate relevance and commitment? As you can see, improvisational theatre leaves us with many puzzling speculations about the theatre of the future.

It would appear, then, that anyone contemplating work in the theatre in a position of leadership will undoubtedly have some important decisions to make. But whatever route he decides to follow, he can be sure that although the director is scarcely one hundred years old, some sort of leader will be a necessary part in making theatre for a long time to come.

BIBLIOGRAPHY

What follows is a minimum list of books with which any advanced student of directing should be relatively familiar. It ranges from discussions of directing and directors at work to the director-actor and director-designer relationships, the theory of dramatic literature, and background historical studies. You will accumulate a knowledge of many of these books as you work through your courses in theatre, but you will need to search out those works missed in the interest of giving yourself as complete a stance as possible for developing your own point of view about directing. Directing is not a display of virtuosity but a highly developed craft firmly based in techniques and backgrounds.

ABOUT DIRECTING

ARTAUD, ANTONIN, *The Theater and Its Double,* trans. Mary Caroline Richards. New York: Grove Press, Inc., 1958.
BAKSHY, ALEXANDER, *The Theatre Unbound.* London: Cecil Palmer, C. Q. Bailey Bros. Ltd., 1923.
BARRAULT, JEAN-LOUIS, *Reflections on the Theatre,* trans. Barbara Well. London: Rockliff Pub. Corp. Ltd., 1951.
———, *The Theatre of Jean-Louis Barault,* trans. Joseph Chiari. New York: Hill and Wang Inc., 1961.
BECK, JULIAN, *The Life of the Theatre.* San Francisco: City Lights, 1972.

BENTLEY, ERIC, *In Search of Theatre.* New York: Alfred A. Knopf, Inc., 1953.
BLAU, HERBERT, *The Impossible Theater.* New York: The Macmillan Company, 1964.
BRECHT, BERTOLT and CASPAR NEHER, *Antigonemodell.* Berlin: Gebr. Weiss, 1948.
BROCKETT, OSCAR, *Perspectives of Contemporary Theatre.* Baton Rouge: Louisiana State University Press, 1971.
BROOK, PETER, *The Empty Space.* New York: Atheneum Publishers, 1968.
BRUSTEIN, ROBERT, *Making Scenes.* New York: Random House, 1981.
CHEKHOV, MICHAEL, *Director and Playwright,* compiled and written by Charles Leonard. New York: Harper & Row, Publishers, 1963.
CLAY, JAMES H. and DANIEL KREMPEL, *The Theatrical Image.* New York: McGraw-Hill Book Company, 1967.
CLURMAN, HAROLD, *On Directing.* New York: The Macmillan Company, 1972.
CLURMAN, HAROLD, *Lies Like Truth,* New York: The Macmillan Company, 1958.
COLE, TOBY and HELEN KRICH CHINOY, eds., *Directors on Directing,* 2nd rev. ed. Indianapolis, Inc.: The Bobbs-Merrill Co., Inc. 1963.
CORRIGAN, ROBERT, *Theatre In Search of a Fix.* New York: Delacorte Press, 1973.
———, ed. *Arthur Miller; A Collection of Critical Essays.* Englewood Cliffs, N.J.: Prentice-Hall, Inc., 1969.
ELIOT, T. S., "The Function of Criticism," in *Selected Essays.* New York: Harcourt Brace Jovanovich Inc., 1950.
FERRES, JOHN H., *Twentieth Century Interpretations of* The Crucible. Englewood Cliffs, N.J.: Prentice-Hall, 1972.
FLANAGAN, HALLIE, *Dynamo.* New York: Duell, Sloan & Pearce, Inc., 1943.
GIELGUD, JOHN, *Stage Directions.* New York: Random House, 1963.
GILDER, ROSAMOND, ed. and others, *Theatre Arts Anthology.* New York: Theatre Arts Books, 1950.
GORCHAKOV, NIKOLAI, *Stanislavsky Directs,* trans. Miriam Goldina. New York: Funk & Wagnalls Company, 1954.
GRANVILLE-BARKER, HARLEY, *Prefaces to Shakespeare,* 2 vols. Princeton, N.J.: Princeton University Press, 1947.
GROTOWSKI, JERZY, *Towards a Poor Theatre.* New York: Simon and Schuster Inc., 1969.
GUTHRIE, TYRONE, *A Life in the Theatre.* New York: McGraw-Hill Book Company, 1959.
HELBURN, THERESA, *A Wayward Quest.* Boston: Little, Brown, 1960.
HOUGHTON, NORRIS, *Return Engagement.* New York: Holt, Rinehart & Winston Inc., 1962.
HOUSEMAN, JOHN, *Run-Through.* New York: Simon and Schuster, 1972.
———, *Front and Center.* New York: Simon and Schuster, 1979.
KNAPP, BETTINA, *Louis Jouvet, Man of the Theatre.* New York: Columbia University Press, 1957.
KOTT, JAN, *Shakespeare Our Contemporary,* trans. Boleslaw Taborski. Garden City, N.Y.: Doubleday & Company, Inc. Anchor Books Edition.
LABAN, RUDOLF, *The Mastery of Movement.* London: MacDonald & Evans Ltd., 1960.
LAHR, JOHN, and JONATHAN PRICE, *Life/Show.* New York: The Viking Press, 1973.
OXENFORD, LYN, *Playing Period Plays.* London: J. Garnet Miller, Ltd., 1958.
PURDOM, C. B., *Harley Granville-Barker.* Cambridge, Mass.: Harvard University Press, 1956.
QUINTERO, JOSE, *If You Don't Dance They Beat You.* Boston: Little, Brown, 1974.
SAINT-DENIS, MICHEL, *Theatre: The Rediscovery of Style.* New York: Theatre Arts Books, 1961.
SCHECHNER, RICHARD, *Public Domain.* Indianapolis: Bobbs-Merrill, 1969.
———, *Environmental Theatre,* New York: Hawthorne Books, 1973.
SHAW, BERNARD, *The Art of Rehearsal.* New York: Samuel French, Inc., 1928.
SMITH, A. C. H., *Orghast at Persepolis.* New York: The Viking Press, 1972.
SPEAIGHT, ROBERT, *William Poel and the Elizabethan Revival.* London: William Heinemann Ltd., 1954.
STANISLAVSKI, KONSTANTIN, *My Life in Art,* trans. J. J. Robbins. New York: Theatre Arts Books, 1952.
———. *Stanislavski on the Art of the Stage,* trans. David Margarshack. London: Faber & Faber Ltd., 1950.
———, *The Seagull Produced by Stanislavski,* ed. S. D. Balukhaty, trans. David Margarshack. London: Dennis Dobson, 1952.
TAIROV, ALEXANDER, *Notes of a Director,* trans. William Kuhlke. Coral Gables, Florida: University of Miami Press, 1969.
WEISMAN, JOHN, *Guerilla Theatre; Scenarios for Revolution.* Garden City, N.Y.: Anchor Press, 1973.
YOUNG, STARK, *Theatre Practice.* New York: Charles Scribner's Sons, 1926.

DIRECTOR-ACTOR RELATIONSHIP

BENEDETTI, ROBERT, *The Actor at Work* (3rd ed.), Englewood Cliffs, N.J.: Prentice-Hall, Inc., 1981.
———, *Seeming, Being and Becoming: Acting in Our Century.* New York: Drama Book Specialists, 1976.
BOLESLAVSKY, RICHARD, *Acting: The First Six Lessons.* New York: Theatre Arts Books, 1949.
CHAIKIN, JOSEPH, *The Presence of the Actor.* New York: Atheneum, 1972.
CHEKHOV, MICHAEL, *To the Actor on the Technique of Acting.* New York: Harper & Brothers, 1953.
COLE, TOBY, ed., *Acting: A Handbook of the Stanislavski Method.* New York: Crown Publishers, Inc., 1963.
CRAWFORD, JERRY and JOAN SNYDER, *Acting in Person and in Style.* Dubuque, Iowa: W. C. Brown, 1976.
GREEN, RUTH M., *The Wearing of a Costume.* London: Pitman & Sons, 1966.
HODGSON, JOHN, and ERNEST RICHARDS, *Improvisation.* London: Metheun & Co. Ltd., 1966.
LESSAC, ARTHUR, *The Use and Training of the Human Voice.* New York: DBS Publications, Inc., 1967.
McGAW, CHARLES, *Acting Is Believing.* New York: Holt, Rinehart & Winston, Inc., 1955.
MACHLIN, EVANGELINE, *Speech for the Stage.* New York: Theatre Arts Books, 1966.
O'CONNOR, GARRY, *Ralph Richardson.* London: Hodder and Stoughton, Ltd., 1982.
PARRISH, WAYLAND MAXFIELD, *Reading Aloud.* Camden, N.J.: Thomas Nelson, Inc., 1933.
PENROD, JAMES, *Movement for the Performing Artist.* Palo Alto, Calif.: National Press Books, 1974.
REDGRAVE, MICHAEL, *The Actor's Ways and Means.* London: William Heinemann Ltd., 1953.
SCHRECK, EVERETT M., *Principles and Styles of Acting.* Reading, Mass.: Addison-Wesley, 1970.
SEYLER, ATHENE, and STEPHEN HAGGARD, *The Craft of Comedy.* New York: Theatre Arts Books, 1946.
SHAWN, TED, *Every Little Movement.* Brooklyn, N.Y.: Dance Horizons, Inc., 1968.
SPOLIN, VIOLA, *Improvisation for the Theatre.* Evanston, Ill.: Northwestern University Press, 1963.
STANISLAVSKI, KONSTANTIN, *An Actor Prepares.* New York: Theatre Arts Books, 1952.
——— *Building a Character.* Trans. Elizabeth Reynolds Hapgood. New York: Theatre Arts Books, 1949.
STRASBERG, LEE, *Strasberg at the Actors Studio,* ed. Robert Hethmon. New York: The Viking Press, Inc., 1965.

THE DESIGN PROCESS AND PLAY PRODUCTION

BABLET, DENNIS, *Edward Gordon Craig,* trans. Daphne Woodward. New York: Theatre Arts Books, 1966.
BARTON, LUCY, *Historic Costume for the Stage.* Boston: Walter H. Baker Company, 1938.
———, *Appreciating Costume.* Boston, Mass.: Walter H. Baker Company, 1969.
BOYLE, WALDEN P., and JOHN H. JONES, *Central and Flexible Staging.* Berkeley, Calif.: University of California Press, 1956.
BURIAN, JARKA, *The Scenography of Joseph Soboda.* Middletown, Conn.: Wesleyan University Press, 1971.
BURRIS-MEYER, HAROLD, and EDWARD C. COLE, *Scenery for the Theatre.* Boston: Little, Brown and Company, 1938.
———, *Theatres and Auditoriums.* New York: Reinhold Publishing Corporation, 1949.
CORSON, RICHARD, *Stage Makeup.* New York: Appleton-Century-Crofts, Inc., 1960.
CRAIG, EDWARD GORDON, *On The Art of the Theatre.* New York: Theatre Arts Books, 1957.
DAVENPORT, MILIA, *Book of Costume,* 2 vols. New York: Crown Publishers, 1948.
FUERST, WALTER R., and SAMUEL J. HUME, *Twentieth-Century Stage Decoration,* 2 vols. New York: Benjamin Blom, Inc., 1967.
GASSNER, JOHN, *Form and Idea in Modern Theatre.* New York: The Dryden Press, Inc., 1956.
GILLETTE, ARNOLD S. *Stage Scenery: Its Construction and Rigging.* New York: Harper & Brothers, 1959.
GRAVES, MAITLAND, *The Art of Color and Design.* New York: McGraw-Hill Book Company, 1951.
HAINAUX, RENÉ and YVES-BONNAT, *Stage Design Throughout the World Since 1950.* London: George G. Harrap & Co. Ltd., 1964.
JONES, ROBERT E., *The Dramatic Imagination.* New York: Theatre Arts Books, 1941.
LARSON, ORVILLE, *Scene Design for Stage and Screen.* East Lansing: Michigan State University Press, 1961.

LAVER, JAMES, *Costume in the Theatre*. New York: Hill & Wang, Inc., 1964.

MCCANDLESS, STANLEY, *A Method of Lighting the Stage*. New York: Theatre Arts Books, 1958.

PARKER, W. OREN, and HARVEY K. SMITH, *Scene Design and Stage Lighting*. New York: Holt, Rinehart & Winston, Inc., 1968.

ROSENTHAL, JEAN, *The Magic of Light*. Boston: Little, Brown and Company, 1972.

RUSSELL, DOUGLAS A., *Stage Costume Design*. Englewood Cliffs, N.J.: Prentice-Hall, Inc., 1973.

_____, *Theatrical Style: A Visual Approach to the Theatre*. Palo Alto, Ca: Mayfield Press, 1976.

_____, *Period Style for the Theatre*. Boston: Allyn & Bacon, 1980.

SIMONSON, LEE, *The Art of Scenic Design*. New York: Harper & Brothers, 1950.

SOUTHERN, RICHARD, *The Open Stage*. London: Faber & Faber Ltd., 1953.

DRAMATIC LITERATURE

ANDERSON, MAXWELL, *The Essence of Tragedy*. Washington, D.C.: Anderson House, 1939.

BENTLEY, ERIC, *The Playwright as Thinker*. New York: Harcourt Brace Jovanovich, Inc., 1948.

BERGSON, HENRI, *Laughter,* ed. Wylie Sypher. Garden City, N.Y.: Doubleday & Company, Inc., 1956.

BRUSTEIN , ROBERT, *The Theatre of Revolt*. Boston: Little, Brown and Company, 1964.

BUTCHER, S. H., trans., *Aristotle on Music and Poetry*. New York: The Liberal Arts Press, 1956.

CLARK, BARRETT H., ed., *European Theories of the Drama*. New York: Crown Publishers, Inc., 1947.

CORRIGAN, ROBERT W., ed., *Comedy: Meaning and Form*. San Francisco: Chandler Publishing Co., 1965.

_____, ed., *Tragedy: Vision and Form*. San Francisco: Chandler Publishing Co., 1965.

_____, and JAMES L. ROSENBERG, eds., *The Context and Craft of Drama*. San Francisco: Chandler Publishing Co., 1964.

FREYTAG, GUSTAV, *Technique of the Drama*. Chicago: Griggs, 1895.

GASSNER, JOHN, *Masters of the Drama*. New York: Dover Publications, Inc., 1945.

MEREDITH, GEORGE, *An Essay on Comedy,* ed. Lane Cooper. Ithaca, N.Y.: Cornell University Press, 1956.

MILLER, ARTHUR, "The Family in Modern Drama," *Atlantic Monthly* 197 (April, 1956), 35-41.

TENNANT, P. F. D., *Ibsen's Dramatic Technique*. New York: Humanities Press, Inc., 1965.

HISTORICAL BACKGROUNDS

ANTOINE, ANDRÉ, *Memories of le Théatre-Libre,* trans. Marvin A. Carlson. Coral Gables, Florida: University of Miami Press, 1964.

ARCHER, WILLIAM, *Masks or Faces?* New York: Hill and Wang, Inc., 1957.

BIEBER, MARGARETE, *The History of the Greek and Roman Theater*. Princeton, N.J.: Princeton University Press, 1961.

BLUM, DANIEL, *A Pictorial History of the American Theatre 1860–1970,* 3rd ed., enlarged and revised by John Willis. New York: Crown, Inc., 1969.

BOWERS, FAUBIAN, *Theatre in the East*. Camden, N.J.: T. Nelson, Inc., 1956.

CAMPBELL, LILY BESS, *Scenes and Machines on the English Stage*. New York: Barnes & Noble, Inc., 1960.

CLURMAN, HAROLD, *The Fervent Years*. New York: Hill and Wang, Inc., 1957.

COLE, TOBY, and HELEN KRICH CHINOY, eds., *Actors on Acting*. New York: Crown Publishers, Inc., 1954.

COLLINS, FLETCHER, *The Production of Medieval Church Music-Drama*. Charlottesville. The University Press of Virginia, 1972.

COQUELIN, CONSTANT, HENRY IRVING, and DION BOUCICAULT, *The Art of Acting*. New York: Columbia University Press, 1926.

CRAIG, HARDIN, *English Religious Drama of the Middle Ages*. Oxford: Clarendon Press, 1955.

DUCKWORTH, GEORGE, *The Nature of Roman Comedy*. Princeton, N.J.: Princeton University Press, 1952.

DUERR, EDWIN, *The Length and Depth of Acting.* New York: Holt, Rinehart & Winston, Inc., 1962.
FRAZER, SIR JAMES, *The Golden Bough,* abr. ed. London: Macmillan Co. Ltd., 1959.
GASCOIGNE, BAMBER, *World Theatre: An Illustrated History.* Boston: Little, Brown and Company, 1968.
GASSNER, JOHN, *The Theatre in Our Times.* New York: Crown Publishers, Inc., 1954.
GORELIK, MORDECAI, *New Theatres for Old.* New York: E. P. Dutton & Co., Inc., 1962.
GRUBE, MAX, *The Story of the Meininger,* trans. Ann Marie Keller. Coral Gables, Florida: University of Miami Press, 1963.
HODGES, C. WALTER, *The Globe Restored,* London: Ernest Benn, Ltd., 1953.
JAMES, HENRY, *The Scenic Art* (1872–1901). New Brunswick, N.J.: Rutgers University Press, 1948.
KERNODLE, GEORGE, *From Art to Theatre.* Chicago: University of Chicago Press, 1964.
KOMISARJEVSKI, THEODORE, *The Theatre and a Changing Civilization.* London: John Lane, The Bodley Head Ltd., 1935.
LEWES, GEORGE HENRY, *On Actors and the Art of Acting.* New York: Henry Holt & Company, 1878.
MESERVE, WALTER, *An Emerging Entertainment: The Drama of the American People to 1828.* Bloomington, Ind.: Indiana University Press, 1977.
NAGLER, ALOIS M., ed., *A Source Book in Theatrical History.* New York: Dover Publications, Inc., 1959.
NICOLL, ALLARDYCE, *The Development of the Theatre.* New York: Harcourt Brace Jovanovich, Inc., 1958.
PICKARD-CAMBRIDGE, ARTHUR, *The Dramatic Festivals of Athens.* Oxford: Clarendon Press, 1953.
ROWELL, GEORGE, *The Victorian Theatre.* London: Oxford University Press, 1956.
QUINN, A. H., *A History of the American Drama: From the Beginning to the Civil War.* New York: Harper & Brothers, 1923.
———, *A History of the American Drama from the Civil War to the Present Day.* New York: F. S. Crofts & Co., 1936.
SIMONSON, LEE, *The Stage Is Set.* New York: Harcourt Brace Jovanovich, Inc., 1932.
SOUTHERN, RICHARD, *The Medieval Theatre in the Round.* London: Faber and Faber Ltd., 1957.
———, *The Seven Ages of the Theatre.* New York: Hill and Wang, Inc., 1961.
STEBBINGS, GENEVIEVE, *Delsarte System of Expression.* Belmar, N.J.: Edgar S. Werner & Co., 1902.
SUMMERS, MONTAGUE, *The Restoration Theatre.* London: Kegan Paul, Trench, Trubner & Co., Ltd., 1934.
WATSON, ERNEST B., *Sheridan to Robertson.* New York: Benjamin Blom, Inc., 1963.

PLAY DIRECTING

INDEX

For a listing of all plays and their authors that appear in the photographs used in this book, as well as the credits for the productions, see pp. xi of the forepages.